TOWARDS A CHRISTIAN REPUBLIC

Towards a
Christian Republic

*Antimasonry and the Great
Transition in New England,
1826-1836*

Paul Goodman

New York   Oxford
Oxford University Press
1988

OXFORD UNIVERSITY PRESS

Oxford   New York   Toronto
Delhi   Bombay   Calcutta   Madras   Karachi
Petaling Jaya   Singapore   Hong Kong   Tokyo
Nairobi   Dar es Salaam   Cape Town
Melbourne   Auckland

and associated companies in
Beirut   Berlin   Ibadan   Nicosia

Published by Oxford University Press, Inc.,
200 Madison Avenue, New York, New York 10016

Oxford is a registered trademark of Oxford University Press

LIBRARY OF CONGRESS CATALOGING-IN-PUBLICATION DATA
Goodman, Paul, 1934–
Towards a Christian republic.
Includes index.
1. Antimasonic Party.   2. New England—Politics
and government—1775–1865.   I. Title.
HS525.G66   1988   366'.1'0974   87–20385
ISBN 0–19–504864–4

1 3 5 7 9 8 6 4 2

Printed in the United States of America
on acid-free paper

FOR OSCAR HANDLIN

Preface

An historical event of no great import in its own right sometimes casts a bright light on complex, fundamental processes of historical development. Such is the case with the kidnapping, disappearance, and alleged murder of William Morgan in 1826 which triggered a national movement—the first mass movement in American history—to destroy Freemasonry, a numerous, male fraternal order devoted to good fellowship and charity but which many Americans perceived as a powerful, insidious conspiracy to subvert the world's great Christian Republic. Sixty years after the first extended published history of Antimasonry, the historian Lee Benson acknowledged that though "some surface facts of the Antimasonic story have been recited many times . . . we have a long way to go before penetrating to the core of what John B. McMaster has called 'the most remarkable' political party in American History."[1] In a study of New York politics in the age of Andrew Jackson, Benson claimed that Antimasonry, which had originated in the western part of that state, "represented an impassioned, leveling attack by members of the 'lower classes' against the village and urban 'aristocracy.' " Later Benson also argued that Antimasonry fused with the movement to establish a "Christian Party" in American politics to impose religious tests of "piety, sobriety, propriety, thrift, 'steady habits,' and 'book-learning,' " derived from "puritanical attitudes."[2]

Benson's understanding of Antimasonry owed much to Whitney R. Cross's study, *The Burned-Over District* (1950), a pioneering effort to fuse social and political history, grounding both in a close examination of local conditions in western New York. "Perhaps the movement may justly be described," Cross suggested, "as an early evidence of rural jealousy toward urban superiority, or at least toward the controlling middle class of the larger villages and county towns. . . ." In western New York's distinctive setting, Antimasonic "leaseholders and renters aligned against the resident agents of absentee landlords." Cross furthermore argued that "the major issue seemed to involve questions of morality," for the churches played a vital role in mobilizing the "religious and moral energies" upon which the crusade depended. Yet Cross did not find "theological divergence" between the Antimasons and their opponents. Class differences within the churches accounted for the

"Antimasonic excitement" which "tended to differentiate rural and lower-middle class folk from their would-be social superiors."[3]

Recognizing the complexity of Antimasonry, Ronald P. Formisano suggested in a subsequent study of Michigan that its "evangelical drive" was central. Acknowledging that class resentment, status anxiety, and rural-urban antagonism figured in earlier accounts of Antimasonry, Formisano insisted that "a religious dynamic provided most of its drive." Like Benson earlier, Formisano saw Antimasons as forerunners of an important strain within the Whig party which made that party "the evangelicals' best hope to Christianize America."[4] In a later study of Massachusetts Antimasonry, Formisano, stressing its mass, democratic character, claimed that "Antimasonry . . . was a middle-class moral populism." The battle over Masonry "was essentially cultural and religious, between descendants of the Puritans who were very similar in socio-economic status, and in many ideas and enthusiasms, but whose values clashed in fundamental ways." Yet while stressing cultural factors more than class, in contrast to Cross and even Benson, Formisano also insisted that Antimasonry was "a new kind of social movement—populist and widely based in the middle- and lower-middle classes." But since Formisano did not find economic or class characteristics that distinguished Antimasons—they were not a " 'displaced elite' " nor an " 'alienated' mass of rootless men," but "were in fact usually upwardly mobile, aspiring individualists, fully attuned to the spirit of 'improvement,' " the clearest basis for delineating them remained religion. In the distinctive Massachusetts context, Formisano found, "a Unitarian-Orthodox division often was the essence of Masonic-Antimasonic polarity." Yet Formisano also acknowledged that "Antimasonry was much more than a by-product of Orthodox frustration, and other denominations also provided Antimasonic votes."[5]

Returning to western New York, Kathleen Smith Kutulowski found, after examining the social basis of Antimasonry at the grass roots in Genesee County, that the leaders "tended to be urban, professional, nonevangelical, commercially prominent, and non-partisan." Moreover, "the party's electoral power lay in the most economically prosperous townships. . . ." Kutulowski's careful study of Antimasonic leadership and mass support compelled her to question the view that the third party drew from "poor, resentful, disadvantaged farmers." Instead she emphasized "evangelical social values emanating from the Second Great Awakening and co-existing with practical material goals which first found cogent political expression, not in Sabbatarianism, temperance, abolition, or Whiggery, but in Antimasonry." But Kutulowski complicated the debate further by suggesting a link between religion and economy: "wherever farm families had begun to cross the threshold of the market economy the countryside throbbed with religious enthusiasm." She concluded that "Antimasonic votes swelled exponentially with church membership." Like Cross, Benson, and Formisano, Kutulowski recognized that there were important religious sources of Antimasonry, yet their precise nature remained unclear, especially since she claimed that the third-party leaders tended to be nonevangelical, though the Second Great Awakening was the work of pietistic Protestants.[6]

If one suspects that the study of Antimasonry carries heavy risk of plunging into a quagmire, John L. Brooke's recent detailed exploration of the social sources of Antimasonry in Worcester County, Massachusetts, confirms suspicion. Massachusetts Antimasons, he tells us, "were men protesting the power of a privileged group in their society." They were "men living in competitive, changing towns, most often of National and Federalist background, and given to an older style of religious orthodoxy." Contrary to earlier historians, Brooke did not find that Antimasonry drew on "the moral immediatism of the latter phases of the Second Great Awakening." Instead he argued that Antimasons occupied "a marginal and often declining position in a rapidly changing economy" and clung "to an older religious tradition which gave priority to the moral harmony of the local community."[7]

This book aims to resolve these and other conflicts over the nature of Antimasonry through a study of the six New England states. They provide a large body of data, permitting comparisons and offering better prospects for making sense of Antimasonry's complexity and heterogeneity as well as its commonalities. The first half, "The Antimasonic Persuasion," delineates broadly the ideological and social sources of Antimasonry, exploring the role of ideology, class formation, religious strain, and gender conflict. These chapters provide a framework for Part II, which examines Antimasonic politics.

Some may wonder why study six states in detail when one or perhaps two might do. The confusing state of the literature suggests that it is necessary to cast a net wide enough to catch a large sample of the movement, yet at the same time to probe its grass-roots nature in sufficient detail to identify its support. Intensive community studies published in the past twenty-five years have been among the most influential contributions to the study of American history because they permit historians to come closer to holistic comprehension of a subject rooted in exhaustive sifting of a limited body of data. Their grave limitation remains the question of how representative the community selected may be in such a large and heterogeneous country as the United States. The chapters on state politics in Part II utilize elements of the community study, but without its depth, a sacrifice required by a desire for breadth not possible in an analysis of a single town, county, or state. Given the variety of New England Antimasonry, one hopes to find here common threads that link together Antimasonry throughout the country, though other wide-ranging studies, especially of New York and Pennsylvania, are necessary.

Since Charles P. McCarthy launched the modern study of Antimasonry in 1902, the subject has daunted many subsequent investigators. If past is prologue, this book will not settle the debate over Antimasonry. One can only hope to narrow the bounds of disagreement and to inspire others to move us closer to the truth.

Scholarly projects are necessarily collaborative even where one person assumes responsibility for authorship, including errors and other shortfalls. I am especially in debt to many who have assisted a work that began long ago as a chapter in a history of New England politics and society in the decades leading to the Civil War. New England archivists and librarians were invariably helpful, especially quick to answer long-distance requests. I am grateful to Vivian Bryan at the Vermont State Library, William Copeley at the New Hampshire Historical Society, Thomas Gaffney at the Maine Historical Society, as well as to others at the Vermont, Rhode Island, and Massachusetts historical societies and at the Massachusetts Archives and Maine and Connecticut state libraries. Interlibrary loan at Berkeley and Davis have also borne a heavy load, and Georgiana Moe and Oscar Burdick went out of their way to facilitate access to the superb collections of materials on the religious history of the northeastern United States at the Graduate Theological Union Library in Berkeley. Susan Wilcox and especially Hal Grade, consultants at the Social Science Data Service, University of California at Davis, never lost patience. Lynnda Pires, Karen Hairfield, and Debbie Shields expertly typed many versions.

Since it was possible to xerox Antimasonic materials from a variety of depositories, such as those noted above, I have collected probably the most complete file for the Northeast, which will be deposited at the library of the University of California at Berkeley for use by others.

I have also benefited from annual research grants from the Committee on Research, Academic Senate, University of California at Davis; a grant-in-aid from the American Council of Learned Societies; and a fellowship from the National Endowment for the Humanities, as well as sabbaticals from the University of California that provided release from teaching.

Along the way Professor Charles G. Sellers of the University of California at Berkeley gave welcome encouragement, and Rachel Toor and Stephanie Sakson-Ford at Oxford University Press superbly edited the manuscript. Finally, Oscar Handlin, who read the manuscript carefully, remains an inspiration and goad for me, as I believe he has been for more American historians of my generation than any other scholar I know.

El Cerrito   P.G.
August 1987

Contents

TOWARDS A CHRISTIAN REPUBLIC

I

THE ANTIMASONIC PERSUASION

Poland will yet drive the Russian Bear back into the dark recesses of his native cavern in the frozen recesses of the North. America has started the bloody Masonic Tiger from his lurking place and will pursue him with increasing and uncompromising vengeance, till driven back into those savage and barbarous wilds from whence he sprang.

Lynn Record, 19 October 1831

I

The Emergence of Antimasonry

No subject has ever spread with such rapidity over the continent, and harrowed up so much ill-feeling in the minds of the people, as the abduction of Morgan. . . .

Groton Herald quoted in the Boston *Masonic Mirror,* 6 March 1830

We will put down Masonry by the sword, if we cannot put it down without.

Jacob Hall quoted in the *Masonic Mirror,* 15 January 1831

On September 14, 1826, William Morgan, a stonemason living in Batavia, in western New York, disappeared and was never seen again by family and neighbors. During the summer of 1826, Morgan, in concert with the editor of the Batavia *Republican Advocate,* David Miller, intended to publish an exposé of the secrets of Freemasonry, a fraternal order which had spread into more than a thousand cities and towns all over the United States, and to which Morgan belonged with perhaps 100,000 other Americans.[1] By divulging the mysteries of Masonry, Morgan violated the oath all Masons take as an Entered Apprentice, the first degree of Masonry: "[to] ever conceal, and never reveal any part, or parts, art, or arts, point, or points of the secret arts and mysteries of ancient Freemasonry . . . under no less penalty than to have my throat cut across, my tongue torn out by the roots, and my body buried in the rough sands of the sea, at low water mark, where the tide ebbs and flows twice in twenty-four hours."[2]

When Masons learned of treason in their ranks, some moved decisively to protect the order and prevent publication, but they were too late. William Morgan's *Illustrations of Masonry* found an extensive circulation throughout the country. A mob of Masons armed with clubs set fire to Miller's printing establishment, but alerted citizens scattered the mob and put out the flames. Masons then had Morgan and Miller arrested, the one for allegedly stealing clothing from a Canandaigua hotel keeper, and the other for an unpaid debt. Before the plaintiff against Miller arrived, the magistrate freed him, but when Mrs. Morgan reached the Canandaigua jail to rescue her husband, he had vanished. Morgan had been released, seized on the street and, despite his cries of murder, was dragged into a waiting yellow carriage by kidnappers, who, through the concerted efforts of dozens of Masons across western New York, transported him to Fort Niagara, an abandoned post, where he was imprisoned. No trace of Morgan ever surfaced.

Early in October, thousands of handbills flooded western New York, publicizing the kidnapping. They touched off a wave of protest meetings that compelled Governor DeWitt Clinton to issue a series of proclamations ordering the arrest and punishment of the wrongdoers and offering a reward to citizens who aided in apprehending the guilty.

By early 1827 there was still no sign of Morgan, and many now concluded that the Freemasons had murdered him. In April, New York State toughened its laws against kidnapping, and in May the state indicted Sheriff Eli Bruce, himself a Mason, who was convicted of participating in the abduction. Grand Juries investigated suspect Masons in five counties; eighteen trials ensued. To avoid prosecution, some Masons fled the state. Many of the accused escaped punishment; a few were jailed briefly. The reliability of the system of justice in western New York in which Masons served on juries and the bench was as much on trial as were members of the Order. Many suspected a cover-up by Masonic officialdom ready to obstruct justice to protect the Order. The Masons themselves took no action to discipline wayward members, their leaders protesting the organization's innocence. Others responded to critics with ridicule, threats, and justifications of Morgan's fate for breaking his oath.

In October 1827, more than a year after Morgan's disappearance, a badly decomposed body turned up at Oak Orchard Harbor, forty miles from Niagara. Three inquests failed to establish conclusively whether the corpse was that of Morgan, as his wife and dentist believed, or of another. No one ever solved the mystery. Some Masons believed Morgan, plied with promises of financial aid, had collaborated in his own disappearance, to escape from family and failure and try his luck in Canada. Witnesses claim to have spotted him in various places, as far away as Smyrna, Turkey. Others believed he had fallen victim to Masonic malevolence. The passage of time has not solved the mystery of Morgan's fate.

In the decade after William Morgan's disappearance, Antimasonry raged like a brushfire, spreading into politics and giving birth to the first third party in American history. It expanded from western New York in an arc that stretched from Pennsylvania to Maine. The flames of Antimasonry burned especially brightly in New England. In Vermont, Antimasons became the largest political party in the early 1830s; in Massachusetts they edged aside the Democrats to become the second strongest party; in Rhode Island they captured the balance of power between Democrats and National Republicans and ruled in coalition with the Jacksonians. In Connecticut they polled at their peak almost a quarter of the vote. In Maine and New Hampshire much weaker Antimasonic movements revealed that no area of New England was immune.

Antimasons believed that Freemasons had murdered Morgan to protect the secrets of the Order, that the murderers had acted under Masonic authority, and that public officials and politicians, bound by Masonic discipline, conspired to cover up the truth. Some Masons insisted that there was no conclusive evidence that Morgan had been harmed. Because Masonic sheriffs, judges, and juries failed to bring implicated Masons to justice, and Masonic leaders were slow to condemn illegal activities—some remained resolutely silent on the subject—there was reason for the growing suspicion that the Order set itself above the law and constituted a conspiracy at odds with republican government and Christian morality.

Though Antimasonry assumed distinctive form in the United States, it had European antecedents. Originating in Britain early in the eighteenth century, it had spread to Europe by the late eighteenth and early nineteenth century, when conservative opponents of the Enlightenment and French Revolution believed that secret societies, most notably Freemasons and Illuminati, aimed to subvert the established order. According to J. M. Roberts, such notions were a "delusion of the directing classes" rather than "a mass phenomenon such as popular antisemitism or a witch-craze." While Antimasonry in the Old World may have been "the aberration of a few hundred writers," in the United States it was a mass movement that had originated at the grass roots and later attracted leading politicians and notables.[3] In Europe, actual conspiracies by political dissidents to strike at conservative rule after 1815 gave substance to the belief that secret societies represented a real threat to social order. Only after Antimasonry showed it possessed political promise did prominent state and national figures in the United States associate with the cause. A former president, vice president, and attorney general joined businessmen, lawyers, doctors, and clergymen well known in their communities to give legitimacy and leadership to a crusade through which militants hoped to rescue the country from the greatest peril, they thought, facing the United States since the American Revolution.[4]

Antimasonic committees sprang up in dozens of towns and counties. Newspapers, almanacs, tracts, reading rooms, and traveling lecturers exposed the alleged evils of Freemasonry. A caravan roamed Vermont performing a mock version of the Masonic ceremony. Lecturers simulated Masonic initiation rites and cheerfully raised hundreds in their audiences into the Order to bring it into contempt. As a mass social movement Antimasonry gravitated eventually towards politics, popularizing a new institution—the party nominating convention—a necessity for a new party since no legislative caucus, no body of elected officials, no group of professional politicians could call into existence a movement that repudiated political establishments. Thousands who had stayed home during the 1828 presidential election went to the polls after 1828 to vote for Antimasonic candidates. Voter turnout soared, demonstrating the new party's ability to mobilize citizens the major parties had failed to activate.

The conflict over Freemasonry ignited remarkably intense feelings among both the opponents and the defenders of the Order. In some communities "neighbor was set against neighbor, friends separated, families made enemies, and the peace and harmony . . . almost wholly destroyed."[5] Fathers disinherited sons, husbands and wives took opposite sides. Dozens of Masons made public confessions in hope of escaping censure by their churches and neighbors. Congregations expelled Masons and dismissed ministers who refused to abandon the order. A few clergymen also lost their pulpits for defying pro-Masonic majorities. Even at funerals Masons and Antimasons formed hostile camps.

What had begun as a response to misdeeds by some Masons and to lapses in law enforcement in western New York threatened to take on the dimension of mass paranoia. Masonic bluff, defiance, and apologetics in the face of sweeping attacks, coupled with the prominence and influence of public officials who were Freemasons, nurtured suspicions that Masonry as an institution, not just a few wayward members, bore culpability in the Morgan case. Moreover Antimasonry perceived the murder of Morgan not as an isolated event, but the tip of the iceberg, merely one of many Masonic crimes. Others were sure to surface now that an alerted citizenry stood vigilant.

In Boston in 1830 a former Mason described in gory detail a murder he had witnessed sixteen years earlier in a Belfast, Ireland, Lodge when another Mason, he claimed, forfeited his life for breaking his oath.[6] When Joab Hunter died at a Masonic Lodge in Boston, Antimasons were skeptical that it was from natural causes, as Masons claimed. What kind of fit "made the eye balls look *blood shot* and as if *started from their sockets*," they asked, or caused black and blue marks around the neck? Why had Masons attempted to prevent people from viewing the corpse, and why did they try to bury it secretly to keep the news out of the papers?[7] In Hartford, New York, claimed Antimasons, Baptist Elder George Witherell was the target of a Masonic assassination plot in September 1830 because he had renounced. Entering Witherell's home "at a dead hour of the night," two men found the wife in bed alone, the Elder not at home. Hearing intruders, a son rushed in to save his terrified mother from a butcher's knife.[8]

Poisonous suspicion filled the air. When the body of Artemas Kennedy, a former Knights Templar, surfaced at "low water mark" in the Milton River near Boston in 1830, some wondered whether he was just a drunk who had suffered an accident or was another victim of Masonry.[9] Reverend Moses Thacher, a former Mason from Wrentham, Massachusetts, told a Rhode Island legislative investigation that a Mason in one of the backcountry towns had illegally initiated a friend for which crime he had been "put out of the way" in a manner "so secretly, that his friends thought he had absconded."[10] When Methodist minister E. K. Avery, a Freemason, escaped indictment for allegedly killing young Sarah Cornell, a chorus of outraged Rhode Island citizens, smelling a Masonic fix, forced a trial. Suspicions of sexual entanglement hung over the Avery case, gaining credibility from repeated allegations that Masonry gave its members license to assault the virtue of women outside of Masonic protection.[11] Likewise a public outcry forced the authorities in Vermont to disinter the body of a Mason who had died in jail to satisfy the Antis that the Order had not sprung the convict.[12]

Antimasonic paranoia led some to fear the worst. In March 1830, Antimasons demanded access to the quarters of the Knights Templars in Boston—one of the higher orders of Masonry known for their stunning military ritual—where they expected to find a private arsenal sufficient to arm two thousand Masons intending perhaps a coup d'état. The excited Antis found only forty-three swords and thirty-four spittoons.[13] Such a frenzied atmosphere poisoned interpersonal relations. "Where once peace and contentment and happiness might be read in the countenance of every villager you met," lamented the *Masonic Mirror*, "you now find distrust, enmity, and hatred. . . . All confidence between man and man is destroyed; families are broken up; neighborly intercourse and interchange of friendly civilities and kindnesses are suspended, schisms have been created in the church. . . ."[14] Not even children escaped. Boston Antimasonic lecturer and editor Samuel D. Greene alleged that parents ordered their children to ostracize his son because the lad distributed Greene's newspaper.[15]

Fear bred intolerance, and intolerance bred acts of violence and intimidation on both sides. In Weymouth, Massachusetts, vandals broke into the Lodge room, stole the regalia and attempted to set the building on fire. Should they be caught, a Deacon in one of the town's churches threatened to use his bayonet to rescue them. In Boston roughnecks defaced the impressive new Masonic Temple and an alert watchman stopped arsonists intent on setting the building on fire. During construction, guy ropes used to hoist large stones were partially severed and after the sashes went in, windows were smashed. In Barnet, Vermont, vandals destroyed the Masonic symbols that graced the tombstone of Sheriff Adam Duncan.[16]

Masons also lost control. In Barrington, Rhode Island, Captain Sylvester Allen, a Royal Arch Mason, entered a church armed with a pair of pistols and threatened to shoot preacher Prentice, a seceding Mason, if he ascended the pulpit. The women in the congregation fled before a magistrate took Allen away.[17] A hostile Masonic mob, armed with guns and firecrackers, chased Avery Allyn, an Antimasonic lecturer, out of Providence, Rhode Island, and followed him into southeastern Massachusetts where they prevented him from speaking. Other Antimasonic lecturers faced repeated arrests to harass and silence them. In Woodstock, Vermont, Masons crowded into the gallery of a church and disrupted an Antimasonic meeting at which Rev. George Witherell, the renouncing Baptist minister from Hartford, New York, spoke. "That's a damn lie," someone shouted, and then missiles followed, first a snowball and then a psalm book aimed at the heads of the sponsoring clergy.[18]

At 11 p.m. at an inn in Hebron, Connecticut, Masons arrested Samuel

D. Greene for debt. Greene had fled to New England from Batavia, New York, where he had witnessed the events surrounding the Morgan case and became a militant Antimason. Masons retaliated by trying to ruin his hotel and tavern business. His butcher refused to sell him meat; vandals smeared his house with filth; they broke windows, ruined the furniture, stole the blankets, secreted rattlesnakes in his granary, and slit the throat of his dog from ear to ear. Greene took refuge in Boston where he edited an Antimasonic newspaper and traveled as an Antimasonic lecturer. Probably alerted to Greene's itinerary, Connecticut Masons lay in waiting, but a rich man saved him from jail by posting the $300 bail.[19] Not even Boston's Faneuil Hall, Cradle of American Liberty, escaped the fury of Masonic wrath. When Massachusetts Antimasons called a meeting in 1830, handbills flooded the city and hundreds of noisy Masons crowded into the auditorium to prevent citizens from exercising freedom of speech and assembly, while public authority stood helpless.[20]

Both sides played for keeps. Antimasons sought the total destruction of American Freemasonry.[21] They encouraged mass resignations, welcomed the dissolution of Lodges, and urged the states to repeal charters of incorporation and to outlaw Masonic oaths. To discover the full extent of Masonic influence, Antimasons secured wide-ranging legislative investigations which gave them a valuable new forum, the public hearing. At these earliest of inquiries into "unAmerican activities," Antimasons made their case for legal proscription. Unwilling to wait for public opinion and government to destroy Masonry, Antimasons proposed that the states place the Order under stringent oversight by requiring annual reports of the names of old and new members, the times and places of meetings and a record of initiations and funds. A century before the creation of internal security concepts and their accompanying apparatus in peacetime, Antimasons advocated the intrusion by government into private association and invasions of civil liberty. Until government acted, Antimasons themselves placed suspected Masons under surveillance, compiling lists which systematically identified Masons occupying public office.

By the early 1830s American Freemasonry was in retreat. Thousands of Masons gave up Lodge meetings. Lodges surrendered their charters, sold their halls, and many that hung on rarely met. States passed laws banning Masonic oaths, and voters turned Masons out of office, teaching the two major political parties that they ignored Antimasonry only at their peril.

By 1836 the Antimasonic frenzy had run its course in New England and the third party disappeared, its work completed. For a generation Masonry languished in the northeastern United States until the 1840s, when there were signs of revival. The number of Lodges almost doubled in that decade, with growth occurring in every region though nowhere to the extent that Masonry expanded in the West and the South. On the eve of the Civil War there were almost five thousand Lodges in the United States, more than twice the number at the beginning of the decade. This rebirth alarmed revivalist Charles G. Finney, who returned to a battle that had engaged his energies forty years earlier in western New York's Burned-Over District. In *The Character, Claims, and Practical Workings of Freemasonry* (1869), Finney insisted that Masonry was as much at odds with Christianity and republicanism as ever. A generation earlier God had blessed both Antimasonry and evangelical Protestantism with a shower of revivals that fell all over the Northeast, but in the Gilded Age, Finney's warnings went unheeded. He seemed an anachronistic voice from another age. In Finney's youth Antimasonry had flourished under circumstances distinctive to the early nineteenth century. By Finney's old age, however, the shift from an agrarian Republic to an industrial society had advanced so far that the ideological and social basis for a popular Antimasonic movement no longer existed. The short-term success and long-term failure of Antimasonry, explored in the following pages, constitute a revealing chapter in the history of this great transition.

At the same time that Freemasonry came under fierce attack and went into temporary retreat, other fraternal organizations such as the Odd Fellows, another English import, proliferated. The fraternal impulse was enduring and powerful. Freemasonry, though it had a distinctive appeal, like other fraternal orders satisfied important needs felt by thousands of Americans who joined these associations.[22]

Late in November 1825, Freemasons throughout New England received from Boston the first copy of the *Masonic Mirror and Mechanics Intelligencer*, one of several regional newspapers reporting Masonic news and spreading Masonic ideas. The appearance of a weekly devoted to Freemasonry was one more sign of the Order's prosperity. The first Lodge in America had been established in Boston in 1733, and nowhere in the colonies or in the early Republic had Masonry become as popular as in New England, which in 1790 boated almost 40 percent of all the Lodges in the country.[23]

Tracing its origins to the brotherhood of builders who constructed King Solomon's Temple and to operative Masons who carried on the tradition of the craft in medieval and early modern Europe, speculative Freemasonry was a product of early eighteenth-century Britain, from which it spread to the continent and America. Borrowing rituals, symbols, and iconography from many ancient sources, modern Freemasonry owed even more to the spirit of the Enlightenment, though the editor of the *Mirror*, like other Masons, stressed its antiquity. "Of all human institutions," he affirmed in his inaugural editorial, "Free-Masonry is the only one that has withstood the wreck of time. All others have sunk into oblivion."[24] Because Freemasonry was in fact an expression of a modern sensibility, with non-sectarian, deistic religious notions and a benign view of human nature and potential, and because its secularist and cosmopolitan tendencies placed it at odds with older patterns of religious belief and social organization—sectarian, parochial, exclusivist in character—Masons stressed their antiquity to disarm critics and reassure themselves. In a world in which the tempo of change had increased bewilderingly, that stratum most attracted by Masonry recognized that uncertainty and risk were inherent in the new social order. In joining this brotherhood, people sought shelter in an institution "founded on the Rock of Ages," old and tested, an asylum of stability in a rapidly shifting world.[25]

Masonry's essential doctrines had weathered the test of time because they offered men "the eternal and invariable principles of natural religion" by which to guide their lives.[26] The principles were as old as the discovery of the laws of symmetry and harmony, Masons believed, and marked a decisive step in the emergence of civilization from the dark ages. Masons claimed for their Order a pre-eminent civilizing mission: they had discovered a universal "science," and their mysteries and rituals constituted "a universal language" wherever art and civilization flourished.[27] To be a Mason was therefore to identify with a tradition that advanced the human race.

Masonry sought to promote human happiness by enlightening men about the paths to virtue. The doctrines of Masonry were "congenial with the best feelings of the human mind," said the *Mirror*, "so mild, and so benign in its principles, so well calculated to assuage the angry passions of man, so consonant with all human views of the attributes of Deity, that its initiates were at once surprised and enamoured, they became a band of brothers. . . ."[28] Masonry distilled the moral essence of religion, and though non-Christians could join, Christianity remained a principal inspiration, purged of obscurantist theology leaving a benevolent God—The Great Architect—whom one could comprehend and approach through reason and ritual by practicing tolerance, charity, and fraternalism, the great commandments of Freemasonry. Masonry counterposed its broadmindedness to the spirit of "the fulminating priests" who divided men and poisoned personal relations. It brought people together on a common platform of "science" and ethical belief and banished "all those disputes, which embitter life, and sour the tempers of men."[29] Masonry admitted Jews, Moslems, deists, and others who believed in God; the Order excluded only atheists. In Europe and America such ecumenical latitudinarianism distinguished Freemasonry in an age when sectarian Christianity still remained the dominant mode, doctrinal differences remained profoundly important, and denominational rivalry and hostility were still strong.

The three great Lights of Masonry were the Bible, the Square, and the Compass. The first was a guide to faith and practice; the second reminded the Mason to square his actions with his beliefs; and the compass symbolized his duty to keep his passions in "due bounds with all mankind, but more especially with our brother Masons."[30]

Each degree in the Masonic hierarchy tested the initiate and imposed new obligations. Only those who successfully passed one trial could ascend further. Most Masons took only the first three degrees, and with each, they gained certification for virtue and probity. The third degree, for example, tested truthfulness and fidelity. The ritual subjected one to assault from mock "threats and violence." The elaboration of higher degrees allowed men who wished further to distinguish themselves within the brotherhood to advance into more exclusive company. The candidate for the fourth degree, the Mark Master Mason, heard the Lodge Master enjoin him to "lay aside all malice, and guile, and hypocracies, and envies, and all evil speakings." Obedience to such injunctions had proved their worth, for they had enabled operative masons—stonemasons—to overcome great obstacles and complete the construction of King Solomon's Temple. Modern, speculative Masonry—ethical, philosophical, and philanthropic—thus traced back to a tradition equally useful for realizing one's ambitions in the modern world.[31]

Masonic ritual offered men an aesthetic experience that appealed to persons who could not find such experiences in Protestant churches or who wanted ceremony without dogma. Masonry developed an elaborate paraphernalia which symbolically expressed Masonic ideas. Masons wore an apron made of lambskin or white leather which was an emblem of innocence "more ancient than the gold fleece of Roman eagle," according to Thomas S. Webb.[32] The Entered Apprentice, the first degree, received a twenty-four-inch gauge, an instrument used by operative Masons which reminded speculative Masons of their duty to partition the twenty-four hours of the day into eight for work, eight for service to God and distressed brothers, and eight for refreshment and sleep.[33] Moral meaning attached to all the regalia and iconography. Claiming that Masonry was "the most moral institution that ever subsisted," Masons taught that "every character, figure and emblem, depicted in a lodge, has a moral tendency, and inculcates the practice of virtue."[34]

Though Masons denied that the order was a substitute for religion, preferring to describe Masonry as "the handmaid of religion," the emphasis on a benevolent and reasonable deity and the insistence that the essence of faith was moral behavior attracted many who found such notions more appealing than those encountered in the churches. This was especially true for people impressed with Masonry's claims to "science" and its devotion to geometry. Through the laws of geometry men discovered "the power, the wisdom, and the goodness, of the Great Artificer of the Universe" and learned to appreciate "with delight the proportions which connected this vast machine."[35] Masonry adopted tools and implements used in architecture and construction such as the plumb, the level, and the square among its "jewels," that is, badges, "to imprint on the memory wise and serious truth. . . ."[36]

Masonry attracted members from various denominations with a high incidence of Episcopalians, Unitarians, and Universalists among the leaders. But members of Calvinist denominations also joined, including clergymen who before 1826 saw no conflict between Masonry and Christianity. Masonry's non-sectarian, vaguely Christian character proved one of its greatest attractions, for in the Lodge one could leave behind "all prejudices . . . on account of religion, country, or private opinion" and find acceptance as a member of "one family."[37]

Because Masonry was a secret organization, prospective members had only a very vague idea where pursuit of the Light of Masonry would lead. It is difficult to know how seriously Freemasons took Masonic ideology when the order was expanding rapidly and recruiting heterogeneous elements. Typically in modern Freemasonry, initiates are unversed in Masonic principles until after they join, though beforehand they must have some vague sense of its Enlightenment character. Masonry drew in people primarily because it offered an appealing fraternalism, which in the early nineteenth century middle-class men might not readily find elsewhere.

In one's Lodge, explained the *Masonic Mirror*, brothers found "a refuge from the storms and troubles of life. In sickness and in health, in prosperity and in adversity, Masonry has its excellencies. . . ."[38] Unlike coffee houses and saloons, Masonic Lodges were private, class-segregated institutions which allowed men to spend leisure time in a respectable, relaxed, and enjoyable setting, entertained by elaborate ritual and good fellowship. At a time when ties based on kinship, locality, religious, and occupational status no longer circumscribed the experience of people who lived in an increasingly geographically mobile, culturally diverse, and economically volatile order, Freemasonry offered businessmen and professionals instant access to a circle of friends, much like themselves, who affirmed their importance. Freemasonry tended to recruit its members from among the upper and middle strata of the community, though as it grew it became primarily middle-class. Admission was particularly valuable to newcomers, for it confirmed their social status, just as it validated that of young men starting their careers. When transiency and social mobility became common experiences, a sorting-out mechanism such as Freemasonry performed an important stratifying function.[39]

For Jews, Afro-Americans, and men who belonged to no church, Masonry could also confer respectability which might otherwise be at issue. Only Afro-Americans failed to break through the admission barriers because American Masons assumed that all free blacks had been rendered unfit for membership in the Order by the experience of servitude. Failing to secure a charter from an American Grand Lodge, Afro-American Prince Hall Freemasons obtained one in Great Britain, but this irregularity left it adrift. These Lodges remained apart from the mainstream of American Freemasonry. Yet through Masonry the black Freemasons sought to identify a black upper class, to differentiate themselves from other Afro-Americans, and to demonstrate to whites and themselves that black Americans were capable of displaying the bourgeois virtues Masonry insisted upon, especially a capacity to acquire property.[40]

Freemasonry thus played an important role in the system of stratification emerging in industrial societies. Masons did not exclude working men, but the dues and fees and the style of sociability made it unlikely that many mechanics or laborers would join. Nor was there any educational prerequisite for membership, but the expectation that every Mason could master a minimum of the complicated ritual assured that Masonry recruited men who possessed superior intellect and literacy and adequate leisure time.[41] Masons saw themselves as among "the better sort" in a social order marked by much uncertainty. In resisting powerful currents which tended to atomize individuals and impersonalize social relations, Masonry offered men an institution through which they might re-establish some sense of community based on social class and a shared set of values and cultural style. "How to be brothers, indeed, in the midst of diversities of race and nation," wrote a leading Southern Freemason in the late nineteenth century, "to be brothers still, loving brothers in a world rent by violence, sundered by partition walls, full of intolerance and party feelings, sectarian strife and exclusiveness of caste . . . is a problem which Freemasonry undertakes to solve."[42]

Within the Order a meritocratic egalitarianism reigned. One advanced up the Masonic ladder through achievement, by earning appropriately each new degree. Those most diligent in the quest for the Light of Masonry won election to office and advanced to the higher degrees, paying, of course, additional fees at each step. Internally Masonic organization rested on a hierarchical structure that emphasized offices, titles, and ritual. A Master, Wardens, Deacons, Stewards, and others presided over Lodge meetings which occurred at least monthly. Meetings at which new members were inducted or old ones advanced to higher degrees were especially rich in ceremony. The rituals were fixed and mastery of the details was essential for leadership. Masons made systematic efforts, especially during the period of rapid growth in the first half of the nineteenth century, to assure uniformity in ritual among the many new Lodges that sprang up after the Revolution in places where few possessed Masonic experience. Lectures, publications, and visiting delegates from the Grand Lodge—the statewide body which chartered all Lodges within its jurisdiction—sought to assure conformity to establish ritual. The distinctive regalia and complicated rites symbolically expressed Masonic ideology and the secretive elements—the passwords, grips, dueguards, and special words, the stationing of a Tyler, or guard, at the entrance to protect the Lodge's security, and the Mason's oath to "ever conceal, and never reveal any part, or parts, art, or arts, point, or points of the secret arts of ancient Freemasonry,"—all set members apart from others and established a sense of community based on access to an arcane set of mysteries. The high value placed on mastery of complicated ritual forms, like the claims to antiquity, served to make Freemasonry appear steeped in history, an institution that linked the ever-changing present to an unchanging moral order. American Freemasons placed an even higher premium on ritual uniformity than did German Freemasons because they lived in a more egalitarian society, experienced greater uncertainty over norms and a greater sense of rootlessness.[43]

Secrecy was one of the distinguishing characteristics which set Freemasonry apart from most other voluntary associations and aroused intense anxiety among outsiders. Secrecy "built a barrier against fear of the dangers of unimpeded individuals uncomfortably shifting within an expansive mobile society."[44] Thus protected, middle-class American men found in Freemasonry an asylum from the marketplace. Secrecy was fundamental; it imposed an obligation on members which tested their faithfulness and emphasized their separateness. That was why Morgan's treason seemed so heinous. One faithless member's reckless deed jeopardized an institution that inspired the devotion of thousands. "Were the privileges of Masonry to be indiscriminately bestowed," explained Thomas S. Webb, "the design of the institution would be subverted . . . ," for its mysteries would soon "lose their value and sink into disregard." Masters therefore solemnly enjoined every initiate to "keep sacred and inviolable the mysteries of the order, as these are to distinguish you from the rest of the community."[45] Bloodcurdling penalties for violating one's oath underlined dramatically the serious obligations Masons assumed.

Freemasonry offered Americans secrecy, ritual, and ceremony which emphasized the importance of order, hierarchy, and social harmony in an aesthetically pleasing setting that satisfied middle-class sensibilities. At the beginning of the Lodge meeting each officer took his appropriate station, and every brother arranged himself by rank according to degree. Such precise adherence to station enabled one to detect imposters, while the vigilance of the Tyler kept strangers out and guaranteed the Lodge's security. Only then could the master give the charge which opened a meeting: "Behold how good and how pleasant it is for brethren to dwell together in unity." After the merchants and master mechanics, the doctors and ministers, lawyers and public officials had completed the work of the meeting, a prayer brought it to a conclusion: "May brotherly love prevail," affirmed the Master, "and every moral and social virtue cement us! *Amen*."[46]

The practical application of Masonic ideas softened everyday experience in an increasingly competitive economic system. Masonry bound brothers together by a kindly code that regulated interpersonal relations and taught them not to be envious of one another or censorious.[47] In a highly litigious society Masons were expected to submit their disputes with fellow Masons to arbitration rather than resort to the courts. Masons in financial need could turn for assistance to their Lodge, knowing that any aid would remain confidential to protect the pride of the recipient and to conform to the Masonic notion that benevolence was a duty, not something to boast about in public. Widows and children of Masons also came within the purview of Masonic benevolence and in other ways Masonry extended protection to the family, for a Mason took an oath to respect the honor of his brothers' women folk.[48]

In death, too, the band of brothers stood together. Masonic funeral services offered men an alternative or a supplement to religious rites.[49] Following a prescribed ritual, Masonic funerals made death less terrifying, treated all the deceased alike, and comforted the bereaved that their loved one had gone to a better reward. Notions of hell and damnation, divine punishment and terror had no part on the Masonic rite. "How many offerings has he made upon the altar of charity! How honorably has he sustained the cares of life! How did he make the hearts of all around him happy," the Masonic funeral orator soothingly affirmed.[50] As churches lost their character as comprehensive community institutions, they were no longer able to assemble a substantial portion of the town to honor the departed. Moreover, since a declining portion of American males became formal church members, at least from the mid-eighteenth century, and many stopped attending regularly, a Masonic funeral assured a respectable turnout. For men whose relations to a church were tenuous, a Masonic service was also more in keeping with the deceased's own beliefs than burial by a wife's minister, a man one hardly knew or perhaps even loathed. And for those without any religious ties, Masonic funerals filled a void. A Mason wishing a Masonic funeral notified the Master of the Lodge and the Master, once informed of the brother's death, fixed a time for the ceremony. This procedure allowed a Mason to remove funeral arrangements from the responsibility of wife and family. According to *The Freemason's Monitor* the entire ceremony "must be under the direction of the Master of the lodge to which the deceased belonged . . . ," which served to subordinate the role of any participating clergy.[51] As a competitor or alternative to the churches in the management of death, the Masonic funeral was another sign of the secular currents that found expression in the organization, yet a secularism that insisted on its Christian respectability and had little in common with popular free thought.

For all the solemnity of Masonic ritual and the somber dignity of Masonic funerals, conviviality was one of the Order's strongest drawing cards. Masonry helped to fill a need for a place where men could relax, let down their hair, eat, and drink among pleasant company. One can get some sense of the Masonic *bonhomie* from Masonic songs. At the St. John's Celebration in Boston in 1834, the brothers raised their voices to sing:

> A Mason's life's the life for me,
> Thus we employ our life with glee,
> Attending every sign.
> But when the glass goes round,
> Then mirth and glee abound.

Alcohol often lubricated Masonic fellowship, as another Masonic verse explained:

> We laugh a little, and drink a little
> We sing a little, are merry a little
> And swig the flowing can.[52]

The growing popularity in early nineteenth-century America of theatre, dancing, music, and other sources of entertainment and recreation often placed people uncomfortably at odds with older standards of religious decorum that rigidly restricted how the pious and respectable might spend their leisure time, especially on Sundays. The Sabbatarian movement of the 1820s sought to curb the increasing popularity of secular activities that compromised the holiness of the sabbath. At a time before the development of mass forms of entertainment, the Masonic Lodge offered men an evening of diversion. Many Masons liked to sing, judging from the Masonic song-books published in the early nineteenth century. The songs celebrated Freemasonry and provided music for different portions of Masonic ritual.[53] The most influential systematizer and champion of American Freemasonry in the early nineteenth century was Thomas Smith Webb, Grand Master of the Grand Lodge of Rhode Island, a key founder of the Haydn and Handel Society in Boston. Since clergymen often served as chaplains of a Lodge, their presence lent respectability to Masonic conviviality. In these ways Masonry offered men a retreat from the cares of the world, the anxieties of the marketplace, and the strains of interpersonal relations. In one's Lodge all were brothers. There the title "brother" took precedence over the titles or social differences that set people apart on the outside. Doctors, lawyers, ministers, and officials, the rich and less-than-rich, prominent and obscure temporarily forgot precise grades of social standing when they participated in the pleasures of Masonic conviviality. The cost of furnishing food and drink revealingly consumed the largest share of a Lodge's funds in the early nineteenth century. Charitable expenditures were relatively small, a measure of the Order's priorities.

Freemasonry was a male institution. Not until the mid-nineteenth century did the Order of the Eastern Star offer women access through a separate branch. The ban on women assured Masons a place unlike taverns and bars, whose respectability was suspect, where men could socialize in the leisure hours exclusively among members of their own sex. Masonry thereby enabled men to rope off one small part of their lives from their wives and mothers. A Mason could not share his secrets even with his most intimate female relatives without violating his oath. Since Masons claimed that they promoted morality and benevolence, there was no reason for women to object if husbands spent one night a month at their Lodge. Not all women, however, were approving, especially because of the attraction Masonry had for their sons.[54]

Freemasonry in the early nineteenth century was very much a young man's institution. Most men joined in their twenties or early thirties, following in the footsteps of a Masonic father or relative; in later years enthusiasm tended to decline.[55] For young men starting out in a career in business or the professions, Masonry offered useful contacts. Becoming a Freemason was akin to a rite of passage by which young males affirmed their independence from women and the domestic universe. Because many women disapproved of Masonry, going against common feminine opinion defied the claims of domesticity. When a son joined his father's Lodge, therefore, he was siding with his own sex in the battle between the sexes.

Despite the emphasis on secrecy, Masonry was in part a public institution. Its members did not hide their membership, its officers were public figures, and some of its ceremonies—funerals and celebration of the birthday of St. John the Baptist, the patron "saint" of Freemasonry—took place in public. Masonic holidays, along with the Fourth of July and a few other public days, were the principal times for public celebration. Freemasons also managed cornerstone-laying ceremonies of important public edifices. On such occasions one saw impressive processions of Masons marching solemnly through the streets to perform their work at the building site.

The growth of Freemasonry after the American Revolution was therefore readily observable to outsiders. In some communities when a new school went up, Masons contracted with the school committee to share the costs and thereby obtained space for themselves. Elsewhere they erected Masonic Halls in communities which had few other public buildings. As early as 1818 the Oriental Lodge in Livermore, Maine, built a hall at the cost of nearly a thousand dollars. The raising of these Masonic edifices, at considerable expense, revealed that the Order commanded extensive wealth. Men unwilling to contribute to the construction of a church readily opened their purses for the erection of a Masonic Hall.

The growth of Freemasonry in the post-revolutionary decades in Vermont gives a concrete glimpse into the process of development in New England. Freemasonry was extremely popular in the Green Mountain State. The number of Lodges tripled during the first decade of the nineteenth century. By 1830 there were more Lodges in Vermont than in any of the other New England states except Massachusetts. Many of the early Masons had served in the army during the American Revolution when officers established military Lodges. After the war some revolutionary veterans sustained old social ties through Masonry. Many of these early Vermont Masons were prominent figures in the early history of the state. Town founders, holders of state and federal offices, they were mostly business and professional men.[56]

In 1794, Vermont Lodges established a Grand Lodge which oversaw rapid growth, maintained standards, and assured quality in the membership, a pattern followed in other states. The Grand Lodge announced it would not grant charters unless the Master and Wardens were competent in Masonic arts. Inspectors from the Grand Lodge, beginning in 1797, visited Lodges to assure uniform observance of rituals.[57] During the decade of most rapid expansion, Vermont Masons took new measures to weed out the unworthy. Beginning in 1808 the Grand Lodge published annually the names of persons suspended for misconduct. During the next twenty-three years, almost 260 men were excluded and 85 suspended.[58]

Until 1824 the Grand Lodge reported no conflict between the Order and

Vermont's churches. In that year Elder Robert Hastings was excluded by his church because he was a Mason.[59] More typically Masonry and the churches avoided conflict. From 1808, the Grand Master appointed a Grand Chaplain each year whose sermon was often published, and who regularly received a donation.[60] Most of the Grand Chaplains who could be identified were Congregationalists, like Jonathan Nye of St. Albans who also served as Grand Master and was a pillar of the Vermont Grand Lodge for many years. In 1813 the Grand Lodge contributed seventy-five dollars to the American Bible Society, the first donation of several to religious organizations. In aiding the work of the Bible Society, the Grand Lodge explained, it sought to spread the Bible on a strictly non-sectarian basis.[61] In 1827, Grand Master Phineas White tried unsuccessfully to expand further the benevolent horizons of Vermont Freemasons by proposing that the Order contribute to the American Colonization Society.[62] In other ways, Vermont Masonry fell under the influence of popular currents. Masonic conviviality eventually came into conflict with the temperance movement. Temperance was a divisive issue for Masons as it was for the churches. In 1819 the Grand Lodge banned liquor, but the next year it repealed the ban only to reimpose it in 1826.[63] Nor could Masons enjoy their music without anxiety. In 1820 the Grand Lodge placed a cap on the cost of hiring musicians not to exceed $4.50 per year.[64] Even dinners fell under a cloud, though that did not last long.

When the Antimasonic frenzy spread to Vermont, the Grand Lodge, which had presided over the order's expansion during the preceding quarter-century, heroically but vainly sought to sustain Masonry. In 1830, sixty-eight Lodges sent delegates to the Grand Lodge; two years later the number dwindled to ten. The Lodge, however, refused to disband, voting down motions to dissolve.[65] A corporal's guard hung on, waiting for the storm to pass. Even should Masonry fall, Grand Master Nathan P. Haswell insisted in 1834, its monument would remain. "So long as brotherly love, relief and truth obtain among men," so long would the memory of Masonry endure. No "waves of popular prejudice" or shouts "of popular clamor" could rob it of honor in the eyes of all philanthropists. Among "the galaxy of social institutions," Freemasonry would ever shine as one of the brightest stars in the "moral constellation."[66] Such brave words could not hide the near-mortal blow inflicted by the Antimasons. For many years no new Lodges were consecrated in Vermont. In consecrating a Lodge, a small chest containing the three Great Lights of Masonry, the Bible, the Compass, and the Square, is uncovered and annointed with corn, wine, and oil. By means of this ritual the Lodge symbolically separated itself from all profane things and was thereby "set apart as an asylum sacred to the cultivation of Masonic principles of Friendship, Morality and Brotherly Love." When the storm of Antimasonry broke, Freemasons were caught unprepared to protect their asylum. The rise of Antimasonry in the decade following the disappearance of William Morgan gathered momentum throughout the northeastern

United States because thousands of Americans came to believe that the evils to which humankind were prone found shelter within Masonry, endangered non-Masons, and threatened the very foundations of a Christian Republic. The extraordinary discrepancy between Freemasonry as conceived by its members and as perceived by its foes gives access to the deep fault lines appearing in the United States as it passed from an agrarian to an industrial society.

2

Guardians of the American Revolution
Republican Sources of Antimasonry

The spirit of anti-masonry can never die; 'tis the spirit of liberty. . . .
The coal that kindled the fire of anti-masonry, is the same that burned
on the altar of freedom in '75.   Amasa Walker, 1830[1]

"We hold these truths to be self-evident, that all men are created equal"—
with these words Antimasons summoned citizens of Massachusetts in 1830
to defend the "fundamental principles of civil and religious rights." "We
have come up to Faneuil Hall, which your Fathers consecrated to Liberty,"
seeking "the political salvation of our country," Abner Phelps told the 245
delegates attending the 1831 Massachusetts Antimasonic convention.
"When in the course of human events, the accustomed safeguards of society
are destroyed," said Antimasons, it was time for citizens to resist rather than
become "willing vassals of this worse than Asiatic dominion of masonry."[2]
Fifty-three years after the birth of the Republic, proclaimed Vermont's
William Slade, the United States was still "the final refuge of persecuted
freedom" but it was now "passing through an exceedingly interesting crisis."
Would the current generation successfully manage the "perilous transition
from the hands of their founders . . . ?"[3] That would depend, said Micah
Ruggles, Antimasonic leader in Fall River, Massachusetts, upon whether
citizens realized that Antimasonry was "but a second declaration of independence." The success of that cause would "prove whether we were worthy
of our sires."[4]

These affirmations of the Spirit of '76 implied that half a century after
the Founding Fathers had taken the first decisive steps to secure the rights
of man, the forces of tyranny once more stalked the land. This time the
enemy was not external—a wicked King and greedy Parliament as in '76—
nor a corrupt and power-hungry executive which Jeffersonian Republicans
in '98 accused of plotting to reinstate monarchy. Freemasonry was a private,
voluntary association, claiming to be a social and charitable institution, but
to Antimasons, this latest enemy of American liberty was more shrouded in

obscurity, more widely diffused, and more dangerous than its predecessors. In sounding the alarm, Antimasons identified as the enemy not a tiny elite but thousands of their fellow citizens who had joined a popular organization that had spread into hundreds of communities throughout the United States. The indictment of Freemasonry was an indictment of central tendencies of the age. Masonry had flourished during the first half-century of American independence because faithless citizens, unworthy heirs of their Revolutionary Fathers, succumbed. Though American Freemasonry traced its origins to the generation before the American Revolution, and Founding Fathers such as George Washington, Benjamin Franklin, and other luminaries had joined, Antimasons brushed history aside. If once pure, Masonry had undergone corruption; if once harmless, Masonry had become a ruthless conspiracy.

A quarter-century earlier, foes of the French Revolution had identified Freemasonry as the secret spring behind that great and unfathomable event. In the United States, some Federalist clergy, supporters of the established churches in New England, sought to discredit their Republican opponents as America's Jacobins by identifying them as agents of the same Illuminist conspiracy that had allegedly drowned Europe in blood, overthrown Christianity in France, and threatened civilized regimes on two continents. The idea of an Illuminist conspiracy, however, gained few adherents in the United States, even among Federalists, but the revival of Antimasonry in the 1820s found a much broader, more receptive public even though the flames of party rivalry had long died down.[5]

Antimasonry was a social paranoia which, like the other paranoias that have captured the imagination of many and stimulated the organization of social movements, had roots in reality.[6] Circumstantial evidence pointed to Masons as Morgan's probable murders. Dozens of suspect Masons in western New York escaped punishment or got off lightly, justifying apprehensions that Masons exercised powerful influence in high places. Moreover, the tendency of Freemasonry to attract membership mostly from the upper half of the social structure gave grounds for thinking that it was a putative aristocratic elite aiming at aggrandizing wealth and power. Finally, Masonry's affinity for natural religion, together with its latitudinarian view of Christian doctrine, furnished grounds for believing it was incompatible with revealed religion just as it was at odds with American Republicanism.

Through Antimasonry Americans hoped first to comprehend and then to arrest disturbing changes transforming the United States in the early nineteenth century. The spread of the market economy wrought the most profound changes Americans had ever experienced. It disrupted the relative stability of the subsistence economy. It introduced people to the volatility of the business cycle and to still more frequent short-term fluctuations in business activity. It encouraged the growth of an entrepreneurial mentality as a societal norm and inspired young people to search for new careers, new occupations, new places in which to live and work where they might pursue the dream of success. It set in motion demographic changes that depopulated some communities and produced mushroom growth in others. It redesigned the nature of the family and the definition of sex roles. It generated un-dreamed-of new wealth and immense private fortunes and yet left some Americans stranded in poverty, dependency, and failure. It shaped a new class structure rooted more in property relations than in community relations. Nothing remained untouched, the culture no less than the economic and social system. A popular, pervasive secularism threatened to erode the influence of religious belief, and at the same time pluralism undermined the cultural homogeneity of communities. The spread of pluralism and the challenge from secularism inspired a sustained burst of creative evangelical activism that intensified people's sense that a great struggle for cultural dominance was underway. As in the marketplace for goods and services, so too in the marketplace for ideas and values, competition became the order of the day.

Rapid changes of such magnitude produced a profound sense of disloca-tion among citizens troubled by the dissolution of an older order, apprehen-sive as they entered the formative stages of a new one whose design re-mained incomplete and unclear. The process occurred slowly and piecemeal, spread unevenly throughout the country and because those living through this great transition did not, could not, clearly comprehend that experience, change was all the more puzzling and threatening.

Freemasonry became a master symbol, the object of people's suspicions because it was both in reality and in their perception closely identified with new currents that were reshaping the United States. Masonry preached the virtues of cosmopolitanism over localism. It offered men on the move a familiar haven wherever ambition and business took them. It provided a streamlined, not very demanding version of Christianity that stressed the centrality of benevolence over doctrine and ecumenicism over sectarianism, tending to secularize religion itself while claiming not to intrude upon the churches. It legitimized a male form of middle-class sociability outside the home, and it enabled members of a newly emergent middle class to identify one another. Freemasonry, like Antimasonry, was a precipitate of the spread of the market, for while its origins preceded the advent of industrial capital-ism in the United States, its rapid growth and widespread diffusion paral-leled the extension of the new order. The Workingmen's party's indictment of "monopoly," like the Jacksonian Democrats' war against the Bank of the United States, revealed a widespread ambivalence towards modernization that, like Antimasonry, sought to identify those half-hidden forces which people sensed radically altered their lives and which seemed incompatible with the social assumptions upon which the American Republic rested.[7]

The revolutionary generation had instructed its successors in the science of republican politics. The security of a republican system, they taught, rested on a virtuous citizenry that balanced private advantage against the common welfare.[8] The identification of the yeoman farmer, in Jeffersonian social thought, as the bone and sinew of a republic, stemmed from a belief that the small, independent landowner, beholden to no man, prized his independence and was vigilantly suspicious of threats to liberty. Because he coveted only a competence, the fruit of his own and his family's labor, the husbandman pursued neither wealth nor power at his neighbor's expense. The American aversion to large cities and industrialism grew out of a belief that, as European example warned, they were incompatible with a free political system because they enslaved the mass while elevating a few. Yet as much as members of Jefferson's generation were apprehensive that the spread of industrial capitalism ate away at the social foundations of republicanism, none could be certain that Americans would forgo the new wealth and opportunities economic development created. The extent of unsettled land covering a vast continent put off the day, "to the hundredth generation," Jefferson once said in a characteristic moment of hyperbole that masked his doubts, when the United States must face the crowding and corruption urbanization and industrialization brought elsewhere.[9] The haste with which Jefferson as President seized the chance to double the size of the United States in 1803 and the persistence of the expansionist impulse that added the Floridas in 1819 to round out the eastern limits of the nation, followed by the press into Texas, revealed a realistic sense that American space was not limitless, that prudent acquisitions today would only postpone the day of reckoning.

By the 1820s, it was apparent that the agrarian Republic bequeathed by the Founders was changing beyond recognition. Anyone searching for an institution whose ideology, social composition, and rapid expansion symbolized the emergence of a new order might well have seized on Freemasonry, whose dynamic growth in the early nineteenth century followed the lines of economic development and centered in the market towns. Between 1810 and 1830 the number of Masonic Lodges in New England jumped from 231 to 388, while in the Middle Atlantic states they grew from 327 to 525 in a single decade from 1810 to 1820.[10] As an institution that served an emerging industrial society, Freemasonry understandably evoked suspicion among those not yet reconciled to the new system.

The Founders had warned that eternal vigilance was the price of liberty. Antimasonry drew support from elements especially sensitive to the successor generation's responsibility to preserve the republican trust in tact. The 1820s was a time of testing—when the fate of the Republic was once again at high risk. "Recreant shall we be to their noble spirit, faithless to their example," warned Amasa Walker, an Antimasonic stalwart from Massachusetts, "if we indulge in sloth, inactivity, and content ourselves with praising, instead of emulating their noble deeds." Masonry was a British import—reason enough for guardians of the American Revolution to be on the alert. The dangers of '26 were as imminent as the dangers of '76. Now as then the agents of tyranny hoped "to lull people into a false security till their chains are made fast forever." Small incidents, singular events should alert every lover of liberty to the danger as did the three-pence duty on tea in 1773, a modest tax, "but a prelude to more odious impositions." The Morgan case in itself was "but a comparatively small thing," but the larger plot that it exposed was of "pernicious and terrific character." Not even George III had dared to seize an American and take his life without observing the forms of law. Masonry was a counter-revolutionary movement that subverted republican order. Against the dangers Antimasons organized "a great revolution" of their own to preserve American liberty, inspired by the same flames "that burned on the altar of freedom in '75."[11]

In answering the call to arms, the Minutemen of 1826 would show that they were worthy of their inheritance. How many citizens would "exhibit anything of the spirit of their Whig fathers" was unclear, observed Edward Barber, a leading Vermont Antimason. Strangely, he noted, many of the "descendants of those who battled for freedom on the field of carnage and death hug to their bosoms a monster stained with the blood of the innocent and covered with the garments of pollution."[12] The post-Revolution generation was squandering its inheritance of freedom and equality, allowing usurpations by "proud aristocratic combinations." A people once content to seek a competence now lusted after "wealth and power." Faithless republicans permitted influence and riches steadily and dangerously to accumulate "into the hands of certain classes in society. . . ."[13] Before it was too late, Antimasons summoned Americans to purge the Republic of a new "haughty aristocracy" and thereby "hand down to posterity unimpaired the republic we inherited from our forefathers." The destruction of Freemasonry would surely secure the American Revolution and thereby give the nation "a Second Independence."[14]

Antimasonic imagery alternated gloomy forebodings of decay with utopian visions of perfectability. Masonry, claimed Edward Barber, was a "wily serpent which had crept insidiously into the Eden of this happy Republic. . . ." The "monster" had deluded people who now "fondle the viper" and allow it to sink its "fangs into the very bosom of the constitution." The triumph of Antimasonry would rescue freemen from "this great moral and political *Boa Constrictor* which was crushing" the people in its "torturous embrace."[15] Antimasonry hoped to "expel from our Eden of social, political and religious privileges, the lurking serpent, the great enemy of the Church, the Constitution, Freemasonry."[16] Americans, warned Vermont Antimasons, "cannot be too watchful of the golden apples which grew in the Hesperidean garden of freedom, or too fearful of the hand that can pluck them either by force or stratagem."[17] Precisely because the United States seemed to be Paradise Regained, Antimasons sensed its unique vulnerability to the forces of darkness. In more sober moments, Antimasons acknowledged that the evils they feared were more prospective than immediate, but that was no reason to relax vigilance.

The Founders taught and Antimasons remembered that the danger to republicanism lay in the very nature of man. "The spirit of denomination, and the lust of power, is not gone," Amasa Walker reminded people. As in the past, so today it "wars against *equal rights* with as much relentless violence and increasing perseverance as ever, only under different forms and with different weapons." Constitutions and laws could check human passions but they alone could not guarantee against subversion. Without virtue no republican system could endure. Freemasonry, however, undermined devotion to the common good. Here was a private association that sought to define rank secretly, elevating a few, motivated exclusively by self-interest to set themselves above other citizens through concert and secrecy.[18] By weakening the restraints doctrinal Christianity imposed on the passions, by giving license to vices such as drinking and debauchery, Freemasonry imperiled the state, the church, and the home.

The spirit of Freemasonry was at bottom the spirit of aristocracy, the Antis argued. Their own movement was "a struggle of republican equality against an odious aristocracy" that had set itself above the law. Masonic "law" required that brothers give preference to Masons at the polling place. Antimasons pointed to the circular issued to Masons by the Grand Master of Massachusetts in 1816 just before the state election, instructing them to "promote a brother's political advancement, in preference to any other of equal qualification." By such means Masons had gained control of "ten times as many offices" as their numbers justified.[19] Masons insisted, in rebuttal, that their rules strictly forbade the introduction of politics into the Lodge, but critics responded that once the formal meeting ended, the brothers broke into small cliques to plot the next campaign, shielded by Masonic secrecy. At a time when Americans still had not reconciled themselves to the legitimacy of political parties, when the Second Party System was yet in an early stage of development, Masonry appeared to be the center of factious machinations by the politically ambitious. It was, indeed, many believed, the animating force behind both parties.[20] Masonic domination explained why both parties refused to condemn the Order and shielded its iniquities, and it explained, too, why "under a government of righteousness, schemes of selfishness and aggrandizement may be carried on."[21]

The legal system no less than the political system fell under Masonic influence. Bound by their oaths to vote for one another, Masons were also bound to favor one another in the courts. It was impossible for Masons to render fair and impartial justice in suits between a brother and an outsider. "Cases almost innumerable can be referred to," claimed Maine Antimasons, "where in legal trials, Masonic influence has turned the scale in favor of the brethren of the craft."[22] That was why, the Antimasons argued, Masons guilty of involvement in the kidnapping and murder of William Morgan had either escaped punishment or suffered light penalties. Likewise in business dealings and in the dispensation of charity Masons favored one another.

Masonry thus set itself in opposition to equality before the law. Deriving republican norms not just from secular principles but from Christian sources, Antimasons posited that God created men equal, whereas Masonry, like other forms of aristocracy, estranged men "from each other and from the common parent."[23] Americans in 1776 had returned to first principles to renew the social contact. Masonry seemed to break that compact. It arraigned one portion of society against another and replaced the republican norm of virtue with other standards, standards which facilitated the rise of "men of feeble talents" into positions of prominence, and allowed "the unprincipled and untalented" to edge aside the deserving.[24] By erecting new barriers between men and women Masonry further excluded from "its advantages the whole female sex—that portion of the human family which is the very foundation of social happiness." Even worse it allowed its members to prey on women unrelated to members of the fraternity whom Masons regarded as outside the limits of Masonic protection.[25] Such was the "spirit and tendency" of an institution that stood at loggerheads with republicanism. In their love for grandiose, monarchical titles, Freemasons betrayed themselves, the Antis agreed. What honest republican would crave such highfalutin names as Grand King, Most Excellent General, Grand High Priest, Sovereign Architect of the Universe, Knight of the Mother of Christ—all titles which Freemasons avidly sought.[26]

How had an institution so at odds with republicanism gained so many adherents in the United States?, Antimasons wondered. Only, they believed, through secrecy and deception. Masonry shrouded itself in mystery because it could not bear scrutiny. Virtually alone among the proliferating voluntary associations in the United States, Masonry dared not take its chances before the bar of public opinion because "virtue and integrity alone can court its glance" whereas "vice and crime die within its presence."[27] A shackled and venal press hid the truth. By the 1820s a competitive, partisan, and vituperative free press had become an unavoidable, some thought a necessary, even desirable, institution in a Republic. Despite its faults, the press stood as a sentinel against abuses of power. The press equalized disparities in the conditions of men. It gave a citizen "however humble his condition . . . free access to the public judgment. . . ." The Revolutionary Fathers understood that in erecting a "superstructure of freedom which should endure the vicissitudes of time," a free press was essential. It therefore was a powerful force to thwart a movement towards aristocracy. Yet, until the Morgan murder, Freemasonry had somehow entirely escaped critical scrutiny. Even then, most papers barred their columns to Antimasons and protected the Order from criticism. Though they subjected every other topic to fearless discussion, American newspapers said little about Masonry, a topic which alone enjoyed immunity from the usual "unsparing scrutiny, and the fiery ordeal" for which American editors were famous. Americans valued press freedom so highly that "the moment an organized power rises up to interpose its veto," they, as in 1798, become aroused.[28]

That moment now arrived anew. Among the hundreds of newspapers in the United States only a few allowed any discussion of Masonry. Of Boston's seven newspapers, for example, only one, besides an Antimasonic journal, opened its pages. When the Boston Antimasonic Committee sent a circular to fourteen editors, only four would print it, and then only as paid advertisement.[29] The editors themselves were caught in the Masonic conspiracy. Dozens were Masons, bound under oath to protect the Order from harm. According to one estimate, one-half of the country's newspaper editors were Freemasons, compared to only one-tenth of other callings. Masonic influence over the press was no accident but the consequence of systematic efforts to hold forth "extraordinary allurements . . . to this profession to induce them to become Masons." A Masonic press gag prevented "a fair and temperate discussion of the merits and demerits of this important question." Any editor who defied the gag faced a loss of advertising and readers. Thus with "a sleepless eye" and "with a flaming sword," Masonry made sure that the press kept mum.[30]

To break this stranglehold on public opinion, Antimasons established their own newspapers. The aptly named *Boston Free Press* joined the *Maine Free Press*, the Hartford *Intelligencer*, the *Boston Christian Herald*, the Danville (Vermont) *North Star* and many other papers nationwide to end Masonic press "monopoly." Yet even the existence of a vigorous Antimasonic press did not guarantee that the truth would freely circulate. Antimasons bitterly complained that "Insurance offices, Banks, Reading rooms, Hotels, all places of public resort, with some few honorable exceptions, are closed to the administration of Antimasonic truth, or the Antimasonic press."[31] A Rhode Island Antimasonic editor suffered indictment for printing a manuscript of a legislative investigation of Freemasonry on the theory that he had violated the monopoly of the state printer.[32]

Supplementing the work of Antimasonic newspapers were reading rooms and tract societies which printed pamphlets, and Antimasonic lecturers who toured the country like itinerant revivalists, exhibiting Masonic ritual to mock them and exposing Masonic secrets to bring the Order into public contempt. Intimidation, mobs and riots, and vexatious arrests tried to muzzle Antimasonic lecturers. In such an atmosphere an outspoken Antimason courted personal danger. "Your business and occupation will be injured. Your interests and prospects will be cut off; a civil war will be created; there will be blood!" Masons threatened, according to the Antis.[33] Fifteen times Masons arrested Avery Allyn, an Antimasonic lecturer, though never once did he go to trial.[34] In Reading, Massachusetts, a deputy sheriff arrested Jacob Allen, an Antimasonic lecturer, charged with inciting riot and making a theatrical exhibition. Only the intervention of Antimasons saved Allen from jail. One hundred Antis stood vigil all night to protect Allen, placed under house arrest, from "the felonious grasp of the craft."[35] Who could forget, Dr. Abner Phelps reminded the Massachusetts Antimasonic Convention in 1832, "the sacrifices of personal feeling, of long-cherished friendships, of business and of reputation"?[36]

Exposing the evils of Freemasonry, whatever the cost, was the first step.

Its destruction would soon follow, the Antimasons insisted. The nation must choose between republicanism and Masonry. Each was the mortal enemy of the other and no compromise was possible with an organization which was "one of the greatest evils that ever existed in any age or country."[37] Hostile to republicanism, contemptuous of the law, inimical to Christianity, and dangerous to women and domestic life, Masonry was irredeemable. In the eyes of Antimasons, Masonry stood convicted of "capital crimes," and "unconditional surrender" was the only acceptable outcome. "Our aim is a war of extermination," announced Vermont Antimasons.[38] To safeguard the legacy of the American Revolution, to pass intact the republican system to the next generation, Antimasons pledged themselves for the duration.

In the forefront of the Antimasonic battalions stood prominent representatives of an older generation, men who represented living links to the Revolutionary Fathers. The Morgan crime had incubated during the fateful summer of 1826 when the deaths of John Adams and Thomas Jefferson on July 4 dramatized the departure of the revolutionary generation and the ascendancy of the sons and grandsons. Antimasons, alarmed at the decay of republicanism, turned in this time of need to remnants of the revolutionary generation for inspiration. In Massachusetts, Rev. Nathanael Emmons, the great Hopkinsian exponent of Calvinist orthodoxy, whose career stretched back to the revolutionary war, endorsed the struggle against Masonry as enthusiastically as he had backed the War of Independence half a century earlier.[39] In Maine, General Henry Sewall, then in his eighties, a veteran of the Revolution, presided over the state Antimasonic convention.[40] In Connecticut, Antimasons nominated for governor Timothy Pitkin, a veteran state leader in the revolutionary and Federalist eras.[41]

Antimasons pointed with pride to the many men in their ranks bowed down by the weight of years such as the "aged and venerable with locks bleached by the frost of three-score winters" who served as delegates to the national convention in 1830.[42] At the start of the Massachusetts state convention in September 1833, delegates deferred to those "advanced in years," chilled by the drafts, and who wished "to sit covered, to wear their hats." Such men, reared in a purer age, were immune to the corrupting influences to which later generations succumbed. At their 1833 state convention Vermont Antimasons boasted the presence of "a large number of the fathers of the State" who overcame bodily infirmity and left retirement, to gather once more "around the hallowed altar of Liberty."[43]

Antimasons worried about the younger generation for whom Masonry had particular appeal. They identified disrespect for age and station as "another alarming feature of the times." Moses Thacher, a leading Antimasonic clergyman in Massachusetts, complained that youth, even children, were impudent and crowded out their elders. "Multitudes of the rising generation," he warned, "seem to glory in their own shame." Youth welcomed the disturbing alien new currents of cultural pluralism and secularism, competitive individualism and careerism. They were as "yet unskilled in the wiles of the common enemy."[44]

Among the Antimasonic leadership one finds members of that transitional generation caught between the ethos of the revolutionary era which had shaped their youth and the turbulent, dynamic advance of industrial capitalism they experienced during their mature years. Typical of those who felt displaced was Timothy Fuller, Margaret Fuller's father, the Antimasonic candidate for lieutenant governor in Massachusetts. Fuller was a lawyer who had attended Harvard, kept close to John Quincy Adams, and served several terms in Congress, but in the 1820s he found himself a man without a niche. He never made much money and suffered from the class snobbery of his wealthier associates, but his self-perception as a man of antique Roman virtues, devoted to public good, sustained him as long as those qualities earned popular favor. He fastened on the popularity of Masonry as one of those new forces which had gained a stronghold among "a large proportion of the younger and more active classes" who in every community formed "a disciplined corp, always ready, on concerted signals, unknown to all but the initiated," to promote one another's interests. It was such a concert that had isolated Fuller. "The thirst for novelty may sometimes betray the country's adventurous sons," he lamented, "into bold and dangerous innovations." Freemasonry explained why some men prospered while others of equal or superior worth, languished. In an uncorrupted Republic, public approbation was "the high regard of those alone, whose ambition is led on by discretion and patriotism," men like himself, Fuller thought. His own isolation was an ominous sign. With the rise of Antimasonry, however, Fuller's hopes revived: "Against this baleful despotism, the free-born sons of the American republic are at last aroused," he proclaimed. Men like Timothy Fuller looked back nostalgically to the revolutionary period as a golden age but they looked ahead apprehensively to a dark future, fearful that the diseases to which republican governments were prone, and against which the Founders had taken precautions, had entered the American body politic through Freemasonry.[45]

The three foremost national figures associated with Antimasonry were repositories of those old republican virtues Antimasons sensed were being swept aside in the 1820s. Though William Wirt, Richard Rush, and John Quincy Adams discovered Antimasonry late, and their relationship to the Antimasonic party was ambivalent, to Antimasons they symbolized the statesmen who had once dominated public life, worthy successors to the Founders and unlike the new breed of professional politicians such as Henry Clay and Martin Van Buren.

When President John Quincy Adams ran for re-election in 1828, he did not attack Masonry though he polled well in Antimasonic strongholds in western New York. Bitterly disappointed by his failure, he used the leisure of retirement to reflect on the deeper cause of his personal defeat to Indian killer and duelist Andrew Jackson: a decline in civic virtue. First he engaged in a vicious brawl with old Federalist enemies in Massachusetts whom he accused of treason and betrayal. Then in 1831 Adams announced: "I am a zealous Antimason." That year he returned to public life as congressman from one of the banner Antimasonic districts in Massachusetts. In 1833 he ran a very strong race for governor as the Antimasonic candidate, giving the National Republicans, and many of his old enemies, a scare. Antimasons welcomed the accession of such a luminary. The Boston Young Men's Association for the Diffusion of Truth reprinted a popular edition of Adams's *Letters on the Entered Apprenticeship Oath,* in which Adams, after reviewing the oath and its penalties, declared it "essentially vicious," at odds with the obligations of Christian Republicans.[46]

Like Adams, Richard Rush was also the son of an illustrious father and leader of the revolutionary generation, Dr. Benjamin Rush. He, too, endorsed the Antimasonic cause, and was talked of as the party's candidate for President in 1836. He drifted to Antimasonry after a distinguished career under Jefferson, Madison, and Monroe, capped by election to the vice presidency with Adams.[47] But of all the national luminaries identified with Antimasonry none more clearly epitomized the Antimasonic standards of Christian Republican statesman than William Wirt, who ran for President on the Antimasonic ticket in 1832. The son of a Swiss father and a German mother, Wirt was born into a farm family of middling status in western Maryland. He lost both parents while still young, but the deep piety of an aunt made a lasting impression on the orphan. Left with a small patrimony, Wirt obtained an education and demonstrated that native talent and hard work paid off. Wirt became a lawyer, settled in Culpeper County, Virginia, and married the daughter of Dr. George R. Gilmer, head of a prominent Virginia family in Albemarle County. Jefferson and his circle identified Wirt as a young man of talent and advanced his career. In 1799 Wirt became clerk of the Virginia House of Delegates, and in 1802 he was made a judge of chancery although he soon gave that up to resume the practice of the law. Wirt earned a growing reputation at the bar, especially for his role in the prosecution of Aaron Burr, but he was not content with a conventional legal career. Public service, not the pursuit of private gain, seemed the only path as the country entered a period of trial. His mentor, Jefferson, encouraged him to run for Congress, which he thought a good preparation for future service in the executive branch. In Washington, Jefferson told Wirt, "You will become the colossus of the republican government of your country." Wirt declined Jefferson's advice but in 1817 President Monroe appointed him attorney general, an office which he held for twelve years, reappointed by President John Q. Adams. Antimasons reprinted the Wirt-Jefferson correspondence because it strongly documented their image of Wirt as an Old Republican, closely linked to the Revolutionary Fathers by personal ties and a common outlook. Jefferson had singled out Wirt for patronage, he explained, "from an ardent zeal to see this *government* (the idol of my soul) continue in good hands."[48]

Wirt neither sought nor desired the Antimasonic presidential nomination. He supported Henry Clay but concluded that Clay could not secure the support of Antimasons and that by agreeing to head the Antimasonic ticket, he might promote union among the anti-Jackson forces. Wirt had been an inactive Mason earlier in life, and though not an early Antimason, refusing to pledge himself to proscribe Masons from public office, he publicly condemned Masonry. Antimasons pronounced him to be precisely the sort of Christian Republican the country needed in the White House.

Wirt's religious and political views set him apart from the professional politicians who by 1830 were becoming increasingly influential. He arrived in Virginia early in the century when deism was in fashion among the gentry, but under the influence of an evangelical wife, Wirt turned towards orthodox Calvinism and became a devout Presbyterian. His reputation for piety made him, in Antimasonic eyes, a model public man. At home he conducted family prayer, read the Bible daily, delved into theology, wrote religious essays, and served as president of the Maryland Bible Society and the state temperance society. His candidacy in 1832 was expected to capture strong support among 120,000 Presbyterian voters in the country, as well as among other pietists.[49]

Crediting his wife with saving him from a life of dissipation and sin, Wirt championed the role of women in civic life, insisting that their piety made them a vital moral force in training future generations of republicans. Women, he concluded, must receive an appropriate education. "The virtues of this country are with our women," he argued, "and the only remaining hope of the resurrection of the genius and character of the nation rests with them." To Antimasons who identified Freemasonry as an enemy of republican womanhood and domestic virtue, Wirt's views on women set him apart.[50]

Wirt's belief that women were the last best hope for perpetuating republican government in the United States was partly the consequence of close observation of his own sex. At the time he accepted the Antimasonic nomination, he was ready to quit public life. There was "so much faction, corruption, intrigue, and impenetrable and imperturbable stupidity and infatuation pervading the community," he complained. The future of the country was bleak. At the age of sixty, ready to retire, Wirt admitted that he was a "disappointed man"—"disappointed in my country and the glory that I thought awaited her;—disappointed most sadly in the intelligence and virtue which I had attributed to our countrymen. . . ."[51]

Wirt was a moralist in politics, which traced to his religious conversion. He was highly critical of Virginia society and the gentry class into which he ascended. Virginians preached " 'equal liberty in church and state,' " he argued, but there was no country "where property is more unequally distributed than in Virginia," with its "stately aristocratic palaces" surrounded by "the little smoky huts and log cabins of poor, laborious, ignorant, tenants" who approached *the great house,* hat in hand, with all the fearful, trembling submission of the lowest feudal vassals. . . ."[52] Wirt contrasted the aristocratic gentry with Patrick Henry, his hero, and the subject of a two-volume biography he published in 1817 to influence young Virginians. Henry's "general appearance and manners were those of a plain farmer or planter of the backcountry," Wirt wrote. The secret of his oratorical power was his moral authority. He filled his listeners "with a kind of religious awe" that "gave him the force and authority of a prophet."[53] But Henry's example failed to set a standard. Though Virginia advanced rapidly in wealth and population after the American Revolution, the state lacked that real source "of solid grandeur" which was "the animating soul of a republic," that "public spirit; that sacred *amor patriae* which filled Greece and Rome with patriots, heroes and scholars." Instead "the one object throughout the state" was *to grow rich:* a passion which is visible, not only in the walks of private life, but which has crept into and poisoned every public body in the state." Wirt's views echoed those of his mentor, Jefferson, who had labored, with limited success, to reform the state along pure republican lines. Like his sponsor, Wirt believed that education offered the best cure for "the aristocratic distinctions" which Virginians "profess to hate," although they were not willing to support "the general culture of the human mind or any other public improvements." Jefferson's wise plan for a system of public education lay neglected because of "a most deplorable destitution of public spirit . . ." among the gentry.[54] Their sons readily embraced deism because it liberated them from the restraints of evangelical Christianity and allowed them to lead lives of indolence and dissipation. In 1832, Wirt's *The Letters of the British Spy* was printed for the tenth time, in a new edition containing a lengthy campaign biography.

Wirt's reputation also rested on his fame as a lawyer and orator. Here, too, he was ever the didactic Christian republican moralist. In 1826 in a memorial discourse on the lives of Jefferson and Adams delivered at the Capitol, he impressed the younger generation with the "moral sublimity" of the two Founding Fathers.[55] In 1830, invited by the Peithessophian and Philoclean Societies of Rutgers College, he warned that public life had degenerated since Washington's day. Now parties, "corrupt combinations," employing slander, falsehood, and "vile intrigues" enabled political mountebanks and jugglers to win office. He urged the young collegians to avoid such models and instead pattern themselves after the Roman virtue of the Founding Fathers. It would take just such qualities to save the country from the "moral earthquake" that loomed unless purged of "political degeneracy." If the rising generation avoided the corrupting influence of selfish ambition, the older generation would hail them "as resurrectors of their patriot hopes, and virgins and matrons will bless you. . . ."[56]

In 1830 Wirt also braved popular hostility to defend the Cherokee nation, whose existence was in jeopardy because of hostile attacts from land-hungry whites backed by the state of Georgia and President Andrew Jackson. The cause of the beleaguered Indians, Wirt believed, had been dear to Washington, Jefferson, Madison, Monroe, and John Quincy Adams, who respected the treaty rights secured to the natives. The "new-fangled notions" that now annulled those rights, Wirt thought, were a most "foul breach of faith on the part of the United States, the disgrace of which the waters of the oceans of Time can never wash out. . . ." To evangelical Christians, especially in the northeast, who were the most conspicuous defenders of Indian rights, Wirt's courageous stand cast him in the heroic mold of the Founding Fathers. Former President James Madison commended Wirt. If Georgia won, "the character of our country will suffer."[57] That year, Congress passed the Indian Removal Act which sealed the fate of the Cherokees and the other four "Civilized tribes" inhabiting the Deep South.

In these ways, William Wirt embodied Old Republican virtues. "Excessive wealth is neither glory nor happiness," he reminded Americans. The "wretch who thinks only of himself," who ventures into the world "only for the purpose of lucre and ostentation" and "who looks upon his fellow creatures . . . with arrogance and insolence, as if they were made to be his vassals," could never be happy. Pursue the golden mean, Wirt advised, for that "is the appropriate region of virtue and intelligence." Seek distinction, he argued; but remember that "wealth is not essential to distinction." That lay in promoting the common welfare.[58]

When he died suddenly in 1833, Antimasons lost a potent symbol of the Christian Republicanism they hoped to revive by purging Masonry from American life. For a moment, Antimasons had argued that the fate of the country hinged on Wirt's electoral prospects:

> Our country calls, let Masonry expire,
> To William Wirt confide the Chair of State.
> His worth a patriot union should inspire,
> To save the Union from impending fate.

"He had none of that intrigue, so common and conspicuous, among mere politicians," recalled the Antimasonic *Lynn Record*. He reminded people of the heroic standard set by the Founding Fathers, a man of perfect moral courage: "Nature never made but two great men in the world, out of that mold, George Washington and William Wirt," summed up the *Taunton Gazette*.[59]

In comparing their own age to that of the Founding Fathers, and in finding it so sadly wanting, Anitmasons registered the painful impact which the birth of industrial society etched on the consciousness of Americans uncertain that change was compatible with republicanism, the Revolutionary generation's most precious legacy. Sensing the dangers that lay in waiting, Antimasons took up their posts as guardians of the American Revolution.

3

The Great Transition and the Social Sources of Antimasonry

The Discovery of Class in Industrial Society

We should make it a principle to extend the hand of fellowship to every man who discharges faithfully his daily duties . . . without stopping to ascertain whether he swings a hammer, or draws a thread. —There is nothing more distant from all natural rule and natural claim than the reluctant, the backward sympathy and forced smile, the checked conversation, the hesitating compliance, the well off are too apt to manifest to those a little lower down; with whom, in comparison of intellect and in principle of virtue, they frequently sink into insignificance.   *Vermont Luminary,* 17 January 1829[1]

"Antimasonry, like the Cholera, it takes only the lower class." Toast at Framingham, Massachusetts, Masonic Celebration.
                    Boston Advocate, 4 July 1832

When in 1831 the Grand Lodge of Massachusetts Freemasonry petitioned for permission to build a larger Masonic hall in Boston, hundreds of citizens protested. Among them were 174 Bostonians whose social status the defenders of Masonry carefully scrutinized. Forty to fifty were transient or unknown and not listed in the Boston *City Directory,* reported the *Masonic Mirror.* Of the rest, "Where are the merchants? where are the lawyers? where are the physicians? where are the clergymen? where are the respectability of the community . . . ?" Masons asked. Out of approximately four hundred professional men in the city, only two obscure names appeared among the petitioners, some of whom were among "the lowest grades of society." Masons found the status of the seventy to eighty petitioners from Roxbury equally suspect. "The remonstrants are generally among the dregs, the offcasts of the community," the *Mirror* observed.[2] As for the Antimasonic leadership in Connecticut, Masons taunted, they boasted "the transcendant talents and preeminent services of William Lynn 3d, James Collins, and shoemaker Sanders" as well as tailor Nathan Dresser. And in Rhode Island, the delegates to the state Antimasonic convention in 1830 included men like Esquire Winslow, "more celebrated as a shoemaker than as a magistrate," a type all-too-typical of the delegates, men without wealth or respectability.[3]

Antimasons just as readily challenged Masonic pretentions though not on grounds of lowly social status, but on fitness for public trust. The voice of Antimasonry sounded the strains of the hinterlands, of the provincials, and of elements in the middle strata—wherever they lived—who felt pushed aside, snubbed by more aggressive, more worldly, better-connected elements. In Boston, for example, Antimasons battled, though with no real success, to wrest control of the Bunker Hill Monument Association from the hands of the state's leading businessmen and professionals whom they accused of permitting that patriotic enterprise to become the handmaid of Masonry. Harvard College, once the servant of the entire Commonwealth, but by the 1820s increasingly the preserve of the metropolis's Unitarian upper crust, likewise came under censure for defying public opinion and loaning fifteen thousand dollars to the Grand Lodge of Massachusetts to erect the new Masonic Hall.[4]

In 1833, a nasty contest to elect a congressman from the towns making up a suburban district near Boston unleashed the raw emotions of class resentment. The National Republicans nominated Henry Dearborn, son of revolutionary war general Henry Dearborn, a resident of Roxbury, but closely tied to Boston's leading families. His Antimasonic opponent, William Jackson, was a self-made businessman and leading Orthodox Congregation-alist layman in Newton. "The higher classes," the Antimasons complained, "had already elected seven of the state's nine congressmen from among their own 'exclusives' "—the exception was John Quincy Adams—men who had "no practical connection with the laboring classes in this whole common-wealth." Dearborn, too, was the candidate of Boston aristocracy. They gave a lavish dinner in his honor attended by the mayor, while most of Boston's newspapers pushed his election. Even Dearborn's persona identified him with elitism: his hands were soft, his aroma perfumed, and he socialized in the homes of the metropolis's first families. Without a single husbandman or "workingman" in the Massachusetts congressional delegation, Dearborn—"who would perhaps be more representative of the genteel and foppish class than of any other"—was not the man, Antimasons urged. By contrast, Wil-liam Jackson was a plain, self-taught, country man, a promoter of manu-factures and railroads, but still a "genuine workingman" who had not been "nursed in the lap of fortune, and taught to pride himself on the riches acquired by a father, or to set himself above the common people." More-over Jackson was a prominent Orthodox Congregationalist; Dearborn was a Unitarian.[5]

Alarmed by the emergence of a monied, Unitarian-tending aristocracy, Antimasons in Massachusetts also worried about threats from below from the newly formed Workingmen's party and emerging trade union movement—additional evidence that the new industrial social order divided communities as never before. Antimasons acknowledged that mechanics had genuine grievances but they deplored resorting to a class-based movement to redress them. Such a tactic violated their communitarian norms, yet it was precisely because wage earners could not rely on employers for fair treatment that they mobilized political and economic power to defend themselves. The *Boston Advocate,* New England's leading Antimasonic news paper, lumped working-class movements together with Freemasonry. The British unions, it noted, employed Masonic-like secrecy, rituals, and conspiratorial tactics. If their American counterparts followed suit, they would become equally dangerous. Antimasons urged mechanics to abandon their class organizations for a communitarian movement such as Antimasonry, which already had taken up arms against monopoly and privilege.[6]

In fastening on Masonry as the foremost evil in the Republic, identifying it with the specter of monied aristocracy, Antimasons were responding to the emergence of industrial society which clashed with the remnants of a pre-industrial order. That order had rested on stable and enduring bonds of family, church, and community rooted in self-sufficient households, cultural isolation, and social homogeneity. By the 1820s the cumulative consequences of the spread of industrialization, the increasing tempo of demographic change, and the heady growth of cultural pluralism, secularization, and supra-local associations alarmed those who clung to an older conception of community which was rapidly passing into history. For Antimasons, Freemasonry embodied currents that were changing their country beyond recognition.[7]

Quincy, Massachusetts, located eight miles south of Boston, was a microcosm of the demographic and economic trends gaining momentum during the early nineteenth century. A stronghold of the Antimasonic party, the home of John Quincy Adams and his son, Charles Francis Adams, who, like his father, dabbled in Antimasonic politics, Quincy experienced many of the long-term changes transforming the country. The younger Adams looked back to the 1820s as a watershed in Quincy's history. At last "the period of immobility and sameness had come to an end," he recalled. The development of the granite quarry to supply markets in Boston and elsewhere brought the town firmly within the orbit of the market economy. The changes, Adams wrote, were "everywhere felt—in habits and modes of life and thought, and in politics."[8] Rapid growth in population, increasing demographic, occupational, and religious diversity, and shifts in political power reshaped Quincy during Adams's youth.

The town's population grew by more than a third in the 1820s and by almost half in the next decade, a substantial advance over growth rates earlier in the century. Industry fueled growth. In 1825 the completion of the Quincy Railroad initiated the efficient transport of granite to Boston and touched off a boom. In 1838 over five hundred men worked in the quarries and together with a large number of boot and shoemakers and persons employed in manufactures, including some sixty women, made up almost 60 percent of the labor force in 1840.[9] The quarry workers included an Irish element and a rough group of native-born transients from New Hampshire who arrived in the summer to work and stayed to vote Democratic in November, before returning to New Hampshire to vote Democratic again in March. The shoemakers were a very different sort. They were not coarse and turbulent, Adams remembered, but worked at home in small groups, in ten footers (workshops) peculiar to their craft, cultivating intellectual curiosity and political independence common to the trade. The old Quincy natives, mainly farmers, were slow and conservative, unable to command deference from the new working class, especially the shoemakers who delighted "to manage things by intrigue."[10] Once overwhelming Federalist in its politics, down through the 1820s, Quincy in the 1830s became sharply divided.

Shifts in Quincy's religious life also mirrored the pluralist currents. The Congregationalist First Church, founded in 1639, had long been the only church. In 1728 an Episcopal church was founded but during the next century no new denomination was represented. Then the dam burst. First came the Universalists in 1831. They represented more than just liberal theological views for theirs was also "a democratic revolt of some from the super-select membership of the First church."[11] Confronted by competition from other denominations, the First Church in 1832 also suffered internal division when Unitarians and Trinitarians split off, ending a long tradition of internal harmony. By 1838 when the Methodists arrived and five years later when the Roman Catholics raised a building, Quincy's spiritual life had been transformed beyond recognition. The multiplication of denominations, the coming of the Irish, the growth of a working class in Quincy as elsewhere measured the degree to which the social order fragmented.[12]

By the 1840s some native sons no longer found Quincy an attractive place in which to live. Thrust aside by newcomers, appalled by the disorderly character of town meetings, the impossibility, Adams said, of conducting rational debate, and by the factionalism that left Quincy more expensively but less well governed, many left.[13] The strength of Antimasonry in places like Quincy and elsewhere in the northeastern United States resulted from a sense of profound rupture of older patterns of community life, which had taken deepest roots in colonial New England.

Masonry became a target of suspicion because it appeared in sharp conflict with older communitarian norms. Those attracted by Antimasonry did not necessarily reject the pull of the marketplace and its values, but they shared a suspicion that an industrial order was subversive of republican order. In singling out Freemasons for attack, containment, and destruction, they focused their anxieties on an institution whose popularity and growing influence was more the consequence of than the cause of change. By shining a spotlight on the alleged evils of Freemasonry, they displaced anxieties about the commercialization of society onto an institution easily identified, pervasive, and vulnerable to attack. It was possible to abolish Freemasonry, whereas one could hardly derail the powerful forces reshaping the United States. Discovering a conspiracy and labeling it as the cause of various social evils, therefore, was one way some Americans confronted the transition from the agrarian Republic of the Founding Fathers to the uncharted new world into which the country plunged.[14]

No set of changes troubled Americans more than the system of social stratification spawned by industrialization. By the 1820s many sensed, even if they did not entirely comprehend, that a new class structure was taking shape, molded by the pressures of demographic change and economic development.[15] Habits of deference to the elderly and to long-established elite families, rooted in stable kinship and communal ties and traditional values, underwent a steady process of erosion.[16] In the colonial period farmers and artisans had deferred to their "betters" but not because they were economically dependent on merchants and larger landholders or other members of the gentry. Indebtedness was common but not bankrupting, tenancy was rare in New England, and production for markets was only marginally important. Wealth alone did not command deference. Piety, education, probity, and ability counted also and though certain families tended to maintain positions of eminence over several generations, they did not monopolize office. Differences in position and power were important but were not as great as they later became. Social stratification enjoyed the legitimacy of being rooted in tradition and in a complex web of community relationships woven by ties of kinship, religious association, and shared values, which promoted a sense of solidarity and constrained individualistic impulses.[17]

The coming of industrialization through the spread of manufactures, commerce, and the advance of capitalistic agriculture slowly shaped a new class structure. Property relations, not community relations, were the hallmark of this new order. One's occupation, not residence in a particular place, counted most in an increasingly differentiated order where personal and social experience became closely linked to work.[18] Labor became a commodity and the drive for personal success, especially among the younger generation, displaced the desire to secure a competency and assure family security.[19] For the first time in the United States a large mass of white, manual laborers, skilled and unskilled, on farms, in workshops, and in factories, together with a smaller but growing mass of clerks and other white-collar workers, depended on wage labor. Though some wage earners might enter businesses or accumulate savings, independent proprietorships, whether on farms or in villages and cities, increasingly lay beyond their reach. Those for whom they worked formed an entrepreneurial class driven hard by the quest for profits, energized by the strains of competition, their loyalty transcending particular communities and focusing primarily on success in businesses and on family prosperity. The most ambitious and successful businessmen were sometimes absentees, as in the Lowell, Massachusetts, textile mills, living apart from those they employed, but even small-scale businessmen and commercial farmers no longer operated under the constraints of older community norms. The self-sufficient household had ceased to be the principal center of economic activity, which had now shifted to production for markets. Moreover, the values derived from competition in the marketplace and the experience of residing in fragmented, diverse communities loosened communal restraints and liberated entrepreneurial energies to maximize opportunity.[20]

Much more than in the colonial period, differences in wealth and occupation counted. By the early nineteenth century there was a pronounced trend in New England, as elsewhere, towards greater inequality, especially evident in older towns such as Bedford, Massachusetts.[21] Even in a relatively recently settled state such as Vermont, shortages of land by the 1820s drove thousands of the younger generation westward.

Compelled to leave ancestral homes, attracted to other places by fresh possibilities, New Englanders faced futures more uncertain than in their previous experience. As they entered the new labor markets, forced or tempted to move from place to place, they discovered, too, the pain of unemployment and the volatility of the economic cycle. The son of a Vermont farm family reported in 1827 to his folks that Boston "is full of men that are out of employ and there was no less than 36 applied in one day" for work at the store where he labored. Those left on the farm also needed to adapt. The son who inherited the homestead and mortgaged it to compensate his siblings spent a lifetime paying off the loan. Nor were the immobile immune to the spread of industrial society, not just because of the increasing commercialization of agriculture but also because the employment of outworkers in shoe-making and palm-leaf hat-making, for example, introduced rural folk to the new industrial marketplace.[22]

Men flocked to Freemasonry precisely because the bonds of locality had grown weaker. No longer so strongly tied to a single place, experiencing an unprecedented degree of geographic mobility, increasing numbers of Americans sought new attachments. Among the many voluntary associations, Masonry held out special appeal because of its cosmopolitan organization and ideology. If professed to unite men "of the most distant countries and of the most contradictory opinions, in one dissoluable bond of affection."[23] Yet to persons outside the Order, this attachment to a supra-local body seemed subversive of local loyalties already strained by the rapid turnover of population. As communities stratified between the transient and the persistent, and between the propertied and the propertyless, Masonry added a further distinction, all the more threatening because of its secrecy.

The high incidence of transiency and shifts in occupation tended to make for indeterminancy of status. Freemasonry attracted men precisely because membership provided a badge of respectability which gave one instant access to professional and social circles even in places where one was a stranger. A Masonic lyric caught the spirit of upwardly striving Freemasons:

> When quite a young spark, I was in the dark,
> And wanted to alter my station;
> I went to a friend,
> Who proved in the end,
> A free and accepted Mason.[24]

In the New England colonial town, one's station was not usually in doubt but in the demographically mobile early nineteenth century that was no longer the case. Rapid change of individual fortunes sowed confusion. Masonry tended to bring order out of confusion but it did so without community authority. To outsiders Masonry dangerously conferred respectability on the suspect. "Many of the highest masons," complained an Antimason, "are men whose relative importance is derived wholly from masonry. Possessing neither intellectual nor moral worth sufficient to secure them from utter neglect among the virtuous part of the community without such adventitious aid, they find their consequences enhanced by being permitted to mingle with honorable men and professing christians, in the lodge room. . . ." Masonry thus introduced a factitious standard of social worth based on superficial appearances.[25]

From its inception, Masonry accommodated the needs of mobile men. Ship captains, for example, had long found Masonry attractive. In the half-century after the American Revolution, when Masonry grew enormously, the tempo of internal migration in the United States also picked up. By 1790, for example, over half of the Concord Massachusetts, Minutemen of 1776 had departed from the town, driven by the shortage of land. By the beginning of the next century, Concord men migrated at an even earlier age than had their forbears, as opportunities at home further shrank.[26] Even in relatively recently settled towns in northern New England the migratory impulse was acute. In Bloomfield, Vermont, the town historian wrote that "few of the early settlers remained in town for any great length of time." The aggregate population data tell the same story. Twenty years before New Hampshire was well settled, outmigration had begun.[27]

The consequences of demographic upheaval were profound. In the eighteenth century, long-rooted, persisting families accounted for a high proportion of a town's residents. In pre-industrial Massachusetts, perhaps a fifth of a town's inhabitants were related to one another.[28] By the 1820s, however, unrelated transients increasingly inhabited communities. Two distinct elements tended to make up a town's inhabitants: a core of persisters and a floating mass moving in and out.

Transiency bore a relation to social class. The children of less affluent or middling families were more apt to leave than those of the better fixed. A group of elite families formed the core. Familial networks, made up of the more persistent and affluent, tended to fashion a style of life, attend a common church, form business partnerships, and social networks through which they assisted one another. Those outside these networks were at a distinct disadvantage, with less access to the resources available to members. Masonry appeared to be a network of men who assisted one another, and to a certain degree this perception was accurate. Masonry was a visible, artificial, in a sense, impersonal network, whereas older community-based elite networks and newer upper-class ones were informal, half-hidden. This exposed Masons to notice, suspicion, and envy.[29]

Early Americans had resided among relatively stable, extended networks of kin and neighbors; by the early nineteenth century many found themselves living among strangers. No institution so explicitly sought to serve the mobile as Freemasonry. When a Mason was "cast upon foreign and unknown shores," when his heart was "desolate, because friends are far away," when a brother was "friendless, and thirsty, and hungry, and naked, and houseless," Masonry supplied "friends, and drink, and food, and apparel, and opens an asylum for the way-worn wanderer."[30] Whereas such were common boasts of celebrators of Freemasonry, many Americans critically identified Masonic cosmopolitanism with demographic instability. By attacking Freemasonry, Antimasons nostalgically recalled an earlier time when local ties sufficed and voluntary associations for the lonely, the peripatetic, the socially insecure were unnecessary.

Freemasons boasted that the Order turned strangers and rivals into friends. "The manufactory, marketplace, and exchange, are made pleasant to us," explained Boston's Universalist minister and active Freemason, Paul Dean, "by the assemblage of friends we meet" at the Lodge. Masonic fraternalism offered middle-class men a means of putting aside temporarily everyday cares and burdens; without it life would be "dreary and lonely." "Therefore," Dean explained, "to make men thus friendly to each other is the grand design of the masonic institution." It "sweetens the disposition, softens the heart and makes the mind cheerful. It checks the angry passions, . . . moves us to delight in another's happiness and share in another's woe."[31] Thus Masonry preferred a universal therapeutic to an emerging bourgeoisie. It softened the edges of competition and helped members in their business affairs; it eased the loneliness of travel; it established a retreat from the pressures of competition; and finally it leveled barriers and overcame prejudices that unnecessarily divided men. "And I bless God, that there is one place on earth where men of different and opposing sentiments can meet as brethren," affirmed Bernard Whitman, a Unitarian minister and champion of Masonry from Waltham, Massachusetts.[32]

Masonic cosmopolitanism and fraternalism did not mean that its doors were wide open. On the contrary, membership criteria were exclusive. Only those who paid the fees, satisfied a test of probity, went through the initiation rituals and fit into the style of Masonic sociability were suitable for admission. A single blackball doomed a candidate. Made up mostly of business and professional men, Masonic Lodges reflected the emerging system of social relations based on a modern class system. It was this aspect that alarmed critics, who saw private association performing a public function, elevating a favored few according to mysterious principles known only to insiders and in sharp conflict with the open character of the earlier American stratification system. In attacking Masonry for its putatively elitist character, without the legitimacy derived from community consent, Antimasons were caught in a dilemma. They looked back to vanishing early American communities where it was comparatively clear to whom deference was owed, but nothing they could do, not even the destruction of Freemasonry, could restore the past, for Masonry was a symptom, not the root of the new stratification system. For critics, Freemasonry became emblematic of a new social structure spawned by industrial society. Freemasonry catered to a mobile, ambitious, rootless new middle class, certifying a man's social position as above the mass, and offering advantages not available to outsiders. Antimasons thus sensed correctly that some profound change was at work. The language of republicanism, the medium of their political culture, directed them to perceive Freemasonry as aristocracy. In a nation without an Old World aristocracy, readily identifiable, rooted in legal privilege, vigilant republicans were ever on the look-out for threats to republican equality. In the 1820s the finger was pointed at an artifact of the emerging American bourgeoisie.

The process of class formation in the early nineteenth century was complex, and though Masonry played a limited role, it attracted attention because of its visibility. In many ways Americans discovered that they were each members of a particular strata, usually linked by occupation, often by lifestyle, and increasingly by place of residence. Master mechanics, for example, formed associations that sought to differentiate them from journeymen by emphasizing their superiority but also registering the mechanic's sense that his interests differed from those of merchants.[33] Likewise wage earners who no longer could look forward to ascending the ladder from apprentice to master mechanic took the first tentative steps toward collective action through trade unions and independent labor politics. By their demands for a ten-hour work day and free public schools, and their avid interest in adult education, artisans sought to improve opportunities for themselves and their families. Employing strategies of self-help and collective action an emerging working class navigated its passage through the uncertain terrain of an industrial order.[34]

Finally those who aspired to positions in the upper strata endeavored in a variety of ways to define and secure that position. As elsewhere throughout New England and the nation in the half-century after the American Revolution, voluntary associations including a Masonic Lodge proliferated in Concord, Massachusetts. These associations tended "to set neighbors off from one another and to nurture attachments separate from the whole community." In doing so they seemed to rob a community "of a certain moral unity." Among the most important in Concord was the Social Club, an organization formed by the town's putative modern upper class to clarify an identity and expand its influence. Colonial elites had no need for such an institution but now the town's leaders, limited to twenty-five members who all resided in the center village and engaged mostly in trade, met regularly to enjoy one another's company and to discuss important issues of the day. The Social Club assumed informal responsibility for directing the town's development and it succeeded in having "a hand in all the important measures to come before the town—at least ideally." In contrast to Concord in the colonial period "now social leaders were distinguished from the common run of mankind not only by wealth or breeding but by membership in a formal organization." Because social change, especially demographic volatility, blurred perceptions of hierarchy, the Social Club tried to re-establish it through new means. In the process Concord's elite felt a need to develop "a distinctive identity as a group and potentially special interests of their own."[35] In other communities a Social Library, more than a hundred of which were chartered by New Hampshire between 1800 and 1815, became a focus of upper-class village life. These library societies were private organizations which charged fees and drew membership from the town's leading citizens who resided in the village center. Formally at least, membership emphasized an attachment to high culture, a desire to transcend provincial isolation.[36] The model was the Boston Atheneum, a private library located in the center of the city's business life to serve exclusively the metropolis's entrepreneurial elite, which passed on shares of stock from one generation to the next as family heirlooms. The Atheneum thus had many provincial imitators.[37] Through the creation of elite institutions and a distinctive way of life, certain families set themselves socially and culturally apart, provided for the continuation of their class, and sought to legitimize their power.

Concord's Social Club also drew its inspiration from a Boston institution, the Wednesday Club, and nowhere was the process of upper-class formation so clearly visible than in New England's metropolis. There a group of families who accumulated large, permanent fortunes derived from successful ventures in commerce, finance, transport, and manufactures emerged on a much grander scale than in the hinterland.[38]

One can perceive more clearly the process of upper-class formation by examining the transformation of Harvard College, which had served the entire Commonwealth during its first two hundred years and functioned as an institution that integrated students into a narrower, class-linked body that helped to define, shape, and reproduce an upper class concentrating in and around Boston.[39] Colonial Harvard had recruited students from all over the colony and from a variety of social strata. The students shared a common religious faith, and Harvard played a vital role in sustaining Congregationalism—which remained the state church until 1833—by training generations of Congregationalist ministers and by cultivating that faith in the younger generation. Its governance and funding reflected its public character. Harvard received state funds and the government shared in administering the college. In the early nineteenth century Harvard began to shed its public character. The split between Calvinists and Unitarians, which had strong sectional characteristics, pitting the western part of the state against the east, touched off a bitter battle for control of the college, which the Unitarians won in 1805. Henceforth, Harvard could no longer serve as handmaid of a weakened religious establishment because it had become identified with one faction within the state church, a split that ultimately helped to undo the establishment. The loss of Harvard embittered Calvinists, who called for severing the links between state and college and demanded their fair share of state assistance for newer institutions such as Amherst and Williams, which still remained true to the faith of the Puritans.

At the same time that Harvard became identified with one denomination its social character also narrowed. Increasingly it drew more of its students from the emerging Brahmin entrepreneurial and professional elite in and around Boston and a sprinkling of aristocratic Southerners. Only the affluent could readily afford Harvard's tuition, the highest in New England and considerably more than costs at Williams, Amherst, and the other newer schools. Moreover, its classical admission requirements gave an advantage to those who attended the private preparatory schools which trained the children of the elite for Cambridge. As Harvard's student body gained a reputation for social exclusivity, the college took a new interest in shaping style and manners. Harvard became the Boston elite's marriage mart and a finishing school for gentlemen, as well as a center for scholarship. Anglophilia also came into full flower. Harvard, like Boston's upper crust, looked to England for models of aristocratic deportment. A Harvard dress code in the 1820s instructed men that a properly attired young man owned a top hat, a cane, and elegant boots. The young swells from Maryland, Virginia, and South Carolina added tone with " 'their swallow-tail coats tapered to an arrowpoint angle' " and " 'their little delicate calfskin boots' " which " 'were objects of great admiration.' "[40] President Everett lectured sniffling students on proper deportment. "In England, gentlemen never blow their noses," he admonished. This new emphasis on personal style was no trivial matter. "The great power of the English aristocracy," explained James R. Lowell in 1846, "lies in their polish that impresses the great middle class who have a sort of dim conception of its value." It was therefore essential for Harvard students to set themselves apart. The rewards were substantial: "A man gains in *power,* as he gains in ease," Lowell observed.[41] The Brahmins and their like did not monopolize Harvard. Country lads and those from families of middling fortunes still attended, but Boston's share of the antebellum grades jumped from 29 percent from 1789 to 1821 to 41 percent from 1824 to 1859. In 1825 the Harvard calendar, previously arranged to allow poor students an opportunity to teach an entire term in winter in a district school, no longer accommodated the impecunious, despite the school's steep tuition. The high cost was unavoidable, because Harvard "had never abandoned the English tradition that a university student should be both a gentleman and a scholar." Henry Adams remembered Harvard in the 1850s as a place that "offered chiefly advantages vulgarly called social, rather than mental." An English visitor in 1862 concluded that Harvard "is to Massachusetts, and I may almost say to the northern states, what Cambridge and Oxford are to England," an institution that "gives the highest education to be attained by the highest classes in that country."[42]

Harvard's governance also underwent change. The power of the faculty and of the clergymen declined once the businessmen and professionals who controlled the governing boards asserted their primacy. This shift was partly a result of a shift in Harvard's sources of financial support. With state aid no longer forthcoming, Harvard had to rely on private benefactors. Two-thirds of the major donors during the first half of the nineteenth century had recently made their fortunes, though many were scions of eighteenth-century families of high status.[43] Eventually the state relinquished any role in Harvard's governance, and New England's oldest college became a private institution identified mainly with a particular slice of Massachusetts and New England society.

Harvard's transformation was the natural result of social, religious, and cultural developments. No single collegiate institution in Massachusetts by the early nineteenth century nor any particular social stratum could serve the interests of an increasingly complex and heterogeneous society. One of the oldest and most important public institutions of colonial America, Harvard by the mid-nineteenth century evolved into a private association, redesigned to reproduce a modern upper class which supplied students, funds, leadership, and ideology. Surveying his alma mater in the 1850s, Charles Francis Adams concluded that Harvard had succumbed to "the cold embrace of commercial conservatism." In 1920, George Santayana still regarded it as "the seminary and academy for the inner circle of Bostonians."[44]

The withdrawal of an upper class into the shelter of elite-designed institutions such as Harvard mirrored a widespread trend in the early nineteenth century for prominent men, who once had played leading roles in local affairs, to alter their commitments. Democratization opened public office to other elements, while private affairs, especially managing business, consumed more time. Horizons also broadened, and some members of the upper class became more interested in national politics and other cultural and philanthropic activities that transcended localism.[45]

Moreover in factory villages and crossroad hamlets springing up within older towns, newcomers who established manufactures and other enterprises pressed their claims to manage public affairs, bringing them into conflict with farmers and prominent families of long-standing settlement in the central village. Fragmentation in the upper strata combined with a high degree of turnover in a population increasingly heterogeneous in occupation, ethnic background, and place of birth. Religious and political attachments further eroded communal solidarity and played havoc with the relatively clear and simple gradations of early American communities. The spread of industrial order brought a "pervasive communal sense of violated norms" that led to struggles over local issues.[46] By the second generation after the arrival of manufactures, communities dissolved into an array of particularistic interests. The idea of a corporate community with common interests was simply anachronistic. Elites were internally divided and made up one among many strata competing to advance private concerns.

The process of class formation in an industrializing society manifested itself in other ways too. Whereas elites in colonial America had exhibited styles of life that distinguished them from others, external marks of class position assumed a new importance because the emerging middle and upper classes were insecure, often newly arrived, not clearly demarcated. Conspicuous consumption became an important strategy for expressing aspirations and asserting membership in a particular stratum. As personal income increased, people gained access to new goods and services most of which were not previously available. Moreover dramatic improvements in communications, especially inexpensive publication, increased awareness of the latest fashions and merchandise, as did geographic mobility. Finally, a shift in values that legitimized consumption reinforced consumer demand.

In the new consumer society patterns of expenditure were linked to patterns of social stratification. "In imitation of the rich," in eighteenth-century England, the first consumer society, "the middle ranks spent more frenziedly than ever before. . . ." "Social emulation and class competition" spurred consumption as people "surrendered eagerly to the pursuit of novelty, the hypnotic effects of fashion, and the enticements of persuasive commercial propaganda." Colonial America was a distant outpost of the first consumer society and participated marginally in the new order, because of stagnation or very slow advances in family income; the dispersed character of the population; the absence of any city comparable to London to diffuse fashion, style, and novelty; and the lack of an hereditary aristocracy to establish trends and whose taste preferences clever manufacturers such as the pottery magnate, Josiah Wedgwood, could skillfully exploit.[47] By the early nineteenth century, the barriers to the emergence of a consumer society in the United States were falling, as the result of the growth in personal income, the emergence of great metropolises such as New York, and the formation of an upper class, characteristically self-made and newly arrived, for whom consumption played a vital role in defining position, as it did also for the new modern middle class. The United States thus followed in the footsteps of the English model.

Conspicuous consumption by the middle classes elicited complaints that families lived beyond their means, that extravagant wives forced husbands into bankruptcy and thus even scared some men into remaining bachelors. These views differed from conventional eighteenth-century complaints about "luxury" because they referred not to an elite whose "virtue" luxury corrupted but to all ranks, especially the middle classes, and not just men but women too. Though American women were said to be "very fond of show, adornment rather than culture," some blamed husbands who indulged their wives primarily to display their own importance. Fashion in dress assumed a new significance for a mass public because being stylish was essential for asserting one's putitive position.[48] *Godey's Lady's Book* imitated earlier English publications and put American women in immediate touch with the latest European styles. Its lavish color plates encouraged and catered to an appetite for modish apparel.

Even farm girls who went to labor in the textile mills at Lowell, Massachusetts, were caught up in this early wave of consumerism. The factories attracted them in part because they now could acquire income for indulging their taste for bonnets, clothing, and trinkets, though of course some of their wages went to help their families.[49] The girls thus joined a swelling army of consumers. Children, too, learned the importance of dress. Timothy Dwight reported in 1821 that "people of fashion in Boston and elsewhere often try to make their children objects of admiration." They paraded them in front of guests to show them off and thereby taught their children "that the end of efforts and existence is appearance only." "Girls are taught to regard dress as a momentous concern," Dwight noted.[50]

Because consumerism sparked competition for clothes, home furnishings, and other marks of position, those with greater resources sought ways to distance themselves from others who could only indulge in popular items. Pianos, explained a writer in a musical journal in 1823, were essential for the affluent because many could not afford them. Pianos, therefore, became "a badge of gentility, being the only thing that distinguishes 'decent people' from the lower and less distinguished kind of folks, known by the name of the middling kind of folks. . . ." Whereas the master mechanic proudly displayed his certificate of membership in the Mechanics Association over his mantlepiece to inform visitors that he belonged "to that enlightened body," so more "ambitious spirits," who aspired "to the elevated ranks and imposing title 'quite decent people,' place a pianoforte in their parlours. . . ."[51]

The itinerant portrait makers who traveled throughout the Northern states in the early nineteenth century displayed in their pictures "the new domestic image of the Northern middle class: fathers and mothers surrounded by their children and their accumulating possessions." These peripatetic limners "by their geographic and social mobility, banished isolation and conservatism in the rural North, and promoted a culture of consumption," served also by numerous mechanics such as watchmakers, cabinet makers, tailors, jewellers, and milliners. Together "they prepared the way for the mass production and consumption of household commodities" and "forged a new culture of commerce."[52]

Even the disposition of the dead bore the imprint of a modern class structure. In colonial times the church graveyard gathered the remains of those who passed out of the community, whatever differences had separated people in life. In the early nineteenth century cemeteries lost their community character and became associated with ethnic, denominational, and class differences. Just as Boston's first families shaped a new way of life, they created in Mount Auburn cemetery—"Gateway to Heaven"—a new way of death. The spacious beauty of Mount Auburn, the tidy cost of a plot, and the exclusive control over admissions assured that those who had mixed rarely with persons of inferior station would go to eternal rest among men and women of their own breed. The middle classes also developed a cult of mourning with elaborate rules that were a mark of true gentility and that differentiated social classes. Rural cemeteries, elaborate caskets, sepulchral art, proper mourning attire and demeanor now became important once death passed from being an occasion for communal ritual and became an occasion for reaffirming the social status of the deceased and the bereaved.[53]

Some Americans were uneasy at the new displays of affluence and the differences in styles of life and death that distinguished classes. Evangelical Christians associated personal display with a worldliness they disdained, and others regarded conspicuous consumption as unrepublican. Masons became known for their penchant for display. They wore elaborate jewels and special dress, which in the higher degrees such as the Knights Templars, drew inspiration from European aristocracy. The same spirit of snobbery and exclusivity that fueled so much of the new emphasis on material possessions was the driving force behind Freemasonry, according to critics. Masonry taught its members to think that they were "better than others," they charged, and encouraged "corrupting" values, ostentatious parades, display of useless badges, adoption of a supercilious demeanor, and consumption of vast quantities of food and hard liquor.[54] Masonry was just one among many modes by which Americans differentiated themselves. Whatever the means, the strategy had similar purposes.

By the early nineteenth century the impulse of Americans to form voluntary associations was so strong that Alexis de Tocqueville identified it as one of the distinctive features of democracy in America. Masonry, of course, was only one among a galaxy of organizations. In Massachusetts alone, over four hundred new associations were created during the first decade of the nineteenth century, and that number doubled in the 1820s.[55] The proliferation of these bodies—economic, religious, benevolent, educational, and social—occurred because family and community no longer adequately served people's needs. Antimasons did not attack the principle of association. They themselves acted on that principle, believing that only through tract societies, newspapers, and party organization would they effectively carry on the battle against Masonry, the one association they singled out for destruction. Of strong conviction, deeply concerned with the direction in which the country was moving, Antimasons probably were more prone than most to join voluntary associations. They made up a significant element in religious, benevolent, and antislavery and temperance organizations.

Many of the new associations were supra-local in character. Whereas almost all those established in the late eighteenth century were local, more than 10 percent organized between 1800 and 1830 were trans-local.[56] These associations harnessed the principles of bureaucratic organization, raised substantial funds, and employed professional staff which published literature, sent out traveling agents, and intruded into hundreds of communities throughout the country. Freemasons were linked with others in the state through a Grand Lodge, which dispatched officers to survey the local Lodges regularly. The active cadre of local and statewide officers, a steady outpouring of Masonic books and periodicals, the construction of Masonic Halls, and circulation of Masonic lectures all vividly exemplified the way supra-local organizations spread as people increasingly looked beyond their communities.

Antimasons voiced the ambivalence many felt towards the proliferation of associations, especially those transcending local boundaries. The association principle, devoted to worthwhile ends in the hands of good people, stood to benefit the country, but in the hands of others it was suspect. Antimasons distinguished Freemasonry from other associations not only because of secrecy and cosmopolitanism, but even more because they doubted that Masonry served the welfare of the community. Masons boasted of their liberal charities, but Masonic benevolence, critics noted, did not serve the entire community: only Masons received assistance. Such a standard of "benevolence" conflicted with an older view that the entire community share responsibility to aid dependent folk. Moreover, charity was a Christian duty; those who limited their philanthropy to a select few fell far short of satisfying religious obligation. Because Masons contributed funds when they were prosperous in expectation of receiving assistance if in need, their charity smacked more of an insurance scheme than of disinterested benevolence.

Masons replied that a voluntary association had the right to care exclusively for its own members, and that Masonry was no different from most other such bodies, but their argument only emphasized the narrow, exclusivist character of the organization. Masonic charity was in fact different from traditional forms of community charity. It sought to aid middle-class folk temporarily in distress, not the down-and-out. The class character of Masonic benevolence underlines once again the nature of the organization. So too did the role that Masonry played in aiding the careers of its members.[57]

Masonry appealed to young men in particular because it introduced them to a prestigious all-male society made up of business and professional men who could be useful outside the Lodge. The decision to join a Lodge, like choice of residence, occupation, or membership in other voluntary associations, was evidence of an expanding range of options not available to early Americans. Industrialization opened new prospects for social mobility. A swelling stream of men and women left their native communities, the families which had nurtured them, and the churches of their ancestors to venture forth and make their own way. A rich, new array of possibilities cultivated a sense of individualism, a belief that people created their own lives through choices they made. This blossomed into the cult of success. For many success meant moving from manual to non-manual occupations and acquiring the gentility and respectability associated with white collar employment. Selling and clerking in cities and the smaller marketing centers became a popular alternative to manual labor since they required little training and no capital. By the 1820s the competition for such jobs alarmed observers who doubted that the supply could satisfy the demand. Even more troubling was the suspicion that dislike of physical labor signified moral decay.[58] Wage-earning artisans reaffirmed the dignity of manual labor, pride in craft, and the republican virtues of the mechanics.[59] Master mechanics also complained that men looked down on manual work and both groups insisted anew that labor alone created value. Exponents of the master artisans' ideology such as Boston printer and publisher, Joseph T. Buckingham, claimed moral superiority for the middle classes who acquired wealth by physically producing it, rather than by appropriating the labor of others.[60] Yet even as Buckingham spoke, master mechanics like himself were under pressure to become risk-taking, speculative, cost-conscious, labor-exploiting capitalists. Some preferred to give up entrepreneurship and work at their trades for wages. Others tried to compete but failed, like Buckingham, and some made fortunes. Exponents of the master mechanic's ideology contrasted his republican virtues—devotion to the common good—with the avarice of businessmen who thirsted for gain and distinction at others' expense. Yet changes within the economy compelled masters to make the transition to a capitalistic mentality in place of a traditional emphasis on craftsmanship and simple commodity exchange. For some this posed difficulties of reconciling republicanism with enterprise. In 1827 William Hilliard put the question to the Massachusetts Mechanics Charitable Association:

> As individuals, forming an important link in the chain, that binds us together as a nation, are we governed by those pure principles of patriotism, that will ever prompt us to fix our eyes upon a single point, the public good?

Hilliard raised the issue because he was no longer sure of the answer.[61]

As the mechanics' associations matured, they opened libraries and offered classes and lectures to employees in hopes of propping up the faltering belief that workers and employers shared a harmony of interest, that the craft ladder from apprenticeship to proprietorship remained intact. In fact, these early ventures in adult education provided manual workers with opportunities for self-improvement through instruction in arithmetic and bookkeeping, useful skills for men interested in white-collar jobs. So while both journeymen and masters reaffirmed belief in the nobility of manual labor, both contemplated avenues through which craftsmen could find an escape.[62]

The young men who migrated to Boston to work as clerks and the farm girls who journeyed to the Lowell mills were members of a "dislocated generation." This, more than any previous generation of Americans, was "forced to strike out on its own, making its way with few family resources . . . with few clear-cut institutions to channel it. . . ." In colonial America the path of the young was clearly marked. In the new industrial order it became "a process of continuing self-construction . . . a kind of vagabondage, moving from place to place and pursuit to pursuit, trying in the words of one particularly battered young man, to 'get a hold on life.' "[63] The development of the professions as illustrated by the example of the ministry reveals how an old calling changed to fit the new order.

In the colonial period young men contemplating a career in the ministry relied on family support or on sponsorship by a local minister who identified a promising young man and enlisted financial aid from affluent townsfolk.[64] By the early nineteenth century this system no longer proved adequate. The demand for trained clergymen exceeded supply in new communities and in the spreading cities, and existing colleges were too small and too expensive. At the same time, farmers' sons who had no prospects of inheriting land searched for alternatives to husbandry. Some gravitated toward the ministry—an escape from manual labor—but lacked the resources. New colleges arose to meet the need for clergy and other professionals and to accommodate the impecunious. The new institutions, whose enrollments boomed, differed from the older colonial colleges. Their students came typically from families who could not finance advanced education. These "rough-hewn, heavy set of fellows, from the hills and woods," Nathaniel Hawthorne remembered, tended to be older than their eighteenth-century counterparts; almost a quarter were in their mid-twenties.[65] They favored the newer New England institutions such as Amherst and Williams which were closer to home and cheaper than Harvard or Yale. Still students had to work to support themselves. The colonial colleges had few scholarships and the new institutions suffered from inadequate financing. To solve the problem, evangelical Congregationalists, anxious to increase the supply of clergymen, established in 1812 the American Education Society. By 1816 the AES gave support to 161 students, and by 1831 to more than a thousand. Dubbing its assistance "parental loans," the AES intruded into a sphere that customarily belonged to families. In the cause of supplying a suitably trained professional stratum, evangelical Christians had "invented a machine that trampled on traditional ties between fathers and sons, families and churches, superiors and inferiors."[66]

The AES, like Freemasonry, was a supra-local institution that shaped the development of a modern social structure. The colleges attended by

the young men reflected class differences. First, there were the elite institutions such as Harvard that appealed to the more affluent, but even within
the newer institutions which recruited more broadly, class differences became painfully manifest. So many impecunious students were now in
attendance that colleges altered their calendars to allow them to take time
off to teach during winter. To further assist them, the colleges allowed
poorer students to live off-campus in cheap rooms and to dine in the Commons at special tables serving less-expensive food.[67]

College graduates who became clergymen entered a profession radically
transformed in the early nineteenth century. The colonial New England
minister had been the spiritual shepherd of an extensive flock. His tenure
typically spanned the lifetime of his contemporaries in the congregation.
His authority was the chief religious authority in the community. The
church was a community institution, supported by tax funds, possessing
privileges as the established church, and encompassing within its ranks a
significant portion of the population, without regard to differences in gender
and station. By the 1820s, however, churches almost everywhere had become private associations without legal privileges, each competing for members and spiritual authority. Denominations also tended more and more
to reflect class differences. Methodism and Unitarianism, for example, did
not appeal to the same sorts of people. And in almost all churches, women
were dominant in the membership as the formal bonds of religious attachment became ever more differentiated by gender. The clergy who presided
over these churches found tenure less secure, their voice one of many, secular
and non-secular, competing to be heard, and their commitment to serve a
single congregation for a lifetime eroding. The laity, too, were restless to try
new preachers with an unfamiliar batch of sermons who might keep people
awake and compete successfully for new members. The ministry, once a
calling entailing a long-term commitment, was becoming a modern profession. Clergymen received formal training in seminaries, then went on
the clerical job market, and moved from place to place in search of better
salaries and more prestigious pulpits. The most successful freed themselves
entirely from pastoral duties by securing professorships, editorial positions
on religious publications, and managerial jobs in the bureaucracies spawned
by organized religious benevolence. The idea of success and upward mobility had invaded the ministry; getting ahead rivaled saving souls.[68]

The birth of industrial order was painful and confusing. Americans were
not equally adept at adjusting to a new world built on a mobility ethic,
conspicuous consumption, a volatile market economy, and modern class
structure. Antimasons sensed that the idea of organic community was in
jeopardy. They sensed, too, that a new class system which located people
on an impersonal spectrum according to wealth, occupation, education, and
appearance fractured communities in ways that social differences had not
in early America. Freemasonry embodied for them many of the currents
sweeping through the United States during the Great Transition. Catering

to transiency and status striving, offering men an asylum from ruthless competition in the marketplaces as well as temporary escape from the constraints of domestic life, and above all by contributing to the formation of a bourgeoisie, Masonry became a master symbol identified with the most profound changes in American history. These changes posed special challenges for the churches and the spiritual life of the country. Antimasonry tapped deep roots of religious faith, yet faith alone did not make Christians Antimasons. Untangling the complex religious sources of Antimasonry brings us closer to understanding why the Antimasonic Persuasion captured the imaginations and the loyalties of a significant fraction of American opinion.

4

Purging the Republic's Churches
Religious Sources of Antimasonry

You might as well expect religion in a brothel, as in a Masonic Lodge.
Lynn Record, 9 September 1834

Antimasonry is bottomed upon rank political hatred and bigoted intolerant sectarianism.   *Masonic Mirror,* 28 May 1831

In 1819 Charles J. Warren, twenty-three, became a Royal Arch Freemason in Attleboro, Massachusetts, having previously passed through six inferior degrees. As in the ceremony for each degree, so in that for the Royal Arch, a Mason blindfolded the candidate and led Warren around the assembled chapter. A voice intoned a passage from scripture: "Now Moses kept the flock of Jethro, his father-in-law, the priest of Midian; and the angel of the Lord appeared unto him in the flame of fire out of the midst of the bush; and he looked and beheld the bush burned with fire, and the bush was not consumed." Warren's guide then removed the blindfold and the initiate suddenly saw "a bush . . . that was made to blaze up, without burning. . . ." It was a bush painted on canvas, which a light suddenly illuminated, Warren recalled. (In other lodges real bushes doused with turpentine burst into flame.) Then a figure impersonating God stepped behind the burning bush and called forth: "Moses! Moses!" Warren's guide answered: "Here am I." "Draw not nigh hither," the Lord commanded, "put off thy shoes from off thy feet for the place whereupon thou standest is holy ground. I am the God of thy fathers, the God of Abraham, the God of Isaac, and the God of Jacob." Warren's shoes were removed and the blindfold once again fastened. "And Moses hid his face, for he was afraid to look upon God," a voice intoned.[1]

Warren recounted his experience more than ten years later as an expert witness before a Massachusetts legislative investigation of Freemasonry in response to Antimasonic petitions demanding that the state outlaw Masonic oaths as blasphemous and subversive. Among the ranks of Freemasons none alarmed outsiders more than the Royal Arch Masons whose oaths, rituals, and penalties seemed particularly dangerous. Warren, as all initiates, had promised to "espouse the cause of a companion Royal Arch Mason, whether he be right or wrong, so far at least as to extricate him from his present difficulty." It was precisely such oaths, Antimasons thought, that enabled Freemasons involved in the kidnap and murder of Morgan to escape punishment because their brothers had kept mum. On becoming a Royal Arch Mason, Warren further pledged: "I will not shed the blood of a Royal Arch Mason, unlawfully, knowing him to be such." Critics inferred that Royal Arch Masons were free to take the lives of persons outside Masonic protection. The punishment for violating one's oath was fearsome, Warren revealed, for he had sworn to bind himself "under no less penalty than that of having my scull smote off and my brains exposed to the scorching rays of the sun." The Morgan case suggested that the oaths and penalties were taken seriously, but in fact there was scant evidence that Masons threatened or harmed anyone except Morgan. Why thousands thought otherwise, succumbing to paranoia, is a central question on which Warren's testimony sheds light.

The year after Warren became a Royal Arch Mason, he underwent "a change of heart" and joined the Congregational church in Taunton, Massachusetts. As a young man, like so many in his generation, he faced the choice of a career with uncertainty. Masonry had briefly played a valuable role in his life, but once he made his choice, Warren "had business of more importance to attend to." He secured a belated education, graduating from Brown, and entered the ministry at the age of thirty-two. His first assignment was at the West Attleboro Congregational Church in southeastern Massachusetts, a hotbed of Antimasonry. There Warren joined the Mendon Association, a regional organization comprised of Congregationalist ministers knit together by adherence to the most uncompromising version of New England Calvinism—Hopkinsianism—and by the powerful leadership of Rev. Nathanael Emmons of Franklin, the foremost champion in early nineteenth-century America of the doctrines of Rev. Samuel Hopkins, Jonathan Edwards's successor.

For several years after his conversion and entry into the ministry Warren still enjoyed the pleasures of Masonic sociability, valuing it especially when he traveled. Not even the Morgan case forced him to reconsider; his first reaction was that it was a political hoax. He knew that dozens of clergymen from many denominations were Freemasons, some even served as chaplains of their Lodge and paraded publicly in Masonic regalia. There was no reason to think that Christianity and Masonry were at odds.[2]

By 1830, however, Warren, like many of his colleagues, had abandoned the Order and joined the crusade to purge the churches of Masons. A generation earlier, sentinels of New England Puritanism such as Yale's President Timothy Dwight and Rev. Jedidiah Morse had echoed allegations circulating in Europe among Catholics and conservatives that Masonry was the secret force behind the French Revolution and the Jacobins' revolutionary assault on Christian faith. Though Dwight and Morse saw Jeffersonian Republicanism as carrier of Jacobin Masonry to American shores, their warnings went largely unheeded even among members of their own denomination. Whatever may have been true in Europe, most Americans in the early nineteenth century perceived no conflict between church and Lodge. Yet from the outset the post-1826 Antimasonic movement drew heavily on a wellspring of Antimasonic sentiment within sectors of American Protestantism. Ministers occupied important places in the Antimasonic movement. They crystallized public sentiment and diffused Antimasonic ideas within their congregations and communities. Some helped to force Masonic colleagues out of their pulpits; others lost their jobs because a majority of their church rejected Antimasonry. They edited Antimasonic newspapers, wrote Antimasonic tracts, and delivered Antimasonic sermons. Prominent laity were active too, and together with religious Antimasons played a major role in the movement. Penitent church members who were Masons made public confessions, which circulated widely in the Antimasonic press; some even signed printed forms that offered the repentant a standard renunciation. These renunciations were akin to confessions of sin except that the penitent addressed not a church but the entire community. They hoped to influence public opinion, encourage other Masons to follow their example, and restore their reputations as Christians in good standing. The confessions vividly demonstrated that remorseful sinners need not fear the awful penalties by which Masonry, some thought, kept thousands in thrall.[3]

Once Antimasonry made the transition from a diffuse popular social movement to a political party, clergy and laity became active in third-party politics. Ministers endorsed the Antimasonic party and participated in its conventions and public meetings. A few even ran for public office. Obscure and famous preachers enlisted in the cause, men such as Charles J. Warren and the greatest evangelist of the day, Charles G. Finney. Finney had also been a Freemason before his conversion, but once he became a Christian, he too abandoned the Order. A member of no church in his youth, skeptical of various competing versions of Christianity, Finney joined the Masons partly to escape loneliness in his peripatetic life. Baptists, Methodists, Presbyterians, and members of other denominations who arrived in an unfamiliar place could usually find a warm welcome from co-religionists, but for a Northingarian such as Finney, Masonry filled a void. Like other Antimasonic converts, he warned Christians that they risked their souls unless they followed his example. In his Lodge, he recalled, the Master had been a Deist.[4] Following his rebirth, Finney advocated sectarian standards in public life: "Christians must vote for honest men, and take consistent ground in politics or the Lord will curse them." Thousands of Antimasons heeded his call and carried the battle against Masonry from the churches into the political arena.[5]

Why Masonry fell under religious ban only in the late 1820s and why only some Christians joined the Antimasonic movement is unclear.[6] Antimasons claimed that Morgan's murder had torn the veil from their eyes. They now saw Masonry clearly: a dangerous threat to Christian religion and republican government. Yet much of the indictment of Freemasonry went far beyond the Morgan case. The claim, for example, that Masonry promoted infidelity was as applicable before 1826 as after. The warnings of Abbe Barruel and John Robinson in the 1790s, popularized in the United States by Dwight, Morse, and others, anticipated most of the arguments of religious Antimasons, some of whom drew directly on these early writers.[7] Yet not until the 1820s did a large body of Christians begin to believe that Freemasonry led to "blank Atheism."[8]

Freemasonry, Rev. Nathanael Emmons told Massachusetts Antimasons in 1832, was the "darkest and deepest plot that ever was formed in this wicked world against the true God, the true religion, and the temporal and eternal interests of mankind."[9] Obviously such a conspiracy must stretch back well before 1826. Masonry had gained respectability by cleverly masquerading as "the handmaiden of religion," by claiming to promote love of God, piety, charity, and benevolence. In reality, critics charged, Masonry insinuated itself as a substitute for revealed religion. By employing such trappings as the open Bible that graced the Lodge room and incorporating scriptural passages into its ritual, Freemasonry actually spread deism and infidelity. By admitting Jews, Moslems, and other non-Christians and by excluding any mention of Jesus from its oaths and rites, Masonry placed itself outside the Christian community.[10]

The god of Freemasonry was the Divine Architect, the First Cause of natural religion, not the mighty, unknowable Jehovah who sternly tested men and women as they trod the rocky road to salvation. "In its whole length and breadth," asserted Massachusetts Antimasons, the Order "is as Anti-Christian as it is Anti-Republican." Unless purged from the churches, Masonry will "corrupt, and, ultimately . . . undermine and destroy all our civil and religious institutions . . . and spread infidelity, despotism, and misery throughout the earth."[11]

Before exploring the reasons for the shift of perception from tolerance or indifference to intense hostility, we must probe more deeply into the religious indictment of the Order. Masonry was "pure Deism," Edward Barber claimed, because it taught none of God's laws, requirements, and sanctions but regarded the Bible merely as a work "of human invention." Through Masonry men sought to escape from the great truths of revealed religion: "the hope of glory and the fear of punishment—eternal life and eternal death— . . . heaven, with all its seraphic joys and choral symphonies, hell, with all its agonizing and burning torments—the blood of the atonement—the groans of Calvary . . . the darkened sun—the bloody sweat. . . ." By banishing these "dread realities," Masonry removed restraints that kept a sinful species in check. Morgan's murder and the escape from justice by hundreds of Masons involved in the crime or cover-up proved that the dangers were neither theoretical nor prospective.[12]

In opposition to the Bible's injunction against swearing, Masonry erected its entire system on a set of immoral oaths that released men from the restraints of Christian and civic obligation. When a Brother lied, cheated, fornicated, stole, or even murdered, Freemasons were oath-bound to protect him, having promised to do so "in the presence of Almighty God." Masonry thereby threatened Christian morality by imposing a new set of obligations that took precedence over all others. Every time a Mason swore an oath "in the presence of Almighty God," he committed blasphemy. He compounded that blasphemy by participating in ceremonies which made "farcical representations of the 'burning bush,' 'the Ark of God,' 'the pot of Manna,' and 'the rod of Aaron.'" Masons, like pagans, even drank blood from a human skull, Antis alleged.[13] Capping the blasphemous oaths and rituals were barbaric penalties. How could any Christian vow to smite off a right ear, to strike off a right hand, to bury people alive, pulling down their house and crucifying them on timbers taken therefrom "until the last trumpet shall sound," tearing out their eyes from their sockets, and quartering the body and throwing the pieces among the rubbish of the temple? And each time Masons swore such oaths, they invoked the name of the Lord, promising, "So help me God, and keep me steadfast to perform this obligation."[14]

Masons pretended to revere Christianity but only, the Antimasons argued, "for the purpose of accomplishing its overthrow."[15] The Order staged as part of its rites a mock murder followed by a mock resurrection which tended to make people look upon Christ's resurrection with "credulity and doubt." And as Masons witnessed other men impersonating God, they debased Him to a level of mere mortality. A frontal assault against Christianity could never succeed but against such "sly insinuation, innuendoes, solemn mockery, sneers and ridicule there is no defence."[16]

Nor was Masonic secrecy compatible with Christianity. Genuine Christianity preached its message in the open to all. "I spake plainly to the World, and in secret I have said nothing," Jesus proclaimed. Antimasons reminded Americans of these words by emblazoning them on the mastheads of their newspapers.[17] Even if Morgan's murder were an aberration, the general tendency of Masonry was to encourage sensuality, overeating, drinking, ribaldry, indecency, and disrespect for women.[18]

In its early days, Antimasons insisted, Christians avoided Masonry as akin to black magic and witchcraft. To overcome such suspicions and to gain respectability, Masons cleverly cultivated the clergy. They invited ministers to join, charged them no dues, and paid them for officiating at meetings. The presence of clergymen attracted other Christians who might have had doubts.[19] The existence of a secret society piqued people's curiosity and exploited their cupidity. Forty-three years ago, explained Aaron Leland, a Baptist minister and president of the Vermont Antimasonic Convention in 1830, he had come to the Green Mountain State as a stranger to preach in the wilderness. Success soon crowned his labors and two hundred to three hundred people gathered into his church. Then fortune went to his head. At the time he joined the Masons, he recalled, "I began to feel myself a man of consequence. I was *hailed* by the members, and was greeted as a *brother* by men of all creeds, or no creeds, by the unprincipled, by infidels." His example led others to join. Soon there were enough Masons in town to form a Lodge. However, years before the Morgan affair, Leland quietly withdrew. He discovered that Masonry "destroyed my devotion to God" for it was "a system of wickedness, which can be summed up in three words—Judaism, Paganism, and Idolatry!"[20] Other renouncing Masons agreed. They too had fallen because they were weak, led by "a vain curiosity," enticed by the trappings of the "harlot," this "idolatrous Jezebel." Above all they were lured "by the selfish hopes of personal advantage and distinction." Masonry was thus only the latest shape which Satan took to entrap Christians "in the unhallowed orgies of his midnight assemblies." Once entrapped, bound by savage oaths, polluted by Masonic "uncleanness," sunk deeply in their guilt, Christians suffered paralysis of will and could not escape. Because the blasphemous oaths and barbaric penalties were secret, none had known what Masonry had in store until they actually experienced their own initiation. By then it was too late to turn back. Few risked humiliation or overcame their fears and doubts by pulling back. And once someone had sworn an oath, the frightening penalties made entrapment complete.[21]

Yet even though some Christians freed themselves quietly, when it came to rescuing others, most faltered. Masonic power was intimidating. Others judged that open confrontation would cause excitement and divisions, antagonize powerful elements, prompt cries of persecution, and certainly throw the churches into turmoil. Yet Antimasons demanded that Christians overcome all obstacles. Every church possessed the power to purge itself by imposing discipline and demanding that members resign from the Order. Should a majority be under Masonic control, the pious minority must withdraw "in obedience to the divine commands" that Christians keep "no fellowship with the unfruitful works of darkness. . . ." "Happy Day," affirmed Antimasons, "when the church, purified from her present guilt and defilement, shall shine in all the beauty of holiness. . . ."[22]

Masons denied that their oaths, rituals, and penalties were anti-Christian. Yet one could no longer dismiss them as harmless considering the fate of Morgan, the secrecy with which Masons shrouded them, and their elaborate precision. How much credit to give Masonic rites, how to interpret them, what religious and moral consequences flowed from them—all these questions puzzled outsiders. Yet the singularity of the Morgan case seemed to justify skepticism that the oaths licensed crime. Freemasons included members of almost every Protestant denomination, and church leaders participated in Masonic rites. They obviously did not regard the oaths and penalties as blasphemous nor perceive Masonry to be in conflict with revealed religion or civic duty. Why Masonry came under such sharp attack from clergy and lay activists puzzled the Order.

Just as political Antimasonry grew out of confusion over the meaning and obligations of being a republican, so religious Antimasonry expressed anxiety over a parallel confusion over the meaning and obligations of being a Christian. Religious Antimasonry was less a quarrel between than within denominations over appropriate standards of Christian behavior and belief. Just as Antimasons sensed that Masonry somehow bore a connection to the emerging system of social stratification, so too they sensed that Masonry carried the seeds of secularization. The churches themselves bore considerable responsibility for the spread of secular perspectives. Assuming that bolstering faith required an accommodation with the scientific and humanitarian currents gathering momentum in the eighteenth century, theologians had de-emphasized the mystical, supra-rational elements in Christianity to stress God's rationality, as evidenced by the popularity of the argument for his existence from the design of the Newtonian universe, and of his benevolence from the steady improvement in the social and material conditions of life. "Yet even while Christianizing the idea of progress," evangelicals "came perilously close to secularizing their divine progressivism."[23] Churches thus adjusted to individualism and materialism, acknowledging the status-striving and worldliness of the populace, while clerical authority continued to suffer steady erosion. Christianity had to compete on increasingly unfavorable terms with a powerful secular culture, spread by newspapers, magazines, and lectures, science, fashion, consumerism, and popular forms of entertainment. The market stamped its imprint on the culture as well as on the social structure.[24]

Antimasonry appealed especially to Christians who clung strongly to Calvinist roots, especially conservative Congregationalists, Presbyterians, and Baptists and others who adhered to an older, communitarian religious tradition that placed a high value on uniform beliefs, revealed religion, and sectarian exclusivity. It attracted, too, people who believed that Christian faith imposed rigorous standards of behavior. The dangers to faith, Antimasons thought, came more from within than from outside the churches, from those forces which secularized faith by accommodating formalism, abandoning or modifying unpopular doctrine, and subordinating rigorous moral standards to worldliness.

Antimasons identified the spread of Masonry among Christians with powerful secularizing currents. Masonry professed not to compete with the churches but it promulgated a vague deism, de-emphasized sectarian and doctrinal questions, opened its doors to an ecumenical membership, and offered opportunities for combining self-interest with good works. How could churches who took seriously their doctrinal and sectarian traditions be tolerant of an institution so at odds with evangelical Christianity? Antimasons asked. For some Masonry represented forces that had spread into the churches, paralyzing them from weeding out the faithless. How churches faced the challenge of Masonry, therefore, became a decisive test in the struggle against devitalization. Antimasonry, consequently, proved to be profoundly divisive. Since Masonry served the needs of an emerging bourgeoisie, an important segment of which clung to evangelical religion, Antimasons attempted to force people to choose, and that was bound to cause trouble.

Moreover, Antimasonry burst on the scene at an especially tense time in the development of American Protestantism. The last quarter of the eighteenth century and the first half of the nineteenth century was a turbulent though formative period in the evolution of denominationalism. No pietist-liturgical dichotomy, such as historians have found in the late nineteenth century, neatly locates Protestant denominations along a spectrum of theological belief, ritual practice, moral concern, and partisan attachments.[25] Important new churches appeared—Universalists, Free Will Baptists, Shakers, Mormons, Christians (Disciples), and others. Powerful currents divided older denominations—Congregationalists, Methodists, and Baptists—and reshaped them in the process. In New England, especially, the relationship between church and state still remained a sensitive question, dividing Congregationalists from evangelicals who had suffered from persecution and second-class citizenship under the religious establishment. Even after Connecticut in 1818 and Massachusetts in 1833 joined the rest of the country and disestablished their Congregationalist churches, conflict persisted among competing denominations, now all equal before the law. In dozens of towns there were disputes over church funds, use of the meeting houses, control of school boards, and efforts to use the state to enforce standards of moral behavior such as sabbatarianism and temperance. Churches became entangled in conflicts between modernist and antimodernist factions which divided over questions of theology, piety, and social practice.[26] Quakers split between the Hicksites and Orthodox factions; Old Side and New Side Presbyterians rended that denomination; Reform Methodists and Protestant Methodists challenged the Methodist Episcopalians in the mainstream; Restorationism split Universalists; and many Baptists adhered to anti-mission principles that rejected organized benevolence, missionary activity, modern revivalism, and a pietism that employed government in the service of religion.[27]

In New England the most important conflicts occurred within the Congregationalist churches of Massachusetts. First, liberal Arminian currents that had emerged early in the eighteenth century culminated in the Unitarian split, though as late as 1830 many Unitarian churches still called themselves Congregationalist and benefited from the historical privileges enjoyed by the state church wherever Unitarian majorities captured them. Then Unitarianism itself fragmented as radical elements came into conflict with the more conservative mainstream and drifted towards transcendentalism and social reform. As for Trinitarian Congregationalists, their struggles against the Unitarians did not inhibit fragmentation into three major fractions, each claiming to adherence to the Calvinist tradition: the Hopkinsians, the moderate Calvinists, and the Arminian-tending elements led by Nathaniel W. Taylor of Yale, Lyman Beecher, and other modernists.[28]

Given these complicated cross-currents within denominations, when Antimasonry burst on the scene, many clergymen and lay leaders strove to remain neutral. There were enough internal strains without adding new disputes between pro- and anti-Masonic factions. Yet neutrality proved difficult, especially in denominations where Antimasonry made deep inroads.

The denominational press in New England preferred to avoid the controversy. The *Connecticut Episcopalian Weekly,* the Massachusetts Universalist *Trumpet,* the *Vermont Baptist Telegraph,* and the Boston *Christian Watchman* (Baptist) were silent.[29] Both the Massachusetts *Christian Register,* a Unitarian weekly, and the *Boston Recorder,* the voice of Trinitarian Congregationalism, excluded the question from their columns. The publisher of the *Boston Recorder* reassured Antimasonic readers that his new editor, E. C. Tracy, was no longer a Mason, but Tracy's failure to renounce left him suspect in the eyes of militant Antimasons. Because the *Recorder* closed its pages to controversy, two new religious papers—the *Boston Christian Herald* and the *New England Telegraph*—gave Antimasonic Congregationalists a press of their own. In Hartford, Connecticut, Rev. Noble D. Strong, a conservative Calvinistic Congregationalist, edited the Antimasonic *Intelligencer,* but in Portland, Maine, the publisher and the editor of the Congregational weekly, the *Christian Mirror,* both loyal Masons, would have no truck with Antimasonry and alienated Antimasonic readers, who then switched to the Antimasonic *Maine Free Press.*[30]

Statistical analysis employing multiple regression reveals no clear-cut relationship between membership in the major denominations and Antimasonic voting. The regression statistics indicate weak or fluctuating relationships. They suggest that Episcopalians and Universalists did not support the Antimasonic party in contrast to Quakers, but the data for most of the major denominations are inconclusive. (See Table 4.1.[31]) Yet we know from other sources that conservative Congregationalists played an important role in the Antimasonic movement, but because that denomination was split over Masonry, as on many theological questions, and membership data do not distinguish among factions within a denomination, regression statistics are inadequate guides.

Biographical data shed more light. In Massachusetts some fifty clergymen were identified in approximately equal numbers who took opposite sides. Unitarians, Episcopalians, and Universalists made up the bulk of the pro-Masonic clergy, and Trinitarian Congregationalists most of the Antimasonic clergy. Likewise in Connecticut, Episcopalian clergymen figured prominently among the pro-Masons, but Congregationalists were divided. In New Hampshire and Rhode Island, Episcopalians, Universalists, and liberal Baptist clergy supported Masonry whereas Antimasonic ministers were more likely to be Calvinists. In Vermont, contrary to the common pattern, Universalist ministers played an active role in an Antimasonic coalition, heavily populated by conservative Calvinists, which underlines the necessity to study specific contexts.[32]

Antimasonry divided some denominations more than others. Many New England Methodist preachers had become Masons before 1826, a useful association for a peripatetic ministry. The *Masonic Mirror* boasted that a majority had joined, partly in gratitude to Masonic devotion to religious tolerance, especially in earlier times when dissenters courted persecution. In 1829, the New England Conference of Methodists, responding to Antimasonic agitation, resolved "not to have any connection with Masonry," instructing the faithful not to "enter the debate for or against Masonry as ministers of the Gospel." The conference directed Methodists to receive itinerant preachers who had been Masons, but refused to condemn Freemasonry. Methodist leaders thus concentrated on avoiding schism, not on fighting Masonry, yet because some Masons interpreted Methodist policy as hostile, New Hampshire Congressman John Brodhead, a Methodist minister and Jacksonian Democrat, together with other Masonic members of the conference, insisted that the denomination did not oppose Freemasonry. Yet in 1831 the *Masonic Mirror* reprinted an appeal to American Methodists from a preacher who complained of an inquisition against those who remained in the Order.[33]

Baptists also split over Freemasonry. As in New York where Baptist conferences divided, so New England Baptists also disagreed. Prominent Baptist ministers and laymen enlisted on both sides of the controversy. In Vermont, the strongly Antimasonic churches which formed the Addison Association in 1833 withdrew from the Vermont Association because it refused to condemn Freemasonry. In Maine, the Wendell Baptist Association declared Masonry evil and denied fellowship with Baptists who failed to quit the Order.[34]

Antimasonry penetrated deeply into the Free Will Baptist church. In 1833 the *Maine Free Press* claimed that most Free Will Baptist elders had quit the order. Like the Methodists, the Free Willers, acknowledging that many of their members were Masons, tried to steer a tactful course. The General Conference in 1830 did not require Masons to renounce, but for the sake of denominational harmony, it suggested that people resign voluntarily. This did not suit the Antimasonic faction, especially in Vermont, whose yearly meeting succeeded in persuading the 1833 Conference to condemn the Order as corrupt, a position re-affirmed in 1844 when all secret societies, including Odd Fellows and Rechabites, a temperance order, fell under Conference ban.[35] Earlier the small Seventh-Day Baptist denomination, whose strength in New England lay mostly in Rhode Island, instructed its members in 1827 to give up Masonry. Three years later those who refused faced expulsion.[36]

The Congregationalists were the oldest, most numerous and influential

denomination in New England, including in their ranks the weight of social and political leadership except in eastern Massachusetts, where Unitarianism competed. The question of Freemasonry proved painful. Many
prominent laymen had become Masons as had some ministers. Prudently
the General Association in each New England state preferred neutrality,
as did the Congregationalist press. Challenged by a proliferation of popular
sects that appealed to the middle and lower strata and by Unitarians and
Episcopalians attractive to the upper strata, Congregationalists were wary
of involvement in another divisive issue. Yet that proved impossible. Many
important Antimasonic leaders were Congregationalist leaders, and though
they could not impose an Antimasonic test of membership in a denomination which fiercely prized local autonomy, they battled to reshape denominational opinion and purge the churches one by one. Congregationalist polity,
like that of the Baptists, made the denomination particularly vulnerable to
internal discord since there was no national or even statewide authority to
lay down the law on Masonry. The battle raged in one church after another.

Apprehensive of Antimasonry's divisiveness, Lyman Beecher, the Congregationalists' foremost figure, opted for caution. When the Antimasonic
furor reached Massachusetts, Beecher had already moved from Connecticut
to Boston, where he led the Orthodox party in a crusade that achieved considerable success in reclaiming the metropolis from Unitarianism. Many
members of the local Trinitarian churches were prominent Antimasons; a
few dominated the party's state committee. Yet for several years, Beecher
kept silent. Then in July 1831, he ascended the platform at a great Antimasonic meeting in Faneuil Hall and invoked divine blessing. All were
breathless, reported the Antimasonic *Christian Herald,* until Beecher revealed "whether his heart was in the great work in which Antimasons were
engaged." Beecher at last proved "plain, full, and unequivocal," causing tears
to well in the eyes of veteran battlers against the Masonic dragon. Their
cause had now won a powerful new endorsement. Antimasons made much
of Beecher's support not just because of his prominence but also because his
earlier noncommittal stand was embarrassing. Yet Beecher still remained
aloof. His sympathies lay with Antimasonry but as a shrewd politician, he
kept his distance, realizing that Antimasonry antagonized influential laymen
attached to both Masonry and the National Republican party.[37]

By contrast, conservative and moderate Calvinists in Massachusetts and
elsewhere took high Antimasonic ground. In 1829 the Suffolk County Antimasonic Committee asked the faculties at Unitarian-dominated Harvard
College and Trinitarian Andover Theological Seminary to judge Freemasonry's claim that it descended from the builders of King Solomon's Temple.
Harvard President Josiah Quincy expressed mild skepticism but tactfully
admitted that his college's faculty had "no precise information." A short
time thereafter Harvard loaned the Grand Lodge of Massachusetts $15,000
to erect a new Masonic Temple in Boston, making clear the sympathies of

liberal Christians. By contrast Moses Stuart and Leonard Woods, leading lights of the faculty at Andover, which the Orthodox Trinitarians had established to counter Harvard's defection to Unitarianism, blasted Freemasonry's claim to antiquity as mere "pretence." A specialist in the Old Testament, Professor Stuart provided Antimasons with an authoritative opinion to undermine Masonry's efforts to link itself to the Biblical epoch.[38] Masons rebutted Stuart's opinion: "Perhaps too much learning has made him mad," fulminated the *Masonic Mirror*. In an enlightened age, the *Mirror* was confident that intelligent people would pay little attention to the uniformed assertions of bigots. Woods's view, it exploded, was an "incongruous mass of nonsense"; Stuart's was mere "intellectual imbecility." Appealing to anticlericalism, the *Mirror* bracketed Stuart and Woods with that "class of men in this country too lazy for manual labor and too ignorant to obtain a comfortable livelihood in any other manner" than by using the pulpit to indulge "their impassioned and senseless raging" to arouse "the passions and unstable feelings of the weak and feeble, and plunge a subsistence out of the credulous poor."[39]

These exchanges occurred at the same time that the Unitarian-Trinitarian conflict reached its culmination in Massachusetts. Woods and Stuart had both engaged in a pamphlet war against the Unitarians. The charge that Masonry was a form of deism in disguise paralleled Orthodox attacks on Unitarianism. Like the Freemasons, Unitarians claimed to be Christians while denying fundamental tenets of Christianity, and, like the secret Order, Unitarians used underhanded, conspiratorial methods to advance their cause, according to the Trinitarians, first by stealing Harvard from the authentic heirs of the Puritans and then by taking over as many Congregational churches in the Bay State as they could with the aid of a Unitarian judiciary and sympathetic politicians.[40]

In 1831 Bernard Whitman, a Unitarian minister from Waltham, Massachusetts, made a strong defense of Freemasonry in an address to hundreds of Masons who defiantly marched through the streets of Boston to celebrate the opening of the new Masonic Temple. Even if a few Masons were guilty of the crimes against Morgan, Whitman argued, that was no reason to condemn thousands of Masons with spotless reputations. By the same theory of guilt by association which smeared all Masons, the Trinitarians were blameworthy for the death of Servetus at the hands of Genevan Calvinists in the sixteenth century, and for the persecution of Baptists and the execution of Quakers by Massachusetts Puritans in the seventeenth century. No sect or group had a corner on virtue, Whitman told the approving Freemasons. "Is there not as much evidence of licentious principle and immoral conduct" among the Orthodox as among others? he asked.[41]

The prime objective of religious Antimasonry was to make Masonry grounds for exclusion from church membership. Whitman rejected the charges of infidelity and denounced the purges. He was not alone. Unitarians, Universalists, and Episcopalians as well as the more ecumenical and anti-evangelical elements in other denominations tended to resist Antimasonry.

The most intense battles were fought, therefore, within evangelical churches. That liberals and latitudinarians were tolerant of Freemasonry did not surprise Antimasons, but the caution displayed by Lyman Beecher, the silence of the religious press, as well as the neutrality of denominational associations distressed them. Since they believed that Freemasonry eventually led to "blank Atheism," it was puzzling why others were so blind. God intervened, however, by sending "delusions, divisions, heresies and strife in their sacred enclosure" to warn the misled that "unless they awake and separate themselves from this abomination, still sorer judgments may be expected." These alarms appeared in the report to the Massachusetts Antimasonic Convention of 1831 by a committee charged to consider "whether intelligent Christians or churches can knowingly fellowship Freemasonry, or its adhering members . . . without becoming accessories" to its "horrid crimes." The convention sidestepped the committee's recommendation that churches expel Masons and adopted a milder resolution declaring Freemasonry "opposed to the principles and precepts of the gospel" and deploring "the direct or tacit encouragement given to this institution by the Clergy and other members of the Christian Church, in almost every denomination."[42] Even Antimasonic partisans hesitated to call for a purge, though purges occurred in churches throughout the northeastern United States.

Since churches were voluntary associations that set the terms of membership, it was anomalous for a social movement such as Antimasonry to intrude into the business of private bodies. Antimasons, however, believed that precisely because Masonry had so thoroughly infiltrated the churches, there was no other way to cleanse them. So divided was Christian opinion, so powerful was Masonic influence, that only by winning the battle of public opinion outside the churches could they win the battle within. Yet in making such public appeals, Antimasons revealed that they depended on community sentiment, which was hopelessly divided. By embracing a mass social movement and political party, religious Antimasons resorted to secular power to purge the churches of secularism.

At the heart of religious Antimasonry lay growing confusion about who was an authentic Christian in a pluralistic society that separated church from state yet still assumed that Christian belief was a foundation of civic virtue.[43] Because the state did not prescribe standards of faith, a bewildering variety of denominations mushroomed in the half-century after American Independence. Denominational competition became more pervasive and reached a new level of intensity in the early nineteenth century. Adding to the strain were new agencies of religious benevolence—newspapers and magazines, tract societies, and missionary and educational enterprises. These institutions, backed by unprecedented financial resources, responded to developments which necessitated new methods to counter indifference and secularism and to advance denominational interests. Reliance on bureaucracy, however, testified to an erosion of Christian community rooted in shared beliefs and loyalty to a common church.

Historians who have appraised the Second Great Awakening—the three decades of revivalism that culminated in the great revival of 1830—as a successful campaign to strengthen evangelical Christianity in the United States underestimate the extensive inroads secularism made within the national culture and within the evangelical churches themselves. That secularism had made inroads was at least the perception of religious Antimasons. They concluded that Masonry flourished because Christian faith and practice had eroded. Widespread secularism among church members necessitated a national campaign to clarify what it meant to be a Christian. Nothing revealed confusion more clearly than the response of pietists to Rev. Ezra Stiles Ely's call for the formation of a Christian party in politics to place pious men in public office in the late 1820s. Ely's candidate for Christian magistrate in 1828 was Andrew Jackson, but to other pietists, Jackson, who had shot several men in duels and was a noted Indian fighter, though a Presbyterian, was even more of an anathema than his rival, Unitarian John Quincy Adams. Though many evangelicals after Adams's defeat in 1828 gravitated towards the National Republican opposition and its leader, Henry Clay, they were uneasy. Clay admitted that he was not a church member nor had ever experienced the Holy Spirit, admissions that, combined with a reputation for loose living, made it difficult for many to support him. If professed Christians could claim that both Jackson and Clay were fit to serve as chief magistrates of a Christian Republic, the hour of danger was late.[44] That the choice was limited to such men might signify that the hour of salvation had passed.

Thirty years earlier Timothy Dwight and others had identified forces outside the churches, Jacobinical Illuminism and Jeffersonian Republicans, as the chief threats to Christianity. In 1830, Antimasons concentrated on the dangers within. Secular currents, they argued, had gained steady influences because churches tolerated lax standards, hypocrisy, and formalism. The acceptance of the theatre, for example, marked a striking decline from Puritan standards. Until the 1790s Massachusetts permitted no theatres in Boston. By the 1820s two had been established. Theatres spread elsewhere in New England. Connected with the popularity of the theatre was the growth of vice. Entrepreneurs erected theatres with galleries physically separated from the rest of the building, fitted with their own entrance. In the "third tier" prostitutes picked up new customers or spent the evening with old regulars before retiring to houses located nearby. When reformers demanded that theatres be purged of vice, owners insisted that without the revenues produced by the third tier, they would go out of business.[45] Female benevolent societies that spread in the 1820s and 1830s and attempted to rescue fallen women, expose male licentiousness, and curb vice, encountered resistance from influential, respectable elements that forced churches that had lent support to the anti-vice movement to pull back.[46]

The popularity of theatres did not depend only on their role as centers of assignation. Men and women also attended for their amusement. The demand for popular forms of entertainment and new modes of relaxation changed the way people spent leisure time. The public appetite grew for theatrical exhibitions, circuses, museums, and shows such as those devised by P. T. Barnum—a Connecticut-born Universalist, Democrat, and newspaper editor jailed for blasphemy, before he switched to show business.[47] The popularity of new styles of sociability, most evident in cities and large towns, played havoc with older notions of how one relaxed, especially on the Sabbath.

By the 1820s the Puritan idea of the Sabbath as a day devoted exclusively to worship was becoming anachronistic for an ever-growing sector of the public. An older view prescribed attendance at church two or three times; during the rest of the day one read the Bible or other religious literature and engaged in family devotions. Novels or other secular literature including newspapers, traveling, visiting family and friends, or frequenting taverns or amusements lay under a ban. In the late 1820s the focus of organized Sabbatarian concern centered on the United States Post Office, which kept the mails moving seven days a week. A nationwide campaign to stop the Post Office from desecrating the Sabbath culminated in 1829 when the House of Representatives rejected the Sabbatarian petition on grounds that it violated separation of church and state. Yet to many pietists, the Post Office campaign, though worthwhile, was hardly an adequate response to lapses in faith. First, it enlisted support from various denominations with differing standards of appropriate Sabbath-day conduct. In Massachusetts, for example, leading Unitarians and Episcopalians joined Orthodox Congregationalists in the petition campaign. In Rochester, New York, even Masons aided the Sabbatarians. By focusing on the sins of the Post Office, Sabbatarians shifted the spotlight from where it was most needed: on lapses by professed Christians and the failure of the churches to discipline them.[48]

The tolerance of the theatre, like lax behavior on the Sabbath, contributed to a moral climate in which Freemasonry thrived. Herein lay a central concern of religious Antimasonry: the declining power of the churches to influence the behavior of their own members. Church membership was becoming a badge of social status in fragmented communities beset by a host of competing denominations. Competition promoted lax standards; churches with loose ones tended to grow at the expense of those with rigorous ones. This allowed pseudo-Christians to masquerade as the genuine article and secular values and behavior to gain tacit acceptance within formally Christian circles.

There were substantial grounds for anxiety also over the disposition of authority within the churches and over the balance of power between clergy and laity. The authority of ministers in the early nineteenth century declined. Short tenures, stemming from careerist strategies among a younger generation of ministers and from restlessness in the laity, were a source of widespread concern.[49] The outburst of revivalism and the flood of converts during the Second Great Awakening failed to arrest erosion in clerical authority. Open mockery of the clergy by secularists such as the Boston printer, editor, and Mason, Joseph T. Buckingham, was also cause for alarm. Buckingham was a devotee of the theatre and started the *New England Galaxy and Freemason's Weekly* in 1817 with Masonic patronage. His repeated attacks on clergy in the 1820s made him the center of a set of libel cases, yet he later stood high in National Republican councils. Buckingham was a Unitarian, but even laymen in evangelical churches, puffed up with pride, defied ministers who preached the difficult truths of Calvinism. They were either purged or worshippers switched to another, more accommodating denomination.[50]

Even more troublesome were lapses in church discipline. Many members resented intrusion into their personal lives. A growing insistence on distinguishing the public from the private led to efforts to circumscribe religious authority.[51] The popularity of Freemasonry among Christians testified to the failure of the churches to satisfy their needs. The churches' teachings were too rigid, too demanding, and too sectarian.

Moreover the churches had become decisively feminized by the early nineteenth century. The trend towards feminization of the membership went back at least to the early eighteenth century. In successive waves the proportion of women grew, climbing from about 60 percent of Congregationalists before the American Revolution to about 70 percent by the early nineteenth century. The feminization of religion and its identification with the separate sphere of women and domestic life provided additional grounds for circumscribing church influence.[52] As many American men came to perceive religion as women's business, they were more resistant to the intrusion of religious authority into the male sphere. Freemasonry, an all-male institution, drew sharper distinctions between the separate spheres of men and women.[53]

Capping all these disturbing developments were the inroads market values made in the leading churches, undermining what was left of their communitarian character, as the evolution of seating arrangements suggests.[54] In 1828 the worshippers at the Amherst, Massachusetts, First Congregationalist church had decided to build a new house and held an auction at Boltwood's Hotel, where the sale of pews raised almost $5500. The price paid for a family pew typically reflected the desirability of its location. By adopting the impersonal mechanism of the market, people no longer had to face the vexing problems of assigning seats according to older, communitarian standards. Those standards had once been appropriate, but by the early nineteenth century they were anachronistic, though some people still clung to traditional modes. Problems of seating called for the election of a seating committee in town meeting to "dignify" the house—determine the most desirable locations—and then assign seats according to agreed-upon criteria usually wealth, age, and sometimes office. An elaborate point system enabled towns to instruct committees in precisely how to balance wealth against the other criteria. Yet the system occasioned chronic difficulties.

In the early meeting houses it was common for men and women to sit separately, with children and young adults in the galleries or in other less desirable locations, to which Indians and Afro-Americans were also consigned. Prominent individuals resisted sitting among the mass and sought family pews. Most churches accommodated, but family pews at first were exceptions; the bulk of the congregation, whether occupying benches or pews, sat segregated and according to ranked designation. The system occasioned not only disputes over the proper application of the ranking system but also opposition to the pretensions of elites. Newton, Massachusetts, for example, instructed the seating committee to observe rank but also to take care "not to degrade anyone."[55] In Franklin, Massachusetts, in 1739–40, "some wished to build pews at their own expense," but the majority refused to allow them. "The *place* is and not the *kind* of seat is sufficient gradation, for the straight bench is the throne of democracy," they admonished the snobbish. Yet even Franklin gave way in 1755 to Capt. John Goldbury's request to build a small pew to the left of the pulpit.[56]

There was no uniform pattern in the eighteenth century but the trend towards permitting family pews and raising funds through their sale became increasingly prevalent, early in the commercialized towns, later in the more isolated ones, especially as the construction of new meeting houses necessitated large sums no longer available through a town tax. The sale of pews became, therefore, the common method of financing construction; seats in the meeting house became the property of families. Massachusetts acknowledged the new situation in 1845 when it permitted incorporated churches to tax pews according to value. The law also made pews subject to attachment, like other goods and chattels, but exempted from execution for non-payment of debts, save for the payment of taxes, "one pew occupied by him or his family," along with other items in the exemption laws, including clothing, furniture, books, farm animals, and hay. Both the new and the old systems of seating reflected prevailing stratification patterns, but the later practice of selling pews gave the arrangement an impersonal legitimacy derived from the marketplace whereas the older system's legitimacy rested on the formal consent of the community. Viewing the contentious history of seating in colonial Woburn's First Church, its historian concluded, "We have cause of congratulation that houses of public worship at the present day are constructed, and seats assigned in them on a plan which supersedes the need of a seating committee." As late as 1830 the Pittsfield, Massachusetts, First Church, though it remodeled large pews into "neat and commodious slips" suitable for families, seated the congregation "by the allotment of a committee." Finally in 1836 renewed dissatisfaction resulted in the triumph of the auction block.[57]

With the authority of ministers and churches weakened, maket values penetrating congregations, grounds of belief shaken by intense competition among rival denominations and by secularism, many young people coming of age after 1800 engaged in a prolonged and tortured search for religious identity, as the careers of such widely diverse figures as Theodore Weld, Orestes Brownson, Charles G. Finney, Abner Kneeland, and the New England transcendentalists suggest.[58] And on a mass level, the thousands who flocked to such come-outer movements as the Millerites who preached that the end of the world was imminent and to the Mormons who promised heaven on earth as well as after death, suggest that the strains generated by social change led some to a search for salvation outside conventional religion. Moreover, the great revivals in the early nineteenth century and the growth of organized religious benevolence—tract and missionary societies, sabbatarian, anti-vice, and maternal associations—were grounds for optimism but, on deeper reflection, sources of despair. A quarter of the converts to Vermont's Calvinist churches during the revivals from 1816–20 were later expelled. Within a few years following the great national harvest of souls from 1830–31, evangelical churches routinely reported coldness, formality, and indifference among converts.[59] The most widespread benevolent organizations—the temperance societies—boasted that thousands took the pledge in the late 1820s, but thousands broke their word soon thereafter. The failure of moral suasion propelled temperance militants towards coercion in the 1830s. The Sunday School movement likewise hardly made a dent in working-class indifference.[60] And within churches such as New England's oldest, best endowed, most prestigious Congregationalist societies there was an unmistakable loss of confidence. Dozens of churches adopted new confessions of faith in the early nineteenth century, ostensibly tightening the criteria for membership. At the same time they published manuals listing members and setting forth their articles of belief, standard of behavior, church order, and modes of discipline. The manuals tried to clarify the obligations of church affiliation but the transiency of membership, necessitating periodic updating of the manuals, suggests that many churches had become bodies of strangers desperately needing some formal mechanism to identify one another and remind all concerned of the grounds of association.[61]

Because standards of Christian belief and behavior were so in flux many failed to discern the "infidel" character of Freemasonry, Antimasons argued. William Morgan's murderers were not infidels or Nothingarians, for "a large number of church members actually participated in the proceedings leading to his death, or openly justified these proceedings." For that reason churches cowered before the "frowns" of Freemasonry and "compromised" with iniquity.[62]

Antimodernist church members sensitive to the spread of secularism and alarmed by religious fragmentation and competition stood in the forefront of the crusade against Masonry. None more so than Rev. Nathanael Emmons, the leading champion of Hopkinsian Calvinism. In 1832, two days before Massachusetts Antimasons gathered at Worcester for their state convention, Emmons informed the delegates that "protracted age, and other uncontrollable circumstances" kept him from "uniting with them in their noble and benevolent efforts to counteract the influence, and destroy the existence of Freemasonry in this our beloved Country." Christian Republicans faced a new test, he claimed, "to stand fast in the liberty wherewith Christ has made him free; to contend earnestly for the faith once delivered to the saints; and to fulfill their solemn and sacred vows to defend the gospel against all the delusion, hypocrisy, and infidelity of the open and secret enemies of the blessed Redeemer."[63]

Emmons was born in Haddam, Connecticut, in 1745 and attended Yale, where he abandoned his Arminian inclinations and fell under the influence of Jonathan Edwards, and later the theological instruction of Rev. John Smalley, a New Divinity preacher who was a disciple of Edwards. He became the foremost successor of Samuel Hopkins (1721–1803), who together with Joseph Bellamy was the leading theologian of the New Divinity school inspired by Edwardsean Calvinism. Hopkins's most distinctive contribution was an identification of self-love as sin and his idea of true virtue, the doctrine of "disinterested benevolence," which required a willingness to suffer damnation for the glory of God. Hopkins's thought inspired social criticism and such reform and benevolent impulses as antislavery and temperance. Emmons trained almost ninety ministers in Hopkinsian Calvinism which he "extended and clarified."[64]

Emmons settled in Franklin, Massachusetts, twenty-seven miles southwest of Boston, where he served as the town's sole pastor from 1777 to 1827, when he retired. The town was an economic and social backwater, attracting few newcomers and thereby preserving its homogeneity. Here were a people willing to sustain the stern Hopkinsian Calvinism of Emmons, who did not bend before popular currents.[65]

Until the end of his life, Emmons wore a three-cornered hat atop his colonial costume, relics of an earlier age. In dress as in beliefs, he paid little attention to changing fashion. For over thirty years Emmons delivered social and civil sermons on Fast, Election, and Thanksgiving days, which chart the reactions of the most influential conservative Calvinist theologian to developments reshaping New England. Once a staunch Federalist who condemned Jeffersonian Republicans for infidelity, Emmons joined Federalist clergy hoping to rally the pious against Jacobinical Illuminism associated with Jeffersonianism.

By 1820 Federalism had collapsed and Emmons shifted focus. His jeremiads now spotlighted corruption eating away at Orthodox Congregationalism. Declension in the Bible Commonwealth had proceeded very far. Once God's chosen, Emmons intoned in the 1820s, the heirs of the Puritans, who now entered their third century in the New World, had fallen further and faster than any other Christians, sinning not only against God "but against the example, the labors and the sufferings of our forefathers." A generation earlier, he claimed, there were few infidels in New England. Now infidelity was brazen and spreading in the large towns and even in the small ones. The greatest peril came not, however, from professed nonbelievers—a small minority—but from professed Christians who disgraced the Sabbath with work and play, who no longer faithfully read the Bible, and who had long abandoned family prayer. From such fallen families came the numerous irreligious youth and "all manner of vice and moral corruption."[66]

Emmons wondered why sin was so much more prevalent in his old age than it had been in his youth and why, too, it went "so little perceived, lamented, and restrained."[67] The cause, he argued, was less the fault of the Unitarians, the religious liberals, the deists, or even the free thinkers—the open enemies of revealed religion—than of the ostensibly Calvinist churches which subtly abandoned, Jesuitically softened, and cleverly modified the fundamentals of faith.[68] As in the past, so in his own time, Emmons argued, Arminianism, which asserted that people had freedom of will to work for their salvation, undermined the essentials of Calvinism: man's utter sinfulness and his entire dependence on God's sovereign will.

Emmons and other Hopkinsians identified as heretics theologians like Nathaniel W. Taylor, leaders like Lyman Beecher, and others who sought to develop, within the framework of Calvinism more optimistic views which enlarged the possibilities of human endeavor in the search for salvation. Taylorism was dangerous, Emmons believed, because it cautiously but relentlessly infiltrated Orthodoxy by professing to reinterpret without abandoning Calvinism. Emmons knew better. These latter-day Arminians cleverly mixed "their poisonous statements" with "some pleasing truths," slowly, imperceptibly undermining the pure faith.[69]

Hopkinsians blamed timid and cowardly preachers afraid to affirm the doctrine of original sin, thinking it impolite to tell men that they were odious and an abomination in the eyes of God.[70] Stern doctrinal preaching had given way to sentimental messages of consolation designed to make people feel good. The laity, who bore much of the blame for the short, insecure tenures of the clergy, forced all but a few stalwarts to tell worshippers what they wanted to hear.

Americans, once the most favored people, had become "the guiltiest of all nations," Emmons argued, because faith in human ability and worldliness had infested the churches. In a purer age pious leaders set high standards and firmly curbed deviations from Christian norms. But now "wealth and affluence have been flowing in upon us, like the waves of the sea," Emmons noted, and "those who have received the largest portion of temporal favors have nearly perverted them to luxury, prodigality and intemperance. . . ." No wonder church members had become "stupid, formal and negligent" for so preoccupied were many with "secular concerns" that they had little time or thought except "to amass property, and become great, magnificent and prodigal." A people whose greatest boast had once been its "fair, religious character," now had become "extremely degenerate," sunk into "selfishness and vanity," led astray by pseudo-Calvinists who instructed them in the awful doctrine that "holiness consists in well-regulated self-love."[71]

On questions of ecclesiastical organization, Hopkinsians also kept their distance from the Congregational mainstream. The churches which made up the Mendon Association stretched from Seekonk, near Providence, Rhode Island, to Worcester in the interior of the state—in twenty-nine towns which preferred this spread-out Hopkinsian body to more convenient regional associations. For twenty-five years Emmons presided over the Mendon Association, which until 1841 refused to join the General Association of Bay State Congregationalist churches formed early in the century. Hopkinsians were fearful that extra-local bodies, such as ecclesiastical councils assembled to mediate disputes between a pastor and his people, tended to undermine local autonomy and give Arminian elements a lever against Hopkinsians.[72] For similar reasons Hopkinsians were ambivalent towards the new religious benevolent associations, perceiving them as instruments of centralized control which tended to promote coalition among diverse elements by smoothing over or ignoring doctrinal differences.[73]

In their approach to pastoral responsibilities, Hopkinsians clung to the ideal of the pastor as a central figure in the community, not just in the church. Emmons was the model. He spent his entire career in one town and knew most of the families. Every part of the parish, wrote Rev. Jacob Ide, editor of Emmons's collected works, "was an object of his almost daily consideration." Franklin's people knew that they were under their faithful shepherd's constant surveillance, and their sins would receive prompt notice and appropriate rebuke. Fiercely independent, Emmons truly "loved his people," Ide concluded, but he did not hesitate to tell them the truth, no matter how painful. Nor did he hesitate to censure ungodly behavior whether committed by the "few or many . . . rich or poor." To assure uncontested authority, Emmons discouraged ministers from other denominations who occasionally fished for souls in Franklin and he discouraged, too, members of his flock who attended them.[74]

Yet not even Franklin could entirely escape change. After "Father" Emmons retired, liberals in the parish voted to open the meeting house on weekdays for use by the Universalists. Suddenly Emmons appeared in the church: "This is not what you have been taught," he admonished. The parish immediately reversed itself. When Emmons finally died in 1840, it seemed as if "the last of our patriarchs has left us. . . ."[75]

Hopkinsians like Emmons sensed that they were at odds with powerful forces reshaping early industrial America. The spread of Freemasonry among Christians, tolerated by the churches, epitomized these currents. Hopkinsians were a shrinking minority within the Congregational fold. Emmons himself trained many Congregational ministers but even he was no match for Amherst, Harvard, Yale, and the master preachers who educated the great bulk. The Hopkinsians had high hopes for Andover Theological Seminary, established in coalition with moderate Calvinists, but those hopes turned sour when the moderates gained the upper hand. The Hopkinsians learned they were no match for Arminianizing, careerist, and bureaucratic elements. "The officers of the great Christian establishments," they complained, were chosen from those who were *"skillful in management."* Such men tended to monopolize "all posts of honor and influence, and almost entirely control the press." The Orthodox consequently felt subordinate to the pseudo-Calvinists in their own denominations. It was precisely those who were so "skillful in management" who argued that Freemasonry, like other expressions of worldliness, "must be connived at and flattered in order *to keep the peace,* and hasten the millennium. . . ."[76]

Long before Nathanael Emmons died, his type had become an anachronism. Students who faithfully followed in his footsteps and stood boldly astride the currents of change tangled dangerously with gentlemen of property and standing in their congregations and risked the loss of their positions. A new, model preacher was appearing in the United States—Henry Ward Beecher became the prototype—who aimed to please the mighty. In an age of improvement, blessed by the steamboat, canal, and railroad, "and almost every other invention, to facilitate their worldly operations," it was only natural that Americans would insist also on "improvements in preaching and propagating the gospel," a Hopkinsian sarcastically commented.[77]

The vital role that Hopkinsians and other conservative Calvinists played in the Antimasonic movement is explored further in Part II, which identifies in detail and context the social sources of political Antimasonry in the New England states. Defenders of Masonry understood that no element within the churches was more hostile to Masonry than were these uncompromising Calvinists who were so at odds with Masonry's non-sectarian tolerance, its doctrinal vagueness, its affinity for natural religion, and its Arminian notion that good works and benevolence formed essential tests of moral worth. Defenders of Freemasonry often singled out sectarian bigotry as the cause of their troubles but one champion of the Order went further. He identified Antimasonry as "bottomed upon rank political hatred and bitter intolerant sectarianism" which was imbued with "the worst spirit of Hopkinsianism" and aimed at introducing "a political religion, a union of Church and State."[78]

Yet as important as Hopkinsians were, they were not alone. Representatives of other denominations, rooted in different theological traditions, also lent fervent support to the Antimasonic cause. Discovering their common ground, despite doctrinal differences, will carry us deeper into the heart of religious Antimasonry.

Among the forty-one honorary delegates who attended the 1833 Massachusetts Antimasonic Convention, only one came from outside New England. He was John Gest, a champion of the Hicksite Quakers, who were also outspoken foes of Freemasonry.[79] In the 1820s American Friends bitterly divided. Elias Hicks, a well-known Quaker preacher, led an anti-modernist element which resisted efforts by the Orthodox faction to adopt a set of doctrines, as did other Protestant denominations, and to turn Quakers outward by accommodating evangelical Christianity and secular forces outside the Quaker fold. The Hicksites resisted. They re-emphasized the mystical side of the Quaker tradition and deeply opposed creedalism and concessions to non-Quaker pressure. They clung to separateness, a plain style of living, and an uncompromising, anti-institutional posture towards both religious and secular organization. Class differences were central to the Quaker split. The modernists found their strongest support in the cities among the developing Quaker bourgeoisie who welcomed Joseph Gurney, son of the great English Quaker banking family, who led a similar movement among British Friends. Gurney visited the United States in the 1830s, met with warm support among the Orthodox, and became, appropriately, a friend and admirer of Henry Clay. The Hicksites drew their following mainly from rural Quakers and modest artisans who believed that the Orthodox betrayed the Quaker way.[80]

In 1835 John Gest wrote a history of the origins of "the late Unhappy Division of the Society of Friends." He blamed Freemasonry. Not until Elias Hicks attacked Masonry, Gest argued, did he come under censure because "too many of our high professors had taken masonic oaths." In 1822, Gest claimed, Masonic Quakers in New York City and Philadelphia conspired to discredit Hicks by denouncing him as a heretic and thereby hoped to end his criticism of the Order. "What won't Freemasonry do?" Gest asked. "And what will it not defile? And in what thing, (however pure) has it not introduced and interwoven its corruptions?"[81] Accused of heresy by members of the Philadelphia Yearly Meeting, Hicks lost his case, for though Hicksites were in a majority, they did not control the denominational machinery. Once again, as the Hopkinsians discovered, those expert in management gained the advantage. The Orthodox proved adept at seizing control of the funds, buildings, and other resources. They disowned the Hicksites and conducted a purge.[82]

American Quakerism formally split in the 1820s because in fact it was already deeply divided at the base. The Hicksites were dismayed by trends in American society. Hicks, a powerful preacher, attacked the spread of theatres, gambling, profanity, prostitution, as well as cattle shows and agricultural fairs. To that list he added Freemasonry, which embodied worldly pride and class snobbery and sanctioned licentious behavior. The Orthodox faction, by contrast, welcomed change, adjusted to it, and prospered. That was Hicks's complaint. Quakers joined Masonic Lodges because "dictation, ambition, promotion, power, wealth, property and money is the principle to which the orthodox is and has been tenaciously devoted. . . ." The attraction to Freemasonry was only symptomatic of Quaker decline just as "the extensive wealth of the Society is now its greatest curse," Hicksites concluded.[83]

The Hicksites were at odds with more than tendencies within the Society of Friends. They clung to rural self-sufficiency and a simple way of life. Every canal, turnpike, bank, and factory was evidence of human vanity, of confidence in man's power to alter God's masterpiece. The Hicksites were quietists who insisted on simplifying human wants, withdrawing from the world, and trusting not in reason but in mystical bonds that tied men and women to God. Human institutions that enlarged people's power over temporal affairs were suspect: schools, agricultural societies, the Erie Canal, and the Baltimore and Ohio Railroad all aroused their doubts. In the case of the canal, Hicks argued, had God wanted a waterway where the canal ran, He would have made one there. The Hicksites rejected "progress" which other Quakers embraced: "Happy is the man who has a good farm clear of debt, and is therewith content and does not know how to write his name!" Hicksites were likewise critical of "mercantile life, when perhaps the hard earnings of many anxious days and sleepless nights are swept away by failures and losses on almost every hand." Rejecting the booster mentality of competitive individualism that proclaimed "Go West, Young Man!," Hicksites replied: "I say to those who have been brought up in the country, stay there."[84]

The Hicksites were not influential in New England, but on the subject of Masonry, their views found an echo in the policies of the New England Yearly Meeting, which had long prohibited Friends from being Masons. Moreover the New Light Heresy, which had developed among Massachusetts Quakers during the second and third decades of the century, shared many of the sentiments of the Hicksites. The New Lights were expelled from New England Quakerism but turned up later as Antimasons in Quaker centers such as Lynn, Fall River, and New Bedford, Massachusetts.[85]

Proceeding from very different theological assumptions and shaped by a different religious tradition, Antimasonic Quakers and Calvinists perceived Masonry as at odds with Christian Republicanism. There were some liberal clerics who also gravitated to Antimasonry, for even among Unitarians there was a minority hostile to Freemasonry. Among them was a preacher called to the rostrum at the opening of the Massachusetts Antimasonic Convention in 1833. George Odiorne, a leading layman in the St. Peter's of New England Calvinism, Boston's Park Street Church, called on Rev. John Pierpont, pastor of Boston's Unitarian Hollis St. Church to deliver the invocation. Pierpont prayed fervently for "a blessing on the deliberations of the Convention, for charity to all mankind, and that the hidden things of iniquity might be brought to light. . . ."[86]

John Pierpont was the stormy petrel of Bay State Unitarianism. Before he attended Harvard Divinity School, he tried careers in law and business but without satisfaction. The ministry, he discovered, was his calling. For twenty-six years he served at the Hollis Street Church and distinguished himself from other Unitarian ministers as a militant reformer, leading a church with a substantial working-class element, atypical for Unitarianism.

Pierpont's activism provoked some Boston liquor dealers to join the church with the intent of silencing him. They accused him of neglecting his parish to participate in "every exciting topic that the ingenuity of a fanatic . . . could conjure up to disturb and distract the public mind, such as Imprisonment for Debt, the Militia Law, Antimasonry, Phrenology, Temperance, and the Abolition of Slavery." In 1838 Pierpont's enemies brought him up on charges before an ecclesiastical council, and for seven years the controversy dragged on until Pierpont resigned.[87]

Pierpont's Antimasonry, like his later abolitionism, set him apart from most Unitarian clergy. He was a radical critic of society ready to challenge conventional opinion and cross swords with men of property and standing, even at the risk of losing his job. Early in his career, he caused a "sensation" in Boston's Ancient and Honorable Artillery Company by an address which condemned the militia for wasting public funds, encouraging militarism, and protecting the property of employers who refused to serve by buying their way out. Pierpont typified a minority current in Unitarianism that led to transcendentalism and communitarian experiments such as Fruitlands, Hopedale, and Brook Farm, which sought alternatives to industrial capitalism.[88] Pierpont was also at odds with many Unitarians who found Freemasonry congenial. Unitarians who were active in the anti-abolitionist and anti-temperance movements in the 1830s stood in Pierpont's eyes as hypocritical Christians.

Hopkinsian and other conservative Calvinists, New Lights and Hicksite Quakers, and a few liberal clerics identified Freemasonry with the secularization of religion and the subordination of the churches to lay power and worldly values. Masonry mushroomed in the early nineteenth century because thousands of Christians had lost their bearings under the impact of pluralist and latitudinarian influences. Religious Antimasonry reasserted sectarian beliefs, clerical authority, and anti-secular values. Masonry had crept into the churches because ministers stood intimidated by a powerful Order drawing support from leading men in the congregations. It was "this Esq., Col., Dr., &c., with their obsequious parasites . . . [who] bind the church with fetters, stop the mouth of the pastor," Antimasons complained. For the sake of "preserving the *peace, numbers, and influence*," churches bowed before "opulent and influential men" and tolerated "popular errors."[89] That was why, according to the *Maine Free Press*, only two religious newspapers in the United States joined the Antimasonic cause.[90] Yet Masonry, insisted the Vermont Baptist, Gov. Ezra Butler, is "a fit subject of church discipline," for "the church can hold no connection with this institution; it must be purified of it."[91]

Antimasons put Masonic Christians on the defensive. They challenged Masonry's benign view of human nature, its complacent notions of progress. They denounced it for encouraging the sin of human pride: pride in man's reason and goodness and pride in one another, an elite that set itself off on grounds of social status, not moral worth. Antimasons looked back to a communitarian Golden Age against which they measured unfavorably churches being transformed into class-bound institutions—social clubs—whose moral autonomy became increasingly vulnerable to those who paid the bills, hostages to demands that churches furnish reassurance and status-certification, not moral guidance and spiritual testing. The murder of William Morgan dramatically demonstrated that when men no longer feared God, whatever their formal religious professions, they lost all restraint. Neither Christianity nor republicanism could long survive tolerance of Masonry. In mobilizing public sentiment, Antimasons appealed to the country's most devoted Christians: American women, upholders of domestic order which, like true gospel religion, lay under Masonic siege.

5

Women and Antimasonry
The Defense of Republican Domesticity

We're true and sincere.
And just to the fair,
They'll trust us on any occasion;
No mortal can more
The ladies adore,
Than a free and accepted Mason.
Masonic song

The ladies claim right to come into our light
Since the apron they say is their bearing.
Can they subject their will—can they keep
        their tongues still,
And let talking be chang'd into hearing?
Antimasonic verse[1]

"The influence of Masonry is not favorable to domestic happiness," Charles Pinckney Sumner, sheriff of Boston, told Antimasons in 1829, because it impaired "fondness for the pleasures" of the home by encouraging husbands to neglect their families and engage in licentious behavior. Sheriff Sumner, once a member of the Order, had visited the home of a Freemason late one night and found the wife alone on a rocking chair by a skimpy fire, with one child in her arms and another in the cradle. "Sir, my husband has not yet returned from the Lodge," she said, as she "bent forward over her child, and with a shawl that hung loosely over her shoulders she absorbed a starting tear." At that moment, her husband might be reveling at his Lodge where the liquor ran freely and the Brothers joined in a favorite song—

We're true and sincere.
And just to the fair. . . .

Sumner left the Mason's home filled with pity for the wife and children and "with lessened respect for an institution which could thus withhold husband and father from the first social duties."

The *Antimasonic Review* confirmed the picture recorded in Sumner's soap opera. Masonry promoted ribaldry, contempt for women and neglect of domestic duty, as another Masonic song revealed:

> There floated a debtor away from his duns,
> And next, father gray beard, stark naked midst nuns.
> Likewise a poor husband, not minding his life,
> Contented in drowning, to shake off his wife.

The Antimasonic *North Star* in Danville, Vermont, alerted defenders of female virtue to another sample of Masonic verse—

> Fair Venus calls, we must obey,
> In love and sports spend night and day.

With a reputation as an enemy of female virtue and domestic harmony, Masonry had committed "insult to the female community" of the Republic when it laid the "Corner Stone of the Monument of the Mother of Washington" according to its "ceremonies and flumeries."[2]

Attacks on Freemasonry as hostile to women and domesticity had dogged the Order since its early days and Freemasons countered detractors and cultivated friendly female opinion.[3] It was not surprising that when Antimasonry developed after 1826 into a popular social movement, allegations that Masons endangered women, children, and the home resurfaced. These attacks fell on especially receptive ears because the spread of industrial society strikingly altered gender relations and generated conflict between the sexes, redefined roles, altered the nature of youth, and carved out a new place for men, women, and the family. The problematic nature of gender relations and family life in an era of unprecedented change spread anxieties that found voice in Antimasonry.[4]

At the same time the American Revolution left a legacy of new ideas and attitudes about the role of women in a Republic. American women during the struggle for independence had demonstrated their devotion to liberty, and republican ideology acknowledged their important contribution to securing freedom. Women bore special responsibility for inculcating children with the virtues indispensable to a republican social order.[5] Antimasons, who perceived themselves as guardians of the American Revolution guarding against corrupt tendencies in a post-revolutionary age, signaled Freemasonry for destruction because they believed it sapped the domestic foundations of republicanism and undercut republican mothers devoted to rearing a virtuous, republican citizenry.

Antimasons identified a conflict between the emerging ideology of domesticity and the behavior of men, a conflict in which Freemasonry played a central role. The domestic ideal postulated the home as women's special sphere, where men found respite from the coarsening, warlike struggle involved in making a living. Women reigned as guardians of gentility, love, caring, culture, purity, and piety. Each day men returned home for moral refreshment before they ventured back into a man's world with its countless corrupting snares. The doctrine of separate spheres conceded to females a vital role in preserving a balanced social order and gave new purpose to middle-class urban women whose labor many no longer perceived as essential as it had been in an earlier system of household production. The "cult of true womanhood" contained, however, radical as well as conservative implications. It constricted female potential and narrowed opportunity by requiring that women center their lives in the home, but it also led some women to question the distinctive sex roles and confined sphere which the doctrine aimed to fix. For if the home were women's castle, an island of purity in a sea of moral danger, diligent women must attend those forces outside the home that threatened to subvert the moral purpose of domestic life. The civic responsibilities of republican women therefore legitimized those who looked beyond a limited domestic horizon because they recognized that the compartmentalization of spheres was artificial and arbitrary.

The spread of Freemasonry in the early nineteenth century, as men by the thousands joined Lodges, made clear the impracticality of bifurcating everyday life between the domestic world of leisure and the extra-domestic world of work. Men joined because they sought recreation outside the home, away from the constricting influence of wife and family. Defying the doctrine of spheres, they fled to the all-male society of clubs, taverns, bars, and Masonic Lodges, where they smoked, drank, gambled, and risked their virtue. Rather than submit to the purifying atmosphere of the home, they escaped from another smothering evening of female society. Though other forms of all-male recreation might be questionable, Masons insisted that the Lodge was a wholesome exception.

If Masonic Lodges offered decorous and respectable forms of sociability, there was no reason, the Antimasons argued, to bar "the gentler sex from its boasted lights and benefits," depriving women of its advantages and men of female companionship.[6] Masonry, for example, boasted of extensive charitable and benevolent enterprises, an activity in which women excelled. To justify exclusion, William Brainard, though admitting that women surpassed men in discharging "the common duties of charity," insisted that "the constitution of Society has divided duties of equal importance among the sexes." There were specifically masculine forms of benevolence that required a Mason to be ready to "dive amidst the storms to rescue his drowning brother, . . . save him in war, from the edge of the sword, tear him from the flames of his dwelling, and visit and comfort him, in the scenes of trial . . . ," all arenas of danger from which female delicacy shrank. By excluding women Masons intended no disrespect. In fact, Brainard conceded, though Masons wore aprons as an emblem of purity, they were "more worthily worn by the other sex than ours."[7]

Brainard's argument left critics skeptical. It was "hollow pretence," to hide the real reason for exclusion: women could not be trusted with "a knowledge of the power and aggrandizement, which Masonry proposed to itself." Intent on erecting a privileged aristocracy, explained the Antis, Masons knew that women were uncorruptible republicans, ever-faithful daughters of liberty, certain to expose Masonry's anti-republican designs. Women's "moral sense" would surely revolt at the means Masons employed, and their presence "would be too great a restraint upon the unseemly orgies, and the Bacchanalian revels of Masonic Lodges."[8]

The exclusion of women, explained Rev. Jacob Eastburn, prevented the spread of false accusations and suspicions that Masons engaged in conduct he was "too delicate to mention." The spread of prostitution and the recognition that vice had become a serious social problem generated an extensive movement by the 1820s to expose the evil, rescue fallen women, and punish licentious men. A Bostonian informed Alexis de Tocqueville that two thousand prostitutes sold their services in the New England metropolis; ten thousand were said to ply their trade in New York City. To scotch apprehensions that Masons shielded licentiousness, Eastburn explained, Masonry barred the fair sex.[9] Any woman seen entering or leaving a Masonic Lodge would instantly expose the Order to public disgrace. Thus, Masons claimed, the bar against women guaranteed that vice found no shelter behind Masonic secrecy.

Incredulous Antimasons pointed to a Masonic oath as conclusive evidence for their indictment. Every Master Mason, the third degree, swore "that I will not be at the initiating of an old man in dotage, a young man in non-age, an Atheist, irreligious, libertine, idiot, madman, hermaphrodite, nor woman." Then he promised not to "violate the chastity of a Master Mason's wife, mother, sister, or daughter, knowing them to be such, nor suffer it to be done by others, if in my power to prevent it."[10] This oath, Antimasons reasoned, gave Masons license to assault women outside Masonic protection. Masons rejected this interpretation, but thousands ready to believe that they had murdered William Morgan and covered up the crime gave it credence. Nor were such fears theoretical. Baptist Elder Nathaniel Colver alleged that a Master Mason, hailed before his Lodge for seducing the daughter of a member, pleaded that he had not known that the girl was off-limits. *Infidelity Unmasked,* an Antimasonic newspaper published in Cincinnati, reprinted the Master Mason's oath side by side a story that described the amorous escapades of two rich Boston gentlemen, one of whom tried to entice the pretty daughter of a poor country family into a life of vice. And the Hicksite Quaker Antimasonic publicist, John Gest, recounted a tale of Masonic seduction to prove that Masonry and vice went together.[11]

Connectitut Freemasons used *argumentum ad absurdum* in a satirical pamphlet full of exaggerated accusations intended to laugh Antimasonry out of court. "Freemasons are guilty of adultery," proclaimed the mock-Antimasons. "Yes! fellow-citizens, the whole force of Masonic infamy is combined against the most lovely part of the species. . . . Yes! there is not an Antimasonic female in this whole country whose integrity has not been assailed by this unprincipled band of ravishers." In Connecticut alone within the last three years, a satirist insisted, Freemasons had raped more than five thousand women.[12]

Antimasons did not regard Masonic libertinism as a laughing matter, nor did it find an outlet only in seduction. Personal indecency, Antimasons argued, was an integral feature of Masonic ritual. Candidates for initiation had to strip themselves of clothing, put on a pair of red drawers, and partially expose their bodies. Levi Chace, a Baptist minister and a manufacturer in Fall River, Massachusetts, renounced Masonry and recounted to a shocked Rhode Island legislative investigative committee his own experience: "I was prepared by being divested of my apparel except my shirt, and a pair of drawers provided and put on. . . . My shirt was ripped off my left arm and my left breast was naked. In this situation I was led into the Lodge Room, and made to kneel at the altar, on my naked left knee, my hands clasping the Bible." Nudity is common in the initiation rites of male fraternal organizations. By exposing candidates to danger, mockery, and shame, men are tested for worthiness. The process of male-bonding in the Masonic ritual of initiation emphasized masculinity and underlined that men enjoyed a retreat remote from emasculating women. But to outsiders, Masons practiced "indecency." Masonic nudity was one more example of the libertine sensuality Masonry cultivated. The initiate "submits to be stripped naked," recalled Solomon Southwick, a leading New York Antimason, "under the indecent and ridiculous pretense of ascertaining his sex and that he has no minerals or metals about him. . . ."[13]

Masonic fondness for alcohol was another reason for excluding women. Antimasonry emerged at the same time that the temperance movement spread into hundreds of cities and towns all over the northeastern United States. Women played an important role in diffusing the temperance ethic and subculture. None suffered more from the evils of drink than women and their families, according to temperance propaganda. Drunken husbands wasted the family's funds and neglected and abused their dependents. Women rallied to the temperance cause in large numbers. They joined societies, formed exclusively female organizations, and mobilized public opinion, often in concert with ministers, to pressure men to take the pledge of total abstinence. Though in its first stage the temperance movement gained broad-based support among both sexes and among members of various religious denominations in the 1820s, increasingly the cause relied on the devotion of women and on coercion. In its later phases in the middle and late nineteenth century, women played a crucial role through such organizations as the Women's Christian Temperance Union and the Anti-Saloon League to impose prohibition on the country.

The temperance question became bitterly divisive. While thousands of men took pledges of total abstinence or joined societies devoted to temperance, the ravages of alcohol continued.[14] Wives might ban liquor from the home, churches might bar members from consuming alcohol, but their authority did not extend outside home and church. Men who drank in public risked exposure, but Masonic Lodges offered a secret place where one could indulge. Antimasons pointed to Masonic songs which celebrated the pleasures of the bottle:

> Let every man take glass in hand
> Drink bumpers to our Master Grand,
> As long as he can sit or stand,
> With decency.

Or:

> This world is all in darkness,
> About us they conjecture,
> But little think, a song and drink,
> Succeeds a Mason's lecture.
> Then landlord pass the hogshead round. . . .

These Masonic drinking songs often accompanied an evening of sumptuous dining and ribald entertainment. Decent men "would be ashamed to sing" such songs "in other company, or even behind a barn or stable," declared one ex-Mason.[15]

Before long, Masons, too, fell under the influence of the temperance ethic in the 1820s. Lodges banned liquor and participated in the temperance movement, yet the Order as a whole, given the autonomy that Lodges enjoyed, never embraced temperance. Moreover outsiders had other reasons to remain skeptical: secrecy might cloak indulgence. To temperance militants, Masonry seemed, therefore, a serious obstacle to the triumph of those anti-alcohol standards so many women championed.

Women had other reasons to suspect Masonic husbands. Loyalty to the Order brought them into conflict with "the duties of the family circle," Antimasons contended. Marriage fashioned an indissoluble interest and neither party dare to keep secrets from the other. Masonic oaths required that men, on pain of having their tongue cut out by the root, never to reveal the secrets of Masonry to their wives. Such oaths violated "the strongest and most enduring covenant which can be entered into by man" and inevitably sowed suspicion and discord between husband and wife. At least once a month a husband deserted his family to spend "his time, till past midnight, in the orgies of the lodge room." Women wondered what transpired in the secret precincts of Freemasonry. While they stayed home and discharged faithfully their domestic duties, men indulged their pleasures. Masonry thereby upheld a double standard. Suppose, Antimasons asked, the laborer came in from the field, the merchant from his store, the attorney from his office tired from a day's labor and found his wife gone. "Where is my wife?" he asks the servant. "We do not know; she did not tell where she was going; but we suppose she has gone to the Lodge." At midnight the wife returned home. "Where have you been my dear," the husband asks.

"O, I have been away, on *important* business to the *lodge,* on business you can *never know. . . .*"[16]

By excluding women, tolerating licentiousness, practicing indecency, shielding intemperance, and sowing distrust between men and women, Freemasonry, critics charged, menaced domestic order. Masons countered that the Antimasonic whirlwind "sundered the nearest ties of social life . . . set father against son and son against father; arrayed the wife against her husband. . . ." Antimasonry threw "the torch of discord into the sacred retreats of domestic repose" and alienated "the affections of our dearest earthly friends."[17]

Yet none of the ostensible grounds of Antimasonic belief that Masonry was dangerous to women and the home are sufficient to account for the intense fear of the Order, the gross exaggerations of its power, the distorted interpretation of its oaths and rites, and the belief that Morgan's murder was no isolated event but the tip of the iceberg. To understand Antimasonry we must neither accept the Antimasonic indictment at face value nor rule out the possibility that Antimasons had reason to be paranoid. In searching for the reasons why Antimasons could mobilize thousands against Freemasonry in defence of republican domesticity we must look beyond the rhetoric to changes in sexual mores, gender relations, and domestic life in the formative period of industrial society in the United States.

The emergence of the domestic ideal in the early nineteenth century both generated and reflected tensions in relations between men and women in a period of rapid change.[18] The domestic virtues were feminine and antithetical to male qualities deemed necessary for success in the competitive struggle. Men were ambivalent towards domesticity, which constrained aggressive "masculine" traits essential to achievement outside the home. Men longed for a retreat from "the manslaughter of reckless enterprise," but the doctrine of separate spheres legitimized domestic controls by women. And it made men uneasy about the discrepancy between their behavior outside the home and the domestic ideal. The concept of separate spheres thereby created a dynamic arena in which both men and women jockeyed to influence one another's behavior.

Men looked to the purifying influence of women to mold the bourgeois family, yet women's ability to fulfill their appointed role depended on the degree to which men accepted domestic constraints and female society when not at work. All could profess allegiance to the doctrine of spheres because it was a set of vague notions, not a prescription for the daily routine. In practice, men and women often spent their leisure time apart, a source of considerable anxiety for women for it limited their influence and aroused anxieties that men exposed themselves to moral danger when they were neither at home nor at work.

The segregation of the sexes, Frances Trollope found, was one of the most distinctive features of domestic manners in America in the 1820s. Men flocked to theatres, women to churches. In Hoboken, New Jersey, while women were praying, men paid six cents to walk in a public garden. In New York "mixed dinner parties of ladies and gentlemen . . . are very rare," a great defect in society, Trollope thought, because the presence of women tended to refine manners. Under female influence men were less prone to swear, drink, smoke, spit, belch, and fart in company. When invited, women were often given short shrift. At a Washington's Birthday celebration in a Cincinnati hotel the men sat down to a splendid dinner while the women sat forlorn on a row of chairs with their plates perched on their laps. On a steamboat, she complained, "of the male part of the passengers we saw nothing, excepting at the short silent periods allotted for breakfast, dinner and supper. . . ." "All the enjoyments of men are found in the absence of women," she concluded. "They dine, they play cards, they have musical meetings, they have supper, all in large parties but all without women." American families rarely went on picnics because "the two sexes can hardly mix the greater part of a day without great restraints and ennui. . . ." Men disliked such outings because they trapped them for an extended period under circumstances "quite contrary to their general habits," preventing them from indulging their favorite pleasures. When at home, men sought the first chance to go out. This sexual segregation, Trollope argued, made American women less influential in society than were their European counterparts. Until both sexes mixed easily in the United States, she concluded, "the tone of their drawing rooms will not improve." But Mrs. Trollope was not optimistic because American women informed her that "the hours of greatest enjoyment of the gentlemen were those in which a glass of gin cocktail, or egg-nog, receives its highest relish from the absence of all restraint whatever; and when there were no ladies to trouble them." Alexis de Tocqueville agreed with Trollope's picture of female isolation. Women in America, he said, lived in a "cloister."[19]

Frances Trollope identified the reverse side of the cult of true womanhood: the cult of true manhood. "Industrialization heightened the importance of gender" and "heightened the importance of defining the criteria of manhood and fulfilling those criteria."[20] Men who worked outside the home, accumulated little or no property, or engaged in occupations they did not transmit to their sons faced new problems of establishing authority within the family, formulating role models, and winning respect from other men. The domestic ideal could threaten emasculation, but through sociability outside the home and new ideas about maleness men sought to clarify gender identity. All-male forms of recreation, such as Masonry, circumscribed female influence and provided places where middle-class men need not be afraid to be "men." This, however, left Freemasonry vulnerable to suspicion because unlike other male locales—the raucous militia gathering, rowdy fire fighting company, tavern, or grog shop—its secrecy inspired doubts. Early nineteenth-century middle-class culture became obsessed with deception, by the "confidence men and painted women" who lurked everywhere, pretending to be respectable only to seduce and corrupt the innocent.

Antimasons saw Freemasonry as one of the many confidence games that lured unsuspecting men, especially the young, to their destruction. Middle-class advice manuals specified an elaborate code of appropriate dress, deportment, manners, and bereavement, which aimed to regulate precisely interpersonal relations. They enabled men and women to distinguish between the genuinely honorable and the fake among the strangers one unavoidably encountered in a mobile social order with an emerging middle class. Masonry seemed at odds with efforts to prescribe standards because it conferred respectability according to its own, secret rules, not those of the advice manuals. Antimasons feared that the Order conferred respectability though it sanctioned departures from the code of the manuals, the churches, and the domestic ideal. The shapers of middle-class culture identified hypocrisy as the great danger. In the parlor women enforced the code of middle-class culture; in the Masonic Lodges their vital influence was absent.[21]

Allegations that Masonry fostered sexual promiscuity registered another tension between the sexes. New notions of sexuality emerged in industrializing societies to reshape patterns of gender differentiation. Whereas in a pre-industrial culture, women were generally regarded as more highly sexed than men, their appetites difficult to satisfy, even threatening to the male's well-being, by the mid-nineteenth century, sensuality became identified as a male quality.[22] The domestic ideal posited a conflict between true womanhood and sexuality. Some regarded women as desexualized, which justified wives in limiting access to their bodies while at the same time it promoted abstinence, a goal of middle-class couples who desired smaller families. At the same time, the age at which men married increased so that for both married and unmarried men, access to licit sexual relations became more problematic. For men who traveled on business and youth who migrated from their home towns where little deviant behavior escaped notice, the cities and factory villages where one was unknown and stayed but briefly offered new opportunities for casual encounters. The emergence of organized vice on a large scale thus suggested that men adhered to a double standard.[23]

When Female Domestic Reform Societies spread throughout the northeast in the 1820s and 1830s to stem the growth of vice, they encountered fierce, even violent resistance from men. Pressure by influential businessmen in New York City, for example, forced clergymen to back off. Opposition to reform, even riots, organized by "respectable" elements harnessed the resentment of young men and others who regarded the domestic reformers, mostly women and "effeminate" men, as prudes who interfered with personal liberty. The evidence that men indulged their passions, betrayed the domestic ideal, and resisted reform made people understandably suspicious that an all-male institution such as Freemasonry was a cover for vice. As in other spheres such as religion and politics, Masonry became a lightning rod that attracted and concentrated the free-floating anxieties of the age.[24]

Maternal anxiety centered on the dangers inherent in identifying sexuality as masculine. If Masonry legitimized suspect male behavior, it posed especial hazards for sons. Charged with raising boys to become uncorruptible men, women sensed that Masonry competed for influence over youth. Men tended to join a Masonic Lodge from age twenty-one to thirty.[25] At a crucial time in the life cycle, young men sought admission to an association disliked by many women but supported by fathers, male relatives, and friends. By becoming a Mason a young man broke free of domestic restraints. Masonry thus aided males in the passage from the domestic shelter of women into an all-male world outside the home. That world was morally suspect for it prized success at the gambling tables, feats in the bar, and conquests in the boudoir.[26] In the all-male, licentious atmosphere of the Masonic Lodge depicted by Antimasons, men who were models of rectitude at home suddenly became reduced to "boys of larger growth" who took delight in the "big words and sentences" and in "the barbaric glitter and pomp exactly fitted to please swelling and half-developed men."[27]

In industrialized societies youth was a troublesome period in the life cycle, a long period of dependency from perhaps age 10 to 21, followed by a time of indecision, perhaps from 15 to 25, when young men finally chose a career. The idea of adolescence did not emerge until the end of the nineteenth century to legitimize an extended period of dependency and clarify its distinctive place in the process of growing up. In early industrial America youth and children were by far the most numerous population element, comprising in 1800 some 70 percent of the total population. The typical pattern in the teen years was for young men to move away from home and then return, only to repeat that pattern. The peripatetic nature of youth made young men and women especially vulnerable to "confidence men and painted women," for there were often no kin nearby to watch and guide them. The spread of maternal associations in the early nineteenth century catered to anxious mothers who sought expert advice and emotional support from other women to strengthen their authority, especially if challenged by husbands. Genteel, cultured, pious, loving mothers armored their sons against the day when they must leave home. Mothers knew that conscience, not direct supervision, must keep sons virtuous, but fathers worried that overprotective mothers weakened the aggressive sense of daring, the willingness to take chances which success in a man's world required.[28]

Further complicating the nurture of youth was the transition from paternal authority to maternal affection "as the focal point of childhood socialization." For fathers and mothers, no less than their offspring, growing up, always a time of strain in modern societies, emerged as an especially difficult one in a period of profound change. The Victorian home "left little place in which" the male head "could exercise his masculine power." The home was woman's sphere and a father "was something of a bull in a China shop, somewhat ill at case with the gentle virtues enshrined there."[29] Yet the home must prepare sons for a man's world where sissies surely failed.

Caught between fathers and mothers, the cult of true womanhood and

the cult of true manhood, the home and the marketplace, young men eventually had to break out of the web of dependency and assume independence.
Because Masonry assimilated middle-class youth into a man's world, Antimasons directed a special appeal to "The Young Men of America" to "rid
our country of the hundred headed hydra, infesting the social circles, and
polluting the temples of justice and religion." Throw off the Masonic
"chains of slavery," they exhorted, which were "more galling and igno-
minous" than those it required "a war of seven years to burst asunder." By
rejecting Masonry, sons would repudiate an institution that was the folly of
their fathers, the despair of their mothers, and the shame of their country.
For every mother who lost a son to Masonry shuddered at the thought that
he had submitted to "all the mummery," including a ritual that enacted his
"mock murder" and the oath that profaned "the name of the blessed God."
Antimasonic women feared that Freemasonry had entrapped sons; its destruction would liberate them.[30]

Further straining relations between mothers and fathers were differences
over the spiritual development of young men. Pious mothers took an intense
early interest in their sons' religious development. Because girls were more
susceptible to spiritual influence, mothers felt a special responsibility for
males. In the maternal associations they prayed for the souls of their children
and received expert assistance in rearing Christian families.[31] Promoting
the salvation of sons and daughters, like most matters religious, was pre-
eminently women's business. Examples of maternal piety and paternal impiety, indifference, or hypocrisy sent conflicting messages to young males.
If a young man submitted to female religious influence, he risked losing
caste in the world of "real" men.

Conservative Calvinists such as Rev. Nathanael Emmons blamed moral
declension on the collapse of family worship and parental neglect. The
primary responsibility rested with the head of the household, but men increasingly sloughed off that duty and women were powerless to resist. "The
declension of religion must generally begin in Families," Emmons intoned,
which modern parents neglected though they spared no expense on secular
education, clothing, polishing manners, or endowing handsome inheri-
tances.[32] The spread of secularism required evangelical mothers to battle
skeptical or Nothingarian husbands for control of children. Secularized,
rationalist fathers, attracted by liberal versions of Christianity, or by none
at all, resisted evangelical wives who struggled to establish the family's religious identity.[33]

In *The Protestant Temper*, Philip Greven describes three types of personality identified with evangelical, moderate, and genteel modes of child-
rearing in colonial America. The evangelicals, obsessed with the sinfulness
of human nature, despised the self and sought purification through rebirth.
Children of evangelicals lived in fear of a stern God and authoritarian
parents who believed that breaking the child's will, imposing total submission, prepared him or her for life and for salvation. Inculcating shame and

guilt, parents internalized rules of strict behavior in the conscience to reproduce the parental sense of sin and alienation from human nature. Only
being born again in Christ relieved the tension. Moderate parents shared a
more optimistic view of human nature, regarded sin as a less powerful force,
and rated more highly people's ability to resist evil. They, too, sought to rear
virtuous children, governed by self-control, and though they believed that
God's grace was essential, they thought grace came slowly, not through a
sudden, tumultuous experience such as conversion. People were frail and
often succumbed to temptation but they were not depraved. Moderates
accept the self as worthy of love and respect. Self-approval, not self-annihila-
tion, the search for happiness in earthly existence, not just in the afterlife,
distinguished moderates from evangelicals. Where evangelicals rejected the
world, moderates were ambivalent. Greven's third type, the genteel parent,
nourished an intensely loving attitude towards children. Self-confident with
themselves, at home with the world, able to enjoy life without a nagging
burden of guilt, genteels expected to die in God's grace but not after a
lifelong struggle against sin. Their optimistic view of human nature and des-
tiny shaped their views of child nurture. They cherished intimacy and
affection between parents and offspring and promoted self-confidence and
self-worth in children. Growing up in households that were at ease with the
world, genteel youth did not experience anguishing guilt nor become painfully introspective, nor were they afraid to indulge themselves in worldly
pleasure. At home with their impulses, they expressed their sexuality more
freely, were more tolerant of diversity, and valued sociability highly. As for
religion, Greven suggests, they invested little feeling in it.[34]

In early industrial America modes of child-rearing were a pressing concern and a cause of considerable anxiety, inside and outside the home.
Evangelical notions met increasing challenges from advocates of more
affectionate relations and more optimistic views of children's ability to
achieve grace through patient nurture. The erosion of Calvinism and its
belief in human depravity and helplessness inevitably affected ideas about
child-rearing. Modernist evangelicals began to move closer to the moderate
position, causing strains within the churches. The history of child nurture in
the early nineteenth century remains obscure; what seems clear is that ideas
were in flux and the balance of power among Greven's three typologies was
at issue. For the emergence of industrial society posed new challenges to
parents, exposed children to new dangers and opportunities, and generated
considerable confusion, uncertainty, and debate.[35]

Religious differences between men and women, and competing views
over child nurture were two among a broader set of issues in gender relations which Antimasonry addressed. In the cult of true womanhood piety
was a feminine quality; in the cult of true manhood, skepticism, indifference, Nothingarianism were masculine. In Antimasonic eyes, Freemasonry
subverted the proper nurture of the young and nourished masculine excess
and infidelity.

By the early nineteenth century religion had become pre-eminently a female sphere and the ministry a feminized profession.[36] Through a devout army of female worshippers, ministers hoped to restore their influence as moral and cultural leaders at the same time that their influence waned in the arenas dominated by men. Church membership data show a long-term trend towards female predominance that by 1830 reached 70 percent in Connecticut's Congregational churches. Religiosity occupied a key place in the cult of true womanhood. Women's piety balanced masculine laxness, indifference, or skepticism. It guaranteed that children grew up in a Christian household and the power of the clergy depended heavily on support from their female parishioners.[37] Though men, a minority of church members, still controlled the governance of churches, they could not ignore the preferences of women, given their sheer numbers and intense convictions, when it came to hiring, firing, and administering discipline. If men feared clerics, it was because there was a reciprocal relationship between pious women and insecure ministers, who strengthened one another in the struggle against creeping secularism.

Frances Trollope offered another explanation for clerical influence over women. American men saw advantages in allowing women to spend most of Sunday in church and a great deal of their other leisure time in religiously inspired activity. The more women did so, the more complete was "the hebdomadal freedom" of men. For while wives attended church or church-sponsored associations, husbands enjoyed themselves at some *reposoire*—Trollope's charming designation for all-male haunts whose masculine aromas of stale whiskey and tobacco blasted passersby. Trollope "never saw, or read, of any country where religion had so strong a hold upon women, or a slight hold upon men," not even in Catholic Spain. Nor did she know another country "where religion makes so large a part of the amusement and occupation of ladies." Women flocked to the clergy because they, alone among men, gave "the women of America . . . that sort of attention which is so dearly valued by every female heart throughout the world."[38] In churches, as in bars, hotels, at parties, and Masonic Lodges, men and women spent their leisure time in separate spheres. Even men who attended church but failed to undergo conversion were suspect as being there in body but not in spirit.

There is further evidence of gender differences in the Trinitarian-Unitarian split that sundered the Congregationalist churches in the Bay State. Both factions competed intensely for control of the town *society* which possessed legal authority over the church. In many towns, the society, made up of the voters—all men who were not supporters of another church—battled the members of the town church, a much smaller body of converts, predominantly women without a vote. In these struggles Unitarians and Calvinists not only counted their strength in the *society* but also calculated on which side women would throw their weight. Trinitarians complained bitterly that all-male societies, dominated by Liberals and Nothingarians, captured town churches from an evangelical majority of the membership, mostly female. The line of division between Trinitarians and Unitarians thus often mirrored gender differences.[39]

There were practical reasons why women had a special affinity for evangelical Christianity, for the pietistic churches adhered to more rigorous codes of behavior and were more likely than were liberal churches to discipline men for intemperance, fornication, non-attendance, Sabbath-breaking, or failure to conduct family prayer. Church discipline strengthened women in the domestic sphere in the jockeying between the sexes for authority over family religion, morals, manners, and child-rearing. Women therefore regarded the conversion of men as vital for preserving domestic order, and they took special interest in the spiritual condition of young males.[40]

Liberals and Orthodox recognized gender as a factor in their rivalry. Unitarian and Universalist churches were less heavily female.[41] Rev. Bernard Whitman, the Waltham Unitarian, champion of Freemasonry, argued that women leaned towards evangelical Christianity because they were more "impressionable," less rational, and more readily swayed by the Calvinist clergy. But Hopkinsian Calvinists argued that women were more pious. "There are comparatively few males that are truly religious," Hopkinsians suggested. Women were not more devout by nature but "their retired circumstances" exposed them to fewer temptations and disposed "them to hear and attend more seriously the call of the Gospel. . . ." Men who spent most of their time outside the home succumbed more readily to "the numerous schemes for the acquisition of wealth, the offices of distinction" which corrupted the heart and rendered "things of religion tasteless and insipid."[42]

When the question of Freemasonry intruded into evangelical churches, women tended to throw their support to the Antimasonic faction which demanded that male members quit the Order. In Wrentham, Massachusetts, the Antimasons failed to get their way and a majority of the female members withdrew with a minority of the men to form a new church. In Cazenovia, New York, one "Young Lady" appealed to Baptist Elder G. to renounce Masonry.[43] And the Hicksite Quakers also rallied women against the pro-Masonic Orthodox Quaker faction. The Orthodox, they claimed, hid their deistic leanings, in fear of repelling women, and resorted to a "stratagem whereby, women Friends, could be enlisted in the work and deceived." In few American denominations did women enjoy such high status as among Quakers. As early as 1741 New York Quakers chose female elders, and in 1777 the Smithfield, Rhode Island, Monthly Meeting allowed women to participate in admission and disowning. Two women were leaders of the New England New Lights, precursors of the Hicksites in the early nineteenth century, a group with a strong affinity for Antimasonry. Hicksites reminded Quaker women that Masonry relinquished "all real human feelings, by discarding one half of the human family from partaking in the least benefit from the institution. . . ." Yet Orthodox Quakers remained devoted to Masonry.[44]

The assault on Freemasonry as an enemy of women and domestic order reflected differences between the sexes over religion, child-rearing, and gender definition as well as tensions over modernist trends in American culture, especially the spread of secularism. It is difficult to measure precisely the extent to which Antimasonry won support among women troubled by rapid change, but it seems likely the female hostility forced thousands of men to drop out of the Masonic Order. The political attacks on Masonry through legislative investigations and legal curbs are not sufficient to account for the sudden, dramatic decline of Masonry in the northeastern United States. The shift in public opinion was crucial and women played an important role in effecting that shift. Women found the Antimasonic Persuasion compelling because it focused the anxieties of domestic life on an institution against which they could mobilize. Antimasonic women were in the forefront of a movement that persuaded thousands of men that for the sake of domestic order no less than of civic virtue Masonry had to fall.[45]

Antimasons made explicit appeals for female support, though the right of women to participate in public life still remained a lively question. Antimasons "invited the ladies" to attend their conventions. The 1830 National Antimasonic Convention in Philadelphia and the Massachusetts Antimasonic Convention in 1832 opened their doors to women while Antimasonic leaders also tailored their messages to female concerns.[46]

Timothy Fuller, father of Margaret Fuller, typified the Old Republican current in Antimasonry which perceived the movement as the guardian of revolutionary principles in a corrupt, post-revolutionary age. Fuller stressed that Masonry was dangerous to youth, recruiting "a large portion of the *younger* and more active classes" whom it exposed to unwholesome influence, and thereby subverted "the great purposes of our schools and seminaries" which were "to make youth into men." Masons took young men, reared by their pious mothers and devoted teachers to become virtuous citizens, and "by its folly and emptiness degrades them into children."[47]

Fuller's defeat as Antimasonic candidate for lieutenant governor was the final failure of an isolated man, at odds with the powerful currents reshaping the country. Like other Antimasonic social critics, Fuller looked on women as Daughters of Liberty, guarantors of the American Revolution. He molded Margaret to become a model of republican womanhood. He cut her off from the middle-class female culture of etiquette books and sentimental novels designed to rear passive, retiring, empty-headed ornaments of domestic subordination. He insisted on rigorous, intellectual training similar to that received by young men intending professional careers or public service. Margaret studied history, especially the Roman republic, a suitable subject for American republicans. Margaret Fuller fulfilled her father's wishes and identified herself with the American eagle, for "she had been trained in the theoretical and political tradition of American revolution." But Timothy Fuller's radical notions of female potential left his daughter, like himself, marginalized. The intractable dilemma of Margaret's life was to reconcile "her historical consciousness with her feminine identity." Trained by an Old Republican father to become a guardian of the Revolution, Margaret rejected the emerging middle-class ladies' culture fostered, for example, by *Godey's Lady's Book* and by romantic fiction which isolated women from reality, trivialized and relegated them to an ornamental role. Conventional female culture was an "opiate" which Margaret found "flimsy beyond any texture that was ever spun or dreamed of by the mind of man." Yet women such as Margaret Fuller who ventured beyond the domestic sphere to confront American life honestly, faced the same hostility as female abolitionists discovered in the 1830s. Through the force of will and intelligence, and with encouragement from her father, Ralph Waldo Emerson, Horace Greeley, and others, she finally found her voice in journalism. Championing the humanity of slaves, Indians, and workers, themes rarely encountered in *Godey's* or in popular fiction, she identified the Americans' passion for "more money! more land!" as the peculiar national disease. "They have received the inheritance earned by the fathers of the revolution," she warned, "without their wisdom and virtue to use it."[48]

Like Fuller, Amasa Walker, a leading figure in the Massachusetts Antimasonic party, espoused the purifying influence of women. Walker was a prosperous Boston wholesale shoe dealer, a devoted member of an Orthodox Congregational church, and a universal reformer involved in the peace, temperance, and antislavery movements. In 1833, at the height of the Antimasonic movement in the Bay State, Walker, president of the Boston Lyceum, addressed twelve hundred young men, many of them country boys far from their mothers whose parting words had been: "Oh, my son, I tremble for you; Boston is such a dreadful place, thousands of young men as virtuous as yourself, have been seduced and destroyed." Walker thus warned newcomers of the "confidence men and painted women," especially the dangers of vice which Antimasons identified with Freemasonry. Walker knew that in Boston Masonry was strong and Antimasonry pitifully weak, a sign of the city's decadence. "We aim to change the MORAL CHARACTER of our metropolis," Walker warned, by offering young men "innocent and rational amusement free of alcohol, such as reading rooms and lectures, libraries and debating societies." But these institutions to succeed must enlist "the sympathies and assistance of the *female mind.*" Walker led the campaign to open them to women. The country was overrun by "avaricious money getting," by a "want of philanthropy," and by a love of caste that raised a few to eminence, leaving them bereft of "any feelings of interest in the great and benevolent undertakings of the age," Walker explained. Women, he thought, had a special affinity for benevolence and an aversion to avarice. Not until women, with their "innate moral and intellectual beauty," occupied a "commanding influence," Walker concluded, would "OUR HAPPY LAND" rest securely "ON THE IMPERISHABLE FOUNDATIONS OF UNIVERSAL INTELLIGENCE, AND PUBLIC VIRTUE."[49]

William Wirt, the Antimasonic presidential candidate in 1832, like Fuller another Old Republican, and Walker a moralist in politics who celebrated the Daughters of Liberty for their devotion to republican virtue, was known for piety and devotion to domestic virtue. The turning point in his life as a Virginia lawyer and intimate of the planter gentry was his spiritual conversion under his wife's guidance. Her "tender exhortations" had saved him "from the horrors of confirmed guilt." By choosing piety over pleasure, Wirt distanced himself from the fashionable deism and easy-going sociability of the Chesapeake elite. "How should I be laughed at if this letter were read by those who were once my wild companions," he admitted to his wife, for they would think him less a man. His conversion synthesized evangelical religion and republicanism, both of which guided the rest of his life.[50]

In 1814 Wirt published *The Old Bachelor*, a set of didactic newspaper pieces, which like his earlier *Letters from a British Spy*, voiced his views on social questions. Women must receive a comprehensive education to prepare them for the difficult task of raising republican children, he argued, for "the virtues of this country" were "with our women." Men, "variously engaged, alas! principally in sordid employment" were susceptible to corruption. Old Bachelor debated the issue with Obadiah Squaretoes, who upheld a conservative view that "a deep and humbling sense of their inferiority to, and entire dependence on the male, should be . . . inculcated in the female." Some women unfortunately had other ideas, Squaretoes complained, because men like Old Bachelor encouraged rebellion. One of his daughters had become a "reading lady" with fatal consequences. Her head filled with subversive notions, she neglected household chores and lectured her sisters on women's rights. When Squaretoes reasserted his authority, his daughter boldly declared: "Have not women souls, have they not reason, is it not given to them for a guide and is it not a duty which they owe to themselves and to heaven to improve their talents?" Old Bachelor agreed: "What is the most beautiful woman in the world, without a mind." Men must accept women as "partners of our souls" and not "debase them into mere objects of sense."[51] Wirt's views on women reflect a Christian Republican ideology, a strong attachment to Jeffersonian republicanism, and evangelical piety, which became the means of reviving civic virtue.

There was a close association between the strains of evangelical Christianity delineated in the preceding chapter and in the Antimasonic defense of republican domesticity. Both saw women and the family as pillars of republicanism and Masonry as an anti-feminine, anti-domestic current that ran powerfully through American life. This thesis gains additional support from an examination of two prominent women who rallied to Masonry.

Freemasonry had few more outspoken champions in the early nineteenth century than Mrs. Ann Royall, a sulphuric-tongued journalist who scourged evangelicals wherever she encountered them. Ann Royall was the wife of a Mason. After her husband's death, Masons patronized her, enabling her to tour the United States in the 1820s and record her impressions in a series of lively volumes. In 1828 she reached New England and filled *The Black Book* (1828–29) with vitriol targeted at evangelical clergy and their female devotees. By contrast she lavishly praised Masons and religious liberals. In Boston, for example, when she learned that her landlady had been converted by Lyman Beecher, she exclaimed: "Oh, shame on my sex." She preferred the company of prominent Boston Freemasons, such as Abraham Dame, whose countenance revealed "a magic sweetness" and whose language was "soft and winning." By contrast the Orthodox Congregationalist minister she met in Middletown, Connecticut, was "little, low, lean, lank, lantern jawed . . . with bigotry and fanaticism marked on every line. . . ." His eyes were "a venemous black" and his complexion was "hard to describe, being a combination of black, white, green and yellow, but the black preponderates." Royall saved her choicest barbs for pietistic women such as the "she monsters" of Newburyport, Massachusetts, enveloped in gloom, cursed with a "squalid, sickly color and a fierce malignant eye—all the contents of hell seemed to boil within them." No wonder there were so many old maids in New England, she concluded. In Vermont she found the people enslaved by "a perfect clerical government." Yet everywhere she encountered religious liberals and Masons who welcomed her. They were invariably "the gentlemen" and the "well-bred people," whereas "the blackcoats" were "always of the lower class, that is, the ignorant." In Wiscasset, Maine, when her Orthodox landlady learned who her boarder was, Royall was thrown out. A Mason, of course, rushed to the rescue. Ann Royall's anticlericalism not only found her an audience among Freemasons but also among Democrats. She spent her later years editing a Democratic newspaper in Washington, D.C., faithfully supporting the party line.[52] The spectacle of a woman such as Ann Royall defending Masonry gave Antimasons further evidence that the secret Order was at odds with revealed religion. The Danville *North Star,* one of Vermont's leading Antimasonic papers, growled: "If so strange a thing must happen under the sun, as that a woman should approve of and praise the institution of Freemasonry, no one can surely object that that woman should be Mrs. Royall."[53]

A much more influential female defender of Masonry was Sarah J. Hale, a leading arbiter of domestic manners and culture in Victorian America. For almost half a century Hale edited first the *Ladies' Magazine* and then, after combining forces with Louis Godey in 1837, *Godey's Lady's Book,* which enjoyed the largest circulation of any American magazine in the mid-nineteenth century.

Personal misfortune nourished Hale's literary career. Born in New

Hampshire in 1788, she married a rising lawyer in 1813 who became Worshipful Master of the Corinthian Lodge of Freemasons in Newport, New Hampshire. In 1822 Hale's husband died and left her with five children. Fortunately Masons came to the rescue. They supported publication of a book of poems, which she followed with a successful novel, *Northwood*, in 1827. The next year Hale moved to Boston at the invitation of Rev. John L. Blake, an Episcopal convert from Congregationalism. He served as principal of a female academy, rector of Boston's St. Matthews Church, and editor of the *Episcopal Register*. Blake conceived the idea, together with the publishers, Putnam & Company, of establishing a woman's magazine. He was also a prominent Freemason who served as chaplain of the Grand Lodge and in 1831 signed the Massachusetts Declaration of 1200 in defense of Masonry. According to Elizabeth O. Smith, a friend of Sarah J. Hale, the Freemasons sponsored the *Ladies' Magazine* in part to provide Mrs. Hale with a suitable position, but perhaps also because they sympathized with her views of true womanhood. In the 1830s Hale threw herself into another enterprise closely connected with Massachusetts Freemasonry and a source of bitter conflict with the Antimasons, the Bunker Hill Monument Association. In the early 1830s the Antimasons launched a campaign to rescue the Association from alleged Masonic domination which they blamed for waste, mismanagement and the failure to complete the memorial to the American Revolution. The Antimasonic attack failed, but the Monument Association remained short of funds. Into the breech stepped Sarah J. Hale, and for a decade she enlisted other women in the cause. She hit on the idea of holding fairs to sell merchandise donated or made by women, borrowing perhaps from the example of antislavery women. Hale raised substantial sums which helped the Association to finish the monument in 1843.[54]

During the Antimasonic movement, Hale defended Masonry and thereby incurred the animosity of Antimasons. The *Lynn Record* attacked her for claiming that Masons promoted "among men the virtues of the heart, sincerity in friendship, confidence and goodwill and charity to each other. . . ." Masons reprinted Hale's endorsement but the *Record* doubted that any woman of sound principle would support an institution that "allures their husbands and sons to its hidden embrace." The Lynn editor, a staunch Antimason, preferred the purifying company of women to the exclusive male society of Freemasonry. Hale's own magazine, he argued, was morally suspect for it published fiction and romances, emphasized high fashion, illustrated by lavishly colored plates, and encouraged questionable activities such as dancing and elaborate female grooming. By stimulating women to become conspicuous consumers of luxury and stressing the ornamental and sentimental functions of womanhood, Hale and *Godey's* were at odds with the severe notions of Christian republicanism.[55]

Sarah J. Hale's sympathy for Freemasonry mirrored the views of a segment of middle-class society, pointing to important divisions among exponents of the domestic ideal. Hale espoused a conservative version that appealed to prosperous, worldly, modernist, and socially ambitious men and women, paralleling her religious and political views. Reared a Congregationalist, Hale shifted to Episcopalianism, as did her colleague, Lydia Sigourney, the Hartford writer who worked as an assistant editor at *Godey's*. A third of the magazine's subscribers at mid-century were Southerners and many were probably Episcopalians or held latitudinarian religious opinions. Hale represented an anti-evangelical current in the middle class that legitimized a lifestyle pietists found suspect. Conservative Calvinists frowned on reading novels. Likewise evangelicals insisted on plainness in female dress and clung to older standards that prohibited dancing or amusing oneself on the sabbath. Hale, however, approved of fashion, dancing, and a sociable sabbath. From the outset Hale reassured men in the prospectus of the *Ladies' Magazine* that she would encourage no "usurpation" by women nor cause them to be "less assiduous in preparing for [the men's] reception" when they arrived home. Whereas the religious weeklies, avidly read by women, filled their pages with articles about vital moral questions such as slavery, intemperance, prostitution, the conditions of labor, as well as theological matters, *Godey's* studiously avoided them.[56] Yet Mrs. Hale subscribed to a coherent set of views about American society that established her as an important voice of anti-evangelical opinion. These views found an early, comprehensive, and artful statement in her novel, *Northwood,* reprinted significantly in 1852 as an antidote to Harriet Beecher Stowe's Christian domestic epic, *Uncle Tom's Cabin*.[57]

The hero of *Northwood* is a New Hampshire Yankee, Sidney Romilly, son of a revolutionary war veteran. The narrative follows Romilly through a series of moral tests which pit the republican virtues of Yankee culture against corrupt tendencies in the aristocratic slave culture of the South. Yet while Hale praises the virtues of her native New Hampshire, whose farmers seek only a competence through "unremitting industry," she is critical of Yankee avarice and duplicity identified with two staunch Northwood Calvinists, Deacon Jones and greedy merchant Skinner. In this way she strives to overcome regional stereotypes, deny Yankees' exclusive claims to virtue, and reconcile the sections. Her Yankee Calvinists must believe in salvation through faith since their selfishness, greed, and hypocrisy make salvation through Christian works impossible. By contrast, kindly Dr. Perkins, a vague, non-sectarian Christian, insists that faith lay in how one lives, not in doctrine. Sidney Romilly himself deserts Congregationalism for Episcopalianism, the result of a radical alteration of fortune that sends him south.

Inheriting a plantation in South Carolina, through an accident of fortune, Romilly rejects New Hampshire's "unsophisticated people where men are esteemed more for merit and usefulness than rank and wealth." His Aunt Lydia, a vain, self-centered girl, had thrown over her devoted Yankee beau for a rich Charleston planter. Lydia, however, cannot adjust to her husband's way of life, his Roman Catholicism, easygoing lifestyle, and paternal relations with numerous slaves who adore the master but frighten the mistress. The couple tries to salvage a barren marriage by adopting Sidney and giving him opportunities unavailable in the Granite State. Growing up in languid Charleston amid luxury, Sidney becomes a lazy, dissipated, fashionable dandy. He inherits the South Carolina plantation and returns for a visit to Northwood, New Hampshire, where he falls in love with Annie Reddington, a pure Yankee girl, down on her luck, who lives with the Calvinist, Deacon Jones. Before the couple can wed, Sidney loses his plantation to a swindler, yet not before generously rescuing a poor Northwood farmer who fell into debt to merchant Skinner, a Calvinist hypocrite who entraps Yankee farmers by over-extending credit and then seizing the bankrupt's property. Skinner also courts Annie, encouraged by Deacon Jones. Sidney demonstrates his moral superiority by abandoning the South to take over the family farm after his father's death: he will earn his living henceforth like his forbears, as an industrious husbandman. But his fortune suddenly changes again, Sidney recovers his plantation, wins Annie, and decides to sell the slaves to spare his Yankee wife. But a deep sense of paternal responsibility compels him to reconsider and sustain the burdens of master to save the blacks from a cruel owner. Then Romilly perfects an extraordinary scheme to solve the problem of slavery.

Northwood is a romance designed in part to advance Hale's anti-abolitionist African colonization views. Slavery, says the elder Romilly, is a great evil, but not a sin, a burden first imposed on Americans by the wicked British. Sidney Romilly discovers the way out. Yankee ingenuity can invent labor-saving machinery, so that whites may grow cotton without slaves. Sidney establishes a fund for his bondsmen into which he deposits their "wages." The slaves gradually purchase their freedom against the day when their master no longer needs their services. Trained to work productively, converted to Christianity in the New World, they will return to Africa and convert their native continent from darkness. Afro-American slavery thereby becomes the means of saving heathen Africa.

In *Northwood* Hale reconciles Yankees and Southerners, the republicanism of independent yeoman farmers with the aristocratic paternalism of southern planters, American freedom with American slavery. True Christian benevolence, untainted by the hypocrisy and greed of evangelical Yankee abolitionism, saves the union and frees the slave. In this astonishing, sentimental fantasy Sarah J. Hale squared the circle. When Civil War approached and then engulfed the nation, no hint touched the chaste pages of *Godey's*. Mrs. Hale's large Southern audience, like her Northern readers, preferred evasion.[58]

Evasion was at the heart of Sarah J. Hale's world. As an advocate of female "influence," she reduced women to the position of "a versatile doll," according to one historian, valuable "because she is able to work a kind of religious transformation," although she "represents nothing finally but a state of susceptibility to very imprecisely conceived spiritual values" that never threaten male power. Entirely dependent "on masculine response for her very being," Hale's female ideal—the polar opposite of Margaret Fuller's—"can as easily be man's victim as his inspiration."[59]

Such self-deception was also at the heart of Hale's role as an arbiter of fashion. Through sentimental culture the new urban middle class in emerging industrial society confronted "the serious social crisis symbolized by the confidence man," that is, the marginal person masquerading as respectable. Sentimental culture insisted on sincerity and sought to distinguish through dress, manners, and other social forms the respectable from the fake. By prescribing appropriate fashions of dress, the middle classes set themselves apart from those beneath them. But because clothes were a surface effect, they could hide moral imperfection and social inferiority. If clothes made the man or woman, character hardly counted. *Godey's* fudged the dilemma by insisting that clothes really did not matter while at the same time it prescribed appropriate fashion. At first *Godey's* sponsored "republican" fashions that emphasized transparency, through relatively simple styles that were revealing yet modest, in preference to the romantic style of the 1820s which were elaborately concealing. But by the 1850s the sentimental critique of fashion gave way to acceptance of self-display. *Godey's,* no longer disparaging the hypocrisy of fashion by which "confidence men and painted women" could hide their real character, now abandoned its ambivalence in favor of forthright acceptance of dress as theatrical costume which projected an image of virtue on the social stage.[60]

Spending most of a long life as editor of *Godey's Lady's Book,* Sarah J. Hale occupied a strategic place from which to carve out a sphere for women that did not challenge masculine authority. "Man never gives his whole heart, even to the object of his choice," she wrote in *Northwood.* "Unreserved devotion" is the virtue of women for while man's "soul is abroad in the world, seeking its employments and riches and honors," women sit "at home and think of him the live long day," designing "all her arrangements . . . in reference to his return. . . ." How could such a woman find fault with Masonry, for she is "the guardian of domestic honor and happiness, friend and companion of men," never stern judge or adversary.[61]

Hale identified hypocrisy as a dangerous national vice. In *Northwood,* she mercilessly flayed the insincerity of Yankee Calvinists.[62] To defenders of Freemasonry, and to others at odds with conservative evangelical culture, hypocrisy betrayed the character of their critics. While Antimasons were sounding the alarm of Masonic designs on female virtue, Masons turned the tables. In Wrentham, Massachusetts, they charged their tormentor, Rev. Moses Thacher, with the seduction of a succession of women in his congregation. Defender of Masonry Ann Royall had warned husbands that it was dangerous to allow their wives to spend so much time unsupervised among "pious men," for the reasons "the blackcoats" were "so very thick" with other men's wives were scandalous. In Connecticut,

Masons noted, Dr. Thaddeus DeWolf, a delegate to the Antimasonic Convention, had just served a term in a New York prison for raping a deaf and dumb girl. And in Vermont Masons claimed that Free Will Baptist Elder Edward B. Robbins, who renounced the Order and charged it with immoral conduct, had "heretofore been a great favorite among the girls," and was notorious for his "smokehouse feats."[63]

These counterattacks did not daunt the Antimasons. They had touched a deep chord of public apprehension when they projected onto Masonry widespread anxiety over gender relations, sexual behavior, the nurture of children, and the rivalry between men and women in the domestic sphere. When fifty women paraded through Brighton, Massachusetts, in June 1834, part of a procession celebrating a Masonic festival, Antimasons wondered how any female could endorse a group so steeped in vice and blasphemy.[64]

The conflict between defenders and critics of Freemasonry revealed divisions within middle-class opinion and fault lines within the ideology of domesticity. The spread of Freemasonry, following the trail of economic development, was important in fashioning the modern American middle class. Sarah J. Hale and *Godey's,* like Masonry, played a role in class formation by delineating values and beliefs by which middle-class people identified one another. Antimasonry voiced a dissenting strain: Masonry was "a selfish and corrupt association," a school for class snobbery, argued Myron Holley. It undermined "the moral sense of the community" and targeted women because "well-ordered loving families are the only stuff that a real republic can be made of." "If the average family is a sham," Holley warned, "so will be the republic." There could be no "patriotism and cohesion in a republic," he concluded, without "love, harmony, order and justice in the family. . . ."[65]

Masonry proved most vulnerable to the Antimasonic Persuasion in those parts of the United States where the spread of industrial society generated intense apprehension that the future of republican government and evangelical Christianity lay in jeopardy. The Antimasonic Persuasion failed to penetrate deep into the South or West but in the Northeast, from Pennsylvania to Maine, a popular movement overflowed conventional political channels to carve out a third stream which became the first mass oppositional party in the United States.

II

ANTIMASONIC

POLITICS

Antimasonry uses politics, as Christianity uses miracles, not to make converts, but to gain attention.

Antimasonic Review, No. 2, 92

And because politics have thus degenerated from morality, many who are opposed to Masonry are opposed to making opposition to it political. They do not wish to see Antimasonry, which they consider a sacred cause, polluted by the immorality of modern politics. But cannot political questions be discussed without descending to immorality?

Maine Free Press, 9 September 1834

6

The Emergence of Antimasonic
Politics in New England

Moral Antimasons! We conjure you to tell us by what means this
murderous institution can be exterminated but by politics.
Maine Free Press, 7 September 1832

Maine must come to the help of the Lord against the mighty.
Maine Free Press, 19 August 1931

Antimasons moved slowly into politics after experience taught them that
spreading the Antimasonic Persuasion and converting citizens to their viewpoint weakened but failed to overthrow Masonry. Tens of thousands agreed
that Masonry must perish, including many ex-Freemasons. But those who
remained loyal—prominent citizens in business, in the professions, in the
press, and in public life—would surely protect Freemasonry. Neither President Andrew Jackson nor the leader of the National Republican opposition,
Henry Clay, betrayed their oaths, giving further grounds for hope to
Masons. By the late 1820s the Antimasons could point to considerable success in shifting public opinion against Masonry, in mobilizing social, religious, and familial pressures that forced men to abandon the brotherhood,
and Lodges to suspend or fold, but they still fell short of final victory. By
the late 1820s they had exhausted the potential of a social movement for
effecting change, and so were pushed increasingly towards political action,
though not without some hesitation.

Antimasons realized that politics had a vital place in the battle against
Freemasonry. They set out to purge public offices of Masonic influence by
refusing to vote for Masons or their protectors. They petitioned for investigations to scrutinize the Order and tried to force Masons to testify. By
pressing the states to annul Masonic charters and to outlaw Masonic oaths,
the Antis believed that government could destroy Freemasonry, or at least
make it difficult for the Order to remain in business.[1] As it became clear
that neither Jacksonian Democrats nor National Republicans were recep-

tive to these actions, Antimasons were forced to embark on independent politics. The issue of Masonry, like the temperance question, was divisive and both parties sought to avoid a split. Because Antimasons initially drew support on a non-partisan basis, they, too, hesitated to make Masonry a political question for fear of dividing their forces. Moreover, many of them harbored antipartisan attitudes, while others who flocked to social movements such as temperance and abolitionism would have been put off if there was a conflict with their partisan attachments or leanings. Even as some Antimasons concluded that formation of a third party was necessary, "moral Antimasons" resisted, but by the late 1820s Antimasonry had either to find a new tactic or relinquish the field. Masonry's hard core resisted suasion; political coercion remained the only way.[2]

Since the Second American Party System was still in a formative stage of development in the late 1820s, many Antimasons reasonably assumed that a new party had bright prospects. The collapse of the First Party System and the ensuing factionalism which characterized contests in the 1820s left most voters unattached to any party. Turnouts were low throughout most of the decade and though the turnout for the 1828 presidential election was double that of the 1824 one, almost half the potential electorate remained unmobilized. Andrew Jackson's election did not immediately establish stable patterns of party loyalty or clearly defined programmatic differences. That happened, but only after a slow, tortuous process in the 1830s, and not until the second half of the decade did the Second Party System achieve maturity. Given the degree of political fluidity in the late 1820s and early 1830s, Antimasons reasoned that they had as much chance as any of becoming an important political force in the country. They possessed a clear-cut program, an ideology and propaganda machinery, and they had recruited a faithful group of experienced leaders who could mobilize thousands of voters indifferent or hostile to the other parties. A two-party system in 1830 was not yet an American norm, and even if Antimasons fell short of displacing the Nationals or Democrats, at the very least they might force concessions especially wherever they gained the balance of power.[3]

Antimasons took advantage of the ambivalence of many Americans towards the party system. On the one hand, antipartisan sentiment persisted throughout the country well into the 1830s and beyond, and some Antimasons shared and were able to exploit this feeling. They pointed to the other parties as exemplars of the worst evils of party politics: corrupt, devious, devoted to personal and special interests, controlled by ambitious but untrustworthy men. But at the same time many Americans were coming to regard party politics in a Republic as necessary to mobilize citizens, offer alternative programs, aggregate diverse interests and make democratic theory practical, and Antimasons defended their own move into politics on these grounds. Formed to promote the common welfare, to protect republican government from subversion, and assure the moral health of the political system, led by a distinterested band of public-spirited citizens—not like the new suspect breed of professional politicians—Antimasons claimed the virtues of party without the vices. No mere officeseekers, Antimasons saw themselves as "a Spartan band," "an inflexible minority," "a blessed spirit," driven by principle, braving great odds for the public good. By contrast the battles between Democrats and Whigs involved "no question of measures of government" because they were just a "personal contest between rival aspirants for popular favors and their devoted followers."[4]

Seeking to preserve their monopoly of the electoral arena, National Republicans and Jacksonian Democrats questioned the legitimacy of a third party. Some conceded that Masonry was a proper issue for public discussion but denied that it was an appropriate political question. If Masonry spread infidelity and threatened the churches, that was a matter for religious bodies, not government. And if Masons broke the law and endangered the civil rights of citizens, that was a problem for sheriffs, judges, district attorneys, and juries. There was no precedent for a third party, let alone one organized around a single issue rather than around the enduring principles the existing parties professed.

Such arguments carried little weight with Antimasons. Convinced that Masonry had infiltrated the bar, the church, and all levels of government, as well as the parties, these Guardians of the American Revolution claimed the right and duty to purge American society of anti-republican evils. But as long as the churches tolerated Masonry, it would be harder to disqualify Masons from public office on grounds of personal unfitness. The battle against Masonry must be fought on all fronts in the churches, families, and the electoral arena.

Antimasons were vulnerable to charges that they advocated a policy of proscribing men for their opinions. They responded that both National Republicans and Democrats rewarded their supporters and proscribed their opponents, strictly on self-serving grounds. By contrast Antimasons acted on principle: "We refuse to vote for a Mason because we believe their adherence to Masonic oaths disqualifies them from civil trusts." Having surrendered allegiance to an institution that claimed to be above the Constitution and the laws, Masons forfeited any right to hold office, Antimasons believed.[5]

An Antimasonic third party seemed necessary because neither of the other parties would allow the question of Masonry on the political agenda. The party leaders excluded Antimasonic opinion or any discussion of the Masonic question from party newspapers, caucuses, conventions, and councils. It seemed arbitrary and undemocratic for politicians to claim that it was proper to fight elections on the tariff but not on Masonry.[6]

By forming a new party on purely Antimasonic grounds, the third party gave citizens a choice, and the support it received at the polls would provide an accurate gauge of public opinion. Since majority sentiment in a Republic was decisive, and public opinion polling lay far in the future, there had to be some orderly means of measuring opinion. "Voting is the expression of an opinion," Antimasons explained, and "the ballot box is the great reservoir of public sentiment by which the people "make known their decision and proclaim their will." Professional politicians who tried to control the political agenda and restrict voters' choice denied "the supremacy of the people."[7]

All roads seemed to lead to electoral politics. Yet Antimasons, nodding to persisting antipartisan sentiment, promised not to seek "the mere triumph of party or the success of their candidates" but rather to work for "the triumph of the moral and political principles [with which] secret societies were at war." On the day that Freemasonary succumbed, Antimasons would disband, a day they "most earnestly desire and court."[8]

By the early 1830s Antimasons had plunged into politics in most of the New England states, meeting varied success. In Vermont they won a plurality and emerged as the leading party; in Massachusetts they captured a quarter of the vote and compelled the National Republicans to pay attention; in Rhode Island, winning 14 percent of the vote gave Antimasons a balance of power to rule in coalition with the Democrats; in Connecticut an equally impressive showing yielded little political influence. Finally in Maine the Antimasonic party never amounted to more than a marginal factor, while in New Hampshire it remained more a social than a political movement. (See Table 6.1.[9])

The spread of industrial society evoked a variety of reactions in the 1820s and 1830s ranging from uncritical enthusiasm and boosterism to ambivalence and resistance. The Workingmen's parties channeled the anxieties of wage earners and others troubled by the commercialization of labor relations. Jacksonian Democrats made the Bank of the United States a master symbol of the spread of the market economy. And the Antimasonic movement, much less class-specific than the Workingmen's and much more rooted in religious sensibility than Jacksonianism, voiced a diffuse but general feeling that the spread of market relationships, demographic instability, and religious pluralism and secularism posed critical dangers to a Christian Republic.[10]

Responses to social change explain a good deal about the social sources of Antimasonry, but they do not explain everything. Competition between the two major parties also shaped the third party's fortunes. In those states where the Second Party System was especially fluid and emerged slowly, the prospects of Antimasons were brightest. In contrast, Maine and New Hampshire, Antimasonry's weakest states in New England, had developed a highly competitive party system by the late 1820s, reviving older cleavages that traced back to the First Party System. In general in New England the Jacksonian Democrats ran very poorly against the regional favorite in 1828—President John Quincy Adams—polling less than a quarter of the vote, compared to Jackson's strong showing in Maine and New Hampshire. (Table 6.2.[11]) In states where both parties were strong, citizens were reluctant to waste a vote on a third party with poor prospects of winning, preferring to back the major party to which they were most attracted—and for Antimasons that usually meant the National Republicans. In Massachusetts, however, National Republican domination was so complete that people allured by the Antimasonic Persuasion could vote their consciences without risking loss of the state to the Jacksonians. Voting for the Antimasons also carried marginal risks where the two-party system was late in developing, as in Connecticut.

In the two most highly competitive states, Maine and New Hampshire, Jacksonian Democrats and their rivals were relatively successful in remobilizing voters along older party lines. Democrats in these states ran especially well in towns where Jeffersonian Republicans had polled well, as suggested by the stronger correlation between voting patterns in the First and Second Party systems than in the four other states. In contrast, in the latter group there was almost no correlation between town-level voting in the two periods, suggesting that where older political loyalties had faded and newer partisan attachments remained weak or unformed, Antimasons had their best chances for electoral success. (Table 6.3.[12])

The Antimasonic party did well where it mobilized non-voters. The third party tended to receive a somewhat larger proportion of its vote from citizens not previously mobilized by the Nationals than from party switchers, though most of these tended to come from the National Republicans. (Table 6.4.[13]) But in states where the major parties had been particularly successful in increasing turnout before the Antimasons entered politics, as in New Hampshire and Maine, the third party's prospects were less auspicious. Thus the large pool of non-voters in the uncompetitive states offered the third party a choice target. (Table 6.5.[14])

There were scattered attempts to establish an Antimasonic party in New Hampshire in the 1830s, but without success.[15] An abortive Antimasonic effort in 1833 was symptomatic of Antimasonry's weakness but also of the National Republicans' hopeful prospects. In the late 1820s New Hampshire emerged as a highly competitive two-party state. In 1828 Andrew Jackson captured 46 percent of the vote, a showing unmatched in New England and foreshadowing the transformation of New Hampshire into a one-party Democratic stronghold in the 1830s. But that outcome was not evident in the 1820s, and Adams Republicans and Jacksonians organized intensively. Well-edited, hard-hitting party newspapers, annual town, county, and state nominating conventions that involved thousands of people gave a mass, participatory character to politics, and produced hard-fought battles and the highest voter turnouts in New England. One-sided elections in the early 1820s gave way to close competition later in the decade. The Jacksonians captured the governorship in 1827, with Benjamin Pierce, an old revolutionary war hero who symbolized the Democrats' claim to be the genuine heirs of '76. But the next year, the Adams Republican candidate for governor, John Bell, brother of United States Senator Samuel Bell, the National Republican leader in New Hampshire, won 53 percent of the vote. Pierce

returned the next year to win narrowly, but 1829 was the last closely contested election for chief executive for the next fifteen years. The Nationals'
vote first declined modestly in 1830 and 1831, but then fell off sharply in
1832. It became increasingly fruitless to contest until the depression of 1837
revived their fortunes.[16]

As early as 1830 signs of demoralization surfaced among the Nationals.
Their opponents, led by Isaac Hill, were masters of the new political tech-
niques, including party organization. The Nationals failed to match them.
In February 1830, Senator Bell received discouraging reports about the
forthcoming election: "The great difficulty is to bring them to the polls,"
wrote a Chesterfield informant. "Such has been and yet is the course of political events that very many of our best men are disgusted, and disheart-
ened, and almost despair of the commonwealth."[17]

By 1833, the Nationals' discouragement opened the way for the Antimasons. A year earlier National leaders had successfully killed attempts to
run a slate of Wirt electors, but Clay did poorly in New Hampshire and the
next year the Antimasons had the field of opposition to themselves. Not
many Nationals chose to vote for the Antimasons in 1833, and turnout
dropped sharply, since the Democrats faced no real contest.[18]

New Hampshire Antimasons were a small band with National Republican leanings, who found the leadership of that party hostile to collaboration
or accommodation. Before 1833 the Nationals harbored hopes of winning
and it seemed imprudent to mix into the controversy over Masonry. New
Hampshire Freemasons included many of the state's foremost citizens, among
them leaders of both political parties. Moreover, most of those serving as
governor from 1824–55 were Masons, another sign of the Order's penetration of leadership circles. Given the precarious position of the National Republicans, and Masonry's support in both parties, the wisest strategy was
neutrality. The editor of the *New Hampshire Sentinel*, a National Republican organ, appealed for Antimasonic support but offered nothing in return. An unbroken wall of hostility by both Nationals and Democrats,
explained an Antimasonic editor, accounted for the third party's weakness
in New Hampshire.[19]

Masonry grew all over the country as a modern middle-class emerged
along with the spread of the market economy, but growth occurred more
slowly in New Hampshire than in southern New England. Masonry lagged
because the business and professional elements who joined the Order were
less numerous in the Granite State. In 1812 there were 110 Lodges in Massachusetts and 50 in Connecticut, but only 19 in New Hampshire. Granite
State Masonry underwent considerable expansion in the early nineteenth
century but still only 28 percent of the towns in 1830 could boast a Lodge
compared to 36 percent in Massachusetts and half or more in Rhode Island
and Connecticut. Only in Maine, New England's least populated state,
was Masonry weaker. It proved more difficult to mobilize Antimasonic sentiment where the target was less visible. For most citizens in New Hamp-

shire and Maine, the controversy over Masonry was not an immediate concern; the dangers seemed remote.[20]

The social characteristics of New Hampshire Masons, judging from the data in a biographical dictionary of New Hampshire Masons biased towards prominents, were eminently middle-class. Sixty percent joined the Order in their twenties and most of the rest in their thirties and early forties, for Masonry was immediately useful in assisting young men as they made their way into the world of business and the professions. Almost a quarter of those for whom we have age data attended college, a remarkably high proportion for the period, and their occupations round out the picture of solid bourgeoisie. More than half (51%) were white-collar professionals, but only 1 percent were in the lower echelons of that stratum, while some 38 percent were businessmen and only 5 percent were farmers. Nearly 60 percent held state office and almost 30 percent held federal or military positions. Finally, membership in non-Calvinist denominations stands out: religious data are skimpy, but of eighteen whose denominational affiliation is given, there were two Episcopalians, one Unitarian and two Universalists, in addition to the four Methodists and one Congregationalist, but no Regular or Free Will Baptists. (Table 6.6.[21])

Masonry's weakness in New Hampshire reflected the state's underdevelopment, a factor which also shaped the fortunes of the major parties, helping to propel the Democrats into the majority. New Hampshire experienced nothing like the sheep boom that spread capitalistic farming into neighboring Vermont. Manufacturing penetrated the southeastern towns by the 1830s and gave Jacksonian Democrats a powerful issue. The party early assumed a critical stance towards development, attacking banks before President Jackson launched the Bank War and opposing tariff protection and government aid for internal improvements. In the early 1840s the New Hampshire legislature obstructed private investment in railroads. The Democrats catered to the state's provincialism, suspicion of Boston capital, and apprehension that industry meant greater inequality and a demographic upheaval that lured young men and women away from family homesteads, destroyed household manufactures, and raised the price of farm labor. If the Nationals met little success in selling the American System in New Hampshire, the state's economic backwardness also made New Hampshire less receptive to the Antimasonic Persuasion. Since Antimasonic sentiment arose partly as a response to the Great Transition, New Hampshire citizens had less reason to be troubled than others caught in the maelstrom of social change. Finally, the Democrats very early pre-empted the cause of Old Republicanism, posing as anti-aristocratic egalitarians, and identifying the Nationals with Federalism, economic development, and aristocracy.[22] The multiple regression statistics suggest that as the proportion of farmers per town increased and land values per capita decreased, the Democratic vote swelled. Masonry was not the danger, Democrats insisted, and pointed instead to an aspiring Whig aristocracy aided by religious bigots. (Table 6.7.[23])

The Democrats cleverly exploited the hostility of Methodists, Baptists, Free Will Baptists, and Universalists towards the once dominant Congregationalist church, the church of the elite. They repeatedly portrayed themselves as champions of the religious settlement of 1819 which separated church and state, and they depicted opponents as men who wanted to restore Congregationalism to its privileged position. The regression statistics indicate that Congregationalists tended to depress the Democratic vote while Free Will Baptists increased it. Baptists and Methodists had a weak and inconclusive impact, probably because these denominations did not unite politically, though the Democrats cultivated their support (Table 6.7).[24]

The Democrats profited from denominational rivalry because the Toleration Act of 1819 did not settle all issues. Sectarian competition persisted in many towns, especially where churches fought over disposition of ecclesiastical property.[25] The Democrats also practiced recognition politics by nominating for high office Methodists such as Congressman John Broadhead and Governor Jared Perkins. They also guaranteed the right of Universalists to give testimony in court; they discontinued the ancient practice of appointing a chaplain to attend the legislature; and they attacked the Sabbatarian efforts to close the Post Office on Sunday. Finally, they proposed to divert the state's literary fund from the support of the common schools to a new college that would end Dartmouth's monopoly of higher education. A new, publicly backed college, founded on pluralist principles, would deprive the Congregationalists of a great advantage. Democratic anti-clerical rhetoric also reached out to Nothingarians, a large fraction of the electorate affiliated with no church and resistant to intrusions by religion into public affairs. Antimasonry's Christian Republicanism, with its emphasis on the spiritual foundations of republican government, made them vulnerable to allegations that they were sectarian bigots seeking to impose a religious test for public office. In New Hampshire a Christian party in politics faced very poor prospects.[26]

Because a well-organized Antimasonic party failed to emerge in New Hampshire, it is more difficult to identify the social basis of the movement there. Fragmentary evidence suggests that Antimasonry drew support from conservative evangelicals with Hopkinsian sympathies, such as former Governor David Morrill who renounced Masonry in 1831 and attended the 1833 New Hampshire Antimasonic Convention. The son of a Congregationalist minister, Morrill was a doctor until he switched to the pulpit. He later entered public life, first as Speaker of the General Assembly, then as United States Senator (1816–23), and finally as governor (1824–26). After retiring from office, Morrill resumed his medical practice in Concord, where he also published the *New Hampshire Observer,* a religious newspaper. Torn between religious and secular careers, Morrill resolved the conflict by devoting himself to both and to organized benevolence. For twenty-four years he served as vice president of the American Bible Society; he was also a supporter of the American Sunday School Union and the Home Missionary Society.[27] In one sense, Morrill was typical, for the most salient characteristic of delegates to the 1833 Antimasonic Convention was leadership in their churches, usually Congregationalist, sometimes Baptist. They often came from towns which had long-tenured, influential, conservative Calvinist preachers. In some cases divisions within the churches over standards of piety, pitting the more rigorous against the more lax, antedated the controversy over Masonry. For such men the Antimasonic claim that the Mystic Order encouraged loose behavior, theological vagueness, and secular values fell on receptive ears.[28]

Yet if some New Hampshire churches provided vital support for the Antimasonic movement, most steered clear of the controversy which threatened to split them. The Antimasons themselves hesitated to criticize the churches for tolerating Masonry. Delegates at the 1833 Convention heeded those leaders who opposed a resolution demanding that clergy join the fight against Masonry to prevent the Democrats from making political capital as defenders of separation of church and state. In New Hampshire where church/state issues remained sensitive, Antimasons sensed they were vulnerable to mixing religion with politics.[29]

In other states, Congregationalist churches generated important leadership in the Antimasonic movement, but their limited support in New Hampshire was a fatal weakness. New Hampshire Congregationalism was very much on the defensive, and not just because of Democratic attacks. By 1830 the denomination had lost its numerical supremacy. Only in Maine were the Congregationalists weaker compared to the other major New England denominations. New Hampshire was the home of the Free Will Baptists, who originated in the Granite State and counted for 20 percent of the members of the major denominations. Along with Methodists, Regular Baptists, and Universalists, the "dissenters" challenged the once pre-eminent position occupied by the Congregationalists. Democratic party recognition gave the rising denominations new prestige. In the face of such formidable competition, the wisest course for most Congregationalist leaders was to steer clear of Antimasonry because of its sectarian divisiveness.[30]

Moreover, liberalism, often identified with deistic currents associated with Freemasonry, had failed to make significant inroads among New Hampshire Congregationalists. The Unitarians claimed ten, the Episcopalians seven, and the Universalists three ministers in the 1830 state register, compared with 130 for the Congregationalists. In New Hampshire, as in other states, ministers of the first three denominations were particularly attracted to Freemasonry, but they did not pose the same threat to Orthodoxy as they did in Massachusetts or Connecticut. The more severe problem facing Congregationalists was internal weakness: a third of their churches in 1830 were without settled ministers. Attacked by the Democrats, facing tough competition from Methodists, Regular Baptists, and Free Will Baptists, Congregationalists clung to the National Republicans.[31]

Neither the religious, political, nor demographic climate was favorable to

Antimasonry. Denounced by Jacksonians as Federalists, ignored by the National Republicans, unable to mobilize extensive support in the churches, New Hampshire Antimasons faced chilling prospects.[32] "The Spartan Band" would have to take hope from political success in other states, such as Vermont and Massachusetts, but in neighboring Maine, Antimasons were only marginally more successful, though not for want of effort by a militant minority to organize a credible third party.

Political Antimasonry arrived in Maine in 1832, preceded by the establishment of an Antimasonic newspaper in Hallowell, a center of third party sentiment. The *Maine Free Press* began in July 1831, following two earlier failures to break the Mason's alleged control of the press.[33] As in New Hampshire, both major parties were hostile. The religious and secular press also proved indifferent or hostile.[34] Masonry's hold over Maine's political and ecclesiastical leadership seemed impenetrable. In March 1832, the legislature rejected a petition to ban Masonic oaths. Both parties also honored Freemasons with nominations to high office. The Democrats named Robert Dunlap, Grand Master of the Grand Lodge, as its candidate for governor in 1833; the Whigs chose Peleg Sprague, a deputy Grand Master. first for the United States Senate and then for governor. In 1832 the Democrats placed five Freemasons and the National Republicans two on their presidential electoral tickets. Frustrated by the major parties, Antimasons established their own.[35] And the Antimasonic party's poor showing in elections it contested from 1832–34 justified the major parties' indifference. The need for educational spadework was evident: in 1833 the Antimasons created a Tract Society, but there is no evidence that it flooded the state with propaganda.[36]

Antimasons attributed their poor showing in Maine to reluctance by National Republicans, who shared their hostility to Masonry, to waste a vote on a third party certain to lose. Most of the 1833 Antimasonic vote came from National Republican voters in 1830 (Table 6.4), but Maine Antimasons were unable to penetrate National strength or mobilize new voters. Voter turnout soared in Maine from 43 percent in 1828 to 68 percent in 1830, before the Antimasons entered electoral politics, but thereafter turnout vacillated, following no trend, advancing only in 1834 when the economic crisis aroused voters (Table 6.5).[37]

The surge of voters after 1828 came in response to the revival of a tight two-party competition. As in New Hampshire, the Second American Party System matured earlier in Maine than in the other New England states. After a series of weakly contested elections in the 1820s, reflecting the demise of the First Party System, Maine experienced renewed polarization as the presidential struggle of 1828 approached. National Republicans divided between supporters of President John Quincy Adams and of Andrew Jackson, and as in the Granite State, the Jacksonians, winning 40 percent of the vote, far exceeded the New England average. Democrats in both states benefited from reactivating older patterns of party loyalty forged a generation earlier. The National Republican vote in 1828, for example, correlated at 0.43 with the Federalist vote in 1810, a good deal higher than in Vermont, where Antimasonry prospered (Table 6.3).

The revival of competition locked Jacksonian Democrats and National Republicans in a closely fought battle for mastery which ended with Democratic domination for a generation. The Adams Republicans captured the governorship in 1829 by the thinnest of margins (51.1%), but the Democrats won in 1830 with 52 percent. Then National Republican fortunes sagged: by 1835 their share sank to 27 percent. Because the major parties were so closely matched at the very time Antimasonry emerged as a political force, there was only a hard core of Antimasons who favored a third party strategy.

The relative weakness of Freemasonry in Maine was also a factor. By 1800 there were only five Lodges in the Pine Tree State, but as northern New England's frontier underwent economic development, and the number and size of cities and larger towns grew, Maine's emerging bourgeoisie gravitated towards the Mystic Order. By 1830 Maine boasted 58 Lodges, but that still left 80 percent of the towns without Masonic outposts, and some of the Lodges were viable only by drawing members from nearby communities. The late development and limited extent of Maine Masonry reflected the uneven spread of the market economy and the laggard pace of modern class formation.[38]

By 1830 manufacturing had made slight inroads in Maine; commerce and the maritime trades were the leading non-farming sectors. Many farmers remained isolated from markets, producing mostly for subsistence, and together with merchants, lumber exporters, and those shipbuilders who preferred free trade, they gravitated to the Jacksonian Democrats. The American System offered little to those involved in fishing, shipbuilding, and the coastal trade. Whereas pietistic manufacturers in industrial communities in Massachusetts, Rhode Island, and Connecticut provided strategic support for the Antimasonic movement, these elements were missing in Maine.[39]

Though Maine's development lagged behind the rest of New England, the social character of the membership and the functions of Maine Freemasonry were similar to other states. Maine's first Lodge, located in its first city, Portland, the commercial emporium, traced back to before the American Revolution, when men prominent in the business, professional, and public life secured a charter. Over three hundred men joined Portland's first Lodge between 1800 and 1830. Most tended to be in their twenties at the time of initiation (60%); the rest entered the Order before they reached forty-five. The typical Mason joined early in his career, and tended to engage in business and the professions. Merchants and retailers were the most numerous occupation (28%), followed by master artisans and manufacturers (27%), and in this port city master mariners were also important, counting for almost a quarter of the membership. Finally public officials and professional men made up 10 percent. The presence of only one clerk, only five (non-master) mariners, and only four farmers and the absence of any laborers or other clearly distinguished wage earners suggest the class-exclusive nature of Portland Masonry. These men were recruited from a wide variety of religious denominations before 1826, but the evidence indicates it held especial appeal for men of latitudinarian disposition.[40]

Maine Antimasons associated Freemasonry with the spread of the commerical economy and the growth of village society. As in other states, restoring Republican equality and defending Christian churches against corrupt, secularist forces were twin themes running through their rhetoric. Towns with Masonic Lodges in 1830 were generally more than twice as populous as the state average; moreover, their economies showed evidence of greater development: over a fifth (22%) of the labor force in "Masonic towns" engaged in manufactures, compared with 11 percent for all towns. The more developed towns were also more hospitable to religious diversity, especially to churches outside the Calvinist fold, such as the Unitarians, Universalists, and Episcopalians.[41]

The voting data are inconclusive, but suggest that the National Republicans received a boost from communities with a large percentage of persons employed in manufacture and with higher per capita assessed valuations—that is, the wealthier towns. (Table 6.8.[42]) Since many Antimasonic voters came out of National Republican ranks, it seems that they gave higher priority to the moral dangers of Masonry than to the party's program for economic development. Masonry was a sinister system "of sapping and mining, which must eventually involve in ruin the very citadel of our national liberties," Rev. Moses Thacher, a Massachusetts Hopkinsian, told a Maine Antimasonic convention, for it "is anti-Christian and anti-republican" and had "trapped many good men."[43]

The statistical evidence points to the saliency of religion in the support received by the Antimasonic party. Congregationalists, Baptists, Methodists, and Free Will Baptists all tended to increase the third party's vote, and Universalists to depress it. Moreover, when one compares the impact of religious and economic variables on the parties in 1830, before the Antimasons appeared on the ballot, with 1833, the major shift was the increased explanatory power of religion (Table 6.8). Yet the numeric data remain inconclusive because the statistics are problematic, denominations are split, and membership figures do not distinguish among rival currents within a church, such as conservative and moderate Calvinists, modernist and anti-modernist Baptists, as well as the liberal or Unitarian currents still present in the Congregationalist fold.

Maine's leading denominations split over the question of Masonry. Several Free Will Baptist preachers renounced the Order and Antimasons polled well in their towns, but the Free Will Baptists as a denomination remained aloof.[44] Likewise, some Methodist preachers appealed to the annual conference in 1832 to force members to abandon Masonry, but the conference remained neutral.[45] The sharpest differences occurred among

Congregationalists. The *Christian Mirror,* the denomination's weekly, defended Masonry against attack by the Massachusetts Hopkinsians' organ, the *Christian Herald,* an Antimasonic newspaper. The *Mirror's* publisher and editor were both loyal Masons, arousing prominent Antimasonic Congregationalists in Hallowell to drop their subscriptions.[46]

The Kennebec Valley was the center of Antimasonic strength and also a stronghold of conservative Congregationalism.[47] Pious laymen, active in the Kennebec Conference, were in the forefront of Maine Antimasonry. One such layman was General Henry Sewall, a delegate to the National Antimasonic Convention in 1831. Sewall was a founder and deacon at South Church in Hallowell, which was an important source of Antimasonic leadership. Old South had once "created the public sentiment in the town," but as the city grew, by the 1820s pluralism and secularism had eroded the church's role as "a spiritual and intellectual element that not only regulated the moral, but refined and elevated the everyday life of the people."[48] Similarly, in nearby Winthrop, Rev. David Thurston's church spawned a remarkable number of associations—temperance, maternal, debating, female domestic reform, and antislavery. The Agricultural Society expressed a restorationist impulse that aimed to combat the emergence of bourgeois disdain for husbandry among "not a few of the young men" who "were beginning to look upon farming as rather a low employment." Rev. Thurston, Hopkinsian-trained, reminded them of Ecclesiastes 5:9: "The profit of the earth is for all; the king himself is served by the field."[49]

Antimasonry flourished also among conservative Baptists in Buckfield, who voted in 1828 to exclude Masons from the church, "they being a wicked and immoral society." When pastor Rev. Ephraim Harlow's brother, Nathan, refused to quit, the church booted him out, but he found a refuge among the more tolerant First Baptist Church. To the upholders of closed communion and strict discipline at the Second, this proved that Masonry had made inroads that subverted Baptist faith.[50]

An important element in Maine Freemasonry was a conflict between modernist and anti-modernist elements in the various denominations. Local histories repeatedly suggest a link between Antimasonry and men and women determined to maintain the bonds of Christian community, based on homogeneous values, adherence to traditional beliefs, acceptance of church discipline, and loyalty to sectarian ties over others.[51] Yet as dependent as Maine Antimasonry was on support from the churches, the religious climate was much less favorable to political Antimasonry than in other states, and that doomed Maine Antimasonry to marginality. Maine was large, recently settled, and lightly populated. The churches of all denominations were on the defensive and faced formidable problems: competition among one another and hostility or indifference from a legion of Nothingarians. The Jeffersonians had capitalized on the discontent of dissenters and Nothingarians and Maine became a Republican stronghold.[52] Separation from Massachusetts in 1820 brought disestablishment. The Congregationalists, pillars of Federalism, faced hard times. Even earlier the Massachusetts Missionary Society had reported in 1813 that more than 200,000 persons in two hundred towns and cities went without regular preaching in Maine. Vast sections of the state in 1825 remained "a moral wilderness." Sensitive to the formidable problems, the Maine Missionary Society instructed agents to refrain from political activity or land specula-tion, a tempting sideline for Jesus' disciples on the frontier.[53]

The Jacksonian Democrats, like the Jeffersonians earlier, shrewdly ex-ploited sectarian rivalry, the weakness of Federalist Congregationalism, and the strength of Nothingarianism. This helps to account for the persistence of town-level partisan attachment from the First to the Second Party Sys-tem. As in New Hampshire, Maine Democrats also made defense of reli-gious liberty their own issue, attacking clerical intrusions into politics, but singling out the Congregationalists, who tended to support the Nationals. Bowdoin College, a Congregationalist institution, had come under severe criticism from Jeffersonians, who altered the governing board when they gained control of the new state after 1820. In 1830 Jacksonian Democrats renewed the pressure, accusing Bowdoin's president, William Allen, and the faculty of throwing their weight behind the "Federalists," that is, the National Republicans. The statistical evidence supports the Democrats' charge that Congregationalists, more than any other denomination, favored the Democrats' rivals. The Jacksonian legislature responded by altering the Bowdoin charter to force out President Allen. Here, as earlier, in the Dart-mouth College case in New Hampshire, the federal courts frustrated Dem-ocratic majorities, but the Democrats continued to bait Bowdoin. In 1834 the legislature cut off further funding for the medical school.[54]

The attack on Bowdoin was one element in the party's strategy of appeal-ing to "dissenters" by sustaining long-standing prejudices against the Ortho-dox. In 1828 Congregationalist ministers refused to read the Governor's Thanksgiving Day Proclamation in retaliation for Democratic hostility.[55] In the face of Democratic attacks, many Maine Congregationalists preferred to stick with the Nationals than weaken the opposition (Table 6.8).

The Democrats also made positive appeals to the other denominations. While condemning Bowdoin, they praised the Baptists' Waterville College and nominated Baptist Elder Hutchinson for senator from Oxford County.[56] In 1834, a Democratic legislature granted assistance to the Methodists' Maine Wesleyan Seminary. They also chose a Methodist minister as pres-ident of the state senate in 1830.[57] Even as they singled out Congregation-alist leaders for criticism, the Democrats cultivated the rank and file.[58] They elected Ether Shepley to the United States Senate in 1831. He was prominent in Congregationalist benevolent activity, as well as the Maine Temperance Society. When the Democratic candidate for governor, Robert Dunlap, a Unitarian and leading Mason, underwent a religious conversion to Orthodoxy in 1834, the Democrats now had a born-again Christian on the top of their ticket.[59]

The vexing question of how to dispose of town ministerial lands offered another opportunity for the Democrats. In 1833 a Democratic leader proposed to weaken the alliance of "the Aristocracy of Massachusetts and the Orthodoxy of Maine" by taking a decisive "stand against the arrogance and dictation of sectarian despotism" which "is spreading itself over the whole community and carrying its ramifications into every business of life," threatening to "swallow up every other interest." Democrats figured that by encouraging the weaker denominations, their party would benefit.[60]

The voting data suggest a good deal of volatility and internal divisions in the partisan preferences of church members except for Congregationalists, who tended to boost the National Republican and Antimasonic votes as did the Free Will Baptists in the late 1830s, though to a lesser degree. The Nationals' best hope was to downplay religious issues in politics to deprive Jacksonians of important talking points.[61]

The closeness of party competition in the late 1820s and early 1830s kept many pietists, attracted by the Antimasonic Persuasion, from straying from the two-party fold. That fatally limited the political progress of Antimasonry in Maine. The Nationals courted Antimasonic votes, insisting that Masonry was already on the skids and no third party effort was necessary. In 1834 leading Antis endorsed the Nationals' Peleg Sprague for Governor after he acknowledged that he was no longer a practicing Mason.[62]

Maine Antimasonry's greatest success came outside politics in the arena of public opinion. Bowing to public clamor, many Masons abandoned the Order. Lodges folded or went underground and only a handful sent representatives to the meetings of the Grand Lodge from 1834 to 1843. In Hallowell, Masons gave up their charter for the sake of communal peace. In North Anson, the Lodge held no meeting for a decade in the face of "politico-religious mountebanks" who "fanned the flames of discord by their frenzied appeals to popular prejudice. . . ." In Livermore, Oriental Star Lodge performed "no work" for fourteen years even though "the persecution on account of Masonry in this vicinity was not carried to such extremes as in some other localities," nor was ever "carried into [their] elections. . . ." Rather than abandon the Order, the faithful preferred to "keep quiet, but stand firm by their principles and their integrity" avoiding "unnecessary disputes, with excited, evil disposed persons" and living "blameless lives."[63]

Because Antimasonry was a social movement as well as a political party, people judged its progress by standards other than victory at the polls. Antimasons in Maine and New Hampshire achieved their greatest success in shaping public opinion. The electoral arena proved inhospitable terrain, but in nearby Vermont, "the blessed spirit" mushroomed into the dominant political force.

7

The Great Green Mountain Purge
Antimasonry in Vermont

Fellow citizens; we want to see masonry *abolished*—EVERY WHERE. And will you not permit us the satisfaction of seeing the work commence with you? of being able to present to the world the glorious example of one State in this Union, in which Freemasonry has *ceased to have an existence?*

Address, *Vermont Antimasonic Convention,* 1833

No party so intolerant and anti-republican, no party so obstructive to social, domestic, and civil happiness, and especially, no party so destructive to religious toleration and religious enjoyment—has existed in our country since the revolution.

Farmers' Herald, 30 September 1829

Approximately one month after William Morgan disappeared in western New York, Joseph Burnham, a prisoner in Windsor, Vermont, died. Friends or relatives claimed the body and buried it in nearby Woodstock, but rumors flew that Burnham was still alive, that witnesses had sighted him in New York City, and that the Masons had sprung him. In 1829 alarmed citizens demanded an investigation and the Vermont legislature appointed three lawmakers to determine the truth. Commissioner John Smith hurried to New York City, interrogated the witnesses, and offered a $500 reward for producing Burnham. The state also promised Burnham a pardon, but he never materialized and the witnesses proved to be without credibility. Yet suspicion still lingered and it was necessary to disinter the body to convince the skeptical that Burnham was indeed dead and that the Masons had not substituted another corpse. The Burnham case revealed that Antimasonic paranoia had swept across western New York and into Vermont. Nowhere in the United States did the Antimasonic Persuasion find proportionately so many adherents who cast their ballots for a third party devoted to the extermination of Freemasonry.[1]

The banner Antimasonic state in the Union, Vermont displayed remarkable enthusiasm for a series of passionate social movements during the second quarter of the nineteenth century when Antimasonry, then abolitionism, and finally the Free Soil party mushroomed, as did Millerite Adventists who believed that the millennium was set to begin between March 1843 and March 1844. Finally in the 1850s the social movements which for a generation had distinguished this landlocked mountain community either subsided or merged with the Republican party. Then Vermont politics froze. For the next hundred years, Vermont rarely deviated from overwhelming attachment to the party of Lincoln.[2]

The erruption of Antimasonry in Vermont coincided with the end of that state's self-sufficiency and isolation and marked the beginning of its integration into the economic and cultural life of an emerging industrial society. This transition left many Vermonters unsure of whether to reject or embrace the new order. Many opted for both, a social schizophrenia that allowed people seemingly to purge the Green Mountains of the evils of modernity, as embodied in Freemasonry, without compelling them to forgo more tangible fruits of modernization.

Antimasonic sentiment appeared in Vermont in 1827. Martin Flint was the pioneer in a course others soon followed. He publicly seceded from the Masonic Lodge in Randolph, Vermont, and that town emerged as headquarters of the Antimasonic party's state committee. In 1828, Flint journeyed to LeRoy, New York, to attend an Antimasonic convention in the heart of William Morgan's country. There he learned first-hand more about the mysterious case and received encouragement from the ardor of the original Antimasons. Between Vermont and western New York there were close, long-standing ties formed by heavy migration for over a generation. One of Morgan's abductors, Orson Parkhurst, had been initiated in a Vermont Lodge, the state's first, in Springfield, only nine months before the kidnapping. Parkhurst's involvement indicated that what had transpired in New York might also occur in Vermont. Moreover, when the going got rough for Masons in New York, Vermont became a natural refuge.[3]

Alarmed citizens discovered that Masons occupied many high offices and exerted extensive influence all over the state, a fact few had previously realized. When President Jackson removed Antimasons from federal office and replaced them with Masons, the power of the Order seemed to reach into the White House. Prominent leaders in both Democratic and National Republican parties were Masons, including Governor Samuel Crafts (1828–30). These discoveries led to the next stage in Vermont Antimasonry: the nomination of candidates pledged against Masonry. Yet even before a statewide party developed, Antimasons in Caledonia County fielded William Cahoon for Congress in 1828 against a National Republican. After eight polls, Cahoon finally won a majority. Then in 1829 county conventions of Antimasons prepared for the forthcoming gubernatorial contest. The Antimasons named Heman Allen, a National Republican. Though

Allen declined, he polled almost 30 percent of the vote. The contest marked the revival of competitive party politics in Vermont.[4]

Earlier in the century, Vermont had develeoped two highly competitive political parties. In 1807 the Jeffersonian Republicans achieved their first breakthrough in Vermont, and though the War of 1812 revived Federalist fortunes briefly, the Republicans reasserted their dominance in 1815. By 1818 Federalism was dead and during the next decade an amalgamated single party captured the governorship without serious opposition. Presidential politics in the run up to the 1828 election stimulated party revival but the Jacksonian forces remained weak and the Nationals swept three-quarters of the popular vote for President John Q. Adams. Even with Jackson in the White House, Vermont Democratic prospects remained poor. Meanwhile the Antimasons forged ahead. By 1831 they won a plurality and the governorship. For five years they remained the largest party in Vermont.[5]

One of the rare third parties in American politics to emerge as the dominant force, even if for only half a decade, Vermont Antimasons benefited from a low level of political mobilization in the state. Large numbers of voters were unattached to either the Democratic or National Republican parties and were disinclined to attend the polls. At the mass electoral base and among the leadership, the Antimasons attracted former Federalists and Jeffersonian voters, but they also garnered a large share of the newer voters who came of political age after the battle of the First American Party System had slipped into history.[6]

Vermont Antimasons rode into power on a surge of increased voter participation. The presidential contest in 1828 had almost doubled the turnout rate generated by the race for governor that year. Subsequent turnouts remained high and reached better than two-thirds of the adult males in the 1832 gubernatorial election, a level not surpassed until 1838. (Table 7.1.[7]) Partisan feelings generated by Antimasonary were intense. "For violence and recklessness of spirit, the excitement has no parallel in our annals," wrote a contemporary. "The ties even of consanguinity have not been able to stay its remorseless hand. It has separated brother from brother."[8]

Regression estimates comparing the 1832 presidential vote with the vote four years earlier point to two principal sources of the Antimasonic strength: about half derived from National Republican switchers and half from persons who did not vote in 1828. (Table 7.2.[9]) When the Democrats and Whigs formed a coalition to crush the third party in 1833, their strategy backfired. Many National Republicans deserted and the Antimasonic governor, William Palmer, won a majority (53 percent), the best showing in the party's history. By 1836, Vermont Antimasonry had run its course.

Antimasonry swept Vermont because many citizens believed that the question of Freemasonry took precedence over the differences between Democrats and National Republicans. At the time that the Antimasonic party was gestating, the programmatic divisions between the Nationals and Democrats were still fuzzy. Even after President Jackson vetoed the Maysville Road bill—opposing federal funds for an internal improvement entirely within one state—revealed his moderate tariff preferences, and moved against the Second Bank of the United States to define national Democratic party policy, he failed to polarize Vermont in the early 1830s or to provide the basis for distinctive issue appeals. On questions of economic development, there was broad consensus in Vermont. Wool production was so central to commercial agriculture that all parties favored tariff protection. Differences over public funding for internal improvements were more likely to revolve around who received benefits than around constitutional scruples or principles of political economy. Finally, neither anti-bank nor hard money policy generated much support in Vermont before 1834, though many who valued appropriately regulated state banks were critical of the Bank of the United States, even if they did not endorse President Jackson's frontal assault. The 1830 Antimasonic Convention ignored national issues and the next year focused exclusively on Masonry because "the evident unanimity of the people of this state on the leading measures of national policy" left "but one main question . . . whether Freemasonry shall, or shall not longer hold her dominion over us." In 1833, Antimasons reaffirmed support for "those leading measures of national policy in relation to the judiciary, currency, protection to domestic industry and internal improvement, of which we have hitherto expressed our approbation."[10] Perceiving Henry Clay and Andrew Jackson as front men for the Masons, the Antis charged that both major parties conspired to suppress the spread of Antimasonry by raising diversions. Clay had originally come forward as champion of the American System, which included a high tariff, but as soon as Mason Jackson entered the White House and favored tariff reduction, Mason Clay abandoned "his honest supporters and faithful friends to the Tariff [who] were left without a compass to guide their political course surrounded with the covering of masonic darkness." By refusing to subordinate Antimasonry to the American System, Antimasons insisted in setting political priorities. They favored pro-development policy but not uncritically, for their fear of Masonry stemmed from an ambivalence towards modernity. Antimasonry was no single issue party, as critics claimed, but no single issue was so important as the destruction of Freemasonry.[11]

For Vermont Antimasons, the central question facing the state was whether the transition from agricultural self-sufficiency to a market economy, and from cultural homogeneity to heterogeneity, jeopardized Christian Republicanism. A plurality of Vermont voters demonstrated that, at a time when loyalty to a national party was still emerging, a popular movement at the state level, at least in Vermont, could shape the political agenda.

Antimasonic strength spread widely but evenly across Vermont. The strong Antimasonic towns tended to cluster in four areas. In the Northeast, Caledonia County was the party stronghold, with Antimasonry overflowing into Orleans County to the north. On the west side of the Green Mountains bordering on Lake Champlain, Addison County was the second epicenter of Antimasonry, extending into Rutland County. Windsor County formed the third center, overflowing into Windham County and among the mountain towns of Orange County. Finally Franklin County, bordering on Canada, had plenty of Antimasonic voters. This clustering of the Antimasonic vote suggests that Antimasonic sentiment extended in an infectious pattern, from one town to an adjoining one, until it reached communities whose soil proved unreceptive. Behind such broad-based geographic support with regional concentrations, together with the tendency for many communities to give landslides to one party, stand complex demographic and leadership patterns that shed further light on who gravitated to Antimasonry and why.[12]

Vermont Antimasons adopted a characteristically anti-aristocratic posture, identifying Masons as an aspiring, conspiratorial, anti-republican elite, and Vermont Antis did not stand alone in sounding the alarm against elitism.[13] A newspaper in Woodstock, Vermont, the home of a strong Antimasonic movement and also a short-lived Workingmen's party, condemned the prevalence of "village aristocracy," which was likely to "end in nothing short of despotism."[14] A leading Freemason blamed the popularity of Antimasonry on the gullibility of Vermonters who avidly read newspapers but failed to separate truth from fiction. "The absurd declamations" filling the Antimasonic press, he explained, exploited "the prejudices of the lower classes." The success of Antimasonry revealed the weakness of the state's elites. "We live under a government, not of bayonets, but of Newspapers," Masons complained, for every day, public opinion, under their influence, grew more perverted.[15] A decade after the decline of Antimasonry, a Congregationalist minister, John Beckley, in his *History of Vermont* (1846), spotlighted the prevalence of intense factionalism among leading citizens. A "system of clan warfare," he said, plagued Vermont and "lessened the enjoyment of social intercourse."[16] Thus from a variety of perspectives the vulnerability of Vermont's upper strata to intense and widespread attack from within and without seemed a feature of the state's social order.

Yet when one compares Antimasonic leaders with staunch Masons, the Antis were neither newcomers, outsiders, obscure or politically inexperienced men, a "mass of stupidity . . . hardly qualified for hog-reeves," according to the *Bennington Gazette*.[17] While Masonry recruited from among the town and village bourgeoisie, including in its ranks businessmen, professionals, officeholders, and other community leaders, so did the Antimasons. A collective biography of leaders suggests that Antimasons were somewhat older than Masons and were more likely to engage in professional occupations than in business. Both drew from the ranks of prominent men, most of whom held public office.[18] Farmers were not an important element in either group. Antimasonry in part grew out of a split within Vermont's upper strata. This had important political consequences because the Antis were able to muster substantial popular support.

Vermont's development in the early nineteenth century nurtured Antimasonry because it strained elite unity and group harmony. Popular acquiescence in elite governance and the collapse of party competition during the Era of Good Feelings (1817–27) did not prove lasting. Antimasonry flourished particularly in towns experiencing relatively high rates of population change. While farmers modestly increased the Antimasonic showing, other measures of economic growth tended to depress the Antimasonic vote. The Nationals were strong in areas with high land valuations, lots of sheep, and where people engaged in commerce, which suggests an affinity between the party and communities in the forefront of economic development, whereas the Democrats tended to run best where there were few sheep, land values were low, and population stagnant. (Table 7.3.[19])

Antimasonry seemed to flourish especially in communities that were neither the most advanced nor the most laggard in economic development but in the middle range.[20] Between 1820 and 1840 the two banner Antimasonic counties ranked fourth and seventh in population growth among the state's fourteen counties. Antimasons supported the American System but they gave priority to anti-aristocratic and anti-monopoly politics, indicating that they were unusually sensitive to the social costs of modernization.

Freemasonry, the Antis argued, was "an aristocratic and monopolizing" system that conferred privileges on a few and made "direct war upon the rights of the rest." It subverted the constitution which placed "every individual in a perfect level with his neighbor as to the enjoyment of all the rights and immunities," elevating an elite on secret principles and without community consent.[21] Why the anti-monopoly theme evoked such strong resonance in Vermont becomes evident from an examination of the state's development from a frontier society.

"The State of Vermont was settled at a comparatively recent period," B. F. Bailey informed the Secretary of the Treasury in 1832, "and though it was believed to exceed most of the northern states in fertility, yet the roughness of the surface of the country, and the density of the forests with which it was everywhere covered, have rendered the task of subduing the soil, and reducing it to cultivation, a labor of very great difficulty . . ." Though there was still little manufacturing in Vermont in 1832, by the 1820s, household agricultural production had sharply declined, evidence of the rapid growth of commercial agriculture.[22]

Vermont experienced the transition to a commercial agricultural economy in less than two generations. The early settlers came from New York, New Hampshire, Massachusetts, and especially Connecticut. The influx came from southern New England towns that had long moved beyond the self-enclosed Puritan village. People poured into Vermont in the late eighteenth century seeking to escape overcrowding and attracted by a free market in land and extensive speculation. Early provisions for town support of religion, in the old New England tradition, failed to inhibit the growth of sectarianism or, conversely, the neglect of the church. Congregationalists, the largest denomination in the founding period, occupied a precarious position. Vermont early won a reputation as a center of popular deism and skepticism and also for its receptivity to enthusiastic forms of Christianity. Rapid population growth further intensified pluralist tendencies.

The state's first great boom took place in the generation following the American Revolution. The population soared from 30,000 in 1783 to better than five times that number by the century's end, making Vermont the fastest growing state in the 1790s. Vermont continued to expand rapidly, registering a 40 percent gain in the first decade of the nineteenth century. Vermont's growth stagnated in the 1830s, reached 300,000 by 1850, but barely exceeded that figure during the next century.

Remoteness and poor transport limited the development of commercial agriculture in early Vermont. Wheat was the leading crop, and in the 1790s, one good harvest could pay for the cost of a farm. In a few years a farmer might accumulate enough to provide farms for his children; even a farm laborer in 1800 could buy 100 acres with a few years' savings. Plant disease and the spread of wheat culture further west doomed Vermont's grain economy, forcing the state to import flour by the early nineteenth century. Vermont farmers turned to raising sheep and cattle, and wool emerged as an important source of revenue. The introduction of merino sheep early in the century was a great boon since Vermont was so well suited for pasture. By the mid-1820s there were almost half a million sheep grazing on Green Mountain grasses, and the number more than doubled by 1840. Propelled by rising prices, especially in the period 1827–35, Vermont emerged as a major producer of raw material for American wool manufacture which centered in neighboring Massachusetts. Because competition from foreign wool was intense and wool manufacturers preferred the cheapest source, the battle over protection for American growers was fierce. Vermont politicians naturally enlisted on the side of the sheep farmers. In addition to sheep, cattle became another important staple. Farmers in southern Vermont supplied dairy and meat for growing markets in Massachusetts and southern New England, and when the wool economy went into decline in the 1840s, dairy farming replaced it.[23]

Transportation improvements early in the nineteenth century gave producers access to markets. From the 1790s, construction of turnpikes in southern Vermont connected the major market towns with the Connecticut River and Lake Champlain. Flat boats carried merchandise down the Connecticut River, but it was access to Lake Champlain that enabled Vermont to partake most fully in the transportation revolution. There the steamboat *Vermont* demonstrated in 1809 the value of the new mode of travel, and by 1823 a system of steamboats plied the lake, giving western Vermont access to the Erie Canal via the Champlain branch, and an all-water route to New York City.[24]

The new wealth generated by the developing market economy spread unevenly. By the first decade of the nineteenth century a sizable portion of the population left the state; over 20 percent of the towns suffered a decline in population. Even during the 1790s, the decade of greatest growth, the Genesee Fever pulled people from southern Vermont into western New York. Thin, unproductive soils that quickly wore out, hilly land unsuitable for agriculture, and the large families produced by the first generation of pioneers resulted in emigration from the older towns. The sheep boom opened new opportunities but it also tended to squeeze people off the land. In the areas most suitable to wool growing, there was a tendency for successful farmers to buy out the less successful.[25]

Within one or two generations the opportunity structure in Vermont changed significantly. The first generation, which had migrated in the late eighteenth century, was confident of its ability to acquire land and provide for their children, but by the 1820s, landlessness, tenancy, and indebtedness were growing problems. The greatest pressure fell on the younger generation. Rising land values priced many out of the market, and those who borrowed often risked their freedom. By the 1820s debtors' prison annually claimed a significant toll, becoming home for hundreds of people between 1827–29, and eventually a movement was started to abolish imprisonment for debt. Mechanics in many villages also faced discouraging prospects. The artisan ladder that had carried apprentices to masterships no longer worked well in communities that stopped growing or grew slowly. There were a few scattered factories, but wage earners there had even poorer prospects of becoming proprietors. A Workingmen's movement appeared briefly from 1830 to 1832 in Woodstock, Middlebury, Burlington, and several of the larger towns, to protest against the artisans' declining fortunes.[26]

Falling birth rates also registered shifts in opportunity. The sharpest drop occurred in the Connecticut River Valley from 1800 to 1810, though birth rates continued to fall during the next three decades. The trend became most pronounced in the market and manufacturing towns and in the best-endowed farming communities. By limiting the number of children families adapted to diminishing local opportunities despite rising national expectations.[27]

The commercial development of Vermont followed an uneven pattern. Wool production was lucrative throughout most of the 1820s and 1830s, but smaller producers found it difficult to compete with larger ones. While many towns stopped growing or experienced decline by the 1830s, one group emerged as dominant. The ten largest cities and towns in 1910, each with over five thousand people, diverged notably from the rest by the 1830 census, when their growth rate considerably outpaced the statewide average. Against such towns the smaller marketing centers, the poorly endowed hill and mountain towns, slipped further behind. Even more important, the social distance between citizens in the two types of communities widened.[28]

The rapid but uneven growth that quickly plunged frontier Vermont into a national market economy made citizens especially sensitive to the contradictions between the assumptions of republican theory that small, independent property holders were the foundations of a republican order and the new realities in the Green Mountain State: thousands had to migrate or accept wage labor and dependency. Governor Jonas Galusha in 1818, observing an increasing flow of requests from businessmen for charters of incorporation, interpreted this as a sign "that secret ambition to aggrandize himself, and promote his own ends" had corrupted civic virtue and chilled a citizen's "general ardor for the concerns of his country." Galusha's warning prefigured later Antimasonic indictments of Freemasonry.[29] The first Antimasonic meeting in Vermont at Randolph in May 1828 condemned the Order for tending to establish "an unnatural and unwarranted distinction, a species of favoritism and aristocracy, derogatory to the equality of a free and independent people." The Masons had fashioned a new form of "close communion," admitting those who possessed only plenty "of the one thing needed—cash."[30] After the great Antimasonic victory in 1831, Masons expressed dismay that "all at once the confidence of thousands seems to be withdrawn from men of the purest lives, the brightest talents, and the most tried integrity and bestowed upon the uncertain, the discarded, and the insignificant."[31]

Antimasonry offered an explanation of why some men prospered and others did not. Masons enjoyed advantages through access to the ambitious and influential, and they aided one another in the competitive race. Outsiders perceived Freemasonry as a network of upwardly mobile men linked by familial, entrepreneurial, cultural, and fraternal ties. The geography of Masonry's progress in the Green Mountain State clearly followed the lines of economic development, confirming such surmises. In the half-century following the appearance of Vermont's first Lodge in 1781, seventy-two more received charters. "Who would have thought?" exclaimed the *North Star*, an Antimasonic newspaper in Danville, "*Seventy three* secret conclaves in the small state of Vermont, devoted to the works of darkness and self-aggrandizement!"[32] More than two-thirds of the largest towns in the state, with populations over 1900 in 1830, boasted Lodges, compared to just under 30 percent of all towns. In Windham County towns with Lodges averaged twice the number of lawyers and doctors as those without Lodges; the picture was similar in Windsor County.[33] In the larger towns the growing central villages, the main locus of business activity, tended to oppose Antimasonry, whereas the smaller eastern or western villages, less commercialized, tended to support the third party.[34]

In 1829 more than 160 loyal Freemasons signed a public defense of the brotherhood in an appeal to public opinion. A quarter of the signatories resided in Burlington and Montpelier alone.[35] Those who vouched for Masonry in its time of trial were generally men in the forefront of Vermont's transformation, including presidents of banks, large-scale merchants, surgeons, lawyers, newspaper publishers, and political leaders, and it was precisely such prominent men Antimasons singled out for moral scrutiny. The most important arenas in which such inquiries took place were the churches. Vermont Antimasons knit together a coalition of various denominations. The *St. Alban's Repository,* a pro-Masonic journal, shrewdly asserted that the Antimasonic party united "heterogeneous ingredients, an amalgamized mass of Calvinist, Baptist, and Universalist preachers."[36] Except for a few Episcopalians and Unitarians, Vermont's clergy split sharply over Freemasonry and there were bitter quarrels within many churches.[37] The grounds of division generally rested on strains between modernist and anti-modernist currents that tore churches apart.

Antimasons did not politicize religion in Vermont. Vermont's constitution established in attenuated form the New England principle of a state church, but from the beginning pluralist and tolerationist sentiment circumscribed the success with which Congregationalists, such as many who migrated from Connecticut, could reproduce the New England Way in the Green Mountains. Ethan Allen, one of the state's founding fathers, was author of the *Oracle of Reason,* the most important popular expression of natural religion produced by an American in the late eighteenth century. Many early Vermonters shared Allen's skepticism of revealed Christianity. The Vermont religious settlement consequently reflected diversity at the outset. The law allowed the first denomination which secured a majority in town meeting to secure the ministerial lands. Each town had the authority to tax its citizens to support the faith of their choice, although during the pioneer period some made no provision for religious worship. Though the Congregationalists were the leading denomination, they failed to resist demands by other groups and by Nothingarians for complete separation, a cause that Jeffersonians cautiously embraced and brought to fruition in 1807. Vermont thus led the way towards disestablishment in New England, and, as elsewhere, churches flourished in the aftermath of separation.[38]

Denominational attachments gave identity to communities. Samuel Robinson, founder of Bennington and a large landowner in the formative era, intended to make the town a Congregationalist haven, but because others arrived, Robinson reconciled faith and profit by segregating Episcopalians in nearby Arlington and Baptists in Shaftsbury.[39] Efforts at promoting religious homogeneity did not succeed. At first religious minorities concentrated in areas of strength but then they moved into rapidly growing, desirable towns, even if the Congregationalists had arrived first.

Dissenters quickly asserted themselves after the downfall of the establishment which Federalist and Congregationalists had sustained. The second largest denomination, the Baptists, rapidly advanced into the political limelight. The Baptists elected one of their own as governor, Jonas Galusha, who served six terms (1812–19), followed by Ezra Butler, a Baptist minister from Woodbury, who was also elected to Congress. He later became an outspoken Antimason.[40] The Universalists also won recognition. Gaining a strong foothold in southern Vermont early in the century, Universalists were proud to see members of their faith chosen to high office.[41] Methodists, Free Will Baptists, Christians also prospered in Vermont's tolerant atmosphere. They too contributed important strength to the Antimasonic movement.[42] Even after disestablishment, quarrels over the uses of town-owned meeting houses, over remaining ministerial lands and funds, over testimony by Universalists in the courts, and over the right of ministers to perform marriage ceremonies generated continued grounds for sectarian bickering, in addition to the ever intense competition for souls.

Voting in the 1828 presidential election showed clear denominational predilections. Congregationalists and Baptists, mostly from Calvinist traditions, boosted the National Republican vote; Methodists and Free Will Baptists, the Democratic vote. Universalism had no statistically clear impact. This pattern reappeared in 1836 and throughout the heyday of the Second American Party System except that Universalism benefited the Whigs.[43] Thus even before Antimasonry became an important political force and after its demise, religion and politics intersected. "To subserve the interests of party, different sects must be made to suspect, and hate, and villify each other," noted one observer of the partisan uses of sectarian division.[44] The appearance of the Antimasons on the Vermont ballot altered some of the 1828 patterns. Congregationalists continued to boost the National Republican vote but the statistics obscure deep divisions over Freemasonry within this denomination. Baptists boosted the Antimasonic vote as did the Universalists. The Free Will Baptists remained strongly linked to the Democrats, and the Methodists were fragmented, yet both denominations contributed prominent leaders to the Antimasonic movement.

Antimasonry divided Vermont denominations as intensely as any issue, for many Freemasons were church members. Half the Masons studied by Randolph Roth belonged to a church, and though they were more likely to be members of a non-Calvinist denomination, they were affiliated with almost every denomination. Moreover, Roth found a close link between Masonic church members and other secular associations: 80 percent of the Masons entered partnerships with brother Masons who were also church members. Participation in each association reinforced the other, distinguishing men more clearly as middle-class modernists and facilitating the formation of entrepreneurial networks. Access to credit and capital became a critical resource for master mechanics and petty merchants risking the transition from simple commodity exchange to capitalistic enterprise. Associations forged in churches and Lodges and elsewhere strengthened the bonds of trust and delineated the lines of patronage.[45]

Vermont clergymen bitterly divided over the issue of Masonry. When one compares the religious affiliation of Masonic with Antimasonic activists several patterns emerge, though incomplete information requires caution. Congregationalists were the most numerous denomination among both groups and divided sharply (13 to 16) whereas all thirteen Baptists and Methodists were Antis and the ten Episcopalians and Unitarians were Masonic loyalists. Eight of the ten Universalists were Antimasons and three listed in the sources as "liberals" not associated with any denomination were Masons. Perhaps most tellingly, the Antimasons were more likely to be affiliated with some denomination (37%) compared to the Masons (25%).[46]

Religious Antimasonry did not spring suddenly out of the air. Since the 1790s there had been isolated attacks on Masonry in particular churches, mostly Calvinistic, yet they did not generate a movement or political party until the growth of industrial society by the 1820s and the accompanying spread of secular values created fertile soil for a reaction against modernist tendencies.[47] As conservative laymen after 1826 became receptive to Antimasonic feelings, ministers who had harbored such sentiments but had kept them under wraps could voice their opinions. Others who had joined the Order suddenly recognized their error. A shift in public opinion shaped the attitudes of clergy and, in turn, outspoken ministers influenced public opinion. Opponents of Antimasonry recognized the powerful role played by clergy and churches, and they denounced Antimasons as "puritans," fanatics, bigots, pious hypocrites, and advocates of a union of church and state.[48]

The battles among Congregationalists over Masonry were among the most heated and revealing. Vermont Congregationalism was diverse, sheltering Hopkinsians, moderate Calvinists, and Unitarians. The state's two leading educational institutions, the University of Vermont, founded in 1799, and Middlebury College (1802), reflected those divergent tendencies. The state university, established as a non-denominational institution in a pluralistic society, had a succession of liberal, Congregationalist minister-presidents, with Unitarian and later transcendentalist tendencies. Middlebury, located in the heart of Addison County, the second strongest Antimasonic county, rallied the Calvinists, who moved swiftly to create their own college when the University of Vermont failed to serve their purposes and its feeble beginning opened an opportunity for another institution. Middlebury quickly gained the ascendancy in wealth, size, and influence and became an important training ground for future Antimasons. Led by moderate Calvinists, Middlebury shrewdly sought to broaden its denominational base. In 1810 Rev. Asa Burton, Vermont's leading Hopkinsian Calvinist, switched from the board of the state university to Middlebury's. Hopkinsian Leonard Worcester followed in 1818. Middlebury honored Baptist leaders such as Rev. Aaron Leland, who served on its board from the beginning. It even made overtures to the Universalists by granting in 1829 an honorary degree to Rev. Samuel Loveland, a leading Antimason.[49]

Antimasonry entered the Congregational churches when some members demanded that Masonic communicants resign from the Order. In Norwich, Dr. Israel Newton, a veteran of the American Revolution, holder of numerous offices, deacon for a quarter-century, and inventor of Newton's Bitters and Pills, refused to attend communion with Masons. In 1829, churches in Weybridge, Addison, and Panton in strongly Antimasonic Addison County, expelled Masons. Congregationalist churches torn between pro- and anti-Masonic factions in the Caledonia, Montpelier, and Orleans Associations appealed for a special council for guidance. A carefully balanced body that included one Hopkinsian, one Mason, and a moderate Calvinist searched for middle ground. It declared that Masonic oaths were "profane and repugnant to the laws of morality and religion," but acknowledged that Masons denied that they took the oaths literally, and many undoubtedly pious men were Freemasons. Yet the council suggested that because Masonry offended some members, Freemasons should voluntarily withdraw from the Order. Christian forbearance was essential if the churches were to avoid damage.[50]

Antimasons rejected counsel of forbearance. Equating Masonry with evil, they insisted on a purge. In Danville (89% Antimasonic in 1832), the county seat and also the county's most populous town—site of the bank, jail, court house, grist mills, and four denominations in 1830—one of the town's foremost citizens, Israel P. Dana, a loyal Freemason, was accused by Antimasons of unchristian conduct. The Danville Congregationalist church, the town's oldest, led for fifteen years by a student of Nathanael Emmons, the Hopkinsian leader, demanded that Dana, a tavern keeper and merchant whose store was a center of the town's social life, withdrew from Freemasonry and publicly renounce it. Dana refused to accept humiliation and his church rejected mediation, expelling Masons unwilling to bow before its authority.[51]

Just south of Danville in Peacham, a town that voted 70 percent for the Antimasons in 1832, the Congregationalist church was also the scene of an Antimasonic purge. Militants insisted that the Masons renounce. When the Masons refused, a majority voted to expel them. By 1831, the Antis had triumphed. Hazen Merrill, a Peacham Antimason, reported that "the subject of Masonry seemed to be settled in the county in the churches especially." After a long contest, the church finally "came to a decision which is thought to be permanent." The Masons agreed that they would "have no more to do with it [Masonry] as long as they live." The controversy pitted a group of Peacham businessmen, including Dr. Josiah Shedd, Deputy Grand Master, bound by marriage to one of the state's leading families, against Rev. Leonard Worcester. Trained by Emmons, Worcester served forty-seven years in Peacham. After two revivals, his church had become one of the largest in the state by 1831, despite its tough discipline. Working his own farm, counting every penny, educating five sons for the ministry and a sixth for medicine, Rev. Worcester was an unworldly, old-fashioned preacher who left his frame house unpainted so no one might think he put on airs. He thereby affirmed his humility and bonds with the less affluent farmers.[52]

Adherence to tradition was also the key to Antimasonry's strength in nearby Barnett and Ryegate (87% and 57% Antimasonic in 1833). Settled in the eighteenth century by Scottish immigrants who gave Caledonia County its name, the towns were still dominated by Scots in the 1820s, led by Barnett's ministers, David and Thomas Goodwillie, father and son, who presided over the Associated Presbyterian church, while Rev. James Milligan preached at the Scottish Reformed Covenanters Presbyterian church in Ryegate. Both towns were especially homogeneous, experienced limited economic development, and enjoyed reputations for an exceptional degree of piety and morals. Because the churches encompassed a large proportion of the populace and the in-grown ethnic community remained a tight community, towns like Barnett became known for better observing the sabbath than other communities swept by the tides of change.[53]

The purges in Congregational churches imposed new standards of membership. By disciplining Masons, evangelicals reaffirmed church authority over private life. This engendered considerable opposition. Democrats and National Republicans, as well as Freemasons, accused the Antimasonic clergy of aspiring to become a priesthood which threatened freedom of conscience. In 1830 Rev. U. C. Burnap, pastor of the Congregational church in Chester, defended ministerial activism. The cry of priestcraft was merely "an epithet" gotten up "for party purposes." Churches were voluntary associations and pastors could only assert moral leadership. In other countries "priestcraft" was a serious evil, but the United States remained "the only place on the face of the earth where priestcraft is unknown." The real danger lay in the erosion of church authority and the spread of secularism. There were too many churchgoers, Burnap complained, who attend to only "the forms of godliness," people who "want something to call religion," even "if they no longer believed in revealed religion" and preferred to "receive a system from man." Burnap did not explicitly refer to Freemasonry but his allusion was plain. He defended those evangelical clergy who struggled against the "unprincipled and lecherous." Despite meager material rewards, such men worked tirelessly for "the preservation of our Republican institutions . . . the happiness of our domestic circles . . . the security of our immortal interests. . . ." Some states such as New York, Burnap noted, denied ministers the right to hold public office and even refused corporate charters to religious societies, preferring to dispense them to "a set of speculating—money-making men" engaged in business ventures. Vermont fortunately welcomed the clergy in public life.[54]

Though many Congregationalist and Presbyterian churches supported Antimasonry, there were others captured by theological liberals friendly to Freemasonry. Liberal clergyman Robinson Smiley of Springfield served as Grand Chaplain of the Grand Lodge of Vermont. He had received his training from Rev. William Emerson, the liberal father of Ralph Waldo Emerson. Likewise Rev. James Johnson of Williston, another loyal Mason, attended Harvard where he studied with Henry Ware, one of the foremost

Unitarian leaders. Similarly there was a connection between Masonry and the liberals at the University of Vermont. Because Vermont's liberal Congregationalists did not split off and form a separate denomination—as Unitarians eventually did in Massachusetts—their claim to be part of the same tradition that included Hopkinsians and other Calvinists confused and compromised standards of faith. The battle against Freemasonry was therefore in part a fight against liberal currents in the Congregational churches.[55]

At the very time Antimasonry swept through Vermont, a wave of religious revivals unfolded, peaking in 1830–31. Over 1600 converts joined Congregationalist churches in 1830 and in the next year almost half of all towns with Congregational churches (99) reported revivals.[56] In the period just preceding the Great Revival, the statewide association of Congregational churches attacked hypocrisy and laxity among church members, especially those who desecrated the Sabbath and violated the new temperance norms. Secularism within the denomination, infidelity and pluralism outside, placed Congregationalists under severe strain.[57] In 1829 the Vermont Legislature appointed a Unitarian to deliver the next election sermon, in keeping with the rotation principle. The *Vermont Chronicle,* the weekly organ of Congregationalists, favored abolishing the election sermon rather than allow the state to confer legitimacy on "heresy." In an extraordinary editorial the editor probed deeply into the national malaise that had just led the United States Congress to reject the Sabbatarian petitions to close the post offices on Sundays. Brushing aside the contention that Sabbath closure violated state neutrality towards religion, the *Chronicle* argued that the Sabbatarian defeat resulted from pervasive moral corruption. Postal workers must work on the Lord's Day "because otherwise, somebody will be in danger of losing five cents a bushel on wheat." Americans had become "an altered people" who viewed moral questions from the perspective of how they affected them materially. "To become rich, or at least 'independent,' has been so easy and so common, that everybody calculates upon it, incited by splendid day-dreams of wealth and greatness for themselves and their children . . . ," the *Chronicle* observed. People judged everything "according to its value in the market." The *Vermont Chronicle,* like the Vermont Congregationalist Association, kept silent on the question of Masonry, but when many Masonic Lodges voted to dissolve in 1834, the *Chronicle* heartily approved.[58]

By 1835 both Antimasonry and the Great Revival had ebbed and the future looked bleak to Vermont Congregationalists, who reported that half the state's churches had no settled pastor and a fourth no regular preaching; ministerial tenures remained insecure, often broken without sufficient cause. Parents neglected religious education of children, everywhere people profaned the Sabbath, and now a new danger loomed—emigration on a large scale. The next year conditions grew worse. Secularism continued to plague the churches. Propelled by "merely worldly motives, mainly to increase their wealth and provide large estates for their children," the Vermont faithful "removed from Bethlehem where the true God was known and worshipped to a pagan country. . . ." Instead of living for Christ people lived for "fashion, pleasure, riches, self-aggrandizement or self-pleasing." Yet such folk stood in good standing in the Christian community as did Freemasons before the Great Green Mountain Purge.[59]

Antimasonry also invaded the peace of Vermont's Baptist churches. As early as the 1790s Baptist Masons encountered hostility. While some churches condemned membership in the Order, there was no accepted denominational position. After 1826, Baptist ministers and laymen became active in the Antimasonic movement and purges, and Baptists were prominent at Antimasonic conventions and in the state legislature. The appeal of the Antimasonic Persuasion to Vermont Baptists stemmed from developments within the denomination in the decades preceding the Morgan case.[60]

By the 1820s Vermont Baptists had experienced striking change since the early days. Descended largely from eighteenth-century New England Congregationalists who had separated from the state churches before the American Revolution, they had weathered persecution and low social status. Some migrated to the much freer atmosphere of Vermont. In towns where Baptists arrived first, they could claim the glebe lands. Unwilling to suffer civil disability at the hands of Congregationalists, Baptists gravitated to the Jeffersonian Republican party. Together with other dissenters, they overthrew the religious establishment a decade earlier than in Connecticut and a quarter-century earlier than in Massachusetts. The Baptists prospered in the years following separation. The second largest denomination in Vermont, they won increasing recognition in local office, the Congress, and the legislature. Vermont inaugurated its first Baptist governor thirty years before Massachusetts followed suit. Thus from a small sect, Vermont Baptists by the early nineteenth century achieved influence and respectability outside their own community.

Within the denomination itself, change proceeded rapidly. In 1824 Vermont Baptists organized their first state convention. In 1828 they formed a Sunday School Union, and two years later a branch of the Northern Baptist Educational Society. Overcoming prejudices against formal education, they founded three academies in the 1830s, including the Vermont Literary and Scientific Institution at Brandon in 1833. But growing respectability exacted a price. As Baptists prospered and assimilated modernist currents, many were apprehensive about the cost. Many Baptists clung to sectarian isolation. They practiced closed communion, adhered to conservative Calvinist doctrine, readily disciplined members, and promptly expelled the recreant. Modernist and traditional currents existed uneasily side by side, especially as many upwardly mobile Baptists moved in mixed company outside sectarian circles. As some Baptists achieved prominence and wealth, others who did not sensed that a gulf was opening within the fold. The price of sectarian purity had been uniformity and homogeneity; earlier in the century churches had even expelled Federalists. In the 1820s and 1830s they split over making teetotalism a test for membership, and after 1826, Freemasonry divided them deeply.

Baptist churches in Addison County, a center of Antimasonry, seceded from the Vermont Association because it refused to exclude Masons from the churches. At its first meeting in 1833, the Addison Association required that member churches treat Masonry as other moral evils. A penchant for radical reform became a hallmark of this association, always alert to forces endangering Christian Republicanism. It welcomed R. B. James, agent of the Moral Reform Society, of New York, the anti-vice organization, and O. S. Murray, president of the Vermont Anti-slavery Society. Here, too, William Miller, later of Millerite fame, found a receptive audience. A member of a church in Orwel, Miller preached among the Baptists, and when his millennialist craze struck, the Addison Association was hard hit.[61]

Two characteristics helped account for the especial affinity of Vermont Baptists for Antimasonry. As practitioners of closed communion, many Vermont Baptists refused to extend fellowship to members of other denominations, however similar theologically. By adhering to sectarian exclusivity, Baptists resisted modernist, ecumenicizing pressures that tended to narrow differences among denominations. Freemasonry was a powerful solvent of sectarianism, for it conferred respectability on a variety of Christians from Unitarians and Episcopalians to Calvinists of all stripes. Masonry eroded the bonds of community that had knit together Baptists. A democratic and egalitarian tradition also made Baptists especially sensitive to people who put on airs, sought a formal education, and desired recognition outside the fold. "While a Mason," admitted Elder Leland, "I once tried to mix Masonry with religion—amalgamate the Lodge with the church but it would never do." "We must wholly give up the church or wholly discard Masonry," Leland told the Vermont Antimasonic Convention in 1830. Antimasonry, affirmed former governor Elder Ezra Butler, was "a work of God," inspired by "the special operation of the Holy Spirit" requiring Christians "to renounce and abandon this worthless institution."[62] The views of Leland and Butler were influential; both served as moderators of the Vermont State Baptist Convention. The Baptist Barre Association set the tone in 1830: "The difficulties of labors and discouraging aspects of the churches . . . is chiefly owing to the alliance of Freemasonry with the churches."[63]

In a Baptist stronghold such as Mount Holly (92% Antimasonic in 1832) cultural homogeneity, material underdevelopment, and geographic isolation on the west side of the Green Mountains nourished the Antimasonic Persuasion. As late as 1830 most families still engaged mainly in subsistence farming, had not developed a central village, and supported only two merchants, two doctors, but not a single lawyer until 1850. A poor backwater, Mount Holly made up in faith what it lacked in worldly accumulation. Led by Elder Daniel Packer, who arrived in 1811, the Mount Holly Baptists became one of the largest churches in the state. Packer, who served thirty-five years, baptized 1600 souls and doubled as town clerk. Even when Mount Holly folk moved away, they called their old preacher to officiate at weddings and funerals. When possible, Elder Packer obliged because "his generous heart yearned towards them; they were like children to him: they had grown up, temporally, as well as spiritually, under his kind ministrations."[64]

Neither doctrine nor ritual alone explains the religious sources of Vermont Antimasonry, for Calvinists, whether Baptists or Hopkinsian Congregationalists, made common cause with non-Calvinists among the Free Will Baptists, Christians (Disciples of Christ), and Universalists. Like many other preachers, Christian Elder Edward B. Rollins of Strafford joined a Masonic Lodge in 1825. Rollins ascended the Masonic ladder to the Royal Arch degree, but failed to find the promised illumination. Then he concluded that Masonry was fraudulent and dangerous. His Lodge admitted "corrupt characters," including "the profane, the drunkard and such like . . . [who] were frequently promoted to office," for they were among the most active members. Masonry's principles tended "to adulterate professors of christianity" and its practices were "sacrilegious and idolatrous," violating "every principle of HUMANITY, MORALITY, and RELIGION." From its earliest days men joined mainly for "gain and promotion."[65] The Antimasonic press widely circulated Rollins's renunciation, which reached Woodstock, another center of Antimasonry, where Deacon Charles Mackenzie, a founder of the town's Christian church, invited Rollins to spread his message. The Christians, like the Baptists, had a strong republican and egalitarian tradition. Preachers often mixed religious messages with attacks on the worldliness of the upper classes. Yet Christians were, like Freemasons, anti-sectarian, anti-dogmatic and practiced open communion. By renouncing Masonry, men like Elder Rollins hoped to "redeem the liberties of my country" and "deliver Zion from the influence and corruption of an Intruder, that has crept within her borders, and polluted her ministers, deceived her sons, and grieved her daughters."[66] Such sentiments also account for Antimasonry's appeal among Free Will Baptists and Quakers.[67]

"Let the preacher of the gospel defend the sacred volume, from masonic interpretation and masonic union," proclaimed Universalist minister Samuel Loveland at the 1831 state Antimasonic Convention.[68] Loveland was one of several Universalists, clergy and laymen, active in the movement. He served four terms in the legislature from Reading (66% Antimasonic). In Massachusetts and Rhode Island, Universalists tended to line up in the pro-Masonic camp but Vermont Universalists divided, with the majority supporting Antimasonry. Opponents of the Antimasons noted the heterogeneous nature of its religious support and taunted Calvinists for associating with Universalists and others they normally scorned, but Universalists worked successfully with others and mobilized their faithful.[69] Randolph in Orange County gave the Antimasons more than two-thirds of its vote in 1832. This town was home to the party's state central committee on which several prominent Universalist laymen, including Martin Flint and Lebbeus Eggerton, served. Eggerton was the Antimasonic lieutenant governor for three terms (1831–34), succeeded in that post by another Universalist, Silas Jennison of Shoreman, who later became governor, leading a coalition of Whigs and Antimasons after 1835.[70]

Vermont Universalists joined the Antimasonic movement because of the distinctive position Universalism occupied in the Green Mountain State. Marginal elsewhere, Universalism was one of the state's major denominations. In 1831, Universalists claimed fifty-seven societies, or one for every four towns. The sect's founders, Elhanan Winchester, Caleb Rich, and Hosea Ballou laid solid foundations, preaching in Vermont in the last decade of the eighteenth and first decade of the nineteenth century. Vermont proved especially hospitable. Many frontier deists or others attracted by natural religion gravitated to Universalism. Ballou himself, according to one student, fell under Ethan Allen's influence. Emerging as New England's most rapidly growing frontier after the American Revolution, Vermont was especially open to Universalist penetration because many settlers were unchurched or anti-sectarian, and the older denominations were weaker there than elsewhere in New England, where they enjoyed state support and elite backing. Vermont Universalists prospered, and as their numbers grew their political influence also advanced. They joined the Jeffersonian coalition with the Baptists and wherever they were numerous, especially in southern Vermont, they tended to secure public recognition. By the 1820s they felt self-confident enough to push for the choice of a Universalist to preach the annual election sermon and for another to serve as chaplain to the Legislature. In 1834 Universalist sponsorship helped to launch Norwich University, which grew out of Captain Alden Partridge's American Literary, Scientific and Military Academy. The school catered to parents searching for an alternative to the denominational academies and colleges which offered sectarian atmosphere, Calvinist doctrine, and classical curricula.[71]

By embracing Antimasonry, Vermont Universalists reaffirmed their egalitarian tradition and rebuked worldly members of the church, who had gravitated to Freemasonry. By joining with Congregationalists, Baptists, and others, Universalists also solidified their claim to respectability within the Christian community. They, too, were sturdy sentinels defending Christian Republicanism. Yet this odd coalition, not duplicated elsewhere, was only possible because other denominations, especially the major Calvinist churches, the Baptists and Congregationalists, extended the hand of fellowship, at least for political purposes, in the war against Freemasonry. Both sides remained hostile to the other's theological views. Vermont Universalists attacked revivals, Sabbatarianism, and Calvinist theology as well as the evangelical machinery, but Antimasons established a common ground which withstood taunts by opponents. Once the third party declined, in the mid-1830s, the Whigs, seeking to win over Antimasons, recognized the strategic importance Universalists played in the third party and in Vermont politics. Silas Jennison became the Whig coalition candidate, and the Whigs gained dominance by combining support from Baptist, Congregationalist, and Universalist Antimasons.[72]

The anxieties generated by rapid change made the Antimasonic coalition with its anti-elitist and communitarian religious appeal the most powerful political force in Vermont in the early 1830s. Here as almost nowhere else Christian Republicans grasped the opportunity to exercise the powers of government. Their experience proved frustrating.

When Antimasonry emerged in Vermont, the Second Party System had not yet established stable patterns of partisan allegiance. Because a two-party system was not yet the norm and because Vermont required candidates for key offices such as the governorship to win a majority, the third party occupied strategic ground from which to prevent an election and bargain for advantage. Elections for governor and Congress frequently deadlocked. Congressional deadlocks resulted in repeated elections, once as many as nine, before a weary electorate produced a majority. The Vermont legislature, however, selected the governor if there was no popular choice. The Antimasons won a majority only once, yet they captured the governorship four times from 1831–34 because the legislature chose William Palmer, the biggest vote-getter.[73]

The Antimasons also organized the House of Representatives from 1831 to 1835. The speakers during the Antimasonic years were St. Alban's John Smith and Salisbury's Ebenezer Briggs. After 1836, Smith went over to the Democrats to win a term in Congress, and Salisbury joined the Whigs. Governor Palmer also joined the Democrats, but many other Antimasonic leaders, such as Lieutenant Governor Jennison and Congressman William Slade, entered the Whig camp. Drawing support from such diverse elements, the Antimasons carefully balanced National Republicans and Democrats on its statewide tickets, but when the party disintegrated after 1835, a majority amalgamated with the Whigs.[74]

The Antimasonic party in power occupied a precarious position. Success gave it governing responsibility without control of the General Assembly. At the beginning of the 1831 session, Governor Palmer's first term, the third party discovered that the other parties could stymie it. Customarily the Vermont Council and Assembly met together in county conventions to nominate before they entered joint session to elect hundreds of local officials—assistant judges, sheriffs, state's attorney, probate judges, and hundreds of justices of the peace. Because the Antimasons in 1831 controlled the Council, the other two parties joined in the Assembly to block the Council from participating in the nominating conventions. In 1833, the Antimasons were fresh from their biggest triumph, and, after much maneuvering, the Assembly allowed Council members to vote in county conventions, a practice reaffirmed in 1834 and 1835.[75]

The advent of Antimasonry paralleled increasing turnover among county officeholders chosen by the General Assembly.[76] During the Antimasonic era there was more open access to office, both elective and appointive. The incidence of popularly elected long-tenured legislators who served four or more terms dropped by half in the 1830s, compared with the 1820s. Somewhat more than half of the long-tenured in both decades came from towns that gave pluralities to the Antimasons, a figure only modestly greater than the proportion of all towns giving Antimasonic pluralities. (Tables 7.4, 7.5.[77]) The central tendency in the 1830s was toward greater fluidity within the officeholding cadre compared with the previous decade, partly the result of party competition but also because men were less willing to serve repeatedly, since it interfered with business, farming, and professions.

Even before the Antimasons achieved political leadership, the Vermont legislature acted on a petition of the party's 1830 convention to repeal the charter of the Grand Lodge of Vermont. The measure was introduced by Peter Burbank of Newbury, a town sharply split three ways among Antimasons, National Republicans, and Democrats, and it raced through the legislature to become law. Even without a charter the Grand Lodge could still function, though less conveniently, and meetings were still held, even if sparsely attended. More central to Antimasonic purpose was to outlaw Masonic oaths. In 1833 the Antimasons pushed through a law that prohibited administering or taking oaths "not authorized by law."[78] Masonry in Vermont was in rapid decline. There were virtually no new recruits for many years and therefore no need to administer oaths. Literal enforcement, moreover, was not so much the purpose as to demoralize the Order. When Masonry revived, Freemasons ignored such anti-oath laws, claiming that their oaths imposed no illegal obligations.

The anti-oath measure passed after two years of skirmishing. In 1831 Governor Palmer recommended prohibition of oaths except "where necessary to secure the faithful discharge of official trusts, and to elicit truth in the administration of justice." The General Assembly took no action and Palmer reiterated his recommendation in 1832. That year a select committee headed by Rev. Samuel Loveland proposed to ban extra-judicial oaths. Though Masonic oaths were voluntary and not legally binding, they might coerce the conscience of an "honest man," who is "drawn into a snare, and chained by an oath" to engage in aberrant behavior. The Antimasons, however, failed to block postponement by the National Republicans and Democrats, but in 1833, with the Antimasons stronger than ever, opposition crumbled.[79]

During their years of ascendancy, Antimasons faced the full range of policy questions that came before the Vermont legislature in the 1830s. Specifically Antimasonic matters occupied little time, generating only two roll calls from 1831–35. By contrast, questions involving economic development, especially the charter of banks, commanded a considerable portion of each session. A study of roll calls on a variety of measures reveals that the Antimasons did not usually vote as a bloc. They divided sharply on twelve roll calls, including proposals to grant new bank charters. But if these roll calls accurately gauge Antimasonic attitudes toward expansion of the banking system, the third party did tend to play a restraining role. (Table 7.6.[80]) Only fifteen of fifty-seven petitions for new banks or renewals of old charters passed between 1830 and 1835.[81]

The conflict over recharter of the Bank of the United States was one of the major issues delineating parties and polarizing the electorate in the early 1830s, but not in Vermont. Vermont Antimasons were widely ambivalant towards the Bank. In 1832 Governor Palmer endorsed recharter in his annual message but the General Assembly expressed no opinion. In 1834, after the Bank War had heated up considerably, Palmer shifted ground. Now he opposed recharter but still favored a national bank in principle, though he was critical of President Jackson's handling of the question. When Richard Rush, Antimasonic vice-presidential candidate in 1832, came out against the Bank in a widely circulated pamphlet, the *Middlebury Free Press* urged Antimasons not to allow the Bank War to divide the party or divert it from attacking Freemasonry, a far worse "monopoly."[82]

Another test of Antimasonic attitudes towards economic development came with the repeal in 1831 of comprehensive road legislation adopted between 1827 and 1830, which shifted control over construction and repair from the towns and county courts to road commissioners chosen annually by the legislature. Better than half of the Antimasons (55%) joined almost three-quarters of the Democrats in favor of repeal. The National Republicans split evenly, indicating that localist sentiment ran strongly in all parties, though most strongly among the Democrats. The creation of the road commissioners was an effort to establish a more effective mechanism to override local obstacles. Repeal was a setback. When the spotlight shifted to securing a fairer share of federal funds for internal improvements, the Assembly instructed the two Vermont senators by a two-thirds vote, but only 46 percent of the Antimasons backed the proposal.[83]

Two roll calls revealed that Antimasons split over abolition of imprisonment for debt. Though Vermont's 1777 constitution condemned debtors' prison, and successive governors, including Governor William Palmer, recommended its abolition, the state failed to act decisively until 1838. It did provide relief earlier for some categories of debtors—such as women and those who took the poor debtors' oath—yet debtors' prison still claimed between 1300 and 1800 debtors from 1827–30, only about half of whom qualified for discharge. Citizens petitioned for abolition and the legislature repeatedly struggled with the issue in the Antimasonic period. In 1835 the Assembly finally passed an abolition measure. The Whigs tried to sidetrack the bill, but the Antimasons and Democrats defeated them. Then the Governor and Council, all Antimasons, insisted on amendments which killed it. The depression of 1837 added new pressure to end debtors' prison; abolition of it finally passed the Whig legislature in 1838. Yet Vermont remained reluctant to follow other states in facilitating risk-taking and promoting entrepreneurship by providing the relief of a bankruptcy law. Not until 1876 did

Vermont adopt one. The Democrats, guided by egalitarian preferences, were the strongest opponents of debtors' prison, but many Antimasons and Whigs, while admitting the law's injustice, clung to older standards of fiduciary obligation that delayed change.[84]

Antimasonic legislators displayed greater cohesion when they faced social policy questions. Antimasons voted overwhelmingly against abolishing the traditional annual election sermon, a link with New England's Puritan past, and voted in favor of a new liquor licensing bill. On two roll calls on the slavery question, they gave more support to the anti-slavery position than did the Whigs and Democrats. Opposition to slavery seemed to hold especial saliency for Antimasons.[85] Yet even on social issues, Antimasons split, and in ways that revealed the heterogeneous nature of the party. Universalists in Vermont as elsewhere suffered from rulings in the state and federal courts that barred witnesses from testifying if they did not believe in divine punishment after death. In 1833 a measure to end disqualification introduced by the representative from Calais, a town populated by Universalists, Christians, and a Society of Free Enquirers, narrowly failed, with 56 percent of the Antimasons voting to dismiss it.[86]

In 1836, when the Antimasonic party was in decline, Vermonters reviewed amendments to the state constitution proposed in 1834 by the Council of Censors. Framed in 1777, the structure of Vermont's constitution largely escaped change until 1836. Earlier efforts to replace the Council with a strong, independent senate, representing the more populous areas, ran into resistance from the smaller towns. As many towns continued to lose population or faced stagnation, and the commercial centers advanced, demands for change mounted, but resistance also persisted. Altering the constitution proved frustrating because the Council of Censors, which met every seven years and was elected on a statewide ticket, submitted its amendments to a ratifying convention in which each town had one vote. The small towns had the power to stymie the growing areas. In 1834 the Censors proposed extensive changes: the creation of a senate; an apportionment scheme that benefited the larger towns; and popular election of sheriffs, probate judges, state's (county) attorneys, and justices of the peace, in place of annual legislative election.

The amendments faced a rough reception in the 1836 ratifying convention. The senate amendment squeaked through, 116 to 113, but the delegates overwhelmingly rejected the proposal for district election of senators apportioned according to population. They also voted down by a narrow margin the amendments for popular election of county officials. Yet the amendments were not clearly partisan issues. Prominent leaders of all three parties tended to support structural changes, but the rejection of most of them and the close vote on the senate indicate widespread resistance. A comparison of how delegates voted on two key tests, the senate amendment and popular election of probate judges, with their town's party preference in the 1832 presidential election, shows that the Antimasonic towns sharply split: the National Republican towns voted strongly in favor and the Democratic towns clearly opposed. Once again as in the earlier analysis of the demographic correlates of party, the Antimasonic towns stood midway between the Whig and Democratic polarities.[87]

The Censors defended their amendments as modernizing reforms. The original constitution had served well "a people, few in number, whose business relations were few and simple, and but little advanced in agriculture, commerce and arts. . . ." But Vermont had changed considerably in the intervening half-century. Its public affairs were more "complicated" and its social structure had lost the homogeneity that had guaranteed liberty in the past. Vermont's growth now made necessary such "artificial" constitutional arrangements as a bicameral legislature to "perfect" the system and ensure balance. Economic and demographic developments generated a variety of conflicting interests that might contest for power and pursue "sinister purposes." Bicameralism would protect Vermont "from passion, party influence, party intrigue, or local interests which are often brought to bear with great force, and exert a powerful and dangerous sway in a single assembly." Finally, it would make it harder to push through "hasty and improvident" changes in the laws.[88]

These arguments did not prevent polarization between growing and lagging communities. If anything, they aroused the apprehensions of those suspicious of change. A senate would shift power away from the smaller towns; limiting the number of justices of the peace would tend to professionalize and centralize business in the hands of fewer men; popular election of county offices, replacing the horse-trading and lobbying that annually engaged the General Assembly, might save time but would alter the paths to public office.

When the constitutional convention ended, Vermont advanced into the mid-nineteenth century with a bicameral legislature at last but with no other major changes. Meanwhile, Antimasonry was ready to expire. The Whigs, sensing its demise, refused to support Governor Palmer for re-election in 1835 when he failed to win a popular majority and the issue came once again before the legislature. Palmer, they complained, was a Democrat and supported Van Buren for President in the 1836 election. The approaching presidential election, certain to be much closer in New England than when Jackson, a Southerner, ran in 1828 and 1832, made Antimasonic support vital. Once the third party decided not to run its own candidate in 1836, Antimasons with National Republican inclinations tended to move towards the Whigs. The Bank War and the financial panic following removal of the federal deposits in 1834 made Whig arguments still more compelling.

The decline of Vermont Masonry further diminished the saliency of third party politics. Yet it is harder to understand why the Antimasonic party lasted as long as it did than why it finally succumbed in 1836. The enactment of the anti-oath law exhausted the party's legislative program in

1833, yet Antimasons lingered. Freemasonry in Vermont in the early 1830s lay in shambles. The Grand Lodge assembled only a paltry fraction of the delegates who had attended in the 1820s. Many of the more than seventy Lodges founded before 1830 collapsed and never revived or only survived along the margins. In 1831 and again in 1833 prominent Masons proposed that Vermont Masonry dissolve. Indignant loyalists attacked politicians who wanted to get Masonry out of the way, the better to bury Antimasonry. Though hundreds of Masons abandoned the Order, defiance by the remaining devotees proved to the ever-suspicious Antimasons that Masonry was not yet dead. Their cause had advanced far, yet total victory eluded them as long as a Masonic revival was still possible. By the mid-1830s Masonry had declined to an irreducible core. From 1836 to 1844 the Grand Lodge did not meet. Few dared run for public office if they retained membership in the Order, and this was surely the Antimasons' most important achievement. The Antimasons had conquered public opinion; they made membership virtually a disqualification; they had purged churches; and they compelled the high and mighty who wished to retain positions of leadership to bow before Antimasonic sentiment.[89]

Antimasonry persisted as long as it did because the underlying forces that had generated the movement, the Christians Republican response to the anxieties produced by social change, were especially strong in Vermont. The weakness of elites and the highly unstable social structure undergoing rapid transition from a frontier to a developed region, with an increasingly diverse cultural life, combined with the collapse of the First American Party System to make politics especially fluid in the late 1820s. Moreover the major parties emerging after 1828 seriously underestimated the depths and staying power of the Antimasonic Persuasion. Their tactics only fed Antimasonic suspicion that on the subject of Freemasonry both parties were hopeless. Both the National Republicans and the Democrats nominated Masons well into the early 1830s, for neither wished to antagonize their Masonic supporters, many of whom were high in party counsels, for the sake of appeasing a new movement that might be transient.[90]

In 1831 the National Republican State Convention recommended the dissolution of Freemasonry, but two years later the Nationals and Democrats buried their differences and formed a coalition to smash Antimasonry. At the 1833 National Republican Convention, which the *North Star* claimed was filled with Freemasons, a prominent member of the Order blessed the new strategy: "Let us say to the Antimasons, We came here to CRUSH YOU—we mean to crush you—and trust we shall crush you!" The 1833 coalition further affronted Antimasonic opinion by naming Ezra Meech as candidate for governor. He was a well-known Mason, one of the state's largest landowners, and a Democrat.[91]

The failure of the coalition made it evident that the superior strategy for burying Antimasonry was absorption. In 1834 the Democrats reorganized. As elsewhere in the country, rivalry between the two major parties intensified as the Bank War heated up and the removal of the federal deposits caused a brief financial crisis.[92] At the 1836 constitutional convention Democrats courted Antimasons, but when the third party collapsed, the Whigs were the main beneficiaries.

After the coalition tactic failed, the Whigs made only token efforts in the 1834 and 1835 elections for governor. Meanwhile leading Antimasons moved towards the Whig camp. The Whigs' refusal to vote for Palmer in the General Assembly in 1835 elevated Lieutenant Governor Silas Jennison, an Antimason who favored amalgamation. In 1836 the Whigs backed him for re-election, and he won the second of his five terms. The Whigs sensed that they needed Antimasonic votes. In 1833 worried Whigs beat the drums of nativism against the Irish and Germans and depicted Van Buren as soft on Popery.[93]

Coalition with the Antimasons did not come easily. The prospective partners had to overcome years of hostility. In the winter of 1836 both parties met in a joint convention and chose a common statewide slate that included many prominent Antimasonic stalwarts. Coalition at the local level, especially selecting candidates for the new Senate, proved difficult. Carlos Coolidge, a rising Universalist politician, shrewdly advised Whigs to be conciliatory, for within a year, he predicted, the Antimasonic party would be dead. Coolidge was correct.[94] The Whig-Antimasonic coalition won easily in 1836 and the Whigs alone, now much strengthened, remained the dominant party for a generation. According to ecological regression estimates, about half of the 1832 Antimasonic voters voted for the Whig presidential candidate in 1836, and most of the rest stayed home. (Table 7.7.[95]) The new Whig coalition was more heterogeneous than the National Republicans'. Multiple regression statistics show that the economic variables had less impact on the Whig vote in 1836 than they had on the National Republican vote in 1828 and 1832, but the religious variables gained in importance. The end of Antimasonry facilitated greater political polarization along denominational lines because the question of Freemasonry no longer divided churches internally.[96]

A small faction of Antimasonic Democrats, charging a Whig takeover of the party's last convention, withdrew and backed the Democrats. The Jacksonians were ambivalent. As much as they wanted Antimasonic votes they would not jeopardize the loyalty of Freemasons who were influential in the party.[97] They added Antimasons to their ticket, but the state's leading unrepentant Freemasons had gravitated to the Democratic party and this made amalgamation awkward.[98] By contrast, Whig leaders who had been Masons tended to abandon the Order, the price of regaining political leadership.

For all its short-term success, Antimasonry was bound to fail in the long run, for it set itself against the powerful currents reshaping Vermont, currents which had nourished the growth of Freemasonry in the early nineteenth century and generated its revival in the 1840s. Yet for a generation,

Masonry in the Green Mountain State entered the wilderness. For a decade, Masons met in secrecy, moved from house to house to escape detection, and hid Lodge property to protect it from mob violence.[99] The bonds of brotherhood forged within Masonry among middle-class Americans withstood the test of persecution. Even among the clergy there were those like Methodist preacher Joel Winch of Northfield who never wavered. He served as Grand Chaplain of the Grand Lodge in the 1830s during the worst of times and led the revival as the first Master of DeWitt Clinton Lodge from 1849–51. Near the end of his life, Grand Master Philip Tucker visited Winch and received his final words: "Tell the world that I died a Mason: that I lived a Mason, as well as I could and I die a Mason and a Methodist."[100]

Vermont Antimasonry survived too, beyond the life of the political movement it inspired. Christian Republican impulses that had found an outlet in the crusade against Freemasonry discovered a new cause, the abolition of slavery. The waning of Masonry left Christian Republicans at loose ends. "A new party has been organized called the Abolitionist, or Liberty party," recalled Nathaniel Haswell, "and the horrors of Masonry have been transferred to the horrors of Slavery." As defenders of Christian Republicanism, Antimasons turned from a declining institution to another national evil in full vigor. As with Freemasonry, some thought, hypocritical politicians and canting preachers worked sinuously to reconcile the sin of slavery with republicanism and Christianity, but abolitionists, like Antimasons, refused to let them.[101]

More than thirty years after the disappearance of the Antimasonic party in Vermont and several years after the abolition of slavery, five farmers, a tanner, and a mechanic from Jamaica, Vermont, joined a new Antimasonic society in Windham County to counteract "the tendency of all secret oath bound Associations . . . to corrupt religion and good morals, circumvent the laws, subvert republican institutions, and destroy the best interests of the people." They elected Hon. Austin Birchard and Judge Laban Jones as vice presidents. Both had served as leaders of the Antimasonic party four decades earlier. The Jamaica Antimasons met annually until 1878 "when they ceased for want of popular interest in the subject."[102]

GRAND LODGE JEWELS.

GRAND MASTER.	DEP. GR. MASTER.	SEN. GR. WARDEN.
JUN. GR. WARDEN.	GR. TREASURER.	GR. SECRETARY.
GR. CHAPLAIN.	GR. MARSHAL.	GR. STANDARD BEARER
GR. SWORD BEARER.	GR. STEWARDS.	GR. DEACONS.
GR. PURSUIVANT.	GR. LECTURER.	GR. TILER.

Jewels or emblems of officers of a Grand Lodge. Robert
Macoy, *General History, Cyclopedia, and Dictionary of
Freemasonry* (New York, 1869), 183.

William Morgan being imprisoned in Old Fort Niagara. *American Freemason*, 8 (Feb. 1859).

MASONIC APRON PRESENTED TO GEN. WASHINGTON
BY MADAME LAFAYETTE.

George Washington: Devoted Mason or casual member? Robert Macoy, *General History, Cyclopedia, and Dictionary of Freemasonry* (New York, 1869), 87.

American Freemason

Vol. 3.   A. L. 5859.—MAY—A. D. 1859.   No. 5.

Romance of Masonry.

MASONIC FAITH AND FORTITUDE.

HUSBAND AND WIFE.

BY ROB. MORRIS, G. M. OF KY.

To his surprise they consisted entirely of works professedly written against Freemasonry. His artful mistress had pur-

A Mason discovering his wife reading Antimasonic propaganda. *American Freemason,* 3 (May 1859).

Rev. Nathanael Emmons, Hopkinsian Calvinist and Antimason. Jacob Ide, ed., *The Works of Nathanael Emmons,* 6 Vols. (Boston, 1842), I.

An Antimasonic view of a Masonic initiation. *New England Antimasonic Almanac* (Boston, 1830).

Due Guard. " Draw the right hand across the throat, the hand open and the thumb next to the throat, and then let it drop down by the side."—*Morgan.* Many call this *a sign.* It alludes to the penalty of the Apprentice's obligations—having the throat cut across, &c. This sign seems more appropriate for a gang of robbers or pirates than a *Religious and Charitable Society.*

MASTER MASON'S DEGREE.

Real Grip.—Take hold of each other's right hand as if to shake hands, and stick the nails of each of your fingers into the joints of the other's wrist where it unites with the hand. This is what the masons call the *Lion's Paw.* It was by this grip that Solomon pulled Old Hiram out of his grave after he was rotten, according to Masonic Chronicles.

MASTER MASONS'

Sign of Distress. Raise both hands and arms perpendicularly, one on each side of the head. the elbow forming a square. The accompanying words are, " *O Lord, my God, is there no help for the Widow's Son.*" At the last words, let the hands slowly fall.—The words are not spoken except in the dark when the sign cannot be seen.

MASONRY AND INTEMPERANCE GO HAND IN HAND.

How many youth who sipped the intoxicating bowl of masonry in the name of Friendship and Brothely love have found the Serpent of Intemperance lurking at the bottom. In masonic language, swearing is called "*labor,*" and tippling " *refreshment.*" The less one has to do with either the better.

Those who applaud Masonry without knowing any thing about it, are called *Jack Masons.* They are likened to this poor animal, for like him they tug and sweat under a heavy burthen without knowing what it is. The Jacks are very annoying, being generally set on by the craft. You may know them by the introductory observation—" I am not a mason, but I know it to be a noble institution."

Antimasonic propaganda. *New England Antimasonic Almanac* (Boston, 1830), 34.

Rhode Island Freemasons' Grand Lodges, 1791 and 1891. Henry Rugg, *Freemasonry in Rhode Island* (Providence, 1895), 620.

Masonic Lodge in Maine. *Gould's History of Freemasonry throughout the World,* 6 Vols. (New York, 1935), 6, p. 54.

Masonic Lodge in Woodbury, Connecticut, 1839. *The Centennial, One Hundreth Anniversary of the Most Worshipful Grand Lodge of Connecticut* (Hartford, 1890), 307.

The pillars of Masonry crush William Morgan. *New England Antimasonic Almanac* (Boston, 1830).

A Masonic funeral rite. *Standard Ahiman Rezon and Blue Lodge Guide* (New York, 1889), 163.

8

Massachusetts Antimasons and the Defense of Republican Community

Secret compacts are formed for the express purpose of gaining some *private advantage*. The motive to enter into such combinations is wholly on the side of selfishness. No persons, who have solely in view, the welfare of *community*, have any inducements to form a secret compact for that purpose.

Moses Thacher, *An Address Delivered Before the Antimasonic Convention of Delegates for Plymouth County . . . 1829* (Boston, 1830)

On February 27, 1830, the body of Artemas Kennedy floated to the surface "at low water mark" in the Milton River near Boston. The corpse of this seceding member of the Knights Templars from Milton, Massachusetts, expelled from the Norfolk Union Lodge the preceding year for intemperance, aroused Antimasonic suspicion that Kennedy, like William Morgan in 1826, was a victim of Masonic malevolence. Morgan's murder, Antimasons believed, was no isolated incident. Masonic oaths were licenses to commit crime but the singularity of the Morgan case troubled them. They needed further evidence.

Kennedy's death upset Samuel G. Anderton, a Boston seaman, who swore before notary John W. Quincy on March 15, 1830, that he had witnessed the murder of another Mason in a Belfast, Ireland, Lodge in 1813. "They said he had broken his oaths," Anderton testified, "called him a damned perjured wretch; said that he forfeited his life. . . ." Anderton recalled that thirty-five or forty Masons were present that night. The Masons cast lots and the execution fell to three foreigners: a Swede and a Dane, both shipmasters, and Anderton. Anderton "begged and entreated" to be let off: "I told them I could not do it." The Scandinavians made ready, and when midnight arrived they posted themselves at the door to the left of the High Priest. The victim, William Miller, approached the Lodgeroom blindfolded, thinking he was about to be inducted into the

Knights Templars. "Who comes there?" someone shouted. "A damned traitor, who has broken his Masonic obligations," another answered. As Miller entered the room, someone forced a cloth bag—a piece of Masonic regalia—over his head, and others choked him with a rope. Miller struggled, fell into convulsions and then, according to Anderton, the Masons slit his throat and cut open his left breast, exposing his heart precisely as the Masonic penalty specified. Then the Brothers threw the mutilated body off Limekiln Dock while Anderton ran away. Horrified by the crime, Anderton tossed his Masonic gear overboard during the voyage back to the United States and fell silent. The discovery of Artemas Kennedy's corpse, another Knight Templar, ignited guilty memories and induced Anderton to reveal his long-kept secret. "Another Masonic Murder!" shouted an Antimasonic handbill that circulated throughout Massachusetts. "Masonry the Same, All Over the World." Anderton offered clinching evidence that Morgan's murder was no isolated event. Nothing that Bay State Freemasons said to discredit Anderton swayed Antimasons convinced of Samuel Anderton's courage and credibility.[1]

Anderton's revelations occurred two months after the first Massachusetts Antimasonic Convention met in late December 1829. The convention, called by the Suffolk County Antimason Committee, brought together citizens who had met in town and regional conventions during the preceding year. In New Bedford, Lynn, Fall River, Wendell, Dedham, Worcester, Boston, and many other towns, Antimasons had assembled in "People's meetings" or "People's conventions" to expose and condemn Freemasonry. In Boston, for example, the Suffolk committee launched an investigation of Masonry in the fall of 1829, established an Antimasonic library, and invited Sheriff Charles P. Sumner, father of future United States Senator Charles Sumner, to tell the public why he had abandoned the Order.[2]

Neither Freemasons nor the state's leading National Republican and Democratic politicians accurately gauged Antimasonic sentiment in the Bay State. The Boston *Masonic Mirror* heaped abuse on Antimasons; pro-Masonic elements hounded, even mobbed, critics; and most newspapers refused to open their columns to the opponents of the Order. In October 1829, the Grand Lodge of Massachusetts voted to spend $40,000 to erect a new Masonic Hall in Boston. A year later over two thousand defiant Freemasons proudly marched five abreast through the streets of the capitol to reaffirm Masonry at the cornerstone-laying ceremony of the new hall.[3] Such Masonic resistance further inflamed Antimasons and pushed them increasingly toward politics.

The first Antimasonic convention met for three days at the end of 1829. It heard reports that affirmed the truth of William Morgan's exposé, commended the courage of seceders, denounced Masonry's claim to ancient lineage, and exposed a "conspiracy" by the press to cover up Masonic crimes and shield the Order from scrutiny. Yet until the state election of 1830, Antimasonry remained a social rather than a political movement.[4]

Antimasons at the first convention nominated no candidates, nor did they petition for legislation, preferring to rely on "moral antimasonry" to shape public opinion. Yet they did elect delegates to a national convention organized to name a candidate for the 1832 presidential election.

Largely ignored by politicians in both parties, especially by the dominant National Republicans in Massachusetts to which many leaned, Antimasons increasingly felt the pull of independent political action. In the spring of 1830, three Antimasons won election to the state senate and some two dozen to the state house of representatives. Antimasons had hitherto refrained from petitioning for a law to ban Masonic oaths or revoke Masonic charters because they recognized their political weakness. Moreover, they hesitated to plunge into politics without exhausting other means. In the fall of 1831, however, Bay State Antimasons nominated a statewide ticket in a bold bid for political influence because suasion had not worked. Governor Levi Lincoln refused to promise he would withhold appointments from Freemasons, making him unacceptable to the Antis, even though Lincoln was not a Mason and expressed disapproval of the Order. The fall elections vindicated the plunge into politics, for the Antimasons garnered a quarter of the vote for governor, edging past the Democrats and demonstrating that they were a significant force. Yet this initial success at the polls, together with the establishment of a Tract Society and a press, did not overawe Freemasons. In December 1831, 1200 Massachusetts Masons published a declaration which flatly rejected every charge against the Order and vowed to sustain Masonry against "infatuated" citizens threatening to violate the civil rights of Masons. Masonic recalcitrance left Antimasons more convinced that politics held the key to the destruction of Freemasonry.[5]

For four years the Antimasonic party remained an important force in Bay State politics, capturing almost a quarter of the vote for William Wirt in the 1832 presidential election. (Table 8.1.[6]) After twice running West Springfield lawyer Samuel Lothrop for governor, a favorite among Orthodox Congregationalists in the Connecticut Valley, the party finally secured the consent of President John Quincy Adams to head the ticket in 1833, though in 1831 Adams had refused. Adams had not wanted to break with National Republicans, but in 1833 he hoped that both parties would turn to him. Strong opposition by Freemasons within National Republican ranks prevented a coalition and reinforced Antimasonic suspicion that the Order held the Nationals in captivity. Adams had returned to national politics in 1831 as congressman from a district that was a hotbed of Antimasonry. The crusty former President embraced the cause, and in 1833 Antimasons published his four polemical *Letters on the Entered Apprentice's Oath*.[7]

Adams ran even better than Lothrop and though Whig John Davis won a plurality, forcing the election into the Massachusetts legislature, Adams bowed out. But he had demonstrated that the Whigs could not secure a majority without Antimasonic support. In the run up to the 1833 campaign, the worried Whigs had made overtures to the Antimasons. The legislature turned down the Grand Lodge's request to modify its charter and it also outlawed extra-judicial oaths. Yet neither measure satisfied Antimasons. The anti-oath law was too vague, failing to specify Masonic oaths. Finally, the Whig candidate for governor, John Davis, refused to pledge that he would not appoint Masons. For Antimasons the battle was far from won, but with John Quincy Adams heading the ticket, the prospects were never brighter. Voter turnout soared that year. The third party's popularity alarmed National Republicans, who now adopted a more accommodating posture. Eight thousand citizens petitioned the legislature for an investigation of Freemasonry. In 1834 the Nationals obliged with a committee stacked with legislators hostile to Masonry. The committee's report echoed most of the familiar Antimasonic arguments: Freemasonry was a moral evil that encouraged insobriety; was guilty of sacrilege; tempted men away from their families; and wasted funds on lavish entertainments, parades, and trinkets which "a well informed savage would blush to wear." Worst of all, Masonry attracted people because it offered them pecuniary and political advantages and promoted "inequality among those between whom no inequality should exist but that which proceeds from superior industry or superior attainments." The committee drafted a bill to compel Masons to report annually the names of new initiates and members, the times and places of their meetings, and the amount of money they collected, but the bill failed in the house by a vote of 106 to 118.[8]

In 1834, Governor Davis made another bid for Antimasonic support by urging that the Masons dissolve. Other Whig leaders echoed him.[9] These more conciliatory gestures, combined with the decline of Bay State Masonry and the growing importance of other issues, such as the Bank War, weakened support for the Antimasonic party. Its share of the statewide vote plunged in 1834, and when the Whigs nominated Edward Everett for governor in 1835 after he had secured the third party's endorsement, the path to accommodation was clear. Everett had courted Antimasons without deserting the National Republican ranks. He earned the enmity of the Freemasons in his own party which in turn endeared him to the Antimasons.[10]

When Governor Davis resigned to become a United States Senator, the Whigs turned to Everett. Overriding the objections of Freemasons, they seized the opportunity to bury the third party, but they balanced the ticked by naming George Hull, a Mason, for lieutenant governor. Everett was easily elected, running five thousand votes ahead of Hull.

Governor Everett disappointed his Antimasonic supporters. Though he forthrightly condemned secret oaths, he appointed Masons to office. By now, however, there was no possibility of reviving the Antimasonic party. The 1836 presidential election approached, making national questions even more salient. The third party's forces had scattered after 1833, drifting into the other two parties or retiring from the political arena, satisfied that

Masonry was in retreat and recognizing that Antimasonry had run its course.[11]

Massachusetts politics in the late 1820s was hospitable to the transition of Antimasonry from a social movement without a definite political purpose into a party. The First American Party System died slowly in the Bay State, lingering into the early 1820s, but after two defeats in 1823 and 1824, the Federalists gave up the battle. The old issues and loyalties that had sustained Massachusetts Federalism for a generation were dead, and new issues and alignments had not yet generated new party loyalties. From 1825 to 1830, Federalists and Jeffersonian Republicans amalgamated behind Governor Levi Lincoln. He was an old Jeffersonian from Worcester and won repeated elections with only token opposition until the rise of Antimasonry.[12]

The disappearance of the Frst Party System and the slow genesis of the Second left Massachusetts politics fluid, a situation as beneficial to Antimasons as it had been earlier to other insurgent groups. In Boston "the Middling Interest" erupted in the 1820s, a coalition of small merchants and master mechanics who teamed up with the Jeffersonian remnant and with disgruntled Orthodox Congregationalists and religious dissenters to defeat Harrison G. Otis's bid to become the city's first mayor. Though Otis eventually succeeded Mayor Josiah Quincy in 1829, "the Middling Interest" exploded once again in 1831 to beat William Sullivan, choice of the National Republican elite, in favor of a builder, Charles Welles, a man with little formal education but popular among the mechanics and small businessmen.[13]

Despite Governor Lincoln's easy victories and President John Quincy Adams's sweeps in 1824 and 1828, factionalism percolated beneath the surface in "the Era of Good Feeling." After he left the White House in 1829, Adams turned venemously on the Boston "traitors" who had betrayed him and whose conduct during the embargo and the War of 1812, he argued, was unpatriotic. Former Federalist bastions in western Massachusetts were also restless under Governor Lincoln's broad National Republican umbrella, which sheltered Boston and Worcester Unitarian elites, Connecticut Valley Orthodox Congregationalists, many old Jeffersonian Republicans, supporters of Senator Daniel Webster, and the friends of John Quincy Adams. Though each of these elements contributed to the National Republican coalition's dominance in the 1820s, they formed an unstable amalgam.[14] The emerging Jacksonian Democrats were extremely weak, divided between the office-hungry faction surrounding David Henshaw and the Boston Customs House crew, and the heterogeneous elements outside the metropolis who professed devotion to Old Republican principles. In 1830, Ebenezer Seaver, a Roxbury Jacksonian, saw only meager prospects for the Bay State Democrats to match the party's success in New Hampshire: "We are split to pieces with Antimasonry, Orthodoxy, and every other Doxey which the enemies of our system of government can invent to destroy it."[15]

The strains of economic and social change soon clarified the confusion and polarized the electorate around new issues. Increasing cultural diversity and rapid industrial development placed Massachusetts in the forefront of modernization during the early nineteenth century. Change produced social fragmentation, divided communities, and propelled new concerns to the top of the political agenda. A restless mass of religious dissenters, strong enough to secure toleration but not to overthrow the last religious establishment in the country, made the final push to separate church and state in the early 1830s. Aiding the minorities was a bitter division between Orthodox and Liberal wings of the Congregationalist establishment.[16]

At the same time there were growing differences over what role government should play in promoting economic development. Once wedded to free trade, many Massachusetts businessmen, especially Boston manufacturers, were in the process of shifting towards protectionism in the 1820s. By 1830, the abolition of debtors' prison, attacks on "monopoly" privilege in banking, disputes over state aid for internal improvements and the temperance movement, and demands by workers for equal rights emerged in the political agenda.[17] In a period of flux, Antimasons pushed forward their own issue. In the late 1820s, neither Jackson Democrats nor the National Republicans had staked out clear-cut policy positions that differentiated the parties. That would happen during the next decade as Andrew Jackson unfolded his program, but until then, the Antimasons had a chance.

Neither the Democrats nor the National Republicans in 1830 commanded deep or reliable support within the electorate. The National Republican vote in the 1828 presidential election correlated weakly in Massachusetts with earlier Federalist votes. Moreover, the level of political mobilization was extremely low. (Table 8.2.[18]) Turnout of adult males in 1828 was only 24 percent in both state and national elections, and weak party attachments thus helped Antimasons to channel Antimasonic sentiment into an independent political movement.

The Antimasons' strong showing in 1831, their first statewide contest, combined with the Democratic vote to hold Governor Lincoln's majority to 54 percent and vindicated the decision to run candidates. From a one-party state, Massachusetts rapidly became a competitive, three-party state. The Antimasons owed much of their success to the mobilization of new voters— ecological regression estimates point to a little less than half of the 1832 Antimasonic vote coming from National Republican switchers and a little more than half from voters who had not participated in 1828. Though the Antimasons could not take sole credit for mounting voter turnout, which surged to 41 percent in 1832, they were an important element in arousing citizens. In 1833, the party's peak year, it attracted twice as many who had not voted the preceding years as those who switched from the National

Republicans. (Table 8.3.[19]) By 1834, however, the Antimasons had exhausted their ability to mobilize voters. The candidates and the issues of the major parties now became the main driving force behind increased participation. Antimasonry's days were numbered.

During its heyday, the Antimasons united a coalition of heterogeneous elements that included former Federalists, Democratic Republicans, and National Republicans as well. The Antimasonic vote correlated weakly with the patterns of support garnered by other parties. Moreover, in the five statewide elections which they contested, Antimasons pulled very uneven geographic support. In the western part of the state, the Antimasons did best in Hampshire and Franklin counties in the Connecticut Valley; in the east, its banner counties were Norfolk, Bristol, and Plymouth; but elsewhere they trailed badly. Moreover, their western strength proved undependable, declining sharply after 1832. In Massachusetts, as elsewhere, the Antimasons tapped, if only briefly, the deeply felt concern of voters, which neither Democrats nor Nationals addressed. Precisely who flocked to their banner and why is a more difficult, though more important question.

As in other states, the new system of class relations, cultural heterogeneity the spread of secularism, and the decline of old communitarian norms focused attention on Freemasonry as an agent of radical change. The Christian Republican perspective provided Antimasons from varied backgrounds with a common platform from which to preserve the moral and political underpinnings of republican order. The party emphasized its character by calling itself "The Antimasonic Republican Party," linking itself explicitly to the republican tradition and to the Jeffersonian and National Republican parties from which it drew support.

Statistical generalization about the social basis of the movement is problematic. The results of multiple regression analysis were inconclusive, though they do suggest some relationship between the parties and demographic variables. In the 1828 presidential race, religious variables were better predictors of the party vote than were other variables. Congregationalists tended to help the National Republicans; Baptists, Methodists, and Free Will Baptists aided the Democrats. The impact of economic variables was slight or inconclusive. When the Antimasons appeared on the ballot in 1832 and in 1833, when they were joined by the Workingmen's party, the pattern changed. Though Baptists and Methodists still boosted the Democratic vote, Congregationalists fragmented, to the disadvantage of National Republicans. After the Antimasonic party disappeared, however, Congregationalists strongly boosted the Whig vote. By contrast, economic variables gained in importance in the early 1830s, perhaps because denominations were sharply split over Masonry or because national issues were much more salient than in the past. During the early 1830s, high rates of population change and maritime employment tended to boost the National Republican showing, while manufacturing and agricultural employment helped the Democrats. Employment in the important boot and shoe industry had no significant impact on party performance from 1828 to 1840, and the effect of employment in textile manufacturing fluctuated or was inconclusive. By the late 1830s the pattern shifted. Manufacturing employment boosted the Whig vote and agricultural employment the Democratic vote. As for the Antimasonic party, population change, maritime employment, and, to a lesser degree, agricultural employment tended to depress the party vote while commercial employment helped it. The complex and inconclusive statistics suggest that available demographic data are too crude and groups were too divided to allow one to discover the social basis of the party through multiple regression. It is more fruitful to employ microcosmic analyses which pay careful attention to divisions within groups and to geographic and local contexts.

Both supporters and opponents of the Antimasonic movement pointed to religious and class antagonism as driving forces behind the third party. The Antimasons, said John Quincy Adams, came "not from the mansions of the wealthy, nor from the cabinets of the great—not even from the Sentinels of the Watch Tower of Zion" but "from the broad basis of the population, from the less educated and most numerous class of the community." This was true, he added "with all great moral reforms." Like Christianity, a telling comparison, Antimasonry rested "upon a pure, precise, unequivocal principle of morals."[20]

Massachusetts Antimasons emphasized the essential selfishness of Masonry. Here were men who placed private advancement over public good, personal interest above civic virtue. They were, the elder Adams argued, "selfish, intolerant, exclusive." They recruited "many individuals possessing a small share of education and property" who hoped to advance their fortunes through Masonry. In business, Masons were responsible for most of the "overwhelming bankruptcies," for though lacking in scruple, they enjoyed access to capital. When failure overtook him, the Mason hid his assets within the secret precincts of the Order "which can never be penetrated by law. . . ." Masonry was nothing more than "a system of unmixed selfishnesses," said Rev. Peleg Sanborn of Reading. By identifying Masonry with cupidity, Antimasons thought they had discovered a new social type, the rootless, competitive individual with only weak ties to community or to fellow citizens. By contrast, Antimasons claimed for their party moral purity and devotion to the public weal. The hallmark of Antimasons was "their simplicity of life, their unobtrusiveness and unambitious deportment, as the minutemen of justice and of liberty." Unlike the aggressive, pushy *arriviste* that flocked to Freemasonry, the Antimasons were ready to wander in the political wilderness and sacrifice political advancement for the sake of principle.[21] At the 1834 Antimasonic Convention—the most democratic, numerous nominating body that had ever assembled in the state, according to the Antimasonic editor and wirepuller, Ben Hallett—the evidence was plain: "Look around, sir, in this assembly. Do you find great wealth or great individual pretensions here?" The Antimasons were representatives of the "substantial, intelligent, moral yeomanry, mechanics, and working men," unencumbered "by wealth and luxury and love of ease, and social influence and party discipline. . . ." The country "in these degenerate days," Hallett intoned, must turn to such "men of moral courage, the middling interest of the Commonwealth" who alone could "secure and perpetuate the institutions."[22]

We need not accept at face value the Antimasons' self-image as disinterested patriots and their view of Masons as selfish amoralists, but should rather try to understand why many perceived themselves and the Masonic order in this light. Antimasons were familiar with recent developments in Massachusetts Masonry, for many were formerly members of the Order or had read about it in detailed accounts prepared by knowledgeable seceders. The Antimasons recognized, in their own distorted and charged way, that Freemasonry's popularity had roots in the emergence of a new system of social stratification based on competitive individualism and extensive geographic mobility. These developments were especially threatening to those people who were unwilling or unable to compete and who believed that Freemasonry eroded the authority of a community's natural leaders, those whose position derived from moral excellence and devotion to public interest and who commanded the confidence of fellow citizens.

The internal development of Massachusetts Freemasonry in the early nineteenth century sheds considerable light on both the growth of the Order and why it evoked such intense opposition. By 1830 there were more than 100 Masonic Lodges in Massachusetts, located in over a third of the towns, enrolling more than four thousand members. Masonry's growth posed serious problems to its leadership. Were the Order to become too accessible, the value of membership might depreciate, since it sought to confer respectability and give men access to valuable but exclusive entrepreneurial networks. For this reason the Grand Lodge, the highest rule-making authority in Massachusetts Masonry, grappled repeatedly with membership standards. In 1815 the Grand Lodge turned down a request from the Portland, Maine, Lodge to reduce the dues. Were fees lowered, it would "render the access to the privileges of Freemasonry and make the Institution undervalued by its cheapness," the Grand Lodge feared. In 1817, tightening membership standards, the Grand Lodge ordered inferior Lodges to demand payment of fees in cash, not notes or credit. And in 1819 a new by-law set a minimum of $19 for initiating, crafting, and raising Freemasons. In other ways, too, the Grand Lodge guarded the portals. In 1816 it ruled that someone rejected in one Lodge was not eligible for admission to another unless six members of the rejecting Lodge, including the Master and Wardens, approved. It also ordered Lodges to circulate among neighboring Lodges the names of men they blackballed. Ever alert to departures from Masonic norms, a committee of the Grand Lodge reported in 1826 that some Lodges ignored the unanimity rule of admission and admitted on a two-thirds vote. It ordered that to cease. The Grand

Lodge also scotched rumors that it had opened its doors to Afro-Americans, a report that spread from the Pennsylvania Grand Lodge. According to rumor, Afro-Americans unable to secure a charter from Grand Lodges in other states turned to Massachusetts, but the Bay State Grand Lodge denied that it had breached the color line.

In 1817 the Grand Lodge petitioned the Massachusetts legislature for a charter of incorporation. Earlier requests had not succeeded, but by now suspicions had subsided. Because the Lodge was growing in wealth, responsibility, and influence, it needed a new Masonic Hall. A charter provided practical advantages. The Masons recognized, however, that grants of charter privileges went only to enterprises cloaked with a public purpose. Masonry, however, was a private association which could make only tenuous claims to serve the Commonwealth, but this time the Order got a charter. Yet in 1824 the Grand Lodge rejected a proposal to establish a Masonic Orphan Asylum. Masonry should not depart from its private, "domestic" purposes for otherwise it might "become an object of animadversion, jealousy and apprehension" which would jeopardize its charter. At a time when other associations raised substantial funds, Masonic leaders pleaded poverty, doubting their ability to finance an asylum. Besides, the poor would try to join, subverting Masonic exclusivity. In the end, the Grand Lodge denied that there was any need for an asylum at precisely the time when Americans were discovering the inadequacy of older modes of caring for the dependent. The Masons should better stick to their own charitable works, aiding their members rather than risk involvement with "the vicious and undeserving," they concluded.[23]

In a variety of ways, Massachusetts Masons underlined the privatistic character of Freemasonry, the tendency to retreat from undertaking new community responsibilities, to restrict access, and to limit function. To adherents of older communitarian norms, the Order elevated self-service into a principle of association. In this sense the Antimasonic perception of the Order as an anti-social body rested on a grain of truth. Where the Antimasons went astray was in failing to understand that privatism, individualism, and the divorce of associational activity from public purpose were deep-seated currents in the United States, not unique characteristics of the fraternal order. Yet by justifying their request for a charter in the language of the commonwealth tradition but narrowly restricting membership and functions to preserve its private character, Freemasons found themselves walking on dangerous ground.

Massachusetts Antimasons voiced the apprehensions of a segment of the middle class. In 1831 over four hundred Bostonians signed a declaration in defense of Freemasonry. With few exceptions Masonry did not attract much support from the emerging Brahmin elite, which had its own modes of self-identification and forms of socializing. From the perspective of the metropolis's upper crust, Masonry was too inclusive, too vulgar, too middle-class, to serve its needs. Two-thirds of the Boston signers were merchants, retailers, master mechanics, and manufacturers. Doctors, ministers, other professionals, and public officials accounted for over a quarter of the signers. Not a single laborer and only ten clerks (3%) joined them. Boston Antimasons were also overwhelmingly drawn from the ranks of businessmen: merchants, retailers, mechanics, and manufacturers made up 84 percent, the rest included a few clerks, laborers, and truckmen or teamsters, but there were few professional men (8%). Both groups were middle-class, but the Masons were occupationally more diverse and better connected.[24] The Masons were also richer. The Boston tax collector rated 22 percent of the Masonic signers as owners of property worth twenty-five dollars or more compared to only 10 percent of the Antimasons. Among these taxpayers, the distribution of wealth was not strikingly different except that a somewhat higher proportion of Masons were assessed for $6,000 or more.[25]

Outside the metropolis, occupational data do not differentiate to the same degree. In smaller communities Masonry often attracted a significant proportion of the community's leading citizens, but the data do not suggest clear differences in social status. Neither group included any farmers or any laborers, yet within the entrepreneurial stratum, dominant in both, there were differences. Masons were more likely to be merchants, and Antimasons manufacturers, but one does not find in the hinterlands much difference in the proportion holding white-collar or professional jobs. The importance of manufacturers among the Antimasons, however, spotlights a social type prominent in religious benevolence, temperance, antislavery, and Antimasonic movements: the moralistic, often evangelical, self-made manufacturer, who professed deep respect for the nobility of labor, strong attachment to community, and a deep sense of social responsibility. Christian Republicanism attracted a significant number of manufacturers, men who found in perfectionist reform movements a mode of resolving the conflict between equal-rights norms and republicanism and the emerging system of social stratification and competitive individualism. Through reform they attempted to purge society of subversive tendencies in conflict with republican and Christian traditions.[26]

Massachusetts Antimasons dramatized their anti-aristocratic pretensions by launching a campaign to capture the Bunker Hill Monument Association, the Bay State's principal memorial to the American Revolution. Seeing themselves as Guardians of the Revolution, the Antimasons tried to purge this patriotic enterprise, freighted with symbolic meaning, of Masonic and elitist influence. Less than a month after the first Massachusetts Antimasonic Convention adjourned, the state central committee, made up of Boston activists, challenged prominent businessmen, National Republican leaders, and Freemasons who dominated the governing board of the Monument Association.

Incorporated in 1823 to erect a memorial to the heroes of the American Revolution, the Association collected over $60,000 in public and private funds and commenced work in 1826. Two years later the money ran out, and by 1832 the monument was still only two-thirds finished. Alleging waste, mismanagement, and Masonic domination, a reform party of Antimasons secured election to the board in June 1831. Since attendance at annual meetings by the six hundred members was usually sparse, it was easy enough for an organized group to concert a coup and elect a new president and eight new directors. The Antimasons justified their takeover by blaming their predecessors for forfeiting public confidence through gross mismanagement. The old directors had bought three times as much land—fifteen acres—as the monument required, intending to make a killing in real estate speculation, but the quick profits never materialized and the Association found itself short of funds because it assumed too large a risk, "a national fault no doubt," argued the Antimasons. Even worse, the Freemasons had gained undue influence. In July 1825, Francis J. Oliver, a Boston builder, president of the American Insurance Company and Past Grand Master of the Grand Lodge, wormed his way onto the board of directors and then onto the arrangements committee that planned the cornerstone-laying ceremony. Hundreds of Masons swarmed into Charlestown for the occasion, marching in a colorful procession with the ancient Marquis de Lafayette, who hovered over the ceremonies like a ghost from the Revolutionary past. Grand Master John J. Abbott conducted the proceedings according to Masonic ritual and the result was a boom for Massachusetts Masonry. Yet the proceedings cost $7,000, an exorbitant amount, because architect Solomon Willard subsequently had to relay the cornerstone properly. For three years there was no progress on the monument. The Antimasons stepped into the breech and promised to restore public confidence, end waste and faulty management, and, above all, purge the Bunker Hill Memorial of Masonic influence. Their immediate aim was to wipe from the inscription table all mention of Freemasonry.

The Antimasons failed. National Republican leaders, members of the Boston's first families and prominent Freemasons quickly mobilized against the June coup with a coup of their own that enlarged the governing board and packed it with reliable men, and prohibited any tampering with the cornerstone. The Antimasons gave up the fight, and at the June 1832 annual meeting, Brahmins and Masons swept the election. Like the patriots who had abandoned Bunker Hill in '75, the Antimasons retired and regrouped to fight on more favorable terrain. But they did not forget their defeat. In 1836, when the Association appealed to the legislature for $23,000 in additional aid, the fiery Antimason from Fall River, Micah Ruggles, remembered the abortive struggle to purge the Association and opposed any further support for an enterprise under Masonic control.[27]

Whether agitating against Masonic influence in public office, in private associations, or in the churches, Antimasons attempted to impose standards of civic virtue and piety at a time when there was growing diversity in public opinion and confusion over civic standards. Men of no religious faith or of questionable principles won office. Unitarians, Universalists, Methodists, and others, once beyond the pale of respectability, now found the barriers tumbling. Ambitious climbers, newly arrived and unscrupulous, pushed their way into positions of honor and trust. Against these powerful tendencies, the Antimasons put forward a simple test—repudiation of Freemasonry—for determining whether a citizen or a leader measured up to the standards of Christian Republicanism they claimed the Founding Fathers had promulgated. If religious diversity or social mobility played havoc with the selection of leaders in the Republic, the collapse of the First American Party System and the slow development of a new one added further confusion and uncertainty. By the 1820s, Jefferson's wish had come true: Republicans and Federalists had amalgamated into an undifferentiated mass.

Christian Republicanism held special appeal to those that occupied positions of marginality in this rapidly changing society, people who felt disoriented by competitive norms and out of step with the popular currents. Marginality was a function of one's difficulty in fitting in with the new trends and social arrangement shaping early industrial America. These marginal men tended to possess a rigidity of temper, inflexible principles, and an inclination to resist the crowd and even risk isolation. The were likely, above all, to be militant moralists, given to judging themselves and others against demanding religious and civic standards.

Dr. Benjamin Waterhouse, who helped to launch Antimasonry in Massachusetts, symbolized, much as William Wirt and Timothy Fuller, the Christian Republican guardian of the American Revolution who found himself increasingly displaced. A professor of medicine at Harvard, Waterhouse's greatest achievement was to diffuse Jenner's cowpox vaccine against smallpox. A Jeffersonian Republican in Federalist Boston, he attacked tobacco and alcohol for causing degeneracy in the morals of the younger generation. He also antagonized his Federalist colleagues at Harvard Medical School, backed a rival one supported by the Republicans, and lost his position. In religion, too, he proved a troublemaker, sympathizing with the Calvinists who lost the battle to name the professor of divinity at Harvard and with Rev. Abiel Holmes, a moderate Calvinist driven by liberals from Cambridge's First Church.

Above all Waterhouse expressed alarm over creeping secularism and growing demographic instability. Fast Days, a traditional Puritan ritual observed twice a year in Massachusetts, devoted to prayer, thanksgiving, and quiet contemplation, had become a holiday for having fun. "I am doubtful if even our minister keeps a fast or any of his hearers," he lamented. The modern Fast Day had surely departed from that "of the ancient Jews and the Primitive Christians," as well as the early New Englanders.[28]

As the country changed, Waterhouse grew pessimistic. In 1833, a young Cambridge man, John Wyeth, returned from Oregon. When Waterhouse learned of Wyeth's bitter experiences, he collaborated with him to publish a narrative of the trip in which the doctor inserted didactic warnings aimed at discouraging "young farmers and journeymen, and mechanics who were so thoroughly imbued with these extravagant notions of making a fortune by only going over land to the other side of the continent." Wyeth had witnessed "more misery in eight months than most old men experience in a long life." Americans were in "great danger *in making haste to be rich,* instead of relying upon patient industry, which never fails to give a man his just deserts." The younger generation must not succumb to that "feeling of discontent" and that "desire to roam abroad" now so current. There was no escape from "sober industry"; any other course led to disaster.

Waterhouse set himself against some of the most powerful currents of the age—the pioneer spirit, the westward movement, the quest for personal achievement. His views, like his appearance, were anachronistic. A dapper, small man with upright carriage, he cared nothing for changing fashions whether in values, mores, or clothing. Like some other Antimasons, he cut a distinctive figure, a relic from the past, with his "powdered hair and queue, his gold-headed cane, his magisterial air and diction," and his familiar coat of shepherd's gray, which had been the latest fashion during his student days in Holland fifty years earlier.[29]

Like Benjamin Waterhouse, a young man studying at the Harvard Law School, just beginning his career, also exemplified marginality associated with the Antimasonic cause. Charles Sumner's interpretation of his republican heritage was formative. It later propelled him into the leaderships of another doubtful and unpopular cause, the antislavery movement in the 1840s. Sumner, reported a friend, holds to Antimasonry "as to the ark of the nation's safety. He feels unutterably on the subject, and he is pricked on by the wrong done his father by the Masons." Antimasonry was not the sort of enthusiasm to sweep through Harvard, but Sumner, like his father, had an independent, moralistic streak. In 1833 Sumner was president of the Harvard Temperance Society, another of his father's causes. He favored William Wirt over Henry Clay in 1832, which must have shocked his Cambridge classmates and may account for his defensiveness about Antimasonry. The Antimasons, despite excesses, he argued, were good men acting on grounds of conscience. In the fall of 1829, his father, Sheriff Charles P. Sumner, wrote a letter circulated widely by Antimasons, which attacked Freemasonry as at best useless and at worst dangerous. The Masons reacted bitterly, roasting him in weekly denunciations in the *Masonic Mirror* which wounded the younger Sumner. "I have been scourged into my present opinions by the abuse which my father has met with," he explained. The elder Sumner had braved the weight of public opinion earlier in his life to support the Jeffersonians in Federalist Boston. The son inherited the father's independence. In 1830 he subscirbed to William Lloyd Garrison's abolitionist weekly, the *Liberator,* displaying an early affinity for antislavery sentiments, a pattern common among Antimasons. Sumner's interest in Antimasonry, like antislavery, set him apart from his peers; Christian Republicanism in 1830 foreshadowed his later break with conservatives. A conventional legal career to make money held no allure, for it seemed cramping, mercenary, and petty. After floundering he finally found his niche in the 1840s, as leader of a revolt against the shoddy compromises of Whigs and State Street moguls who sacrificed American republicanism to appease the Slave Power.[30]

John D. Williams, a wealthy Boston businessman, exemplifies still another kind of Antimasonic marginality. Williams served on the party's state central committee and ran as a Wirt elector in 1832. Assessed for over $115,000 in 1830, he was one of Boston's richest men, prominent in the city's business and voluntary institutions. His wealth brought him into contact with the metropolis's leading men, yet he clearly was not one of them. Charles Francis Adams, who encountered him in the Antimasonic movement, remarked: "He is one of our rich men, yet exceedingly illiterate at first sight, and as I suppose somewhat sensible of the superiority of some who have greater advantages of education." Yet Williams did not defer to his social betters, certainly not to Boston's National Republican elite. In 1836, Williams, then in his mid-sixties, attacked the Bank of Ten Million, a scheme concocted by leading National Republican businessmen to establish the largest bank in the Commonwealth. Williams joined Robert Rantoul and other Jacksonian Democrats to rally the country members of the legislature, regardless of party, to defeat the proposal. He described himself as "a real friend to the industrious young men with small capital, just beginning in trade," who were misled if they imagined the bank would help them. His own career pointed to the virtuous path to success. As a self-made man, a farmer's son, Williams had arrived in Boston without friends or relatives. He sold vegetables, and from such small beginnings accumulated a large fortune. Unlike other men of fortune, Williams was proud to engage in physical labor. "Some think labor is an evil. But I consider labor one of the great blessings conferred on man," he advised. People sneered at him, Williams recalled. "Who are you, for I can remember when you went to market?" someone once told him. Williams replied: "So can I; and when I sold potatoes for twenty five cents per bushel, and carried them on my back nearly half a mile, into the bargain . . . !"

The current mania to increase bank capital—there were petitions for twenty-four new banks besides the Bank for Ten Million in 1836—was dangerous. The multiplication of banks only encouraged more borrowing and speculation, which sent interest rates higher. This get-rich-quick mentality was bound to result in disaster. "The whole duty of man is the duty we owe to our Heavenly Father, ourselves and our fellow men," Williams argued. His views were heresy on Boston's State Street. Defeated by one vote in the house of representatives, the Bank of Ten Million obtained the backing of all fifty-nine Boston Whig representatives. Not a single Whig leader spoke against it, but as a veteran Antimason, John D. Williams never flinched before the powerful.[31]

Like Williams, Sumner, and Waterhouse, the Antimasonic state committee resisted the mainstream. Leading that charge and directing the Antimasonic movement throughout its existence was Dr. Abner Phelps, who had briefly won the presidency of the Bunker Hill Monument Association on the Antimasonic ticket. Phelps, described by Charles F. Adams as "the chief of the Antimasonry Party in this State," earned degrees at Williams College and Yale and then practiced medicine in Boston, where he joined Old South Church, an Orthodox stronghold. Phelps was also a prominent advocate of state aid to railroads. In 1853 Phelps deployed his professional expertise in the service of piety in a book called *The Crucifixion of Christ Anatomically Considered* (1855), a novel approach to a familiar subject. "He seems to transfer the application of his belief in *human depravity* wholly to the devoted heads of those 'under' the influence of Masonic oaths," complained the *Masonic Mirror*. Driven by energy and ambition and with some organizational talent, he tried in 1831 to convince John Quincy Adams to run for governor on the Antimasonic ticket.[32] Joining him was George Odiorne, another perennial on the state committee and in the Bunker Hill Monument fight. Odiorne was a Boston merchant who headed a bank, sat on the Board of Alderman in 1823 and 1824, and was a founder of the Park Street Church, Orthodoxy's most important counter to Unitarian dominance in Boston. Odiorne also became active in the temperance and antislavery movements and ran for mayor and lieutenant governor on the Antimasonic ticket.[33] Orthodoxy united Phelps and Odiorne and joined them to John French, another fixture on the state central committee. A member of Phelps's church, he became its clerk in 1842.[34] These men were among a dozen Boston delegates to Antimasonic state conventions who worshiped at Park Street, Hanover Street (Lyman Beecher's), and Old South churches, three bastions of Orthodoxy in the metropolis. The important place that these and other prominent Orthodox Congregationalists occupied in the Antimasonic movement becomes clearer from an examination of religious sources of Christian Republicanism in Massachusetts.

9

Religious Sources
of Massachusetts Antimasonry

Watchman in Zion should awake, and sound the alarm. The evil is one which threatens to overwhelm the church. Those very principles of illuminism, which flooded France and Germany with infidelity, and deluged one of the fairest portions of the globe with human blood, have taken deep and extensive root in this country.
Moses Thacher, *Masonic Oaths, Neither Morally nor Legally Binding An Address . . . 1830* (Boston, n.d.), 28

In Massachusetts special circumstances shaped the third party's development and broadened the religious appeal of Antimasonry. Antimasonry emerged in Massachusetts at a critical period in the evolution of church-state relations. The movement to end the last church establishment in the United States finally succeeded in 1833 through a constitutional amendment that dethroned the Congregational churches. An increasingly bitter battle after 1819 between the Liberal (Unitarian) and the Orthodox (Trinitarian) wings of the state church gave dissenters new encouragement and allies. By the late 1820s many Trinitarians concluded that they stood to gain more from a voluntary system than would be gained by their Unitarian rivals.[1] The special strength of Liberalism in eastern Massachusetts, where Unitarianism and Universalism achieved a broader popular base than anywhere else in the country, strongly colored the sources of religious Antimasonry in the Bay State. Studies of the church affiliations of Masonic loyalists and Antimasonic activists show a sharp polarization along Liberal and Orthodox lines. More than half of the Antimasons identified were Trinitarian Congregationalists and another 30 percent were Quakers and Methodists, whereas a third of the Masons maintained Unitarian affiliations and 40 percent were Universalists or Episcopalians. Both of these last two denominations, like Unitarianism, offered a refuge from Calvinism. Moreover, Antimasons were almost twice as likely to be lay leaders in their churches as were Masons, suggesting that they made a deeper commitment to religious institutions.[2]

Denominational differences had long injected religious issues into politics, but Antimasonry gave religion a new edge, for it cut across denominational lines to unite a diverse body of Christians. Some Massachusetts politicians in the late 1820s sensed that a rising tide of religious intolerance threatened to upset the political equilibrium. The Federalist party had disintegrated partly because it could no longer harmonize its eastern Unitarian wing with its western Orthodox wing. Congressman Edward Everett, a Unitarian minister turned ambitious politician, sensitive to the shifting winds of public sentiment, found himself in a difficult position when the Sabbatarian movement reached Congress in the late 1820s and forced him to take a position on banning Sunday mails. Trinitarians were the strongest supporters of rigorous standards of Sabbath observance, but closure of the Post Office also received backing from some Unitarians and Episcopalians in Massachusetts. However Everett voted, he courted trouble. "I agree with you," he wrote to his brother, Alexander, in 1830, "on the impolicy of driving the Orthodox to rally as a party." Yet being in the middle proved uncomfortable. "To one who holds there is as much bigotry and fanaticism on the Liberal as on the Orthodox side, this is peculiarly vexatious," Everett confessed.

More than other National Republican politicians, Everett angled for Antimasonic support without abandoning his party. Anxious to succeed Governor Lincoln, preferring residence in Boston to Washington, he spoke out forcefully against Freemasonry and urged the Order to dissolve, incurring the enmity of Masons, especially those in National Republican ranks who could hurt him. The Antimasons proposed to run him for governor in 1833, but he refused unless the Nationals put him on their ticket too. The Masons vetoed that, which further raised his stock with the Antimasons. In 1835 Everett's strategy for mobilizing Orthodox sentiment behind his banner finally paid off.[3]

In performing a balancing act, Everett correctly appreciated that sectarianism threatened to pull apart the National Republican coalition. Throughout the 1820s, Orthodox Congregationalists nursed mounting grievances against Unitarian domination of the National Republican party and the machinery of state government, and growing confidence that they could serve their interests better by displaying political independence. Antimasons capitalized on this discontent. They deplored that virtually every member of the state's congressional delegation was a Unitarian. Moreover, Governor Levi Lincoln (1825–32) was a Unitarian; his running mate, Thomas L. Winthrop, was an Episcopalian Boston blueblood. Both symbolized the political subordination of Trinitarians.

Bitter disputes in dozens of communities fed sectarian divisions in politics. The battle between Liberals and Orthodox for control of the Congregationalist churches reached a climax in the 1820s when forty-five towns experienced division; another thirty-six split during the next decade. The Orthodox had suffered a stunning defeat at the hands of the Supreme Judicial Court. The judges, all Unitarians, ruled in the Dedham case (1819) that voters of a parish, a political body, not the church members, controlled church property and selection of the minister. The decision allowed the Liberals to mobilize majorities in many parishes—those voters not affiliated with another church, yet not necessarily born-again Christians—to gain control over Orthodox churches. Thus Unitarians, often a small minority among the converted, because of political influence extending to the state's high court, managed to govern dozens of churches.[4] Harvard, the preserve of eastern Liberals, occupied an anomalous position in a pluralistic commonwealth. Without an accommodation, warned Professor Moses Stuart of Andover Theological Seminary, the Orthodox, having a large majority in the State, could become a formidable political force. "But I dread such a contest," Stuart added.[5]

A careful examination of the gubernatorial election returns in the late 1820s should have warned National Republican leaders that there was trouble brewing. In 1826, and again from 1828 to 1831, Governor Lincoln ran behind, sometimes far behind, his statewide vote in one or more of the Connecticut Valley counties where Orthodox discontent was strongest. Then in the fall of 1831, the dam burst when the Antimasons polled a huge vote in Hampshire and Franklin counties, carrying the former, a feat they repeated in 1832.

The revolt in western Massachusetts had slowly gathered momentum. For a time Trinitarians hoped to reverse the Dedham decision, but by the late 1820s that appeared illusory. Increasingly, some threw their weight behind the Universalists, Baptists, and others who favored ending the religious establishment. The Orthodox had previously hesitated to enter the political arena for fear "that religion may suffer from a political contest," but their rivals showed no such restraint. Unless they broke Unitarian political power, the future of Orthodoxy was bleak. The decisive battle was for the younger generation. If the Liberals retained control over public office, together with their grip over Boston, the press, large corporations, and major voluntary associations, their patronage and influence would prove overwhelming. Young people would discover that advancement required Liberal patronage. The Liberals had employed secrecy and cabal, just like the Freemasons, to infiltrate strategic positions in church, state, and college in the generation before the Unitarian-Orthodox split came into the open. They had cleverly exploited Orthodox fears of the Jeffersonian peril, but as soon as the danger passed, they dropped Governor Caleb Strong, an Orthodox Congregationalist from the Connecticut Valley, for liberal Governor Christopher Gore, a wealthy eastern aristocrat. Then in the 1820s they joined with the Jeffersonians to back Liberals such as Worcester's Levi Lincoln. By such maneuvers they relegated the majority to a subordinate position in public life.

Parsons Cook, a Trinitarian minister in Ware, a strong Antimasonic town in western Massachusetts, summoned the Orthodox "to question the infallibility of the Unitarian aristocracy" and to strike down the anachronistic religious establishment. Without state funds, the Liberals would have to fall back on voluntary support, but their tepid piety was no match for the intense devotion of the Orthodox.[6]

In 1831 and 1832, the Antimasons ran Samuel Lothrop of West Springfield for governor and tapped a ground swell of anti-Liberal sentiment in western Massachusetts. Lothrop was an experienced politician who had represented western interests in the Federalist and National Republican parties. He had run for governor in 1824 and lost, served in Congress, and presided over the state senate. Lothrop's usual role was as mediator between east and west. A National Republican, he had first backed Henry Clay for President, and when he deserted to the Antimasons, surprised National Republicans taunted him for disloyalty, inconsistency, and opportunism.[7]

The Nationals now faced a politically aroused segment of Orthodox opinion. John Lowell reported that the Orthodox had formed "a combination among the sects, to seize the civil power. . . . No man is to be elected into any office of honor or trust, who is not a believer. . . ." Daniel Wells reported from Greenfield that Lothrop ran "as a candidate of a religious party, united with the Antimasons, and that he will be supported by those who differ from Governor Lincoln on religious grounds." "Neither sectarian zeal, nor political prejudice, nor the unreasonable requisitious and proscriptive spirit of anti-Masonry" would prevail, one National predicted.[8] To make sure, the Nationals in 1832 dropped Lieutenant Governor Winthrop, a Harvard overseer and Episcopalian, and replaced him with Samuel T. Armstrong, deacon of Boston's Orthodox Old South Church and prominent in many religious and benevolent associations, having made his fortune by printing and selling Orthodox literature. He was also popular among many of Boston's small businessmen and master mechanics. In 1833, the Antimasons, recognizing a hot political property, tried to pair him on their ticket with John Quincy Adams, but Armstrong turned them down. Armstrong's nomination was a clever bid by the Nationals for continued Orthodox support. Charles F. Adams rated him as quite a "political catch."[9]

Orthodox opinion was not monolithic. The question of Masonry divided the Congregationalist churches as it split other denominations. Many Congregationalists, whether liberal or conservative, remained convinced that the tariff, banking, and other questions of economic policy were more important than Masonry. The Antimasons proved especially successful in tapping Orthodox support where sharp conflicts between Unitarians and Trinitarians at the local level produced alienation from the statewide National Republican leadership, which had a bias in favor of Unitarianism. In the Connecticut Valley, an Orthodox stronghold, the demand for separation of church and state mounted, but in 1831, the National Republican senate defeated a constitutional amendment. In 1832 the legislature finally adopted an amendment which easily won popular approval, but Unitarians were still the main opponents, though some accepted change as inevitable. Boston, the center of Liberalism, cast 25 of the 90 votes against separation in the house of representatives. Five of seven Freemasons identified in the Boston delegation also opposed the amendment. Outside the Hub, the Nationals carried twice as many towns whose representatives opposed separation as did the Antimasons.

The end of an already much-weakened religious establishment carried important political consequences, for it robbed Antimasonry of one of its principal appeals in the Connecticut Valley. The Orthodox advocates of religious voluntarism had won an important victory, and in 1833 the third party's vote fell off sharply in the Valley. That year an eastern Liberal, John Quincy Adams, replaced Lothrop at the top of the Antimasonic ticket, while the Nationals replaced Governor Lincoln with "Honest" John Davis. A member of Lincoln's Unitarian church in Worcester, he escaped close identification with Boston Liberalism. Moreover, there were signs that the Liberals had learned a lesson, for in 1832 Orthodox Amherst's request for state aid received a warmer hearing in the legislature. Success seemed likely in the near future.[10]

The revolt of the Orthodox in western Massachusetts had political parallels in Boston, where Trinitarians had launched a counter-attack against Liberalism from the Park Street Church, founded in 1809. "You can form no adequate idea of the strength of Satan's kingdom in this vicinity," recalled the church's first minister in 1810. "Our church has been overwhelmed with contempt," he reported.[11] By the 1820s Orthodox prospects in the metropolis were on the upswing. The arrival of Lyman Beecher from Connecticut in 1826 was a turning point. An 1823–24 revival won over hundreds of new converts, especially among the country folk streaming into the city. Alarmed, Unitarian husbands forbade their wives and children from attending Orthodox meetings; the Unitarian propaganda machine churned out fresh attacks against the "absurdities" and "cruelties" of Calvinism. Yet Beecher sensed that the tide had turned. The defeat of Harrison Gray Otis for the governorship in 1823, Beecher thought, "has broken, and will, in its consequence, break forever their power, as a Unitarian party to proselyte and annoy, and defend by perverted legislative and judicial influence" their illegitimate privileges. Yet the burdens of being a Trinitarian in Unitarian Boston still remained formidable. "The whole weight of influence was turned against us, and the lash of ridicule laid without a stint," remembered one Orthodox worshipper.[12]

In 1825 and 1831 new revivals swelled the ranks of the Calvinists and strengthened their resolve. Beecher, well schooled in politics from his Connecticut days, instructed the Orthodox in Boston that Unitarian power rested on organization and patronage. Under his tutelage, the Orthodox entered city politics. Because they had previously avoided caucuses, the Orthodox had exercised little political influence. Now they attended nominating

caucuses and backed their own men and those of other denominations, anyone except Unitarians. In 1827 some young Orthodox men met secretly to
form a moral improvement society, the first of several. They plotted to kill
lotteries, bar liquor from Boston Commons on holidays, and expose Sabbath-
day violations. To gauge accurately the Unitarians' strength, they visited
Liberal churches, counted those present and discovered to their surprise that
those attending Trinitarian services outnumbered the Liberals.[13] The *Spirit
of the Pilgrims,* a sharply edited magazine which Beecher and others founded
in 1827, argued that as long as evangelicals avoided "the bustle and dissipation of political life," Liberals would make sure that Trinitarians received
"so small a share in the honor and emoluments of office." Trinitarians did
not seek political domination; they wanted only "a fair distribution of offices among several denominations of the state."[14]

The Bay State's leading Unitarian preacher, William Ellery Channing,
was not so sure. Channing warned against Orthodox intolerance and bigotry, for once "skillfully organized, trained to utter one cry," they were dangerous. Bernard Whitman, a Unitarian minister, controversialist, and the
foremost clerical defender of Freemasonry in Massachusetts, echoed Channing. He deplored the licentiousness of press and pulpit that allowed evangelicals to defame Unitarian clerics, public officials, and institutions such as
Harvard. Whitman accused the Orthodox of dividing communities into re-
ligio-political parties. Unless checked, the state's "best" men would avoid
public life, making room for those of mediocre abilities. Party competition
was healthy, Whitman advised, but political discussion should focus on the
tariff, banking, and internal improvements, not sectarian questions. He
pointed to a small town with an Orthodox majority in which sectarianism
infected everything, the schools, the lyceum, even domestic life for "the wife
attends one church, the husband another, and the children a third. . . ."
The result was a community cursed by endless "disputes, backbiting, slanderous imputations, and impious denunciations." Whitman responded to
the mobilization of Christian Republicans with a call for a new organization—the American Society of Christians—to unite "all who would conscien-
ciously endeavor to do morally right in everything . . . made up of some
from all religious parties and some from no religious party." Whitman's ecumenical, latitudinarian proposal only stamped him in Orthodox eyes as a
Liberal sectarian. His projected society smacked of Freemasonry.[15]

In eastern as in western Massachusetts, Antimasons tapped Orthodox
discontent. Their indictment of Freemasonry closely paralleled the Trinitarian indictment of Liberalism: both, they claimed, were latitudinarian, hostile to sectarianism, tolerant of lax morals and low standards of Christian
decorum; both employed secretive, conspiratorial methods to monopolize.
And as soon as evangelicals ripped off the façade of religious respectability
from Freemasonry, Liberals jumped to its defense.

The odyssey of Lewis Tappan provided further ammunition for both the
Orthodox and the Antimasons. Lewis Tappan, a Boston merchant who had

moved to New York City, renounced Freemasonry not long after he renounced Unitarianism. Reared as a Trinitarian in his native Northhampton, Massachusetts, he abandoned the faith of his ancestors for the more fashionable Liberalism of Boston, where he sought a fortune in trade. In 1827 Tappan announced his reconversion and caused a sensation. An account of his spiritual journey went through four editions and evoked widely reprinted responses by Reverends Henry Ware and J. P. Blanchard for the Unitarian side.

In New York, Lewis Tappan and his brother, Arthur, operated the largest silk importing firm in the nation. They became financial angels and driving forces behind a variety of benevolent organizations and now occupy an important niche in the history of antebellum reform, especially the abolition of slavery. Lewis Tappan's reconversion to Orthodoxy was a prelude to his renunciation of Freemasonry and commitment to militant reform.

Tappan had little interest in the theological disputes which preoccupied Unitarian and Trinitarian protagonists. He applied a simple, practical test. In Boston during the 1820s he closely observed the behavior of both groups and concluded that Orthodoxy produced better people. Unitarians, like Freemasons, argued that doctrinal differences were less important than Christian living. Tappan, however, maintained that doctrine and practice were closely connected. The Unitarians, he found, were often puffed with "Pharisaical pride," ready to impeach other people's motives, and rarely prayed in private or with their families at home. On the Sabbath, the Liberals boarded the boats and road the coaches, strolled down to the newsrooms and crowded into the theatres. And when it came to charity, they could match neither Orthodox donations nor their efforts to spread the gospel among the poor, domestic servants, children, and the heathen. Tappan found the Liberals to be worldly and self-centered, with little piety. They seemed to lack that warm sympathy for others which he found in members of the Orthodox churches. The difference Tappan saw was between a dead, secularized faith versus a living, burning, evangelical conviction.[16]

Neither the metropolis nor western Massachusetts proved to be Antimasonry's most fertile ground. The party's sudden decline in the west after 1832 left southeastern Massachusetts the banner Antimasonic region. Here a coalition of Hopkinsian Calvinists was centered in the Mendon Association, led by Nathanael Emmons. This coalition, as well as assorted sectarians including Christians, Calvinistic Baptists, Quakers, and New Lights, appeared highly susceptible to Antimasonry.

Antimasonry sprung up suddenly into a mass movement because it tapped grass-roots sentiments and channeled existing divisions into political directions that gave them fresh meaning. Churches, clergymen and laymen provided Antimasons with a ready-made organization and with leadership capable of mobilizing public opinion. At the grass roots Antimasons sensed that people faced disruption in the continuity of American experience. The spread of cultural pluralism and a market economy, the social and geographic fragmentation in towns experiencing development, the exodus of natives and the influx of birds of passage, the sudden appearance of new mill villages and marketing centers, each with new churches competing with the old town centers—changed forever the world of Antimasons.

Nowhere was resistance to modernizing currents in Massachusetts religious and social life more evident than among Hopkinsian Calvinists who formed the Mendon Association. The Hopkinsians resisted both the radical repudiation of Calvinism by Liberals as well as the efforts by modernizing Trinitarians to modify Calvinism without abandoning it. The Mendon Association played an important role in preserving Hopkinsian influence, resisting Arminian tendencies by buttressing the authority of Hopkinsian ministers in their churches. Towns with strong Hopkinsian leadership tended to gravitate to Antimasonry. Emmons endorsed the Antimasonic cause. Rev. Ethan Smith of Hanover, for example, prepared a report for the first Antimasonic State Convention which linked modern Freemasonry to infidelity and the Illuminati, resurrecting old allegations that tainted Masonry with French Jacobinism. Likewise, Rev. Moses Thacher of Wrentham, another Hopkinsian, was one of three Antimasons elected to the state senate in 1830, the first major electoral victory for the third party. Thacher emerged as the most active Antimasonic clerical politician in New England.[17]

Recently graduated from Brown, trained by the Hopkinsian from Rehoboth, Otis Thompson, Moses Thacher settled twenty-seven miles southwest of Boston in 1823 as pastor of North Wrentham's Congregational Church. Wrentham, a town of almost 2700 people in 1830, supported two Orthodox Congregational churches which had never compromised standards by admitting half-way members.[18]

In time Thacher joined the Masons, like many Wrentham men. Then suddenly he renounced the Order, won election to the state senate, and became a prominent Antimasonic activist. He edited newspapers, addressed Antimasonic conventions, and led the 1831 national convention in Philadelphia in prayer. No New England minister fought harder against Antimasonry, incurred such intense opposition, or suffered so much for his efforts.

Antimasonry propelled Thacher from an obscure country parson into prominence, but success turned to ashes. His church split over Masonry, and when he led the minority to form a new one, he alienated colleagues who shared his opposition to Freemasonry but could not stomach his ultraism. Isolated, embittered, Thacher struck back. Since 1829 or 1830, rumors had circulated that Thacher was an inveterate adulterer. Because Masons were the source of these reports, Antimasons discounted them, but once the Antimasonic movement ebbed, fresh rumors surfaced. Thacher tried to silence his defamers by prosecuting one of them for libel in 1836. He won the case, but the trial became a personal disaster. His name dragged through the mud and a year later he left Wrentham for good.

Thacher's Wrentham underwent only modest changes in the early nineteenth century, compared to other towns so close to Boston. It escaped de-nominational rivalry until 1830, when a Universalist church finally appeared. Wrentham also lay outside the mainstream of industrial development. In the 1820s its population declined slightly (4%) and then grew modestly (8%) in the 1830s. Agriculture dominated the economy, though later it became more diversified. By the 1830s there was a bank, and over a hundred people worked in cotton and woolen manufactures, while others made boots and shoes, hats, axes, and chairs.[19]

Early in the nineteenth century, some of the town's leading citizens formed a Masonic Lodge. It is puzzling why Thacher became a Freemason *after* the Morgan case had made Masonry suspect, and in face of opposition from nearby clergy. It is especially strange since he later admitted that Morgan's fate and the failure of top Masons to repudiate Masonic wrongdoing had turned him against Freemasonry. He blamed others for inducing him to join, assuring him that Masonry was respectable and that the furor over Morgan was a political diversion. Whether Thacher joined in good faith or as an infiltrator is unclear.[20]

In any case, Thacher became a zealous Mason. Unlike most who advanced only through the first three degrees, he took seven, including the Royal Arch degree. There were obvious practical advantages. The minister strengthened his standing with some of the most influential men in his church, for a third of the male members were Masons. In return he gave clerical approval to the Order and demonstrated that he was one of the boys. Wrentham's St. Albans's Lodge made him chaplain, charged him no dues, and compensated him for his services.

Masonry's growing popularity must have aroused Thacher's curiosity, especially since it attracted many members of his congregation, but it seems that he had other objectives. At the time of his induction he claimed that he was unaware that Masonry promoted infidelity and immorality, yet he had read William Morgan's exposé beforehand. Moreover Reverend John Ferguson of nearby Attleborough testified that both had concluded that Masonry was evil. "Our fathers in the ministry, had long agitated the subject, before we came upon the stage," and they had settled the matter, Ferguson noted. He assumed that Thacher shared his view that Masonic oaths were "wrong in principle," that the Order was a disguised form of Illuminism and infidelity. Therefore, when Thacher joined, Ferguson was astonished. American Calvinists since the 1790s had been in the forefront of Antimasonry, and Thacher had been familiar with the anti-Illuminist argument. Yet Thacher claimed that he had studied Freemasonry closely only just before he renounced in the spring of 1829. Moreover, Thacher admitted that he disapproved of Masonic funerals and celebrations, even while a member of the Order. The evidence suggests that Thacher became a member for clandestine reasons.[21]

The manner of his joining was curious. Instead of seeking admission to St. Albans's Lodge in Wrentham, he applied to a Providence, Rhode Island, Lodge, where his uncle, Moses Richardson, a high Mason, and his cousin, William E. Cutting, vouched for him.[22] Thacher must have feared that if he applied in his own town, religious liberals and Nothingarians might blackball him. Once inducted, however, he easily transferred to Wrentham Lodge. Thacher criticized Masonry because it admitted men "too *liberal* in their views of religion," but he did not discover that by affiliating.[23] Liberal ministers and laymen were prominent in the Order, including Unitarian Rev. Luther Wright in nearby Taunton. Thacher chose an indirect mode of joining because his own proscriptive attitude as a Hopkinsian must have been well known. He further feared the liberals because his motives were suspect.

When he quit Masonry, Thacher acted deviously. First he consulted with Rev. Nathanael Emmons and other neighboring ministers, including five who were Masons. He read them an address prepared for the Wrentham and Medway Lodges explaining his renunciation. Two Hopkinsian colleagues, Rev. Charles J. Warren of Attleboro and Rev. Preston Cumming of Dighton, endorsed the published version of the address. Emmons also must have encouraged him.[24]

Thacher's renunciation betrayed him. He claimed that he still cherished the Order, for Masonry in its pure, original form was a worthy institution, but immoral men had perverted it "from its primitive designs" in order to promote Illuminism, personal interests, and "sensual gratification." Yet Thacher pretended to hold out hope for reclaiming Masonry. The Masons at first took his criticism with good grace, unaware that Thacher acted in concert with local clergy and intended to publish his renunciation and blast "the fair fame of Masonry forever."[25]

Masonic members of his church accused him of deception, and some refused to renounce. Less than two weeks after his address to the Wrentham Lodge, Thacher forced the issue in the church. Joining the Freemasons was a sin, he insisted. He begged forgiveness for his own waywardness, denounced the Order, but unctuously insisted that he intended to stir no "unnecessary excitement" nor to wound "the feelings of any individual." With Antimasonry raging throughout the northeastern United States, especially in the churches, Thacher deliberately precipitated a crisis, since a sizable fraction of the male church members were Freemasons.

Thacher's confession brought the issue to a head. How could others remain in the Order if their pastor declared Masonry to be "a blood-stained body," a nursery of intemperance, selfishness, elitism, and infidelity. Thacher had thrown himself on the mercy of the church: "I ask the forgiveness of this whole congregation and of the world," he pleaded. He had succumbed to the "Anti-Christ," but he now saw the light. "Can you forgive . . . one of the grossest false steps I have ever taken?" he begged. The minister now expected others to follow his example.[26]

Reverend Moses Thacher had made Antimasonry a test of his leadership and of church membership. By December 1830, six members abandoned Masonry, but two refused. All were among the most influential townsmen, two manufacturers, a deacon, and the postmaster. Once before Thacher encountered resistance when he agitated the temperance question. His opponents struck back in a series of letters that accused him of "duplicity," "double-dealing," and acting with "impetuous rashness."[27] For weeks "false charges, slanderous reports, and insidious misrepresentations," Thacher complained, circulated widely for the purpose of destroying "my character."[28] The *Masonic Mirror* pilloried him mercilessly. Members of his church accused him of "carrying on a war of extermination" against a benevolent institution which he falsely misrepresented as anti-Christian and anti-Republican.[29]

Thacher demanded that the church discipline Anson Mann, one of his leading opponents, for accusing him of infidelity and atheism. A majority found Mann guilty, but the anti-Thacher elements refused to accept the verdict and appealed to an ecclesiastical council. The Thacherites rejected the council's jurisdiction. Hoping to prevent a split, the council, which included Lyman Beecher, found Mann guilty but persuaded him to sign a confession, which Mann watered down and Thacher dismissed "as a consummate trifling." Thacher turned on the council, accusing it of shielding *"six Freemasons* in the church acting in perfect *concert,* and making the most assiduous and persevering efforts to clear the seventh from censure."[30]

A split was unavoidable. On October 24, 1830, forty-eight Thacher supporters withdrew. "When a church becomes so corrupt either in sentiment or practice, that the discipline of the gospel *cannot be maintained,* it then becomes the duty of all those members, who are friends to gospel truth and gospel order, *to come out* and be separate . . . ," they explained.[31] Thacher accused the Masons of plotting his dismissal by recruiting into the church Freemasons from other towns. A second council reviewed the separation, found it "precipitate and irregular," and urged reconciliation, but the time was past. Most ministers with whom Thacher had customarily exchanged now shunned him as a dangerous ultraist. Even though most of the Masons in his church had resigned from the Order, Thacher doubted their sincerity and insisted on a purge.[32]

Eleven men and thirty-seven women followed Thacher into the new church—a minority of the men, but a majority of the women in the old church. The women saw him as a martyr in the struggle against Masonic subversion of Christian Republican families. Thacher had cultivated female support. Masonry, he preached, was dangerous to women and the family: it taught that the fair sex was "the lawful game of masonic concupiscence." The Masons, too, noted Thacher's frequent references in his diatribes to "abandoned wives, infamous characters, pimps, mistresses, and divorces" and to "virtue and divinity" becoming hostage to Masonic libertinism. They accused him of pitting wives against their husbands and subverting paternal authority. That may be why Thacher moved swiftly and secretly to form a new church, hoping to catch the male majority off-guard before husbands could pressure wives to desist from following the embattled minister.[33]

Thacher's Hopkinsianism helped him to explain and endure his isolation. Some ministers modified the doctrine of original sin to accommodate their congregations, but he stood fast. Nor would he compromise on Masonry. The clerical profession was full of cowardly, insecure men. There was "even more quackery in *morals* than in medicine," he observed. The buffoons and sycophants, he insisted, usually attracted "the largest share of public patronage." His weekly, the *New England Telegraph,* took sharp aim at Nathaniel W. Taylor, Lyman Beecher, and the New Haven theology for betraying Calvinist Orthodoxy. A majority of the Orthodox, he argued, had deserted their Calvinist heritage. It was the "character of multitudes to preach disinterested benevolence and practice selfishness," he lamented.[34] Yet even Hopkinsians and Antimasons deserted him. In 1831 he lost his bid for re-election to the state senate while other Antimasons triumphed in Norfolk County.[35]

Time dealt unkindly with Moses Thacher. The *New England Telegraph* failed in 1836, and Thacher's career in Wrentham drew to a close. Thacher's last years were painful. Scandal had haunted him since 1829. Caleb Sayles, a Wrentham manufacturer and one of the Masons in the church, accused him of multiple acts of fornication. According to Sayles, Thacher forced a woman to sign a certificate stating that he was not the father of her illegitimate child.[36] Antimasons discounted these rumors as Masonic defamation. But when General Preston Pond, a Wrentham storekeeper who had earlier called Thacher "an old whoremonger," circulated a new round of allegations in 1837, Thacher could no longer remain silent. He sued Pond for slander for accusing him of having "criminal intercourse" with Adeline Hawes, a young woman who resided in Thacher's household; for soliciting "the chastity of Jerusha Pond," the wife of General Pond's brother; and for "indecent levities and familiarities and obscenity of conduct" with Arsenath Holbrook, Susan Holbrook, and Lavonia Hall. During the trial, tawdry tales of Thacher's alleged indiscretions titillated the public and amused the Masons who avidly followed the prurient details in the Masonic press. The secret of Thacher's success with women, they could chuckle, was now in the open.[37]

The key witness for the defense, the source of General Pond's information, was Jerusha Pond, his sister-in-law. She had been a member of Thacher's church until September 1836, when she discovered his "immorality" and resigned. Adeline Hawes had told Jerusha Pond that Thacher repeatedly committed adultery with her. After each episode, she said, "Thacher was always very penitent" and engaged in long periods of fasting and prayer. He even contemplated "making himself a eunuch." In the witness box, General Pond admitted that some of the charges against Thacher were false, but he vouched for the veracity of Hawes's allegations.

Pond claimed that he himself had confronted Thacher: "Mr. Thacher, you have ———— more than a hundred times, no I won't say a hundred but a great many times" with Adeline Hawes, he recalled. Moreover, Jerusha Pond reported that she had discovered Thacher's right hand "where it had no right to be." Thacher acknowledged that he had sinned, Pond claimed, but he had repented and begged forgiveness. But Pond weakened his testimony by admitting that Thacher had confessed to committing adultery with Adeline Hawes only "in [his] heart," not in the flesh.[38]

The trial reached a dramatic conclusion when Adeline Hawes, the final witness, took the stand. She flatly contradicted Jerusha Pond's testimony on every point. Thacher had never seduced her; he had never "wet" her; he had never "humbled himself in the dust" before her, nor contemplated castration. The jury rendered an ambivalent verdict. It found General Pond guilty of slander but fined him only $5.00 damages and $1.25 in costs, not the $3,000 Thacher had sought. Pond had failed to make truth a successful defense. Hawes's testimony and the arguments of Thacher's counsel struck at the credibility of the Ponds. Yet the trifling penalty suggests that the jury found persuasive the arguments of Pond's counsel that Thacher's reputation was so badly tarnished that not even Pond's words could further injure it. The defense presented a succession of witnesses—ministers and prominent citizens—who testified that for years Thacher's reputation was under a cloud. Other witnesses rebutted their testimony, but nothing could clear Thacher's name. In the end, Moses Thacher won a dubious victory.[39] He secured legal vindication, but his position suffered damage beyond repair. The days of his usefulness to the cause of Antimasonry, abolitionism, and Hopkinsian Orthodoxy were over in Wrentham. In 1838 he left and by 1840 he had found a church in Wysoc, Pennsylvania, the first of several outside his native region, the scent of his greatest triumphs and defeats.

The emergence of a growing Antimasonic movement in southeastern Massachusetts where Hopkinsians were so strong encouraged Thacher to push himself forward, win public office, and become a shaper of public opinion. Other Hopkinsians also flocked to the Antimasonic cause, but more discreetly. They avoided doubting the sincerity of church members who quit the Order; nor did they insist on total purges. Thacher stretched his authority beyond the limits which laymen, even in conservative Calvinist churches, would accept, and courted isolation.

Thacher could look back to better days. How his pride must have swelled when party leader Abner Phelps, in his report to the 1831 Antimasonic State Convention, celebrated Thacher's heroic work. His name was "engraven on our hearts, and is destined to live in the history of our country." He had led "the forlorn hope of Antimasonry in Massachusetts, and gone up over his enemies in triumph." Confronting such a mighty opponent, the Masons employed "all the formidable engines of falsehood and slander" to destroy his character, but nothing could stop him from "fearlessly vindicating the liberties of his country."[40] That was the view in Lynn, Massachusetts, among other Antimasons who closely followed Thacher's case.[41] In Lynn and other new manufacturing communities, some citizens turned to Antimasonry to reconcile the new industrial order with Christian Republicanism.

10

Antimasonry and the Emergence of Industrial Society in Massachusetts

The Antimasonic party are the political salt of this country. . . .
They are mostly shoemakers, whose employment will insure them a
living, from which they cannot be driven. Threats . . . are in vain
attempted on them.   *Lynn Record,* 19 November 1834

Throughout Massachusetts, the most important industrial state in the
union, Christian Republican businessmen struggled to reconcile piety with
profits, capitalism with respect for labor, republicanism with growing inequality. In Worcester, Massachusetts, the wire-manufacturer Ichabod
Washburn devoted himself to evangelical Protestantism, temperance, abolition, upholding the dignity of manual toil, and Antimasonry. On the family
crest adorning his autobiography stands the ancient artisan cry, "By Hammer and Hand, All Arts Must Stand," a bow towards the doctrine that
labor creates wealth. Further west in Ware's Factory Village, home of a
textile mill financed by Boston capital, cabinet maker Thomas Thwing,
deacon of the Calvinistic Congregational church and twice elected Worshipful Master of Eden Lodge, abandoned the Order because he realized
that Masons "had forgotten the ties which bind us together" and had failed
to "live in the practice of 'Friendship, Morality and Brotherly Love.'" And
in the region around Fall River and New Bedford as well as in the shoe-
manufacturing capitol of Lynn—all Antimasonic strongholds—Christian
Republican entrepreneurs found in Antimasonry an antidote for the social
strains created by the coming of industrial society.[1]

Located on the Taunton River, close to New Bedford, Fall River (called
Troy before 1833) became a hotbed of Antimasonry, giving the third party
majorities from 1832 to 1834, and casting two-thirds of its vote for William
Wirt in 1832. Antimasonry surfaced here in the fall of 1828, when a crowd
overflowed the new schoolhouse to attend one of the first Antimasonic
meetings in Massachusetts. Elder Job Borden, a blind Baptist preacher of
many years standing, opened the proceedings with prayer. The audience

then heard accounts of recantations by seceding Masons, condemnations of secret societies and their blasphemous and subversive oaths, and it adopted an address to the people.[2] In December 1828, the Antimasons chose delegates to the "People's Convention" at Dedham and in January 1829, established a reading room.

The Antimasonic Reading Room was an innovation characteristic of this age of associations. Religious and benevolent organizations often established such places as a way to spread their ideas and to provide a meeting place for the curious and the faithful. The Fall River Antimasonic Reading Room opened at 9 a.m. and closed at 10 p.m. seven days a week. It gave people quick access to newspapers from around the country, not just Antimasonic journals but others printed in Baltimore, New York, Albany, Providence, and Boston. An agent managed the Room and was under instruction to rush down to the post office to fetch the latest newspapers. The Reading Room exemplified the breakdown of provincial perspectives, the emergence of a national arena of public opinion, and an eagerness to know what was happening around the country. Here, too, Antimasons found a social circle. The rules gave precedence to reading over conversation. Reflecting the religious sentiments of Fall River Antimasons, the Room welcomed clergy free of charge, prohibited lighting a fire on the Sabbath, and banned smoking.[3]

The Antimasonic leaders of Fall River were prominent businessmen engaged in transforming this previously sleepy backwater into one of the most dynamic smaller industrial communities in New England. Exploiting the abundant waterpower, a textile industry developed, and as workers flocked to Fall River, the town's population more than doubled in the 1820s, exceeding 4,100 by 1830. By 1840, 70 percent of the work force found jobs in the mills. By 1827 a regular line of steamers connected Fall River with nearby Providence, Rhode Island, the first of a series of transportation improvements linking it efficiently to the national market.

With growth came cultural diversity. Until 1816 the Baptists had the only church in town, but in that year the Trinitarians established a Congregational church, and by 1835 there were also Unitarian, Methodist, and Christian churches. An old Quaker community had long been resident in the region. With nine cotton factories and several other textile works, a bank, and an insurance company, by 1835 Fall River had undergone a sudden transformation within one generation.[4]

Industrial development created wealth, but it also brought class conflict. In 1832 a Mechanics and Workingman's Association in Fall River and New Bedford demanded a reduction in hours. Joseph and Jesse Eddy triggered a strike when they tried to lengthen the thirteen-hour day by half an hour. A fourteen-year-old girl in one mill had recently died and the doctor blamed her death on overwork. Besides grievances over hours, workers labored under a harsh discipline in this region where the family labor system was widespread. Benjamin Pierce remembered that at the age of eight, he and his older brother left school to work eighty-four hours a week for fifty cents. If a child fell asleep, he risked a beating. A worker who sued his employer on account of assault or mistreatment risked blacklisting.[5]

Antimasons, like other employers, opposed the strike. They argued that the turnout was the result of "a momentary excitement, and a misapprehension of" the workers' true interests, rather than "a settled determination to overturn the established custom of the place." The peculiar nature of the textile business—expensive technology and intense competition—required long hours. Capitalists acknowledged that they owed their success to the honesty and faithful service of employees, but they insisted that wages were fair and working conditions showed due regard for the health of employees. They blamed the troubles on "the inexperience which tends to sever the bonds of society, and array one class in hostility against another." Demanding a restoration of harmony and deference, the employers were confident that the mechanics had "no inclination to separate themselves from the interests of the whole, feeling as they do that their obligations to society are no less strong on one class than on another."[6]

In this setting of rapid industrial and community development and incipient labor struggle, some of Fall River's leading entrepreneurs gravitated to the Antimasonic movement, as did many manufacturers elsewhere. The most prominent was Micah Ruggles, an abrasive character who served on the Antimasonic state committee in 1829, was a vice president at the 1831 and 1833 conventions, and was a delegate to national conventions in 1831 and 1835. In 1831 he ran unsuccessfully for Congress against Joseph Hodges, a Freemason, but won election to the state legislature. Ruggles had close associations with two important groups in Fall River: the new industrial elite and a group of ex-Quakers, the New Lights, which overlapped. He was president of the Fall River Institution for Savings on whose board sat other Antimasons, but his most important position was as agent and treasurer of the Pocasset Company, the first large-scale mill in Fall River.

Before Ruggles joined the Quakers, he had served as a militia captain and was active in local politics. His religious awakening led to withdrawal from worldly affairs. The New Light tendency had originated in Lynn and spread southward to the New Bedford area through the powerful preaching of Quaker women. Ruggles and others rallied to the New Lights, who accused Friends of sinking into "a dead formality" and claimed that Quaker leaders imposed an authoritarian rule. The New Lights called for the relaxation of discipline, which they believed had subverted the primacy of the inner light, one of the well-springs of Quaker piety. Many New Lights eventually gravitated towards New Bedford's Unitarian church, but these New Bedford and Fall River New Lights were not searching for a safe, comfortable faith. Emerson, who preached in New Bedford in 1834, found an especially receptive audience for his transcendentalist message. Emerson's ideas, according to the historian of the New Bedford Unitarian church, was "intellectualized Quakerism, pure and simple."

The New Lights anticipated the Hicksite movement of the 1820s which led to a split within the Quaker fold. The Hicksite separation did not spread to New England, because the New Lights had already drained off similarly discontented elements. The New Lights, like the Hicksites, damned Freemasonry for corrupting and secularizing faith. When Ruggles ran for Congress against a Freemason, the National Republicans attacked his piety. They accused him of being an infidel, a "Unitarian Quaker" who held to no particular creed. Ruggles, they said, believed man could not sin because his mind was pure. Ruggles replied that he had never mocked Christianity, only fake Christians. "The doctrine of change of heart, and regeneration, I believed in, and professed it long ago," he averred.[7]

In 1831 and 1832, at a time of labor unrest, Ruggles contested James L. Hodges for a seat in Congress. The race was very close, but neither commanded a clear majority and repeated elections were necessary. The Nationals attacked not only Ruggles's religious beliefs but his social position. He was a man of fifty, yet had no accomplishments to his credit, little experience in public life, and had accumulated no fortune. His views on important national issues were unpredictable, his character capricious, and he suffered from being "an erratic visionary." During the sixth election in October 1831, Ruggles, in desperation, violated the older norm against personal campaigning by attending the meetings of mechanics, mingling with them, smiling, and shaking their hands. The Nationals hoped to undercut Ruggles anti-aristocratic appeals by claiming that when a tailor refused to support him, Ruggles cast aspersions on his lowly status. The Whigs were the genuine party of workingmen, they contended, for they had elected a mechanic—master builder Charles Welles—as mayor of Boston.[8]

It was men like Ruggles who pioneered Fall River's industrial development, men who perceived Freemasonry as at odds with a Christian Republican order. They projected onto it their apprehensions of the dangers posed by undemocratic class distinctions and moral disorder associated with rapid change. In adopting Antimasonry, Fall River entrepreneurs distinguished themselves from other businessmen.[9] Through Antimasonry, a segment of Fall River's elite affirmed devotion to more exacting standards of Christian belief and conduct than those attracted by Freemasonry's latitudinarinism and easygoing morality. The emergence of industrial society in Fall River had nourished fears that fed Antimasonry. A similar process was at work in the shoemaking capital of the United States, Lynn, Massachusetts.

For five years Antimasons dominated Lynn politics, pulling nearly half of the three-party vote in the early 1830s and sending large delegations to the third party's state conventions. Their success resulted from ambivalence over Lynn's remarkable growth. Lynn's boosters in the early 1830s were proud of the town's tremendous advance. Its population swelled by over 35 percent in the 1820s, which was prelude to a still greater boom in the 1830s, when it mushroomed by better than 50 percent. In the single year

1833 more than a hundred new buildings rose to accommodate the enormous expansion in the shoe business. But Lynn's celebrators praised more than its physical and material progress. They claimed that unlike other dynamic communities, Lynn did not sacrifice republican virtue. "Aristocracy is frowned upon," reported the *Lynn Record,* the town's Antimasonic newspaper. "An idler or a drunkard is scarcely known and would not be tolerated. There are *comparatively,* no poor nor rich" in this city of simple, neat homes, "without beggarly tenements." Unlike the cotton manufacturing towns, Lynn's business was more stable, less dependent on fluctuating tariff protection, and though profits were not as great, they ensured "a comfortable living, without furnishing the means of extravagance, or eliciting that thirst for speculation, which has often but unfortunately been engendered by the sudden and short-lived profits of cotton and wool manufacture."[10]

Yet such boosterism could not hide anxieties that industrial development even in Lynn, as elsewhere, carried considerable risk. In 1826, the Society for the Promotion of Industry, Frugality and Temperance, organized by the town's prominent businessmen, came into existence to promote in the populace those virtues one could no longer take for granted. Into the town hundreds of newcomers flowed without solid links to local families and households that could monitor and discipline behavior. The efforts of the Society fell short of expectations, for by the early 1830s a new temperance movement surfaced that made Lynn one of the first towns in the county to deny licenses to liquor sellers. Yet in 1831, the Overseers of the Poor expressed dismay that though temperance had gained ground, the expected payoff—a decline in pauperism—had not materialized and expenses seemed headed upwards.[11]

Like the Society, Lynn's Institution for Savings hoped to encourage thrift and hard work to secure people against the hazards of hard times and the miseries of dependency.[12] But here too the advocates of industrial morality ran into difficulties. First, male shoemakers organized a Cordwainer's Society in 1830 to protest low and fluctuating wages. The female shoe binders also organized to raise wages. Some thought the solution was in cooperative workshops that eliminated exploitation by the shoe bosses; others objected to the practice of truck payment which offered employers new opportunities for chiseling. Underlying these early working-class organizations in Lynn was opposition to being treated as a commodity. Workers expected that an honest day's toil yielded a competency; yet that was not always true. Neither temperance nor industry paid off, let alone produced savings, when wages fluctuated wildly without apparent reason and fell below the artisans' notion of just compensation. Even when the shoe business prospered, the women of the Society for the Protection and Promotion of Female Industry complained that their wages fell. "Equal rights should be extended to all—to the weaker sex, as well as to the stronger," they argued, translating their demands for economic justice into the language of gender-blind artisan republicanism.[13] But neither of these early organizations was successful or lasted long.

Lynn workers lacked cohesion and unity, and, like capitalists elsewhere, Lynn's rejected working-class notions of moral economy that insisted that labor was not merely a factor of production. Impersonal market forces, not grinding shoe bosses, determined the worker's compensation, the *Lynn Record* instructed. At a Fourth of July celebration sponsored by Antimasons, Chief Marshal Captain William Abbott expressed one view of Lynn Antimasons towards unionism: "Trade Unions of the North and Disunion of the South, children of 'Old Rebellion.' May they speedily land in a 'six foot grave.'" Yet Antimasons had to admit that cordwainers still suffered unjustly from the contempt with which "the purse proud" and the idle looked down on manual labor. Middle-class spokesmen, who ritualistically celebrated the sturdy independence of the mechanics, acknowledged that "the fetters of prejudice, forged by the aristocracy of the old world" persisted in the new.[14] The mechanics were republican exemplars, seeking only a competence and shunning "the vice and gorgeous temptations of a fashionable life." Yet their future was bleak, for the apprentice who hoped to ascend to an honorable station by virtuous industry could no longer count on a fair reward. Apprenticeship seemed to some "the alphabet of servitude and degradation," though the system had once been "one of the best symptoms of the long continuance of our republican institutions."[15] For Lynn's five thousand shoemakers in the late 1830s—half the population—the prospects to escape drudgery were diminishing.

While the experiences of the emerging working class increasingly diverged from the rhetoric of artisan republicanism and counsels of bourgeois thrift and industry, the lifestyle of the emerging middle class made more evident and painful the growing gulf between classes. People of moderate fortune, reported the *Boston Journal,* indulged in conspicuous consumption, insisting on the latest fashion because "a man's clothing is of more consequence than his character, for his credit could depend on it." Daughters could not do without the latest "French hats and blond veils" for fear of hurting their social prospects, and these attitudes filtered down to the working classes. Likewise, the passion for recreational travel and public amusement had killed the old, simple modes of leisure. Mechanics neglected their jobs and abandoned their debts to board the steamboats to "take a peep at the great canal, or the opera-dancers." And mothers even left their children in the care of others so they could "improve their minds at the Mountain House or The Spring."

The temperance movement, in which Lynn Antimasons played a major role, was another sign of moral disquiet, for it was much more than a strategy for squeezing labor out of cordwainers. It sought as much to reform the behavior of the middle and upper classes, and its greatest success was among these elements. The *Lynn Record* called for an end to genteel tippling at the hotels and public houses by the trend-setters. "Rum drinking was first made *fashionable* by the personal example of *fashionable* people." Reform must begin at the source, with "the dandies—tight pants, tight-laced gentry which lounge about the hotels and fashionable drinking places on Sundays. . . ." Lynn Antimasons complained that Governor Levi Lincoln displayed "an overseeming fondness for parties, balls, military parades and *display* of all kinds." His example set an unwholesome moral tone and reflected patrician pretensions.[16]

Lynn's Antimasonic leaders came from a segment of the business community which insisted on temperance, piety, and simplicity, but also respect for the nobility of labor, the worth of the mechanic's art. In the mid-1830s Quaker manufacturers, led by Antimasonic leader Jonathan Buffum, proprietor of the *Lynn Record,* established manual labor schools for males and females. Concerned with improving the physical and moral development of their children, this fraction of Lynn's bourgeoisie imposed on the rising generation a regimen aimed at inculcating republican virtue. Like similar schools that spread elsewhere in the 1820s and 1830s, Lynn's manual labor institutions combined academic instruction with manual exercise, but whereas schools typically offered poor young men a chance to acquire education inexpensively, the Lynn schools, serving local youth from prosperous families, had a somewhat different purpose. Lynn parents did not aim to prepare children for careers of manual toil but to inculcate virtue. The schools would toughen the bodies of softies whose social position spared them physical labor, especially women. Moreover, the regimen would channel youthful energies, otherwise dangerous, into wholesome activities and thereby protect young people from the temptations of vice and the risk of mental disorder. Above all, the schools reaffirmed the dignity of labor at a time when invidious distinctions among classes and disdain for manual jobs were growing. Theodore Weld, the great evangelist and abolitionist, wrote tellingly that the manual labor movement hoped to overcome differences which "have so long operated to estrange" the working classes from others. Only if children from more advantaged backgrounds, not intended for manual labor, appreciated the virtues of toil would the two classes "approach each other with looks of kindness, and form a compact, based upon republican equality, and the interchange of mutual offices of courtesy and of kindness." Women from homes where servants performed most of the hard chores stood in special need, for someday they would assume the principle responsibility for rearing republican children.[17] For leaders of Lynn's new industrial bourgeoisie, the manual training movement, like Antimasonry, offered opportunities for reaffirming republican norms. The growth of Masonry in Lynn made evident the spread of corruption and the need for reform.

Masonry's popularity in Lynn stretched back to the beginning of the century. Lynn's Mount Carmel Lodge dated to 1805. In the 1820s it was prosperous enough to erect a Masonic Hall, but Antimasonry soon made life impossible for Lynn Freemasons. They eventually dissolved the Lodge and sold the Hall in 1835. First they temporized by opening the Hall to public functions, but that failed to satisfy critics. Masons found themselves subject to intense personal pressure. The Lynn Committee of Correspondence—a name borrowed from days when republicanism was born in America—wrote to Masons beckoning them to renounce. Under social pressure, in March 1830, William F. Ingalls, a cordwainer, complied, and so did William Luscumb, a sign painter. In 1831 James Pratt, a prominent Quaker businessman, also made his peace with the committee. In the close world of the shoemaking capital, it was not easy to resist public opinion.[18]

The structure of Lynn society helps to account for the weight of conformist pressures. Lynn was nearly a single-industry town. Neither large-scale commerce nor other kinds of manufacture competed with shoe production. The town was inbred. An unusually high proportion of Lynn folk remained rooted in the community, intermarrying with other old Lynn families. Seven family surnames accounted for 1,260 people in 1834, a degree of inbreeding, the *Lynn Record* speculated, few towns matched. Individuals sharing common surnames were not necessarily of the same family, but there were clusters among these large families which shared close economic, religious, kinship, and political relations. There is extensive evidence from other New England towns in the period that members of a numerous family in a town tended to vote for the same party. Adding to the force of family influence was neighborhood clustering. Many Quakers lived on Quaker Hill; the fishermen concentrated in the Swampscott section of town and were known to march *en masse* to the polls to cast two hundred solid votes for the Democrats. Because of its unusual degree of inbreeding and economic homogeneity, Lynn attracted few foreign-born people in the early nineteenth century. Yet when rapid growth in the 1820s and 1830s propelled hundreds of newcomers into the town, the unusually stable, familistic, deeply rooted segments proved especially sensitive to the disturbing presence of so many birds of passage. They were also concerned that the younger generation of Lynn natives did not pick up bad habits from outsiders. The bonds of community among old Lynn families thus remained strong and inhibited the development of an impersonal system of social relations, even as Lynn underwent industrialization.[19]

Antimasonry was a movement to impose civil and moral standards on people, much as other reform movements, as well as to reaffirm faith in republicanism. Lynn was proud of its contribution to winning the American Revolution. Now a new generation tested its mettle against the latest enemy of American republicanism.[20] Aristocratic forces might gain mastery in Boston to the south and Salem to the north, both commercial centers where Antimasonry made little headway, but Lynn was different. It became Antimasonry's stronghold in Essex County. Some people looked down on Lynn for its peculiar ways, noted the *Lynn Record*, but they "no doubt begin to see the folly of despising the poor cordwainers, since they find them to be so intelligent and patriotic as other people." Their devotion to Antimasonry proved that. While some people scoffed, "Lynn shoemakers—what do they know about political affairs?," Lynn's affinity for Antimasonry rendered such attitudes "contemptible." If Lynn stood nearly alone in the region strongly embracing the Antimasonic cause, that was because Essex County had one of the highest proportions of aristocracy in the United States.[21]

By focusing on the aristocratic dangers of Freemasonry, Antimasons diverted cordwainers from other manifestations of class inequality, a pressing concern in view of the propensity of some shoemakers, men and women, to organize trade unions. Competition, not price fixing, was the order of the day, capitalists argued. The Workingmen's parties in other communities were subject to manipulation by non-mechanic elements, they added. Lynn's cordwainers should be wary of anarchists, Fanny Wrighters, and radicals who exploited workers' grievances for their own ends.[22] In Lynn the Workingmen's party made no inroads, for Antimasons pre-empted the field and constructed a broad-based coalition that combined shoe bosses and shoe workers, an early example of the political collaboration which inhibited the development of class parties in the United States.[23]

In Lynn, the Masons were a more exclusive group than the Antimasonic activists. Almost half (46%) of the Masons were proprietors of businesses compared to 38 percent of the Antimasons. Slightly more than half the Antimasons were manual workers, mostly cordwainers, compared to a third of the Masons. The Masons also owned more real and personal property to judge from tax assessments. Almost a third of the Antimasons studied owned no real and 38 percent no personal property compared to 20 percent and 30 percent respectively for the Freemasons. A higher proportion of Masons occupied the top strata of the wealth distribution. A list of Democratic supporters allows further comparison, though it was composed of those protesting election irregularities and was a less exclusive list than the Antimasonic list derived from candidates for office. Half the Democrats were also manual workers but fewer were shoemakers and fewer were proprietors than among the Antimasons. Moreover, shoe manufacturers were much less common among Democrats, while fishermen formed a major element. The Democrats were somewhat less wealthy than the Antimasons: almost half (45%) clustered in the lowest stratum of real property holders; conversely a higher percentage of Antimasons occupied the upper strata of the real and personal wealth distribution. When Antimasonry declined, the third party's supporters tended to amalgamate with the Democrats, making them the leading party in Lynn in the late 1830s, but earlier the third party successfully claimed the popular mantle.[24]

Lynn's leading Antimasons also had important links to the town's major religious denominations, ties which distinguished them from the Masons. The most prominent Masons tended to be religious liberals associated with the Unitarian, Universalist, and Episcopalian churches. The *Lynn Record* reported that the Masonic Lodge included 55 Methodists, a dozen Orthodox Congregationalists, 44 Unitarians, 9 Baptists, and a couple of Quakers. The Antimasons attempted to pressure Christians to abandon Masonry, but they had more success in influencing members of some other denominations than others.[25]

The religious basis of Lynn Antimasonry, like the class basis, was diverse. The National Republican newspaper *Lynn Mirror* described the Antimasons as "composed of seceders and Quakers, old darks and new lights, and . . . Anti-Christians . . . and anti-republicans. . . ."[26] Lynn was a stronghold of New England Methodism, and when Masonry proved divisive among Methodists in many parts of the country, Lynn was no exception. The Methodists had been a major source of strength in the Jeffersonian Republican party early in the century. The limited success of Lynn Jacksonians in reviving the party after 1828 suggests that they no longer could count on a solid phalanx of Methodist voters. The partisan loyalties of other denominations also shifted. Orthodox Congregationalists and Quakers had been pillars of Federalist strength, but both these groups, especially the Quakers, leaned to the Antimasons. The Quakers were especially prominent among the Antimasons. It was a Quaker who "strutted through our streets, exclaiming in the most boastful and disgusting manner, 'I am the father of Antimasonry in Lynn.'" Critics of Quaker Antimasonry turned tables on those who charged Masonry with shielding men of loose morals. The Quakers had perfected hypocrisy and now projected their own deficiencies onto the Masons, they claimed. Particularly exasperating was the willingness of Quakers to make common cause with the New Lights who had originated in Lynn some fifteen years earlier. Jonathan Buffum, a leading Antimason, disrupted the Quaker meeting house in 1822 and landed in jail with other New Lights convicted of riot. The *Lynn Mirror* taunted Antimasonic Quakers for allying themselves with Buffum, who, a decade earlier, had called them "the sons of Belial" who "thurst for our blood" and engaged in "Spiritual Cannibalism." Yet Buffum became the commander-in-chief of a large Antimasonic party, which included many he used to denounce.[27]

Uniting elements from different denominational traditions was the view that a church that tolerated Masonry tolerated infidelity, undermined its ability to impose discipline, and legitimized hypocrisy. Lynn Unitarians came in for especial criticism. When Antimasons sought permission to hold a meeting at the Unitarian church, six of the seven trustees at first agreed, as did the minister, but once they came under Masonic pressure, they reversed themselves. The matter went to the membership, many of whom were Freemasons, and they voted to close the house to the Antimasons, though they opened it to Universalists.[28]

It was characteristic of Lynn Antimasons to give strong support to other causes of moral reform. "The Antimasons are in favor of a wholesome reform in all its branches," proclaimed the *Lynn Record*. "Republican *liberty* is their object—Freemasonry, Intemperance, Slavery are the leading obstructions—which they are struggling to remove." Devoted to the common welfare, in contrast to the Whigs and Democrats, Antimasons sought neither personal benefit nor to advance the interests of a segment of society. "We are not partisans," they boasted. "Antimasonry is virtuous democracy—pure, rational, well-informed democracy—without radicalism, without licentiousness," aiming for "a real, rational, thorough reform, moral and political." Their success against Freemasonry in Lynn pushed Antimasons in other directions, especially against liquor consumption and slavery. The temperance cause was as vital as the destruction of Freemasonry to assure that a sober and virtuous citizenry could meet taxing republican obligations. Just as many churches temporized over Masonry, so they hesitated to ban liquor for fear of losing members, antagonizing powerful supporters, and causing a ruckus. But genuine Christian Republicans must condemn drinking as a sin just as they must root out Freemasonry which was a system "of selfishness, of falsehood, of adultery and fornication. . . ."[29]

The American middle classes divided sharply in the early nineteenth century over questions of moral reform. In most communities, for example, only a minority backed immediate abolition of slavery, preferring to support the colonization movement, which did not threaten southern slavery, jeopardize party unity or sectional harmony, and proceeded on racist assumptions that blacks, free or slave, should be removed to Africa. Colonization sought to direct antislavery sentiment into harmless channels that enabled the guilt-ridden to deceive themselves that they served the cause of Christian conscience and republican justice without disturbing anyone. Such hypocrisy got short shrift in Lynn. From the outset William Lloyd Garrison found Lynn especially receptive to his abolitionist message. The town became a stronghold both of abolitionism and later of the Liberty and Free Soil parties of the 1840s. There were two large antislavery societies in the 1830s, one for men (founded in 1831) and another for women (1837). A third of the male abolitionists were Antimasonic leaders, compared to 10 percent who were Freemasons. Like Antimasonry the abolitionist movement attracted shoe bosses and shoemakers. This overlap in leaders and similarities in popular support grew out of the perception that slavery, like Masonry, was an enemy of Christian Republicanism. "There is more slavery in the United States," proclaimed Daniel Henshaw at the 1834 Antimasonic Fourth of July celebration, than in monarchical Europe. Slavery, like Freemasonry, denied equal rights and legitimized crimes against humanity. When mobs assaulted the abolitionists in the 1830s, Antimasons blamed the Freemasons. The Masons had resorted to mob rule earlier when they tried to suppress Antimasonic lecturers and meetings. "Riots are the *masonic mode* of answering the arguments of adversaries," Antimasons argued. The mob spirit, manipulated by gentlemen of property and standing, even infested Lynn. In August 1835, anti-abolitionist vandals tried to suppress a meeting of the female antislavery society, tossed eggs at the office of the

Lynn Record, and then broke some windows before invading the building. Christian Republicans turned back the rowdies.[30]

By 1834 success had taken the wind out of Lynn Antimasonry. Temperance and abolitionism now appeared as more salient causes, still facing great resistance, while the Bank War made the question of national economic policy harder for Antimasons to subordinate. In 1830, Antimasons had persuaded voters that the old partisan loyalties were no longer relevant.[31] Lynn, once a strong Jeffersonian town, experienced party amalgamation in the 1820s, as did the rest of the state. Andrew Jackson's election stimulated only a modest revival of the Democratic party's fortunes. Antimasons made their principal inroads among the majority of voters accustomed to supporting the National Republican ticket. The *Lynn Record* backed Henry Clay for President but then switched to William Wirt. The next year a "young men's" ticket, whose leaders were Democrats, unsuccessfully challenged the Antimasons in the election of town officers.[32]

Hopes for revival by the major parties faded until 1835, when the Antimasons finally went into decline. For the first time since 1830, the third party failed to win the town elections after several ballots. Thoughts turned to coalition with one of the other parties. As elsewhere in Massachusetts, Lynn Antimasons joined with the Democrats. Opposition by some Democrats to the anti-liquor position of Antimasons was an obstacle to amalgamation, but the pro-temperance faction among Democrats prevailed and that smoothed the path to unity. The Democrats emerged as the leading party in the late 1830s. Antimasonic leaders split: of those who could be traced, half became Whigs and half Democrats. The majority of Masons (88%) became Whigs.

The Lynn Democrats welcomed the infusion of Antimasonic strength. They recognized the third party element as "moral operatives," noted champions of peace, abolition, and temperance, and now worthy partners in the quest for Jacksonian Democracy. Analyzing the Whig defeat in 1838, the *Lynn Freeman* reported that former Antimasons shook hands with Democrats at the Jacksonian rally: "Workingmen drank wine with the Gentry, and amalgamationists chatted with the regulars."[33]

The pattern of party transition in Lynn differed somewhat from the rest of the state, where the statistical evidence indicates a more complicated reshuffling of voters. According to ecological regression estimates, half of those who voted for the Antimasons in 1832 and also voted in 1836 split between the Whig and Democrats, but a larger body of Antimasonic voters stayed home. (Table 10.1.[34]) Antimasonry mobilized an element that voted for a moral reform movement in the form of a party, but many of these antipartisans were not deliverable by Antimasonic leaders to the two major national parties, especially since the Antimasons had played down the importance of other issues. Those who remained leaders of the third party after 1833 tended to endorse the Democrats, and because that party was so much weaker than the Whigs, the influx of Antimasonic support was proportionately more important.[35]

Regional variations had roots in demographic factors. An important difference between the multiple regression statistics for 1836–40 and those for 1831–33 was the tendency for manufacturing and maritime employment to depress the Democratic vote sharply. Even more noticeable were shifts in the impact of religious variables on party fortunes. In 1836 and thereafter, Orthodox Congregationalists boosted the Whig vote more than did any other variable. No longer divided over Masonry or troubled by the now-settled issue of religious establishment, the Orthodox once again emerged as the relatively unified political force they had been in the 1820s. By contrast, the Baptists, who earlier had boosted the Democratic vote, no longer exercised a statistically significant impact on that party's fortunes. This suggests that some Baptists were moving away from earlier Democratic proclivities while others retained them. The Baptists no longer gravitated to the Democrats as a bloc since they no longer experienced persecution or suffered from second-class legal status. On moral issues, such as Sabbatarianism and the liquor question, they moved closer to other groups sharing a Calvinist tradition, such as the Orthodox. Still there were elements of continuity among religious denominations. Methodists and Free Will Baptists typically boosted the Democratic vote throughout New England in the early 1830s, and continued to do so in Massachusetts in the late 1830s, though to a lesser extent. The Universalists also boosted the Democratic vote, but the Unitarians, who earlier had advanced the National Republican vote, no longer exhibited significant statistical impact in the late 1830s. Perhaps with them, too, separation of church and state and the decline of Antimasonry lessened tensions with the Orthodox, though the temperance question was a persistent irritant. (Table 10.2.[36]) Whigs recognized that denominational shifts altered voting demographics. They credited Nathanael Emmons's endorsement in 1836 with winning conservative Calvinist votes for the Whigs. In Lynn, the arrival of Rev. Parsons Cooke added a strong voice against the town's ultraists, and he leaned to the Whigs. Likewise, in Newton, William Jackson, the Trinitarian Antimasonic leader who had successfully battled for a seat in Congress the Unitarian Henry Dearborn, a National Republican, moved into the Whig camp.[37]

Both Democrats and Whigs, following the third party's poor showing in 1834, angled to sweep the remaining Antimasons into their column. As the weaker of the two major parties, the Democrats had more incentive to court the Antimasons. After the fall 1833 election, Democratic leaders and Antimasons explored a coalition. Members of both parties collaborated in the General Court, especially in the senate, where they attempted to block the Whigs from picking only Whigs to fill the seats not chosen by a popular vote.[38]

The prospect of an Antimasonic-Democratic alliance worried the Whigs.

Senator Daniel Webster, pushing his perennial quest for the presidency in the run up to the 1836 election, curried favor among the Antimasons in Massachusetts and in other states where they were important.[39] In 1835 the Whigs made sure that a coalition did not threaten their grip on state government by running Edward Everett for governor. Everett had long advocated Antimasonic sentiments at considerable political risk, but once in office, Everett proved a big disappointment. He continued to appoint Masons who were good Whigs, and some Antimasons cried betrayal. John Quincy Adams's defeat for the United States Senate in the Massachusetts General Court gave Antimasons further grounds for discontent with the Whigs.[40] Once in office, Everett's Antimasonic sympathies appeared skin-deep. Finally Everett's attack on abolitionists in his inaugural address affronted political moralists and reminded them that while in Congress, Everett had curried favor with the slaveholders. Many Antimasons agreed with Charles F. Adams, who pegged Everett as "a double hearted man if ever there is one on the face of the earth."[41]

Still in 1835 the Antimasonic state committee declared that the third party had achieved its objectives. Freemasonry was in decline and there was little need now for an independent third force. Masonry seemed beyond recovery. At a recent meeting of the Grand Lodge, only a handful assembled. "The enemy have either surrendered or hid, run away, or mingled in our ranks," claimed the *Boston Advocate*.[42] The best strategy for assuring that Masonry did not revive was collaboration with the Democrats. In 1834, by going it alone, the Antimasons had failed to elect a single state senator; the Whigs installed fifteen Masons. By joint efforts, however, in 1836 the Democrats and Antimasons elected eighteen out of forty senators, and there were only six members of the Order in that body. Coalition also produced the "Report on Secret Societies" by the senate, which exposed anew the evils of Masonry. At the local level, too, Antimasons found the Democrats tolerant. The Democrats nominated for Congress Antimasons such as Nathaniel Borden of Fall River and Amasa Walker of Boston. They included Antimasons on their 1836 presidential electoral slate and incorporated other Antimasonic leaders into the party ranks. Most of the surviving Antimasonic newspapers backed Van Buren in 1836, with Ben Hallett's *Boston Daily Advocate* in the forefront. Hallett's journalistic fortunes linked him to the third party's fortunes. Since most newspapers were party organs, deriving advertising and patronage from partisans, Hallett had special reason to worry. Coalition gave Hallett a new lease on life as a Democratic editor, with special influence among the Antimasonic Democrats. In 1836 Hallett told a Democratic gathering at Palmer that he was a Democrat because he was an Antimason. "Antimasonry has been one of the most efficient pioneers of Democracy in New England," he proclaimed, because its basic principles were those of the Democratic party: opposition to "a secret monopoly for the benefit of the few at the expense of the many." Rhetorically, at least, it was not difficult for Antimasons to adapt their equal-rights talk to Democratic themes that stressed the dangers of corporations and bank monopoly, especially now that Masonry was in decline.[43]

In 1836 the coalitionists controlling the Antimasonic party's statewide machinery endorsed both Marcus Morton for governor and Martin Van Buren for President. A minority held a counter-caucus to oppose Van Buren. In the able hands of an editor like Hallett, both Morton and Van Buren emerged as original Antimasons. Morton had always opposed Masonry; his father had voted against a charter for the Grand Lodge in 1812. As for Van Buren, he had moved swiftly when he was governor of New York to punish Masonic wrongdoing. On the slavery question, Van Buren's record posed real difficulties because of his long record in appeasing Southern Democrats, but Hallett argued that he was nevertheless preferable to the two leading Whig candidates, both regional nominees, Hugh L. White of Tennessee and William H. Harrison of Ohio, both pro-Southern and pro-slavery. In the fall of 1836, Massachusetts Democrats could point to Antimasons in their ranks as proof that theirs was the party of moral, social, and religious reform. The Antimasons, champions of the producing classes against aristocracy, had finally found their natural home. For years the Antimasons had led the battle against "exclusive privilege and anti-Republican titles and distinctions, and in steady support of the supremacy of equal laws. . . ." In Hallett's version, the Antimasons were the original Jacksonians.[44]

Whatever political course Massachusetts Antimasons pursued, they could feel they had won the day. Leading Whig Masons throughout the state publicly resigned from the Order and urged its dissolution. To secure their political future, Whigs had to turn to Edward Everett over strong Masonic opposition. And the Democrats, too, assiduously courted the Antimasonic remnant.

As Antimasonry ebbed in the Bay State, a much-reduced band of Freemasons patiently bided their time. In 1833 the Grand Lodge, having lost its charter, sold the newly completed Masonic Temple in Boston to the wealthy businessman, Robert G. Shaw, for $35,000. The Masons then thought up a new arrangement. They created a Board of Trustees and authorized it to repurchase the Temple from Shaw and hold it in trust for the Grand Lodge. Though hundreds of Massachusetts Masons abandoned the Order and some Lodges folded, a remnant maintained the faith. In 1834 the Grand Lodge rejected a proposal by some members that it dissolve in deference to public opinion to restore the "tranquility of society." The Masons refused "to surrender the Imprescribable Right of Association," and urged their members "to maintain peace and self-respect" and "avoid . . . any political controversy or speculations." The Grand Lodge assured surviving Lodges that it "is still in active existence."

On December 28, 1835, at 7:30 p.m., twenty-four Masons, a pathetic remnant, assembled at the Masonic Temple in Boston to install a new Grand Master. Reverend Samuel Barrett, a Boston Unitarian, celebrated the birth of St. John the Evangelist, delivering "an interesting and animating discourse on the character and Masonic relations of that distinguished Apostle." Afterwards the brothers formed a procession and solemnly followed the Grand Marshall into the next room to enjoy some "suitable refreshments." At 10 p.m. they returned to the Hall, closed the meeting "in ample form," and streamed into the night, confident that they were as good Christians and loyal Republicans as any Americans.[45]

Though much reduced in numbers, having suffered a decade of attack, surviving Masons looked to the future. In the long history of Freemasonry, which they traced back to King Solomon's Temple, the latest time of trouble would occupy a minor place. In Massachusetts the Antimasons had triumphed in many towns and churches, but voters never entrusted them with power, as in neighboring states. In nearby Rhode Island, Freemasons had to face a rougher time, for a coalition of Antimasons and Democrats gained a majority and ruled for five years.

II

"An Inflexible Minority"
The Antimasons of Rhode Island

But be it known, that none but such a Governor as the antimasons
approve, will ever again be elected in Rhode Island, until the 'voice
of the dead,' [i.e., William Morgan's voice] ceases to cry or until masonry has ceased its career of infamy.

Rhode Island American, 1 May 1832

June is an important month in the calendar of active Freemasons. Nearly
coinciding with the summer solstice is the Masonic Festival of St. John the
Baptist. New England Masons customarily assembled at their halls in full
regalia, marched through the streets to a nearby church, and after the
service reassembled for feasting and merriment. On this day, Masonry went
on parade.

June 24, 1835, was a special day for Rhode Island Freemasons. For almost six years Freemasonry had retreated before the Antimasonic attack.
Lodges suspended meetings and Masons were anxious about gathering in
public for their annual festivals. A coalition of Democrats and Antimasons
had gained control of the Rhode Island government, enacted a series of
antimasonic laws, and purged Masons from public office. The coalition
banned Masonic oaths, revoked the charters of the Lodges, and compelled
Masons to make annual reports of members, new initiates and funds.
Placed under state surveillance like criminals or subversives, excluded from
juries, Rhode Island Freemasons tasted the bitter draught of persecution.[1]

In the palmy days before the Morgan case exploded, Masonry had spread
into half the towns and recruited three thousand members, but by the mid-
1830s, membership had shrunk by two-thirds.[2] Though they believed themselves devoted to the love of God and their fellow men, like the saint they
celebrated, Masons had "been slandered, reviled and persecuted." For the
two hundred Masons from thirteen Lodges who crowded the First Congregational Church (Unitarian) in Providence in June 1835, the recent spring
elections offered hope. The coalition had just suffered a major defeat and

the house of representatives elected a Masonic speaker, an augury that mis-
guided fanaticism was on the wane.[3]

Though Providence was a stronghold of Freemasonry, lingering animus
marred the Festival. The city's Antimasons, alert to efforts to revive Masonry, engaged two sturdy Afro-Americans, Black Jack and Cuffy, to dress
up in the gaudy regalia of the Knights Templars, one of the most brilliantly
attired branches of Masonry. Resplendent in colorful red sashes and aprons
bearing the skull and crossbones, the two mock Masons, comporting themselves as gravely as the Grand Master of the Grand Lodge, audaciously took
up the rear of the Masonic procession as it marched from Masonic Hall to
the church. Everyone along the route, reported the *Boston Advocate,* died
with laughter, except the Masons. The prank sought to achieve what no
proscriptive legislation could manage: by employing outlandishly attired
black folk to mimic the foolish pretentions of white folk, Antimasons hoped
to puncture the balloon of Masonic self-importance with the sharp edge of
racial mockery.[4]

Antimasons in Rhode Island polled only 15 percent of the statewide vote,
but through coalition with the Democrats, they exercised power. Demographic and political circumstances were especially favorable to the alliance.
Competition between the Democrats and National Republicans revived in
the later 1820s just as the Antimasonic movement emerged. In a small,
closely divided electorate, Antimasonic votes held the balance of power.
First they swung behind the National Republican candidate for governor,
Lemuel Arnold of Providence, who challenged Arthur Fenner, son of James
Fenner, head of a long-standing dynasty that had dominated politics since
the Jeffersonian era. Because Antimasons supported the American System,
and their base was in the northern industrial towns, the Nationals seemed
the more appropriate partners.[5] Moreover, the Nationals were underdogs
against the Fenner machine and sought additional votes to oust an en-
trenched Democratic party. In 1831 the Nationals, with Antimasonic support, finally captured the governorship, but they had no intention of attacking Freemasonry. Masons were prominent in the leadership and among the
party's electorate, more than among the Democrats. Yet the Antimasons expected a pay-off. When the Nationals betrayed them, they concluded that
Freemasonry had influence in both parties, and in 1832 they fielded their
own statewide ticket, preventing the election of a governor.[6] Rhode Island
voters went to the polls four times that year, but no party squeezed out the
necessary majority. The Nationals passed the Perpetuation Act which continued the old officers in place until the spring 1833 elections. This time,
the Antimasons, joining forces with the Democrats behind John Brown
Francis, swept to victory. The coalition remained in power until 1838.

For the Democrats, the coalition was a godsend. The party's long-term
prospects were not bright because the balance of demographic forces was
shifting decisively against the landholders of the southern towns, the party's
principal base. The most important division in Rhode Island politics was

between the rapidly expanding towns of the industrial north, with Providence at the head, and the static or declining agricultural towns in the south. The Rhode Island colonial charter, not replaced in the Revolutionary era by a new constitution, stacked the deck against the growing towns by lodging the franchise in freeholders and their eldest sons and by apportioning the house of representatives to favor the stagnant areas. To block constitutional reform, attempted repeatedly after 1820 by elements in northern Rhode Island, was the top priority of the Democratic party. The Democrats recognized that National Republican economic policies were popular, and until the mid-1830s Rhode Island Democrats did not clearly embrace Jacksonian economic policy. From the late 1820s and throughout the 1830s, all Rhode Island representatives and senators in Congress were National Republicans, faithfully supporting protectionism and resisting Jacksonian bank policy. Should the Nationals capture the state government, too, they were certain to rewrite the rules of the political game and impose permanent subordination on the landholders.[7]

Antimasonry came to the Democrats' rescue because it split their rivals. Rhode Island Antimasons drew their principal support from the northern part of the state, especially from industrializing communities and influential manufacturers. They also attracted a following among evangelical Christians who might otherwise have gravitated to the National Republican and Whig parties. Because there were relatively few Masonic Lodges in southern towns and correspondingly few Masons in Democratic ranks, the party was in a strong position to exploit the falling-out between the Nationals and the Antimasons. Finally, the structure of Rhode Island politics gave a small number of men enormous leverage to influence electoral outcomes.

Money and influence were especially important in Rhode Island, which resembled the eighteenth-century England recounted in the pages of Sir Lewis B. Namier.[8] Though Rhode Island held frequent elections, and most officials served annual terms subject to removal by the General Assembly, beneath the outward forms of republicanism lay an oligarchic system. A very restricted electorate enabled large landowners, creditors, monied men, their relatives and business associates, to form "connections" that commanded an army of venal or dependent voters.[9] Yet as in Namier's England, there were many independent electors who added a popular and unpredictable element. Banking and currency policy, tariffs and taxes, temperance, slavery, and Antimasonry, as well as other issues, all figured in politics, their saliency varying from year to year, and the anachronistic and undemocratic features of the Rhode Island political system always begged for reform. There was restlessness, too, among the growing industrial labor force, which by the 1820s began to assert itself, groping towards economic and political organization. A fraction of the commercial and industrial elite in northern Rhode Island also displayed unease and dabbled in constitutional reform. By 1820 just over 30 percent of the labor force engaged in manufacturing, edging out Massachusetts and making Rhode Island the most highly industrialized state in the Union; twenty years later, the proportion in manufacturing reached just over half. Providence County, the center of the industrial revolution, contained more than half the population by 1840 and cast more than half the vote in statewide elections, yet it chose only 30 percent of the house of representatives. Even Democrats sensed that they could not put off reapportionment or suffrage reform forever, yet constitutional reform stalled repeatedly.

Most of northern Rhode Island's business leaders were ambivalent towards constitutional revision, for they would clearly benefit from reapportionment which shifted power from south to north only if they could control those newly enfranchised by abolition of the property qualification. Some favored reapportionment without broadening the suffrage, but once the state tampered with its old colonial charter, it might prove impossible to block more radical changes. For such reasons propertied interests of all kinds resisted universal white male suffrage. Finally, Rhode Island was a small state and the balance among competing interests and elites was delicately poised and easily upset by constitutional change.

Rhode Island's resistance to an expanded suffrage left it an anomaly. Here alone in the United States, the coming of industrial society preceded the democratization of the vote. The presence of a large propertyless mass, including a growing stream of persons born outside the state, some hailing from other countries, aroused greater resistance than suffrage reformers encountered elsewhere.[10]

The unreformed system gave landholders disproportionate weight, but it worked well enough to satisfy other interests. At the nation's capital, Rhode Island representatives faithfully advanced the views of the manufacturers. At home a tax on banks relieved landowners and shifted the burden to others, while generous grants of bank charters soothed capitalists. The National Republicans dared not tamper with the fiscal settlement of the 1820s when they came to power in 1831; not until the Jacksonian Bank War heated up in the mid-1830s did national economic policy become a significant issue in Rhode Island. When that happened, the coalition between Democrats and Antimasons frayed, then collapsed, and cleared the way for a Whig revival in 1838.[11]

Rhode Island Antimasonry sprouted at the grass roots with meetings in several towns towards the end of 1828 and early in 1829. Two short-lived Antimasonic newspapers appeared in Pawtucket and Newport, and in January 1830, the *Rhode Island Free Press* began to publish in Providence. The first statewide convention assembled in Providence in March 1830, shortly before the spring elections, but Antimasons approached electoral politics cautiously and did not nominate a slate. Another convention met in December 1830, and this time named a ticket headed by a wealthy landholder, John Brown Francis of Warwick, whom the National Republicans also endorsed. Francis declined, however, as did others slated on the Antimasonic ticket for the senate, a body chosen statewide. Rejecting a third-party strategy, the Antimasons preferred an alliance with the National Republicans and endorsed Lemuel Arnold of Providence and a senate list that included three Antimasons, five Nationals, and two Democrats. Arnold won and the senate candidates with Antimasonic backing ran well too.[12]

The Democrats pushed the Antimasons into the arms of the Nationals by abandoning a policy of playing down their ties to the unpopular Jackson Administration. In 1831, Governor Fenner, facing the strongest challenge in years, attacked the American System, hoping thereby to rally the landholders by stirring up anti-manufacturing sentiment. Fenner's strategy backfired. Since the Antimasons endorsed the American System, they had additional reason to move towards the Nationals. The Nationals, moreover, courted them. Arnold was no Freemason and convinced Antimasons that his party was sympathetic. Antimasons had no prospect of winning power on their own and their experience with the Democrats had soured them on that party. In 1830 the Antimasons had petitioned the General Assembly for an investigation of Masonic Lodges incorporated by the state, but the Democrats ignored them.[13]

The Antimasonic strategy seemed to pay off. Arnold and the Nationals in control of General Assembly investigated Freemasonry. The month-long hearings turned into a whitewash. One National leader denounced the Antimasons as "a pestilence" while another repeatedly abused Antimasonic witnesses and called them "vermin."[14]

The coalition collapsed, its prospects never very good. Even during the 1831 campaign, Arnold's supporters circulated a secret letter to reassure Freemasons.[15] Rhode Island Masons recruited largely from an emerging bourgeoisie, especially in towns where the Nationals were strong. Every town in Providence County boasted a Masonic Lodge, compared to only one among the seven towns in the Democratic stronghold of Washington County. Democrat E. R. Potter, Sr., probably reflected the views of Democratic landholders who identified Freemasonry with the entrepreneurial interests of industrial Rhode Island. "They let in a parcel of small fry," Potter complained, "that injure the community." Landholders did not need a secret fraternal society to distinguish the better sort. "The difficulty was that all Masons were not honorable men," Potter argued, for "such persons join the lodge to accomplish an object as the worn-down harlot joins the church merely for the privilege of drinking tea with the Parson's wife."[16]

Betrayal by both major parties inflamed Antimasons, confirming their suspicions that Freemasonry exercised power over both. First spurned by the Democrats and then by the Nationals, the Antimasons nominated their own ticket in 1832, headed by William Sprague, Jr., a powerful industrialist. Sprague captured 14 percent of the vote, enough to precipitate a deadlock.[17] "An inflexible minority" winning fewer than a thousand votes now commanded the balance of power.

The stage was set for a reversal of alliances and the formation of a coalition of Antimasons and Democrats. Now the Democrats needed Antimasonic votes. They included fewer Masons in their ranks than did the Nationals and therefore had greater freedom to accommodate Antimasonic demands. James Fenner, the perennial Democratic candidate, stepped aside for John Brown Francis, on whom both parties united.[18] Francis was the ideal coalition candidate for governor. Formerly a National Republican, a Clay supporter, and advocate of the American System, Francis was also a large landholder, came from a distinguished family, and was related to the owners of Brown and Ives, a leading Providence mercantile house. He got along well with Democratic leader, E. R. Potter, in nearby South Kingston, and his own Spring Green estate in Warwick put him in close proximity to the Spragues, who also had extensive interests in that town. Wealth and family connections, together with backing by the Spragues and others, represented formidable electoral strength.[19] For the Democrats, the coalition also possessed long-term strategic value, for it not only assured them of a majority but also guaranteed against constitutional reform by splitting off a fraction of the manufacturing and commercial interests from the National Republican base. Francis dreaded reapportionment and suffrage reform as much as Potter did.[20]

The new coalition was victorious in April 1833 and laid solid foundations for a partnership that lasted five years. The Democrats accommodated the tariff preference of their allies and supported eight Antimasons on a common electoral slate. The victorious coalition chose William Sprague, Jr., as speaker of the house of representatives and awarded other important legislative posts to Antimasons. A purge of state officials followed. Almost two-thirds of the offices annually chosen by the General Assembly changed hands, compared to only a handful the previous year. Only two of the thirty-three notaries named in Providence County in 1832, for example, won reappointment by the Coalition Assembly.[21]

The congressional election in 1833 soon tested the durability of the alliance. Each party nominated its own ticket, but after the Nationals captured one of the state's two seats, the Democrats withdrew and cleared the field for the re-election of Congressman Dutee J. Pearce, a National Republican who had switched to the Antimasons. The Antimasons reciprocated and backed Democrat Elisha R. Potter for the United States Senate.[22]

A series of legislative blows against Freemasonry sealed the alliance. Lodges with revokable charters lost them and the legislature placed others under close surveillance. In 1835 even the National Republicans went along with proscriptive legislation.[23] Meanwhile, the electoral fortunes of coalition prospered. Governor Francis won re-election with regularity, facing only token opposition from the demoralized opposition in 1836 and 1837. The Democrats carried the state for Van Buren in 1836, and the coalition captured both congressional seats in 1835 when William Sprague, Jr., joined Congressman Dutee J. Pearce in Washington.

Rhode Island's "inflexible minority" discovered an appropriate political strategy. The party, claimed the *Masonic Mirror,* "was composed of the most incongruous material . . . a mixed medley. . . ." A glance at the leadership finds prominent manufacturers joining forces with farmers and well-known Quakers, Free Will Baptists, and others.[24]

The third party's electoral strength centered in eleven of Rhode Island's thirty-one towns in which they polled 20 percent or better in 1832. A band of contiguous towns—North Kingston, Warwick, and East Greenwich—where the Sprague and Francis connections were influential were the Antimasonic strongholds. In the cities of Providence and Newport, the Antimasons garnered only 9 percent in 1832, substantially below their statewide record of 15 percent.

There are too few towns in Rhode Island to justify giving much weight to multiple regression analysis of voting, and missing data further compound the problem. The voting data are less problematic. Simple correlations reveal a weak, negative relationship between the Antimasonic vote and the Federalist vote a generation earlier, and a weak, positive relationship with the National Republican and Whig votes in 1830, 1838, and 1840, but there is considerable variance among these elections. The ecological regression estimates replicate a pattern found elsewhere: the bulk of the Antimasonic vote for President in 1832 came from persons who had not voted in 1830, and the rest from the National Republicans. Rhode Island Antimasons thus mobilized new voters much more than they attracted support from party switchers. The regression estimates also demonstrate that Antimasons shifted their support to the Democrats in 1834 and 1836 when the third party did not run its own ticket, though in the presidential year many Antimasons stayed home. (Table 11.1.[25]) The mobilizing function of the Antimasonic party contributed to rising levels of voter participation. Turnout of adult white males in Rhode Island was exceptionally low throughout the antebellum era because of franchise restrictions, yet it jumped by 50 percent from 1830 to 1831. It did not increase much thereafter, peaking at 33 percent in 1835, a rate not significantly surpassed until after the adoption of a new constitution in 1842. The Antimasons helped to make Rhode Island a politically more competitive state, after more than a decade of lopsided gubernatorial elections following the decline of the First American Party System. (Table 11.2.[26])

Hundreds of Masons and Antimasons made public avowals, allowing us to construct collective biographies which offer important clues to their demographic differences. Some two-thirds of the Masons and almost 90 percent of the Antimasons resided outside the state capitol of Providence, the Masons in thirteen and the Antimasons in sixteen towns. This distribution reflected the relative strength of Masonry and weakness of Antimasonry in the capitol. Tracing both groups to the 1850 census suggests that Antimasons were somewhat less geographically mobile than the Masons (39% vs. 30%). Occupational differences offer a clue to differences in residential mobility. The Antimasons were more than twice as likely to be farmers; Masons tended to engage more in the professions, business, and skilled manual occupations, including master mechanics who headed small shops. The Masons also drew more support from older cohorts and they were a bit more likely to own real property, though the differences were modest.[27]

With fewer than a quarter of the Masonic loyalists engaged in husbandry, in a state whose political system heavily favored landholders, Freemasonry's demographic base left it politically vulnerable. Masonry held less attraction for farmers than for businessmen and professionals because Lodge meetings were not convenient for persons living at a distance from village centers where Masons met and also because the class-stratifying function of Freemasonry—identifying members of an emerging middle class and offering resources to entrepreneurial networks—held less attraction to farmers. Rhode Island farmers were a heterogeneous group and crude classification by occupation obscures important variations. Some diversified and invested in non-agricultural activities, though they listed themselves as farmers in the census. Some aggressively pursued market opportunities and tried to expand output while others practiced more conservative husbandry. Masonic farmers tended to be in the upper strata of the real wealth distribution compared with Antimasonic farmers. The farmers in Washington County remained largely impervious to Masonry, Antimasonry, and National Republicanism, too. This Democratic party stronghold was the region least touched by industrial development. A poll book for South Kingston, the home of powerful Democratic party leader Elisha R. Potter, Sr., sheds light on that party's base and provides a further contrast to the Antimasons. South Kingston, like most towns in Washington County, did not grow in the 1820s. Just over 80 percent of the labor force engaged in farming in 1820, a proportion virtually unchanged twenty years later. There were only five Antimasons, four farmers, and a cooper in 1832. The National Republicans were much more heterogeneous than the Democrats. Whereas almost three-quarters of the latter were farmers, some 55 percent of the Nationals were husbandmen, and most of the rest were businessmen or skilled artisans. Voters with the same surnames tended to vote overwhelmingly for one of the two major parties in 9 of 16 large "families." Thus, 11 of 13 Watsons chose the National Republicans, while all 13 Gardiners voted Democratic.[28]

While most Antimasons were farmers, others had occupations that were quite diverse. Antimasonic farmers inhabited rapidly growing industrial towns and this distinguished them from the Democratic farmers. Close proximity to the spread of industrial society may account for why some Rhode Island farmers found the anti-modernist, restorationist rhetoric of Antimasonry particularly persuasive. While the spread of factories opened new markets for husbandry, economic development posed dangers. The factories competed for labor and bid up wages. The owners of textile mills and other factories, relying on water power, dammed streams and precipitated long battles over riparian rights among farmers, artisans, and mill bosses.

Farmers who invested in local industry risked their savings and sometimes suffered great losses, as in Pawtucket during the devastating depression of 1829. The result was an estrangement of farmers from industry.[29] Historians of politics in the Jacksonian era have located farmers along a spectrum of attitudes towards economic development. At one end were those inclined towards the National Republicans and uncritically enthusiastic for economic development; at the other stood Jacksonian farmers who felt threatened by the spread of the market economy. Rhode Island's Antimasonic farmers may best be located between these polarities, attracted by the opportunities for economic growth but fearful of the cost.

The Antimasons enjoyed less success in the city of Providence than in the hinterlands. The metropolis was a stronghold of Masonry, boasting two Masonic Lodges. Almost 30 percent of the Masonic signers in 1831 lived in the city, which accounted for only 11 percent of the Antimasonic petitioners. The Antimasons drew their support from socially inferior strata compared to the Masons. Businessmen account for nearly half of both groups, but the Masons were more likely to be merchants and the Antimasons grocers. Both attracted similar proportions of professionals and artisans, but Antimasons were not as wealthy. A much higher proportion of the Antimasons (47% vs. 28%) did not appear on the tax assessment list, and among those assessed, the Masons tended to own more property. Almost half the Antimasons owned no personal wealth compared to 35 percent of the Masons, who also tended to be in the top wealth strata.[30] Membership in voluntary associations, with data drawn primarily from Providence, also indicated that the Masons were far better connected than the Antimasons. Masons accounted for 68 associational affiliations, including 29 with banks and insurance companies and 15 with professional and occupational organizations, compared to only 20 affiliations for the Antimasons and only eight with financial institutions. Providence Antimasons tended to resist integration into the dominant Whig elite; one observer described them as "the middling interest." Tracing Antimasons to the 1840 Providence poll book indicates that 59 percent voted Whig, whereas the Whigs who dominated the city polled 80 percent citywide. Moreover, more than half of the Antimasonic voters resided in Wards V and VI. Ward VI, the banner Antimasonic Ward in 1833, was the maverick in city politics throughout the 1830s, usually resisting the Whig tide. Physically set off from the center of business and from the affluent neighborhoods, distinguished from the other five wards by its high proportion of small, property-owning master mechanics and shopkeepers, Ward VI became the most strongly Democratic ward later in the decade and the most sympathetic to the Dorrite movement for constitutional reform after 1840. Its insurgency traced back at least to the rise of Antimasonry.[31]

The demographic data for both Providence and the hinterland suggest that the Antimasonic party formed a coalition of elements among the lower middle classes in Providence and insurgent farmers and manufacturers in the industrializing hinterlands, knit together by the ideology of Christian Republicanism.

An exploration of the social sources of Rhode Island Antimasonry leads also to the churches, for both laymen and ministers occupied prominent positions on both sides of the battle lines, and the language of Antimasonry used a rich Christian vocabulary. The *Providence Journal,* the leading National Republican newspaper, viewed the coalition as the means whereby Antimasons hoped to pursue "their peculiar view and sectarian tenets." The Antimasons made an issue of the religious sympathies of Lemuel Arnold, the National Republican candidate for governor in 1832. The *Journal* admitted that Arnold had lost votes because his wife antagonized Orthodox Calvinists by refusing to accept a tract. In 1833 the coalition made further political hay out of Arnold's latitudinarian sympathies. Campaigning in a Warwick bar, William Sprague, Jr., charged that Arnold had joined the Universalist church and had broken down in tears three times when he rose to address the congregation. The link to Universalism was a link to Freemasonry, for the state's leading Universalist preachers were prominent defenders of the Order.[32]

In Rhode Island, as elsewhere, Antimasonry bitterly divided the churches. Masonry found its warmest defenders among ecumenically minded, anti-Calvinist elements. Besides the Universalists there were other preachers who remained faithful to Masonry such as the Unitarian Rev. Henry Edes of Providence's prestigious First Congregationalist Church; Episcopalians such as Alexander Griswold, George M. Randall, N. B. Crocker, and Pawtucket's George Taft; broadminded Baptists such as Providence's Stephen Gano and Zalmon Tobey, and Pawtucket's David Benedict. As proof of their devotion to Christian faith, Masons could also point to laymen who were leaders in their churches.[33]

In 1831 Universalist preacher Jacob Frieze spoke for many when he told the Grand Lodge that Antimasonry "is chargeable alone to the intolerance of bigotry, the frenzy of fanaticism, and the lust of power." His colleague, David Pickering, had earlier warned at a Fourth of July celebration that "there is no dark fiend to moral purity and freedom . . . to be dreaded, as the unbending spirit of religious bigotry." There were those, he argued, who "would hurl from the seats of authority the highest dignitaries of the nation" and "close every avenue to preferment against the enlightened, liberal and independent citizen. . . ."[34]

The bitterest battles over Masonry were within denominations with strong modernist currents that engendered anti-modernist reaction. Rhode Island Baptists, the state's oldest and largest denomination, were especially hard-hit. Rev. Stephen Gano in Providence and his son-in-law David Benedict in Pawtucket led churches that included many of their community's leading citizens. Gano had early accommodated the liberalism in the First Baptist Church by abandoning the laying-on of hands. Benedict followed suit in

Pawtucket. In the early days the Baptists in Pawtucket lived "in the back part of town," dressed outlandishly, and were objects of derision, an old resident reminded Benedict. More recently, she noted, "your society are more like other folk now than they were." Gano's devotion to Freemasonry did not threaten his tenure, but Benedict's cost him his pulpit.[35]

Benedict swam with liberal currents seeking to transform the Baptists in the early nineteenth century. In Providence, he recalled, some members of the First Church had deserted to the Unitarian church. Unless Rhode Island Baptists adjusted doctrine and ritual, they would continue to suffer losses. Facing competition from a broad spectrum of anti-Calvinist opponents, not just Unitarians and Universalists but also Free Will and Seventh-Day Baptists, some Baptists welcomed Fullerism, an Arminian-tending reinterpretation of theology, imported from Great Britain, that insisted on its Calvinist orthodoxy much as Taylorism did among the Congregationalists.[36]

Benedict's career illustrates the price modernists paid who ran into strong, unexpected resistance. Benedict's church became a stronghold of Antimasonic sentiment. Masonic Baptists like himself found themselves "in an embarrassing dilemma in consequence of the new church laws, to which they had never subscribed, and against which they entered a solemn protest." Without the protection of ecclesiastical hierarchy to restrain the laity, men like Benedict stood at the mercy of their congregations. Deacon Remember Kent led the Antimasonic faction which demanded that Benedict and other Masons renounce the Order. The Masons were defiant and accused the Antimasons of stirring up strife, infringing on freedom of conscience, and "alienating the affections of our dearest earthly friends"—the women. The Antimasons prevailed. Benedict resigned and a revival blessed the church.[37]

Benedict was one of a new breed of educated Baptist clergymen. A convert from Episcopalianism, he attended Brown University in 1804 and served as trustee of the university for thirty years, a sign of high standing among denominational leaders, including the socially prominent Baptist elite. In 1806 Benedict settled in Pawtucket, a rising industrial village still part of North Providence. There he took over the Catholic Baptist Society. Established in the 1790s with sponsors such as Nicholas Brown and Moses Ives, two affluent Providence Baptist businessmen, the church was open to other denominations on the principle that "discussion upon both sides of every question" advanced truth. When Benedict assumed charge, he moved the church to the center of town, built a more attractive house of worship, and installed an organ.

In other ways, too, he pushed Pawtucket Baptists in a modernist direction. He advocated open communion with members of other denominations at a time when many Baptist churches still practiced closed communion. In 1824 Benedict published *All Religions,* intended as an impartial, accurate account of the beliefs of all Christian denominations. He argued that "admidst the various forms which I observed, there was not so much difference in the feelings and purposes of good men of every name, as many suppose."[38]

Benedict's anti-sectarian sympathies were more common among Unitarians, Universalists, and Episcopalians, denominations whose members had a particular affinity for Freemasonry. The eruption of Antimasonry among Pawtucket Baptists caught Benedict by surprise. He had nurtured modernist trends only to face a powerful backlash. Antimasonry he saw as a divisive wave of perfectionist fanaticism that included abolitionism and other "anti-isms" that came out "against any of the evils of the land, real or imaginary." Looking back half a century from the Civil War, Benedict recalled that Baptists had once sharply distinguished between the church and the world and had punished violations of discipline. By Benedict's old age such restraints had lost their force. The older conception of a church as a gathered community of men and women who were "brothers" and "sisters," titles that expressed communal affection, gave way to the same cold, formal modes of address common to other denominations. In 1800, Pawtucket Baptists expected members to settle disputes with one another by arbitration; by 1860, Baptists, like others, went to law. "Elders" used to preside over Baptist communities; by mid-century, "Reverends" replaced the self-trained ministry. In the long run, modernist tendencies gained ascendency, but in the 1820s, Benedict, a college-educated, well-connected, anti-sectarian, was caught in the cross fire. After twenty-five years, he resigned. It "was forced upon me by a severe pressure of one of the high excitements of those times," he explained. Benedict remained in Pawtucket as postmaster.[39]

Antimasonry also divided Free Will Baptists. In Pawtucket's Masonic Lodge, Benedict met Elder David Greene, a leader of the Free Will Baptists. In 1827, Levi Chace, a Methodist turned Baptist, renounced Freemasonry and pleaded with Greene to follow his example because, though the Masons were not deists, "such is the tendency and design of the Masonic Institution." The Masons had murdered William Morgan because they had repudiated Christian morality, he added. Greene, however, insisted that Morgan "had suffered his just deserts, according to his obligations." Morgan's death was "an awful thing before God," he admitted, but Masons should not suffer for the sins of a few "bad members." But who could trust anyone like Greene who, upon becoming a Knight Templar, consumed wine (representing blood) from a human skull. An angry Greene responded: "I do not know that it can affect the interest of anyone, WHETHER I DRANK WINE OUT OF A SKULL, A TIN CUP, OR A BASIN!"[40]

Greene's embarrassment must have gratified an old enemy among Pawtucket's Free Will Baptists, Rev. Ray Potter. Like Chace, Potter renounced Masonry, pleading that friends had lured him into the Order by claims that it promoted "pure morality." He intervened in the hot 1832 gubernatorial campaign to urge Christians to vote the Antimasonic ticket and slay "the Red Dragon."[41]

Potter and Greene had fought for control of the first Free Will Baptist church in Pawtucket in the early 1820s. After shifting from one religious persuasion to another, Potter, the son of a poor Rhode Island carpenter with little formal education, lost out to Elder Greene whose father, David Greene, was a prominent manufacturer and member of the congregation opposed to Potter's enthusiastic revivalism. Potter established a new church and agreed to arbitrate the differences. The arbitrators ruled in favor of the Greene faction. Later, one admitted, "Masonry was thought by some to have had an influence in the affair," for the Greenes were staunch Free-masons.

Potter attributed his defeat to the rich. "Do not let rich men oppress you," he told his followers. "Lo to ye rich men, weep and bow for the miseries that shall come upon you," he warned. In 1829 Potter published his memoirs, which received endorsements from prominent Antimasons in Pawtucket. Potter, self-conscious of his lack of education, insisted that his writing was "sufficiently elegant to make *common people* understand what I mean. . . ." If the learned had trouble, he wryly advised, "they may ask the illiterate to teach them." Potter's Antimasonry only exposed him to fresh abuse at the Rhode Island Legislative Investigation, whose chairman treated him "with great disrespect and gross insult." In what kind of a republic, he protested, were poor men like himself denied "decent treatment"?[42]

Class resentment combined with a complex spiritual odyssey led Ray Potter to Antimasonry. Like many early nineteenth-century youth he grew up without any firm religious moorings and drifted through periods of infidelity and loose morals. He claimed that this generated intense guilt that led him to repent and adopt some version of the gospel, first the Sixth-Day Baptists, then the Free Will Baptists. He repeated this process several times until he finally embraced Calvinism. Only an omnipotent God could "ever bring such a perverse wretch as himself to heaven."

Potter's popularity derived from his courageous, anti-elitist stance. He opposed the Rhode Island Quarterly Meeting of the Free Will Baptists. He combined belief in a democratic ecclesiastical self-government with Calvinism and a vivid millennialism. "An awful judgment and calamity will soon visit the world generally," he warned. Though the United States had so far "escaped national judgment," he predicted, "let us not suppose that we will not yet be visited." The spread of Masonry was just one sign of national corruption; the existence of slavery was another.[43]

Potter found support from other clergymen such as Elder Henry Tatem. Like Potter, Tatem was a Free Will Baptist minister. Ordained in 1816, he preached in Cranston and then Warwick, both towns where the Sprague family was powerful and Antimasonry strong. Tatem finally settled in Warwick, supporting himself as a tailor, where he established the Tatem Meeting House in 1829. In 1825, Tatem, Potter, and John Prentice, all later Antimasons, with two other Free Will Baptist preachers formed the Union Conference, a body independent of the Rhode Island Quarterly Meeting. As independents they need fear neither powerful laymen nor intrusion by higher ecclesiastical authority. Tatem, like Potter, had also joined the Masons and then suffered disillusionment. In February 1832, the Royal Arch Masons in Providence summoned him to stand trial for un-Masonic conduct. His crime was revealing the truth about "blasphemous" Masonic rites and vouching for Ray Potter's veracity. For a long time Tatem had kept silent, fearful of the awful penalties threatened by the oaths he had sworn. The emergence of the Antimasonic movement emboldened him. His duty was clear, for Masonry was "the cause of many of the dissentions that exist in the Church and State. . . ."[44]

The Quakers were one of the oldest and most influential denominations in Rhode Island and their position on Freemasonry became a hot question. Moses Brown of Providence, the great Quaker businessman, was the venerable patriarch of Rhode Island Friends. In 1831, Antimasons sought to clarify on which side he stood. Brown had been a founding member of Providence's first Masonic Lodge during his youth, but after his conversion to the Friends, he quit the Order, preferring Quaker benevolence. Because he had never broadcast his separation, some Masons still claimed him. To end public confusion, William Sprague, Sr., and Daniel Mathewson, acting for the Antimasonic state committee, visited Brown. He told the "two respectable countrymen" that he had long ago abandoned Masonry. The Quaker Book of Discipline, which he helped to revise periodically, forbade membership; Quakers had a long-standing ban on secret societies, public parades, and other expressions of human vanity.

Brown's disavowal did not mean that Rhode Island Quakers voted for the Antimasonic ticket or felt strongly about Masonry since membership in the Order was not, as among other denominations, a source of internal dispute in this state. The *Providence Journal* courted the Quakers for the National Republicans and claimed that many Friends voted for Governor Lemuel Arnold in the great struggle of 1832. The *Journal* pointed to Elisha Bates and Ethan Foster, both Quakers, who appeared on the National Republican statewide slate, but the Antimasons could also point to Quakers prominent in their ranks. Anson Potter, a Cranston Quaker, testified against Masonry at the legislative hearing. Rhode Island Quakers did not suffer a formal split between Hicksites and Orthodox, as did Friends outside New England, but the prominence of some Quakers in the Antimasonic movement suggests that, as with other denominations, anti-modernist elements favored the cause. Antimasonic Quakers tended to hail from outside the metropolis.[45]

There was also support for Antimasonry among the city's Congregationalists. Congregationalists were not numerous in Rhode Island, and in

Providence their theological complexion was less clear-cut than in Massachusetts, where by the 1820s a formal split occurred between Unitarians and Trinitarians. Yet the liberal/conservative conflict also appeared in Rhode Island. In Providence the Unitarians captured the First Congregational Church which kept that name and affiliation. They also founded the Westminister Congregational Church, for the demand for a liberalized, secularized Christianity in the metropolis was strong.[46]

Whatever their other differences, an ambivalence towards modernist trends in the churches bound together Antimasonic clergymen and pious laymen. A parallel ambivalence towards modernizing tendencies in Rhode Island society also figured in the attitudes of the state's most influential Antimasonic family, the Spragues, father and sons, who established a powerful dynasty of manufacturers in the early nineteenth century. The patriarch, William Sprague, Sr., presided over the 1832 Antimasonic State Convention and ran for the state senate on the third-party ticket that year. His son, William, Jr., was the Antimasonic candidate for governor in 1832 and won election as the coalition's speaker in the house of representatives from 1833 until 1835, when he went to Congress. The Spragues played a key role in the third party's fortunes, providing funds, negotiating the terms of alliance with the Democrats, and mobilizing voters.

According to William Sprague, Jr.—the politician in the family—his father led the family into the Antimasonic movement. The son had joined a Masonic Lodge but the patriarch's violent opposition forced him to resign under threat of disinheritance. Precisely why the elder Sprague suddenly discovered the evils of Masonry remains obscure, but the family's political ambitions, its paternalistic relations with its employees, and its image as countryfolk, self-made mechanic/entrepreneurs who prized their distance from Providence's elite offer the best clues.

In Cranston, five miles from Providence, the Spragues diversified their agricultural holdings by adding grist, lumber, and textile mills. They became one of the earliest calico printers. Until they joined the Antimasonic movement, the Spragues were not conspicuous in Rhode Island politics, but from that time through the Civil War era, they played a distinctive role in politics. They were wealthy outsiders, dissidents who possessed great resources and marketed themselves as champions of the masses, sturdy country men who resisted integration into the elite centered in Providence. They were the wild cards in Rhode Island politics, supporting one side, then the other, and often coming out on top. Their tariff and financial views were closer to the National Republicans than to the Democrats, but they preferred the Antimasonic movement which made them kingmakers. Then, in 1838, sensing the decline of the third party, increasingly unhappy with Jacksonian economic policy and radical, Loco-foco Democracy in Rhode Island, they switched. William Sprague, Jr., became governor on the Whig ticket, defeating his former ally, John Brown Francis, in 1838. In the late 1830s the Spragues also gave encouragement to constitutional reform; they even sympathized with the Dorrites until they realized that a mass movement for democratic change might get out of control and undermine their own power. Frightened by the Dorr rebellion, they joined conservatives in both parties to turn back the populist tide.

The Spragues pictured themselves as popular tribunes. The elder Sprague was patriarch of numerous employees and dependents who took meals around an immense table at which Sprague presided. A stocky, five-foot-ten figure, tipping the scales at 200 pounds, he dressed so plainly that strangers took him for a farmer. He never disdained physical labor, and so preoccupied was he with managing his many enterprises that, according to reports, Sprague rarely smiled. He also put on no airs or pretensions, and payed his workers promptly, unlike others. Before becoming a politician, William II ran the Natick works in Warwick. His brother, Amasa, concentrated on the family business. Like his father, Amasa had no use for fine clothes or mingling with the Providence gentry. As a boy he had worked for his father and when he became the boss, he remained on familiar terms with his employees. Like the elder Sprague, Amasa was "a big, burly gentleman," who maintained paternalistic relations. He preferred that employees call him by his Christian name, yet they must never forget who was boss, or "he will be, after you sure, wid those big boots of his . . . ," an Irish worker remembered.[47]

The Spragues' attraction to Antimasonry seems rooted in a desire for political power, in fierce independence from other members of their class, and in paternalistic relations with their employees that harked back to earlier communitarian values and social relations. They illustrate, too, divisions among capitalists in the forefront of Rhode Island's transformation, which provided the third party with vital leadership as in Pawtucket, one of the seedbeds of the industrial revolution in the United States.

"There is probably no spot in New England of the same extent in which the same quantity or variety of manufacturing business is carried on," reported Timothy Dwight after visiting Pawtucket. A center of textile manufacture in the late eighteenth century, Pawtucket had material advantages which made it a leader. Located not far from Providence, on the Pawtucket River, Pawtucket tapped abundant water power. These advantages attracted Samuel Slater, the English architect of early American textile manufacture. From Pawtucket, textile manufacturing spread through the Blackstone Valley into northwestern Rhode Island and southern Massachusetts. By 1820 Pawtucket boasted eight mills; and by 1835, twelve cotton factories as well as machine shops and iron works employed some two thousand workers.[48]

Pawtucket became a hotbed of Antimasonry. The town spread out on both sides of the river, splitting the population between two states. In Pawtucket, Massachusetts, incorporated in 1828, the Antimasons polled 36 percent of the vote in 1833. There are no election data for Pawtucket, Rhode Island, because it was part of North Providence, where the Antimasons polled 13 percent of the vote, slightly below their statewide average in 1832, but Pawtucket spawned an important group of Antimasonic leaders in Rhode Island drawn from the town's manufacturers.

In December 1828, Pawtucket citizens crowded into the Brick School House to "pronounce Free-Masonry to be unchristian, anti-republican, a hindrance to the cause of religion, and dangerous to our liberties." They also elected delegates including prominent Pawtucket manufacturers, to the People's Convention in Dedham, Massachusetts. Though Antimasons denied "most unequivocally any feelings of prejudice, ill-will or unkindness against members of the Fraternity in our village, or within our acquaintance," Pawtucket suffered bitter divisions.[49] A parade of Freemasons and Antimasons from Pawtucket squared off against one another at the 1832 legislative investigation. The Antimasons alleged that the Masons attempted intimidation to keep critics quiet. The Masons counter-attacked by depicting Antimasons as reckless libelers and paranoids. Abraham Wilkinson, a manufacturer, had called one Masonic Lodge "The Slaughter House." He claimed that Masons had murdered five hundred innocents and he denounced Masonry as "an abominable bloodstained, stinking Order." The Antimasons sought to establish that Masonry subverted fairness in the legal system because Masonic judges and juries showed partiality for their brethren. On this point the Rhode Island legislative investigation produced conflicting testimony. Rev. Daniel Greene, a Freemason, insisted that he had testified on behalf of Wilkinson in a suit against a Mason, but when Wilkinson cross-examined Barney Merry and asked, "Would not a mason, on trial, have secret means of communication with a masonic judge or juror, which one not a mason could not have?" Merry refused to answer.[50] Antimasons also charged that Masonic debtors who failed favored their brothers over other creditors when distributing assets.

Pawtucket was a highly litigious community. Farmers and artisans, since the 1790s, sued mill owners whose dams diverted streams and injured them, but powerful capitalists with political connections, such as Almy and Brown, enjoyed an advantage. In the 1820s a new conflict over water power erupted as the result of competition among mill owners. With every mill site occupied and seven factories tapping power generated by two dams, Pawtucket's future development lay clouded. When a court finally resolved Sergeant's Trench Case in 1826, the village's elite was left "divided and fragmented." The Wilkinsons were party to the dispute, and a son-in-law and business partner, William Harris, acknowledged that the case had generated "strong party feelings in Pawtucket."[51] Freemasons, including another branch of the Wilkinson family, were prominent on the other side. Antimasonry provided an explanation of divisions which pre-dated the furor unleashed by the Morgan case. The underlying sources of fragmentation and factionalism in Pawtucket, as elsewhere, lay embedded in the village's recent history.

The trail in Pawtucket, as in other industrial communities, leads back from the Antimasonic period to earlier developments which had a long-term effect on the social order. Though iron production had deep roots in Pawtucket, until the end of the eighteenth century farming predominated, and market relationships were subordinate to the subsistence economy. Industrial growth after 1790 transformed Pawtucket's economy and social structure. At first the mills employed children from local families, but increasingly they recruited labor from outside, including entire families. Businessmen established banks, built turnpikes, and won public office. The religious and cultural life of the community also changed. In addition to the Baptist church formed in the 1790s, by 1830 there were Episcopal, Free Will Baptist, Universalist, and Congregationalist churches. In 1809 the Masons established Union Lodge, the tenth in the state, led by such Grand Masters as Barney Merry, David Wilkinson, Samuel Greene, and Ebenezer Tyler, each deeply involved in the town's industrial development. Manufacturers also promoted a new industrial morality by establishing Sunday schools for children and supporting the temperance movement.[52]

The most portentous development was the emergence of a modern industrial class structure. In the pre-industrial period there were few wage earners or capitalists. Most adult males were property-owners and possessed the vote, and the political system was open to men of middling fortune. Industrialization brought sharper social divisions. The influx of workers who owned no land and the creation of new fortunes in the hands of an emerging industrial elite left Pawtucket highly stratified. Wealth was much less evenly distributed in 1820 than it was a generation earlier; now three-quarters of the adult males could not vote. Access to public office also tightened. Those who won positions in the early nineteenth century on the average tended to serve longer terms than had their predecessors at the end of the eighteenth century.[53]

The most dramatic evidence that Pawtucket had entered a new stage of its history was the strike by weavers in 1824. In the pre-industrial era, master mechanics worked side by side with journeymen and apprentices and incorporated them into their households, paying a customary wage. A web of mutual obligation and responsibility knit together the artisan community. Even in 1810 the line separating wage earners from capitalists was still not clearly drawn, for both groups were eligible for membership in a new organization of mechanics and manufacturers. Early industrialists typically had backgrounds as master artisans, and journeymen might still plausibly dream of moving into the ranks of masters, even becoming manufacturers. By the 1820s, however, the artisans formed their own Pawtucket Mechanics Society, denoting growth in the wage-earning population and increasing distance between them and the mill owners. Some of the bosses erected impressive mansions that symbolized their eminence as a class apart.[54]

In 1824 the trade cycle hit Pawtucket. Over-production and falling prices led mill owners to lower costs, to stretch out the work day, and to cut wages.

Women weavers rebelled and attracted widespread community support. There were public disturbances and windows smashed at the Yellow Mill, which someone tried to burn down, the latest of several acts of arson against factories. Demonstrators marched on the mill bosses' mansions. The mill owners found themselves on the defensive. Unable to count on community support, they backed down. The strike was successful because of the persisting strength of egalitarianism deriving from the American Revolution—a heritage endangered by industrialization—and because of enduring preindustrial values that resisted the treatment of labor as a commodity. In this transitional period, the triumph of the market was not yet complete, and, for the moment, employers had to accommodate to pressures from below.[55]

In 1829 the business cycle struck again, causing some of the town's leading manufacturers to fail. Farmers who had invested in the mills also suffered losses and soured on industry; a decade passed before Pawtucket achieved full recovery. Drawing lessons from the recent experience, the *Pawtucket Chronicle* asserted: "Need we look twice in the circle around us, for distress and poverty among those who have lorded it with a high hand over their poor neighbors?" The *Chronicle*, which was hostile to Antimasonry, observed, "Every village, as well as every monarchy, has its tyrants," men who employed wealth and talent "to domineer over the multitudes, and to keep down the poor and indigent." Pawtucket was no exception. A critic taunted the Wilkinsons for dabbling in Antimasonry and throwing their energies into the Antimasonic movement instead of paying off their creditors.[56]

In the quarter-century before the emergence of Antimasonry, Pawtucket had experienced its first boom, accompanied by increasing social complexity, stratification, and conflicts within the elite and between capitalists and labor. Politics also changed. Elections in the pre-industrial era were typically uncontested; by 1830 factionalism was fierce. At the center of the Antimasonic party stood a group of the town's leading industrialists, especially the Wilkinson brothers, Abraham and Isaac, who acquired textile mills and other properties throughout the Blackstone Valley. Isaac was prominent in the Baptist church which ousted Rev. David Benedict, who defended Masonry.

The Wilkinsons developed extensive business and family connections which aided them in the Antimasonic movement.[57] Whereas their family connections and the Baptist church were centers of Antimasonic sentiment, Pawtucket's Episcopal church included numerous Masons, among them Samuel Slater's partner, David Wilkinson, and his branch of this large and prominent family.[58]

While the Episcopal church in Pawtucket proved to be a safe refuge for Freemasons, the Baptist church suffered lacerating wounds. Rev. Benedict's successor, Calvin Philleo, maneuvered perilously to avoid a split. In April 1830 the church voted to "know no brother as a Mason, or Antimason, but

hold an even balance," but neutrality only inflamed the Antimasonic faction.[59] Philleo struggled with a divided congregation and in 1831 coun-
seled both sides to renounce their allegiance. The Masons must resign from
the Order without violating their oaths or repudiating Masonry. They had
deeply offended other Christians by joining an organization that embraced
"Infidel, Jewish, Mahomet, Catholic and Pagan Masons. . . ." The Antimasons also must abandon their crusade. Then "the church of God might
be at peace," Philleo hoped. "I do not think the world would suffer loss,"
he concluded, "if Masonry and Anti-Masonry . . . were blotted from creation."[60]

Yet Philleo realized that the dispute was much more than a parochial
affair. Social stratification, class divisions, and elite factionalism had an important bearing on the emergence of Antimasonry. The minister strove to
restore unity to the social fabric. "I call on the farmer and mechanic—the merchant and manufacturer—the scholar and clown—the father and mother—
the daughter and son—the high and the low—the rich and the poor—I call
on all who do not wish to be buried in the ruin of this land, to awake. . . ."
An apocalyptic millennialism framed Philleo's perspective. None of the
"wars and struggles" the United States had yet experienced "compared to
the present awful portentous period," he intoned. "The world is convulsed;
the unbridled passions of selfish men are impatient of restraint, and threaten
to break over the lines of equity and ancient land marks, and deluge the
earth in blood. . . ." Were "the patriots of seventy-six" to revisit the Republic, "how would they weep to see their labors lost—their fondest hopes
blighted in the ruin of this last retreat of man from the reign of tyrants,
and the scourge of despotism." "O America, America," he pleaded, "what
shall be done for thee?" In the end, only the Savior of mankind could save
mankind's best hope on earth: "O Prince of Peace," he prayed, "look down
on this land, and save this nation from the yawning gulf in which republics
have been lost. . . ."[61]

The heterogeneous Rhode Island Antimasonic coalition of politicized
pietists and moralistic entrepreneurs lost political vitality as it gained political success, robbing the cause of urgency. Meanwhile national issues such
as bank policy and the financial crises of 1834 and 1837 gained saliency,
which undermined third-party politics. By 1837 Rhode Island's "inflexible
minority" had run its course. Always wedded to Whiggish policies, especially tariff protection, the Antimasons' coalition with the Democrats underwent increasing strain as radical, Loco-foco Democracy gained influence in
the party. In 1834, for example, the Sprague family and other Antimasons
deserted their allies briefly to join the Whigs to protest removal of the
federal deposits from the Bank of the United States. No admirers of a
powerful central bank that restrained state banks in which they held invest-
ments, the Spragues still blamed the financial crisis on the national Democratic Administration. Once the fiscal stringency passed, the pressure lifted
on the coalition. As for Rhode Island Democrats, preserving the alliance

in order to block constitutional reform remained a top priority, while for the Antimasons, the alliance remained the ticket to power and to repression of Freemasonry.[62]

The Whig decision to cosset Freemasons left the Antimasons little choice. In 1834 the National Republicans threw their support for governor behind a ticket pledged to constitutional reform and the election of United States Senator Nehemiah Knight, a Freemason. Knight lost, but came closer the following year. The Whigs won control of the house of representatives in 1835 and replaced William Sprague, Jr., as speaker with Newport's Henry Y. Cranston, a Freemason. They also purged state offices: few sheriffs, militia officers, or justices of the peace who had secured appointment under the coalition in 1833 escaped removal in 1835.[63]

A new economic crisis in 1837 and the growing strength of anti-bank and hard money sentiment among Rhode Island Democrats eventually strained the coalition to the breaking point. The Spragues opposed President Van Buren's Independent Treasury scheme and hard money ideas. The Fennerites, who had long dominated Rhode Island Democracy before the coalition, bid for a comeback by appealing to radical Democrats in Providence, where Loco-foco notions gained ground. When the movement for banking reform spread to Rhode Island, some Democrats pushed for tough regulation of state-chartered institutions. The Spragues grew more unsettled. Finally, renewed agitation of the tariff question in Washington disturbed them. Governor Francis recognized that his re-election in 1837 required that the tariff issue remain dormant; otherwise the Spragues would bolt.[64]

For one last time, in the spring of 1837 the Spragues and the Antimasons backed Governor Francis, who won a fifth and final term. But by August, when Rhode Island chose two congressmen, the coalition was dead. The Spragues came out against Van Buren and two Whigs swept both congressional seats. In April 1838, Sprague headed the Whig ticket and defeated Francis. A bitter faction fight within the Whig party in the mid-1830s facilitated the reversal of alliances. By nominating Sprague, the Whigs avoided a choice between rival factional contenders. Sprague won 53 percent of the vote in a heavy turnout, but he did not carry Antimasons with him *en bloc*. The correlation between Sprague's 1832 and 1838 vote is weak; Francis won four of the eleven banner Antimasonic towns, but in Providence he ran very close to the Democratic vote in 1832, suggesting that big-city Antimasons either voted Whig or stayed home. Ecological regression estimates show that Sprague polled almost a fifth of the Democratic votes which Francis had captured in 1836. These were probably Antimasonic voters who, before the coalition broke up, had voted Democratic. (Table 11.3.[65])

Sprague brought the family's formidable resources into the new coalition. The Spragues had strong temperance views which they could more fruitfully push as Whigs than as Democrats. In cultivating the rising tide of

pietism in Rhode Island, nurtured by the growing temperance and abolitionist sentiment, the Spragues and the Whigs broadened their appeal.
Finally, the Spragues, who had once spent money lavishly on behalf of the
old coalition, now spent lavishly for the new.[66]

The disappearance of the "Inflexible Minority" and incorporation into
the Whig party, with its strong ties to Masonry, seemed to vindicate those
who regarded Antimasonry as little more than a smokescreen by which the
ambitious hoped to gain office and preferment. That element is rarely missing from popular social and political movements, but the success of Antimasons in other states as well as in Rhode Island rested on more than
personal influence and private ambition. Antimasonry, proclaimed the
Chronicle of the Times, "is the war of the few against the many."[67] Here
were Christian Republicans unfurling the banner of "genuine" Christianity
and "true" republicanism.

12

A Frustrated Minority
Antimasonry in Connecticut

Shall Connecticut be behind her neighbors in the good work of resistance to Masonry? She has not been accustomed to let others go before her, when freedom was in danger.
Address, Connecticut Antimasonic Convention (1830)

For six years an inflexible minority of Antimasons struggled for civic and religious purification in Connecticut, but unlike their counterparts in Rhode Island, Vermont, and Massachusetts, they experienced chronic frustration. The prospects for the third party at first seemed bright. Antimasons attracted as much as a quarter of the vote in the gubernatorial election of 1831, but thereafter their electoral fortunes declined sharply. Yet opponents of the Order refused to give up, pursuing concessions from the major parties, especially the Whigs, and running independent candidates when coalition proved unpromising. Finally, in 1834 a Whig governor and legislature elected with Antimasonic help launched an investigation of Freemasonry that condemned the Order and recommended a law banning extra-judicial oaths. The bill failed narrowly and was never revived. By 1835 the third party was virtually dead, with little to show for its efforts in the political arena. But in the battle for public sentiment, Antimasons could point to real success. They pushed Masonry on the defensive; they induced prominent Masons, especially Whig leaders, to recommend dissolution of the Lodges; and they purged churches of Masonic loyalists. The seventy-five Lodges in existence in 1830 shrank to just eleven by the end of the decade. Yet this decline of Connecticut Freemasonry did not satisfy Antimasons. The loss of membership, the closing of Lodges, the drying-up of new recruits, and renunciations by prominent members might only be temporary. The Masons preferred tactical retreat, sly maneuvering and crafty adjustment, the Antimasons warned. Public opinion was fickle and though the current ran strongly against the brotherhood in the early 1830s, unless the state adopted proscriptive measures, future revival remained possible.[1]

Confident that the people supported them, Connecticut Antimasons blamed their political frustration on the unprincipled partisans of Andrew Jackson and Henry Clay. Both parties were unwilling to lose votes by embracing Antimasonry, though some Whigs boasted of being "moral Antimasons." Two-party double-talk left no alternative to independent politics. "If Antimasonry fails, our country is lost," Antimasons argued, for "a commingling of Antimasonry with either of the political parties of the day, in political matters, is paradoxical. . . ." Amalgamation with the major parties was certain to betray "the great cause itself."[2] Despite William Wirt's poor showing in 1832, polling 10 percent—not enough to keep Connecticut out of the Clay column—the third party persisted. Antimasons agreed with the National Republicans that Jacksonism was dangerous, but the original political sin was Masonry. They agreed also with the National Republican program for economic development, but they refused to subordinate such matters to "the purposes of moral reform." Antimasons perceived themselves "not as a party devoted to the acquisition of political power" or personal gain, but a union of men and women agreed on principles on which "the patriotic and the Christian can unite." They did not reject the idea of party, but those "mere political parties" which enjoyed "only an ephemeral existence" because no deep social purpose or moral truths gave them life. A Christian Republican party was the model for Connecticut and the United States.[3]

Failure at the polls perplexed Connecticut Antimasons. They attributed it to the effects of prosperity on national character. "Too many of our children have become proud and prodigal in their self-indulgence—exclusive, overbearing, and persecuting in their conduct towards others—and inordinately anxious" for office and honor. All the Masonic vices were in full flower. Civic virtue, "the tutelary genius of freedom, is nearly merged in the groveling pursuit of wealth, or the dangerous aspirations of unlawful ambition," Antimasons intoned.[4] The "baneful effects" of prosperity "have been amazingly aggravated and extended by the institution of Freemasonry" which legitimated acquisitiveness, advanced elitist pretensions, and subverted devotion to commonwealth. Freemasonry had become a dangerous force, since even those outside the Order were so busy minding their personal affairs that "the designing, the unfaithful, the selfish and the profligate" took command of public affairs.[5] Antimasons targeted the "sincere, grave and honest" who sought no favors from government, citizens who judged others "less by their wealth, titles and outward appearances, than by their good sense, candor, and public spirit. . . ." But in summoning voters who "cultivate the sympathies and exercise the thoughts of their immortal nature . . . ," the Antimasons doomed themselves to slim pickings.[6]

After battling with Freemasonry and its protectors in both major parties, Connecticut Antimasons had ample grounds for despair. By 1834 they had committed themselves to cooperating with the Whigs. Their electoral fortunes had further dimmed when the economic crisis of 1834, which many blamed on President Andrew Jackson's removal of the federal deposits from the Bank of the United States, strengthened the motivation for coalition. The financial strains cut into Antimasonic strength, as some portion of "the inflexible minority" deserted. Once again a shrinking band of faithful found a moral explanation for their slipping fortunes. "When the love of money prevails more in any man's mind than the moral sense," the *Free Elector* argued, "the spirit of liberty dies within him." At a large public meeting in Hartford in April 1834 to protest Jacksonian bank policy, Antimasonic speakers emphasized the underlying moral dimensions, whereas others "dwelt too much upon the love of property, business success, and outward prosperity." The anti-Jackson movement could not rescue the country as long as it remained tainted by "the general prevalence of *private* interest over *public* interest."[7] The murder of Morgan and subsequent cover-up had polluted the rivers and streams "with blood," tainted the churches, and corrupted the government. Freemasonry had launched a "reckless, factious, self-seeking, treacherous, lawless and murderous spirit." From the original sin of 1826 "sprung forth upon the land, with a new ferocity," a reign of "irresponsible power and unnatural cruelty."[8] President Jackson's arbitrary exercise of executive power was just the most dramatic example.

As Whig fortunes advanced and Antimasonic prospects dimmed in Connecticut, third-party rhetoric became even more shrill. "Never did Mammon enter so deeply into the hearts of a nation," the *Free Elector* warned. Everywhere "the sordid slaves of avarice"—speculators, misers, and usurers—"suddenly awoke from their neglect of public duty to defend the Bank of the United States." And though Antimasons condemned Jackson's Bank War, they still suspected the newly mobilized opposition of being tainted by "predatory hoards, born of the spirit of Freemasonry, nourished upon bank stock. . . ."[9] By 1835 the remaining handful of political Antimasons in Connecticut concluded that national deliverance will not come from politics but from moral reform. The fate of the Republic did not depend "on the success of an election."[10]

For six years Connecticut Antimasons had believed that politics held the key to final victory. The first Antimasonic convention met in Hartford in February 1829, following well-attended town meetings at the grass roots.[11] As in other states, the initial efforts to mobilize Antimasonic sentiment stopped short of electoral politics, concentrating on influencing public opinion. Following defeat in the legislature of a bill to impose prison terms for kidnapping—one of the crimes against William Morgan—members sympathetic to Antimasonry caucused and called a state convention.[12] Delegates numbering 140, representing more than a third of the state's towns, assembled in Hartford the following February to nominate a statewide ticket and choose delegates to the national presidential nominating convention. "We have sometimes been called the Old Federal, and sometimes the old Democratic party, sometimes the Jackson, and sometimes the Adams party, but we are neither of these; we are the Antimasonic party, embracing individuals of all the parties that have hitherto existed in this country . . . ," the delegates proclaimed.[13] The Antimasons had good grounds for asserting multi-party origins. Most of the 1832 Antimasonic vote came from citizens who had not voted in 1828, and the rest from National Republicans. (Table 12.1.[14]) Turnouts were usually low in Connecticut in the late 1820s and early 1830s; barely more than a quarter of the adult white males went to the polls in 1828. The advent of Antimasonry did not greatly arouse non-voters. The big upturn came in the presidential year of 1832 when turnout soared to 46 percent. The revival of two-party competition galvanized the new voters, and the third party drew the lion's share of its support from them. In 1828 the National Republicans had captured three-quarters of the vote for President; by 1832 the party's share dropped to 55 percent. After slow gestation, Connecticut suddenly became a hotly contested two-party state following a long period of one-party rule. This development created both opportunities as well as stumbling blocks for the third party. (Table 12.2.[15])

A generation earlier the Toleration party had broken Federalist rule and given Connecticut a new constitution that separated church and state, accommodating discontented interests and making possible a decade of placid one-party government. In the 1820s old party lines further blurred because the Tolerationist leadership was moderate and preferred to amal-gamate various elements under a broad Republican umbrella. The new constitution left intact the practice of electing senators on a statewide ticket, not in districts, and Connecticut law established the same mode for choosing congressmen. A constitutional amendment in 1828 required senators to be elected in districts, inhibiting deals among statewide power brokers. Since senators and representatives together selected county and local officials, this change eventually rearranged the paths to power in Connecticut and en-couraged party development at the grass roots. The emergence of new issues in state and national politics, resulting from the Jackson/Clay rivalry and the conflicts among demographic interests, further promoted party develop-ment. Differences over tariff and bank policy, temperance, and church-state relations all contributed to the revival.[16]

The Antimasons were first to challenge the one-party system. In 1830 they endorsed Governor Gideon Tomlinson (1827–31) for re-election. He was an old Toleration party leader who quietly cultivated Antimasonic sup-port, but the Antimasons refused to accept his runningmate, another Toler-ationist veteran, Dr. John S. Peters, a Chesire physician, Episcopalian, and Freemason. They named their own ticket, replacing Peters with William T. Williams. Peters won, and after Tomlinson became United States Senator, Peters became governor in 1831 with both National Republican and Demo-cratic votes. The Antimasons ran their own man, Calvin Willeys, who polled 26 percent. In the race for lieutenant governor, the Antimasons, with

16 percent, blocked a majority. Refusing to support either of the two stronger candidates when the contest went into the legislature for resolution, the third party caused a deadlock that left the office unfilled that year.[17]

Until the further growth of major party competition, the Antimasons polled too few votes to make a difference in the governor's race. Yet once competition between Democrats and National Republicans or Whigs became keen, "moral Antimasons" who leaned toward the Nationals were wary of "wasting" a vote on a third party. In 1833 the Democrats abandoned amalgamation and chose Henry W. Edwards, formerly a Tolerationist United States Senator (1823–27), to contest Peters, who barely edged by Edwards in the popular vote but fell short of a majority. In the legislature, the Antimasons threw their support to Edwards in a futile effort to exercise a balance of power.[18]

Elements in both parties cultivated their support, yet neither would push through Antimasonic legislation. In 1832 a committee headed by an Antimasonic senator, Stephen Palmer, recommended legislation compelling annual reports from all Lodges, but that proposal did not pass. The next year the Democrats rewarded the Antimasons with a legislative investigation of Freemasonry, but once again no legislation passed. Connecticut neither repealed Masonic charters as did Rhode Island, nor banned extra-judicial oaths as did Massachusetts. In 1834 the Whigs dropped Peters and named Samuel A. Foot as their candidate for governor. As he was no Freemason, they hoped he could appeal to Antimasonic voters, but the third party still contested, its vote tumbling from 14 percent the previous year to just under 7 percent. Foot, like Edwards, fell shy of a popular majority. Now the Antimasons backed the Whig who became governor. Once again the third party experienced frustration: a bill outlawing extra-judicial oaths narrowly failed. The Whigs did reward their allies with appointments to local office, but the Antimasons, claiming they were not office-seekers, were dissatisfied. By 1835 political Antimasonry expired in Connecticut. The Bank War continued to dominate public attention, and the closeness of the two-party battle made voting for a third party too costly for Antimasons who leaned to the Whigs. In 1835 the Whigs put a leading Antimason, John M. Holley, on their congressional ticket, a move aimed at bringing the remaining Antimasonic strength into the Whig fold. A few members of the inflexible minority held out, but most drifted into the Whig column. (Table 12.3.[19])

The slow development of the Second American Party System had facilitated the birth of the third party; its maturation killed it. Gideon Welles, a Jacksonian Democratic leader, attributed the growth of the Antimasons to the existence of a political vacuum. Without a two-party system offering Connecticut a clear choice, voters were vulnerable to Antimasonic agitation. Welles thought that hostile public opinion gave Freemasonry no future in the state. That may also explain why many with Antimasonic sympathies refused to make it a political question. The battle seemed already won, and other, more compelling questions attracted them to the major parties.[20]

The course of party development goes far to explain the reasons for the Antimasonic party's frustration, but understanding the social basis of Antimasonry is also vital. The party's electoral strength centered in the two eastern counties, Windham and Tolland, which accounted for 42 percent of the Antimasonic vote in the 1832 presidential election. These two counties formed part of an extended region of Antimasonic strength that stretched into northern, industrial Rhode Island through Pawtucket into southern Massachusetts. Throughout this region, the persistence of conservative evangelical Calvinism, dating from the struggles over the Great Awakening in the eighteenth century and the development of industrial society, generated restorationist impulses that sought, through the destruction of Freemasonry, to rebuild the civic and religious foundation upon which many believed American Republicanism rested. Even outside this epicenter of Antimasonry, the strength of the New Light evangelical tradition and the spread of small-scale manufacturers provided fertile soil.

Yet Connecticut's demographic history in the early nineteenth century was not as favorable to the growth of Antimasonry as other parts of New England. Among the state's major religious denominations, the Congregationalists found Antimasonry a divisive intrusion. Modernist elements were in the ascendancy. Facing competition from Episcopalians for upper- and middle-class support, and from Methodists for lower-middle-class- and working-class support, many Congregationalists preferred to avoid the question of Masonry. Liberalism of a Unitarian or Universalist strain was much weaker than in Massachusetts, in part because the consociational polity of Connecticut Congregationalism placed limits on local autonomy, and unorthodox opinion had difficulty making inroads. The Unitarian/Trinitarian split which figured so prominently in Massachusetts had no counterpart in Connecticut. Moreover, Episcopalianism, whose male adherents had a strong affinity for Freemasonry because of its class character, elaborate ritual, anti-sectarian and latitudinarian attitudes, was strong in Connecticut.[21] Antimasons found important support within the churches, but it remained limited for political purposes. Finally, the state was relatively slow in undergoing industrial development, at least before 1840. The slow pace of the transition to industrial society combined with the halting development of the Second Party System doomed Connecticut's "inflexible minority" to marginality.

The statistical clues to Antimasonry are suggestive but inconclusive. The weak correlations with Federalism and Whiggery suggest an unusual degree of electoral discontinuity and fragmentation. The multiple regression statistics are also problematic. They indicate that few variables had much impact on the Antimasonic vote, though Congregationalism and Episcopalianism both tended to hurt, while manufacturing and money-at-loan tended to help. (Table 12.4.[22]) Biographical information is more helpful. The delegates to the 1830 Antimatonic Convention tended to be mature, well-established men, prominent in their communities. More than half were fifty years or older and most of the rest were over forty.[23] In 1831, Antimasons named Timothy Pitkin, a veteran Federalist leader, as their candidate for governor against John Peters. Though Pitkin declined, his selection suggests a restorationist strain in Connecticut Antimasonry that looked back to an earlier day. Another older leader from the state's Federalist past, Gen. Nathaniel Terry, was prominent in the party. He had led the anti-Tolerationist forces in the 1818 constitutional convention where he and Pitkin tried to avert complete separation of state and church. Terry, a veteran of many previous battles, sounded the restorationist note when he told the third party's 1832 State Convention that though "an old man," he championed the Antimasonic cause because he could not "leave my children a more precious inheritance than Freedom unshackled by Freemasonry."[24]

More than half the Antimasonic leaders identified were in business, but they were more likely to engage in manufactures than commerce. These Antimasons were not outsiders, but possessed experience in public life and were often leaders in religious, charitable, and benevolent associations. Yet their most telling characteristic was their religious proclivities: three-quarters were Congregationalists, and references to personal piety and devotion to their church crop up frequently in the sources.

The religious sources of Connecticut Antimasonry are complex, because while Congregationalists and Baptists tended to have the greatest affinity for Antimasonry, most denominations hoped to avoid this dangerously divisive question. Some religious leaders, however, played a central role. In their propaganda, Connecticut Antimasons gave the religious argument great weight. In 1830, for example, the Antimasonic state address declared Masonry to be "a cunning device of the Powers of Darkness, to deceive and ruin the souls of men." Antimasons were certain their cause enjoyed divine blessing, arguing that William Morgan's death was the means by which God turned "a great private calamity" into an occasion for awakening Christian Republicans to danger.[25]

For churchmen convinced that Freemasonry was "a heaven-daring impiety and blasphemy" incompatible with genuine Christianity, the unwillingness of most denominational leaders, especially within the Calvinist traditions, to form a united front was vexing. Antimasons targeted evangelical opinion as a major battleground. "Many of our brethren are deceived, and human nature is stubborn; men are proud, and they are selfish," Antimasons explained.[26] The *Boston Recorder,* for example, came under fire for excluding Antimasonic opinion from its columns. The General Association of Congregational churches maintained a prudent silence on the question. The disinclination of churches to take a stand appeared in Plymouth, where an Antimasonic leader, Ely Terry, Jr., appealed to the Litchfield Association to advise his church to take a tougher line. Some church bodies, such as the Litchfield Association, took a strong Antimasonic position when pressured. So too did the New London Association of Baptists, which recommended that Masonry was grounds for exclusion. Likewise, individual Baptist and Congregationalist churches conducted purges, but neither of these denominations acted with any uniformity. And therein lay the dilemma facing religious Antimasonry.[27] The problem, wrote Rev. Noble D. Strong, was that men who "committed whoredom with this Mother of Abominations . . . find it hard to confess it and bear the disgrace. Hence the efforts of thousands to chastify the courtesan."[28] As late as 1834, Antimasons complained of apathy in the churches "in respect to the licentious, dangerous, and anti-Christian institution of Freemasonry." Even worse, the direct connection among ministers and laymen with this "sinful association" was "rapidly undermining the moral sense and vitality of the community."[29]

The Connecticut Antimasonic Tract Society, hoping to enlighten Christians, published General Chauncey Whittlesey's *Renunciations of Freemasonry and Appeal to the Public.* Whittlesey was a Middletown lawyer who joined the Masons in his youth and became a devoted member. The Morgan case trigged feelings that Masonry was "incompatible with Christianity" and was of "pernicious tendency." As his health deteriorated, the approach of death made him even more remorseful and eager to save others from his mistake. Whittlesey thanked God for sparing him long enough to dictate a renunciation of Freemasonry, an act of repentance which might weigh heavily in his favor on Judgment Day. "When the final hour came," God would remember that Chauncey Whittlesey had not "neglected important duties," nor placed his "hopes for Eternity upon false foundations," as Masons did. Whittlesey's public confession brought him peace of mind, for "when almost every earthly comfort was withdrawn, he was not cast down, for he looked to his inheritance among the saints."[30]

Behind these efforts to make Antimasonry a test of Christian orthodoxy lay deep fissures within the evangelical churches and increasing rivalry between them and other denominations growing in influence in the early nineteenth century. The stakes were high, for at issue, they believed, was the separation of real Christians from fake. The Antimasons adopted a simple objective test: persons who remained Masons could not be genuine Christians, for in Masonry one found "no confession of sins, no acknowledgment of the influence of the Holy Spirit, no seeking for justification through faith in the Son of God. . . ." The Lodges, moreover, welcomed the "unprincipled and profligate," who mixed with true Christians, uniting both "in a sustenation of an irreligious, heartless cosmopolitanism." Masonry's latitudinarian spirit and heterogeneous membership were symptomatic of the erosion of Connecticut's Puritan heritage.[31]

The election of Governor John S. Peters, an Episcopalian and the first to break the nearly two centuries' monopoly by Congregationalists, exemplified the weakening of sectarian exclusivity. "It is not at all surprising" that some traditionalists preferred the Antimasonic Calvin Willeys for governor, "when you consider Gov. Peters' religious Sentiments are Opposite to the Orthodox," explained a Democrat.[32]

The growth of Episcopalianism in Connecticut alarmed many Congregationalists, though in 1830 they still claimed two-thirds of the state's churches and over 40 percent of the membership in major denominations. Episcopalianism had made important inroads in the eighteenth century, more so in Connecticut than anywhere else in New England, and by the beginning of the nineteenth century, it demonstrated remarkable ability to attract support from the upper strata, especially in fashionable places such as New Haven and Hartford, draining off elements that elsewhere drifted towards Unitarianism. People seeking a more secularized faith, less constrained by Calvinism, Puritan discipline, and sectarian prejudice, unable to find a liberal alternative within the Congregationalist churches, switched denominations. This had serious political effects in Connecticut, where Federalist hegemony had rested on close ties between political and ecclesiastical authority. When Episcopalians abandoned the Federalists for the Tolerationist party, they assured its triumph and gained unprecedented influence. In 1817, Tolerationist Governor Oliver Wolcott invited an Episcopal minister to give the annual election sermon—a break with Puritan tradition. Likewise, the Episcopalians' Washington College overcame strong opposition from Yale's Congregationalist supporters and secured state aid. Finally in 1831, Peters became governor.[33]

The obvious successes of Connecticut Episcopalians encouraged the Methodists. They, too, surmounted Congregationalist opposition and obtained a charter for Wesleyan College in 1831.[34] Even the Universalists, not numerous in Connecticut, obtained relief from an appellate court decision barring testimony in court by witnesses who did not believe in punishment after death. Because Nothingarians and liberal Christians—as well as Universalists—felt threatened by the decision, there was broad support for overturning it. Likewise, when P. T. Barnum, a Democratic editor of the Universalist *Gospel of Freedom,* landed in jail for tangling with the Congregationalist elite in his community, those opposed to the old Standing Order cried religious persecution.[35]

While the emerging Jackson party was especially appealing to the more vulnerable denominations, emerging National Republicans, with solid support from mainstream Congregationalists, recognized that too close an association with the remnants of the Standing Order was risky. In the late 1820s the Connecticut legislature took a series of steps that moved further in the direction of religious pluralism. Besides ending Yale's monopoly on higher education, Connecticut fashioned a compromise that allowed witnesses who professed to be Christians to testify at trials. Since the legislature did not define Christianity, Universalists, Nothingarians, and others were unlikely to face exclusion. Thaddeus Betts, a Congregationalist who later became lieutenant governor on the National Republican ticket, was the architect of the measure.[36] With both parties avoiding narrow identification with sectarian positions, and with many churches and laymen adopting more tolerant, latitudinarian, secular attitudes, those who clung to older notions of Christian community had understandable grounds for alarm. The Constitution of 1818 had formally eliminated a single sectarian standard as a civic test and the change was irreversible, but by agitating against Freemasonry, some hoped to reimpose a non-denominational test for Christian magistrates. Masons perceived their opponents in precisely this light. The *Masonic Mirror* pointed to the proposed Antimasonic statewide ticket, designed by Rev. Noble D. Strong, which contained only Congregationalists, and called it an affront to the thousands of Episcopalians, Methodists, and Baptists.[37]

The post-1818 settlement had encouraged increasing pluralism in Connecticut, which strained the tolerance of conservative Calvinists. The Episcopalians continued to draw away members from the Congregationalists, including some of the most prominent who sought refuge from Calvinism, strict discipline, and female majorities, similar to the refuge offered by Masonic Lodges. The Episcopal seminary in Cheshire sent forth a stream of ministers to spread the faith. The number of Episcopal ministers doubled in the 1820s and a new academy, established in Hartford in 1830, further expanded the supply. The *Episcopal Watchman,* first published in 1827, gave laymen their own weekly, further evidence that the 1820s was a time of growth and consolidation for the denomination.[38]

There was an affinity between the spread of Freemasonry and Episcopalianism in Connecticut. From the Antimasonic perspective, the same secularist, anti-evangelical impulses that led people away from the Puritan churches drew them toward Masonic Lodges and Episcopal churches. Lodges were most prevalent in those parts of Connecticut where Episcopalianism had made its greatest advances. Towns with Masonic Lodges were likely also to have an Episcopal church, and Episcopal ministers and laymen were prominent in the Order. In Kent, the first master of the Lodge (founded 1806) was an Episcopalian worthy. In Newton, the Episcopal church dated from 1733, and Universalists arrived early in the nineteenth century. The Episcopal parson, Daniel Burnham, was active in the Lodge. Cheshire, whose Masonic Lodge dated from 1790, hosted the important Episcopal Academy and members of that denomination were prominent both in town government and in the Lodge. Even after the rise of Antimasonry, when clergymen of other denominations steered clear of Masonry, two Episcopal parsons helped Masons celebrate the Feast of St. John in Oxford in June 1833. Finally, Governor Peters reminded Orthodox sectarians of the link among religious pluralism, Episcopalianism, and Freemasonry.[39]

The inroads made by modernism in Calvinist churches were even more alarming to traditionalists than was the growing influence of the non-Calvinist denominations. Some sensed a radical discontinuity in Connecticut's spiritual life. In 1816, an astute historian of Connecticut Episcopalianism reported that it was still common for the most fashionable people in a town to attend church, for ministers to occupy positions of authority, and for churches to oversee matters of faith and morals. Geographic and social mobility, population turnover, mushrooming pluralism and indifference, political factionalism, and increasing class differences played havoc with the idea of Connecticut as the Land of Steady Habits, a homogeneous, corporate Christian commonwealth.[40] Precisely because their influence over morals had declined, Congregationalists especially turned to voluntary associations to fight Sabbath breaking, intemperance, neglect of family prayer, and the religious education of children. Though they had no monopoly over the temperance movement, for example, Antimasons perceived themselves as more devoted to the cause than others, who merely gave the movement lip service. Masonry encouraged moral laxity, they reasoned, and whoever was not thoroughly Antimasonic was an uncertain ally in the war against social disorder. In New Haven, they pointed out, the Freemasons ran a "Republican ticket" pledged to oppose the temperance society and the anti-lottery movements. "Thus Masonry and rum acted together," Antimasons insisted. At the same time, half the Old Federalists who were Masons also voted for the Masonic "Republican" ticket, and, even worse, all the Masonic Congregationalists marched together with the "rummies."[41]

New Haven was home of Yale and its theological department, from which Rev. Nathaniel W. Taylor and others fashioned a modernist reformulation of Calvinist theology, accommodating popular preference for free will in the search for salvation. The Taylorites hoped to resist defections to the Arminian churches such as the Episcopalian church, which did not hold to the Calvinist view that man lacked free will. At the same time, modernists adopted a less sectarian, more tolerant stance towards other denominations. In 1825 the Grand Lodge of Connecticut elected Rev. Charles Boardman, a Congregationalist, as chaplain, succeeding two Episcopalians. Boardman denied that Masonry was an anti-Christian institution and boasted that Masonic benevolence was valuable because it encouraged charitable impulses in men beyond the reach of the churches. Boardman's example illustrated "the trend toward increasing accommodation of Masonry" by elements of Connecticut Orthodoxy. Boardman succeeded Nathaniel W. Taylor as pastor of the Third Church in New Haven. Taylor's *Quarterly Christian Spectator* kept silent on the question of Masonry throughout the Antimasonic period, though it was outspoken in opposition to another social movement, abolitionism. Antimasons polled few votes in New Haven and recruited few leaders. An exception was the venerable Noah Webster, an unrepentant Federalist and devout Christian, whose roots traced back to the Revolutionary era. It was precisely among such men who looked back to a golden age that Antimasonry found some of its most influential and articulate voices.[42]

Connecticut Antimasons recruited Rev. Noble D. Strong in 1828 to edit the *Antimasonic Intelligencer,* published in Hartford. His father, Rev. Nathan D. Strong, had presided over the city's First Church for over half a century and provided the son with a role model. The elder Strong, a conservative Calvinist, arrived in Hartford in 1744 and found the First Church weak. A successful evangelist, he generated a series of revivals. His influence eventually spread beyond the parish, for he took a strong interest in public affairs. He enlisted in the resistance to Great Britain movement, joined the army during the American Revolution, and, after the war, entered the struggle on behalf of the federal Constitution. A founder of the Connecticut Missionary Society and editor of the *Connecticut Evangelical Magazine,* Nathan D. Strong set a standard as a public man. His son, Noble, who had migrated to New York, returned to Hartford to lead the Antimasonic movement, for now the greater need lay in his native state. Strong had come to Antimasonry first-hand, having seceded from Royal Arch Masonry. He blamed tolerance by the churches—ministers who refused to repent—for the limited success of the Antimasonic party in Connecticut. Professed Christians, eager for personal advancement and public office, clung to Masonry, and churches went along for fear of temporal losses.[43]

Yet Noble Strong knew that there were clergy and laymen in Connecticut, especially among Congregationalists, who were faithful to the Puritan past. In the forefront stood Rev. Daniel Dow of Thompson. Dow delivered one of the first clerical attacks against Freemasonry and in 1829 participated in efforts to remove Rev. Ralph Crampton, a Masonic preacher in Woodstock, whom he had earlier helped to install. Dow typified the Orthodox Calvinist who rejected Taylorism, sought to sustain tight bonds between church, pastor, and community, and advocated strict adherence to the painful truths of Calvinism. He was Connecticut's closest counterpart to Rev. Nathanael Emmons, the leading clerical Antimason in Massachusetts.[44]

In 1833 conservative Congregationalists established the East Windsor Theological Seminary to combat the perceived Arminian take-over at Yale, dominated by Taylorism. Dow was a founder of the seminary and in 1834 he published an extended attack on Taylorism, denying that it was consistent with the Westminster Platform or with the Calvinism of Jonathan Edwards, Joseph Bellamy, Samuel Hopkins, or Timothy Dwight. Dow challenged Taylor's right to retain a Yale professorship, claiming that he had strayed too far from Orthodoxy. East Windsor's largest benefactor was James Hosmer, a Hartford Antimason who contributed $100,000 for a professorship and made the seminary his residuary legatee. Noble Strong, Dow, and Hosmer typified the conservative Congregationalists who occupied an important place in Connecticut Antimasonry.[45]

Baptist leaders also joined the third party. In 1829 the New London Baptist Association staged a debate between supporters and opponents of the Order, and though it favored Antimasonry, other Baptists resisted. "It is pleasant to think that all the really religious, as soon as they get information, withdraw," and only the infidels remain, said Rev. Joshua Williams. "The present, Sir, is a season of darkness, and of sore affliction," consoled Noble

Strong to a Baptist who suffered for his Antimasonry. "Many of our breth-ren are deceived," he explained.[46]

Both Baptist and Congregationalist Antimasons wrestled with the prob-lematic question of who was a Christian. Outward conformity to evangelical standards was no adequate guarantee. The tendency towards secularization in the churches subordinated godly concerns to worldly affairs. Antimasons proposed a new litmus test that separated the "really religious" from the fake. Hypocrisy plagued the evangelical fold. This became most apparent after the great 1831 revival, but it had long bothered many pietists. In 1831 and 1832 Connecticut Congregationalists boasted the greatest harvest of souls in their history—more than eight thousand. When the revival ended, a gloomy pessimism filled the annual reports which struggled to explain why the harvest had ended. Some blamed "the worldliness of Christians," others "the coldness and inaction of pastors." Certainly the mobility of the population and the large number of non-residents in every congregation ac-counted for why many were "cold and worldly, and at length relapsed. . . ." In 1835 the General Association complained of a great increase in travel and recreation on the Sabbath, the frequent dismissal of ministers and "neglect of public worship." Once again in 1836 the problem was growing "worldli-ness—an eagerness to monopolize their full share of earthly gain. . . ." The post-awakening let-down and self-examination made clear how powerful were the secularist currents among the saints, currents which not even the most successful revival in American history had reversed.[47] An antimodern-ist, restorationist perspective linked religious leaders in the Antimasonic movement, but it also linked others whose Antimasonry is not reducible to religious anxieties.

Farmington, not far from Hartford, was an important center of Antima-sonic leadership; it had also played a comparable role in the period of Fed-eralist dominance. In 1830, Farmington sent ten men to the Antimasonic convention, the largest delegation from any town. The state's leading in-land trading community in the late eighteenth and early nineteenth century before Hartford displaced it, Farmington had long been accustomed to carrying great weight in public life as an unofficial center of Federalist/ Congregationalist leadership. Farmington's native son, Governor John Tread-well (1809–11), led the Federalists until his defeat in 1811, when the state chose for the first time a man who made no professions of being a born-again Christian. Treadwell's loss heralded the end of a system of co-optation within a small circle of Orthodox by which the state customarily chose its rulers. Treadwell resisted reform at the 1818 Constitutional Convention along with another Farmington delegate, Timothy Pitkin, a former Federal-ist congressman and party stalwart, descended from one of the town's early-eighteenth-century ministers.[48] Both were founders of the American Board of Commissioners for Foreign Missions.

Neither Treadwell nor Pitkin played a role in the Antimasonic move-ment—Treadwell died in the 1820s, and Pitkin, though nominated for governor by the third party in 1831, declined—but other Farmington leaders threw their weight behind the cause, enabling William Wirt to poll almost a third of the vote in 1832. When citizens petitioned a Democratic-controlled legislature in 1833 for a bank charter, a Jackson leader urged its defeat because a new bank for Farmington "would be no more or less than a fund for the support of an Antimasonic Tract Society."[49]

Before 1830, Farmington demonstrated an exceptional degree of cultural uniformity measured by the failure of other denominations to make inroads. The world around Farmington, however, was changing rapidly. Governor Treadwell's defeat in 1811, followed shortly by the fall of Federalism, dramatized that. The town was not only losing its political and moral influence but also its commercial importance, as Hartford passed it to become the leading emporium in the region. Religious pluralism finally punctured its homogeneity. Antimasonry promised to restore a Christian Republicanism which Farmington's leaders took to be the foundation upon which the Revolutionary generation had raised the Republic. In 1834 they reaffirmed their devotion to Antimasonic principles, "second in importance to no cause which has risen since the days of the American Revolution."[50] Antimasonic prominents in other towns, too, had strong links to the Federalist past which, usually combined with adherence to Orthodoxy, made them feel stranded, outside the mainstream of Connecticut development.

Hartford cast few votes for the Antimasons, but it contributed important leaders. General Nathaniel P. Terry, who had strong ties to Federalism, headed a large delegation to the Antimasonic convention in 1830, occupied the chair, and served as a delegate to the 1831 presidential nominating convention. At the 1818 Constitutional Convention, Terry, Treadwell, and Pitkin worked to head off the collapse of the standing order. Terry had graduated from Yale, entered the bar in the 1790s, and quickly ascended the Federalist ladder, combining public service with astute business leadership. He sat on the bench, went to Congress (1816–18) and served as mayor of Hartford (1824–31). He married a daughter of Col. Jeremiah Wadsworth, another of Hartford's leading families. Terry organized the Governor's Foot Guards, which he commanded for almost a dozen years, and he served as president of the Hartford Bank, the Hartford Asylum for the Deaf, and as director of an insurance company, a savings bank, and an academy.[51]

Antimasonry also drew support from industrialists in the forefront of the state's economic transformation who were keenly sensitive to the problems of preserving moral order. The concentration of Antimasonic strength in the eastern counties coincided with the center of early manufacturing. The factory villages of Toland and Windham counties formed part of an industrial region spreading into northern Rhode Island and southern Massachusetts, Antimasonic strongholds. Industrial society spread more slowly in Connecticut; in 1840 the U.S. Census reported that two-thirds of the labor force still engaged in agriculture, compared with approximately 40 percent in Massachusetts and Rhode Island. The persistence of farming explained the comparatively slow population growth during the first four decades of the nineteenth century. With its farmlands long settled, forcing many native-born to migrate, and without rapid growth in the commercial, transport, or industrial sectors, there was little to keep many of the native-born or to attract immigrants. The later development of metal and textile manufactures, brass, iron, farm equipment, and clocks helped to lay foundations for Connecticut's rapid development after 1840.

Salisbury, a strong Antimasonic town (47% in 1832), was the home of the Holley family, party leaders and prominent iron manufacturers. John Milton Holley, Jr., a son of iron manufacturer John M. Holley, attended Yale, became a lawyer, and then migrated to western New York in the 1820s, along with thousands of other Yankees. In the early 1830s he returned home, became active in the Antimasonic party, ran for lieutenant governor twice, and served as a delegate to the national convention in 1831. In 1835 he won a spot on the Whig congressional ticket. His brother Alexander, born in 1804, entered his father's iron business, became a pioneer manufacturer of pocket cutlery, and after Antimasonry, gravitated to the Whig and the Republican parties. In 1857, he won the governorship, following a lifetime's devotion to temperance, abolition, Antimasonry, and the town's Orthodox Congregational church.[52]

Myron Holley, cousin of Alexander Holley and John Milton, was the leading reformer in the family. Also the son of a prosperous iron manufacturer, he attended Williams College and prepared for the bar, but he practiced only briefly because he could not reconcile a legal career with moral obligation. In 1803 Holley settled in Canandaigua, New York, as a bookseller, joining De Witt Clinton to mobilize support for construction of the Erie Canal. He served as a member of the Canal Commission and, living near where the Morgan case erupted, Holley joined the Antimasonic movement at its source. He attended the party's 1830 national convention, drafted its address, and edited an Antimasonic newspaper near Rochester, returning to Connecticut in 1834 to edit the Antimasonic *Free Elector*. He wrote the report of the Connecticut legislative committee which investigated Freemasonry and drafted a bill outlawing Masonic oaths.[53]

Holley's affinity for Antimasonry had roots in radical egalitarian abhorrence of class snobbery. He celebrated the nobility of labor and the moral superiority of the "producing" classes. He worshipped republican equality, but believed Freemasonry obstructed justice and sought to elevate some citizens above the rest. He insisted that the fate of Christian Republicanism rested with America's women, and therefore he rejected an "institution which segregated a body of men from the rest of the world, including the wives and daughters of their own families. . . ."[54]

Myron Holley's social thought had deep roots in his religion of benevolence. He never joined a church, despised revivalism, the idea of human depravity, and a punishing God. Rejecting all creeds and theologies, he believed in a loving God and universal salvation. He preached a social gospel that made benevolence the ultimate test, a test most church members failed because they made absurd theologies, bigotry, rituals, and social exclusivity the basis of faith. It is hypocrisy, he argued, for revivalists to preach that sinners must renounce the world when they converted Freemasons who *"secretly,* in a state of indecent nudity, with a rope round their necks and bandage over their eyes, kneeling before a mock altar, laid their hands upon the open bible. . . ." Masonry was a school for snobbery that flourished in an age in which "Mammon has more devoted worshippers here than any other God."[55] Antimasonry failed in Connecticut, he concluded, because too few citizens subordinated selfish "interests and appetites" to the moral obligations of civil society. The result was "suppression of the moral sense of the community."[56] It was among the poor and uneducated that Holley found hope, for they, unlike "the high born and the high bred," loved God and their fellow men.[57]

In Holley's scheme, the family was the nurturing ground of Christian Republicanism. Families governed by "hoops of theological creed" must generate governments that were "arbitrary, plutocratic, and theocratic, as well as military." Without "love, harmony, order, and justice in the family," there could be no "patriotism and cohesion in a republic." Though he stayed out of the churches, Holley conducted family prayer faithfully and preached in a Rochester Court House and later in a schoolhouse outside the city. People from every rank attended his meetings, including humble laborers who shunned socially pretentious, hypocritical churches. When he died in 1841, laboring for the Liberty party, its members placed a monument over his grave which read: "He trusted in God, and loved his neighbor."[58]

The strongest Antimasonic town in Connecticut was Pomfret, which went for Wirt in 1832 by 65 percent. Smith Wilkinson was the town's leading Antimason. He was a manufacturer, one of the five sons of Oziel Wilkinson, the prominent Pawtucket, Rhode Island, businessman whose family stood on both sides of the battle line. From the early days of industrial development, Americans were mindful of England's oppressed factory population and feared the degradation of labor in the United States. Yet some entrepreneurs believed that the advantages of industry were available without social cost. Among them was Smith Wilkinson, who argued that a factory regimen could improve morals, as his own experience in Pomfret demonstrated. Wilkinson recruited workers from poor, large families who lived on worn-out farms or in run-down rented houses. The families were "very ignorant, and too often vicious," but once under Wilkinson's control, they changed. Working twelve hours a day, he explained, left "no time to spend in idleness or vicious amusements."[59] Wilkinson's control extended beyond the workplace. He tolerated no drinking in bars or taverns and no gaming, not even ball playing. He also strictly limited employees' credit, forcing them to live within their means. And he made sure that workers strictly observed Sabbath and Fast days; in the 1840s he donated land for a Baptist church. The results were exemplary, he claimed. The houses in Factory Village were neat, there were no loafers, morals were beyond reproach. Should a loose woman infiltrate, workers demanded her immediate ouster. In twenty-nine years, Wilkinson boasted, "I can assert that but two cases of seduction and bastardy have occurred." The company purchased more land than it needed just to prevent taverns and grog shops from gaining a foothold nearby, and it built a school and encouraged religious worship. John Holbrook, deacon of the First Congregational church, joined Wilkinson in the Antimasonic movement.[60]

Wilkinson's paternalism had other sides. No absentee capitalist, he lived among his workers. His house was open "to his people" and many thronged there. Wilkinson hoped to fashion "a family connection," a paternalistic bond, which tempered his authoritarian rule. A young man who graduated from Wilkinson's school of industrial morality was thought likely to succeed later in life. Wilkinson won his people's affection, for they took "pride in the place, even in the peculiarities of its master, which furnished inexhaustible discussion and anecdote."[61]

Wilkinson was a social engineer, convinced that by careful control, he could reconcile industrial society with Christian Republicanism. He had only to point at nearby Willimantic in Windham, a town that spurned Antimasonry and was synonymous with moral disorder. Willimantic was another new factory village, financed, as was Pomfret, by Rhode Island capital. The arrival of industry occurred without the planning or oversight of a Smith Wilkinson and the result was disaster. Manufactures emerged "like a spring freshet, tearing down the old landmarks and sweeping everything before it." Not many people had inhabited Willimantic before the factories went up; then "the few previous residents of the hitherto quiet valley were almost dazed by the onset." Economic growth generated conflict—an "eruption of many clashing enterprises and interests" which proved "quite overpowering." Without careful provision for decent housing, for example, shanties suddenly sprang up. The first public building was not a church or town hall, but "The Lighthouse"—a grog shop Wilkinson would never have allowed.

The nature of the work force added to disorder. Employees came from "many different communities" and formed a very "heterogeneous population" which "refused to be blended." In Pomfret, Wilkinson's regimen "blended" equally inauspicious elements, but his discipline was missing here. The teamsters who hauled in the raw cotton and carried the finished goods away provided further patronage for bars. The result was "much disorder and drunkenness, and bad elements seemed for a time to predominate."

The forces of pietism and social order did not overlook Willimantic, but they stumbled on rough terrain. Temperance workers complained of bitter opposition. Rival religious denominations, quarreling with one another, failed to carry their appropriate weight. There was such indifference towards preachers that they had difficulty finding meeting space. Baptists, Congregationalists, and Methodists clashed with one another and Nothingarians and skeptics joined with one or more church faction to close the schoolhouse to preaching.

In Pomfret, children were model little Christian Republicans; in Willimantic, they were ungovernable. "Rampaging" boys taxed the ability of all the town's schoolmasters, forcing the school committee to recruit tough disciplinarians elsewhere. Parents contended unsuccessfully with unruly and disobedient offspring. "Insubordination at home was quite as subversive of progress as Windham's resistance," wrote the town historian.

Yet there were serious efforts to reclaim Willimantic. The Congregationalists' Domestic Missionary Society targeted this latter-day Sodom to establish an outpost. In 1827 Rev. Denis Platt arrived, built a church, and recruited a hundred souls, but it languished for a generation, ever weak and dependent on outside help. Willimantic needed a Smith Wilkinson to mobilize its citizens under the banners of industrial order, temperance, pietism, and Antimasonry. Without such leadership, making industrialism compatible with republicanism remained problematic.[62]

In September 1834, Smith Wilkinson chaired a meeting of Antimasons at Nichols' Inn in Pomfret. They resolved that "in as much as the Whig party have not met the views and feelings of the Antimasonic party, it is wholly improper for the Antimasons to support their nomination."[63] Rejected by the Democrats, frustrated by the Whigs, Connecticut Antimasons failed to become a balance-wheel in the state's political system. Purists like the Pomfret Antimasons preferred isolation even if that meant defeat.

The Antimasonic dilemma in Connecticut derived in part from the strength of Freemasonry in both parties. The Democrats made any alliance impossible, for they nominated a Freemason on the first purely Jacksonian state ticket, courting Masons, Nothingarians, and others. Bidding for votes from those at odds with the social and moral pretensions of the Congregationalists, the Democrats carefully built a Jacksonian party on ethno-cultural appeals—rejecting tough temperance legislation and breaches in separation of church and state—as well as on populist reforms such as broadening the suffrage and regulating the banking system. By 1833 the Democrats had become strong enough to abandon amalgamation and pursue an independent course.[64]

Antimasons leaned towards the National Republicans but found them wary. Like the Democrats, the Nationals would not risk antagonizing Masons, yet they angled for Antimasonic support. They avoided putting Masons on their tickets; in 1835 they nominated John M. Holley for Congress; and when they controlled the state patronage, they generously rewarded Antimasons. But there were limits to collaboration. The Whigs ignored Antimasonic senatorial district slates; they tried to take over Antimasonic meetings and impose their own candidates; and a Whig legislature failed to enact Antimasonic legislation. The emergence of a competitive Jackson party, the Whigs calculated, made it too costly for "moral Antimasons" with Whiggish leanings to waste a vote on the third party. On such questions as temperance, black rights, and national economic policy, the Antimasons and Whigs were close. Once Connecticut became sharply polarized, the third party's prospects faded.

A small group of Antimasonic diehards, including Smith Wilkinson, remained outside the Whig fold. By retaining their independence, militants in 1834 and 1835 hoped to demonstrate that their support was indispensable to Whig victory. The economic crisis of 1834, however, further weakened Antimasons and gave the Whigs a popular new cause. In the fall of 1835, even with John M. Holley on the congressional ticket the entire Whig slate was defeated; the previous spring the party also lost the state elections—not even Antimasonic support saved them.

"We contend for correct principles, and correct principles may sometimes be as surely advanced by an inflexible minority as by an overwhelming majority," was the consoling hope for Connecticut Antimasons. Calling on Christian Republicans to shun the Whigs, diehards argued that any who collaborated "will soon find himself engulfed in the turbid stream of modern Whiggery, without a compass rudder."[65] Yet even after the third party's demise, Antimasons did not drift aimlessly, for there were other causes worthy of their energies. "The two greatest evils which afflict us," proclaimed the *Free Elector,* "are Freemasonry and domestic slavery." Slavery, like Freemasonry, had mushroomed since the American Revolution, even though "most men of sense and character" opposed it. It, too, was in "the interest of men, numerous, wealthy, and widely scattered, in the union. . . ."[66] To restrain selfish interest, reconcile ambition and material progress with Christian Republicanism remained Antimasonry's vexing legacy.

13

The Antimasonic Legacy

I go for the immediate, unconditional and total abolition of Freemasonry.   William Lloyd Garrison, 7 September 1832[1]

How came I to marry that negro sir: Why sir, my sister has done infinitely worse than that. . . . Why sir, *she married an antimason.*
Masonic Mirror, 8 April 1833

The Antimasonic Persuasion outlived the demise of the third party. Before 1826, attacks on American Freemasonry as a branch of French Jacobinism and Illuminism—infidelity unleashed—failed to touch a popular chord in the United States. By the late 1820s popular suspicion that Masons had indeed kidnapped and murdered William Morgan and then covered up the crime with assistance from members of the brotherhood in high places, ignited the country. Experiencing the most profound changes in their history—the birth of industrial society—many Americans found the Antimasonic Persuasion a powerful guide for comprehending puzzling, complex, and new experiences. A modern, market-designed class structure and a pluralistic popular culture, shaped by intense competition among Protestant denominations and spreading secularism, seemed to subvert the Revolutionary heritage. Antimasons saw Freemasonry as undermining a social order which they understood to rest on a synthesis of Christian and republican principles. They perceived themselves as Guardians of the American Revolution, sentinels who alerted a slumbering, half-corrupted nation to dangers most failed to comprehend. Tens of thousands responded enthusiastically to the Antimasonic Persuasion with an outpouring of activity—educational, agitational, interpersonal, and political. Yet because many refused to make Antimasonry the central issue in American politics, they confirmed the militant minority's suspicions that Masonry held the country in its grip.

Though Antimasons fell short of their explicit goals of destroying Freemasonry and failed to alter the currents of change for which Masonry served as the master symbol, they dealt a body-blow against Masonry in hundreds of communities throughout the Northeast. Their success owed much to women who joined male allies to defend republican domesticity against the alleged Masonic threat.

The failure of Antimasonry to penetrate significantly into the southern states, paralleling the failure of other antebellum reform movements, highlights different ways Northerners and Southerners experienced change.[2] In the South the market system failed to penetrate extensive areas. The growth of the plantation economy, utilizing slave labor, did not involve a majority of white families. This left the South less vulnerable to social tensions that elsewhere encouraged varieties of perfectionism. The Southern social order was peculiar, as contemporaries and later observers recognized, half capitalist and half pre-capitalist, an order some thought blissfully, others woefully, at odds with the system of free labor and the culture of Christian Republicanism in the rest of the country. In any event Masonry flourished in the South, unchecked by a powerful Antimasonic movement.

The United States, alone among industrializing nations in the nineteenth century, experienced the Great Transition after it had developed a well-rooted tradition of republican politics and a popular culture deeply shaped by the language, emotions, and institutions of evangelical Protestantism. Everywhere the advent of industrial society met with resistance and inspired widespread ambivalence. In the United States the reactions took distinctive forms which reflected the country's pre-industrial experience. Antimasonry emerged as a powerful social movement because thousands experiencing the unsettling process of modernization found that it offered a chance to voice their anxieties and a tangible adversary to attack.

The view of Freemasonry as a serpent which had invaded America's republican garden reflected a perception that a new pattern of social relations was emerging in the United States. While systems of stratification exist in all societies, in early nineteenth-century America, as in other early industrial capitalist societies, class became "an immediate and in some sense a directly experienced historical reality. . . ." In previous periods when most people sustained only weak connections with the marketplace, the links "between what people actually experience as economy, polity, or society, and what actually constitutes the wider economic, political, etc., framework within which they operate" were not so clear.[3] In industrial society, however, wage earners and employers, buyers and sellers, producers and consumers, debtors and creditors, the upwardly and downwardly mobile, the domestic and the extra-domestic arenas of family life, transformed social relations. The new patterns were not unfamiliar, but not until the early nineteenth century did they penetrate sufficiently to become dominant. The closed, corporate communities found in Puritan New England had long become unravelled, yet communitarian notions of social order retained remarkable life, surviving well into the mid-nineteenth century in parts of the country touched only marginally by the market.[4]

In the early nineteenth century many Americans believed that Freemasonry carried into the United States the European seeds of aristocratic social relations, commercialized values, and secularized faith. Masonry was dangerous because no manifestly anti-republican or infidel movement had any chance of making headway. For that reason secrecy and stealth, obscurantism and mumbo-jumbo were necessary tools of Masonic conspiracy. Masonry hid its real purposes, critics argued, behind a façade of respectability which offered the ambitious, the upwardly mobile, and the cunning invaluable advantages that furthered and legitimized ambition, selfishness, and worldliness. It also served the psychic needs of an emerging bourgeoisie seeking association and fellowship to offset the strains of competitive individualism and chronic geographic mobility.

Evangelical Christianity was another fount of the Antimasonic Persuasion. The break-up of once culturally homogeneous communities, the declining authority of churches and pastors, and the transformation of congregations into social clubs—class-certifying agencies—deeply troubled people who looked back to corporate Christian community. The Second Great Awakening did not "cause" the spread of Antimasonry, for the movement pre-dated the great religious revival of 1830–32. Moreover, leading religious Antimasons, such as the Hopkinsians, were ambivalent or opposed to Charles G. Finney and other advocates of the New Measures as well as to the Arminian-tending theology central to the revival's success. Moreover, Antimasonry deeply divided evangelical churches, just as abolitionism split them later. Finney himself recognized the dangers to continued growth and prosperity of the revival churches if converted sinners thought personal salvation required radical social reform. He pulled back from abolitionism and other controversial reform movements. Antimasons regarded the churches as complicit in the spread of Masonry because they tolerated membership in the Order, an order which, like other sins, was incompatible with Christian order. As a competing voluntary association, emblematic of the new class structure, Masonry made people conscious of class differences in the churches. Finally, latitudinarian, ecumenical Masonry open only to males was linked to gender conflict between pious women and worldly men. Churches concerned about earthly fortune, afraid to antagonize wealthy and prominent Masons—all men—were the only ones to remain silent. Neutrality permitted Freemasonry to survive and even to flourish, before 1826.

Masonry's alleged aristocratic and infidel character made it the chief enemy of Christian Republicanism in the United States. There was simply no place in a Republic founded on equal rights for a Masonic elite, serving personal ends, unsanctioned by the community, unlegitimized by virtue and piety. Nor could Christian Republicans allow a non-sectarian, warmed-over version of natural religion clandestinely to subvert faith and undermine civic virtue, the twin foundations of a Christian Republic.

The Antimasonic perspective alerted Americans to the dangers of all secret associations, not just Masonry. In 1829 Rev. Peter Sanborn, an Antimasonic Congregationalist in Reading, Massachusetts, warned of a connection between the Order and Phi Beta Kappa. Like Masonry, the scholarly society gathered an elite behind curtains of secrecy. Masonic lecturer Samuel Knapp lavishly praised Phi Beta Kappa, recognizing a kindred spirit. Sanborn noted that the group clandestinely inducted each year "a third of college youth," young men "of the first order, for talent, industry, enterprise, and literary acquisition." Within half a century they would become "a mighty Host," and because most also joined Masonry, Sanborn warned, they would "form a *powerful* auxiliary to that *secret* corps," that required the closest scrutiny lest, at some "unhappy moment," Phi Beta Kappa and Freemasonry combined to blow "up all our civil and religious *rights*" and bury "in promiscuous ruin, the fair temple of American freedom, and the *last hope* of man."[5]

In 1831 Edward Everett, John Quincy Adams, and Supreme Court Justice Joseph Story took the lead to purge Phi Beta Kappa of its secret features. Adams and Everett, both sympathetic to Antimasonry, hoped to clear the society from further suspicion and bring it into conformity with republican norms.[6]

The implications of Antimasonry for Phi Beta Kappa highlight a central dilemma facing Americans in the early nineteenth century. As the older bonds of community weakened and those of a much more complex industrial society replaced them, numerous voluntary associations sprang forth. Masonry was just one among many. Antimasons, troubled by the spread of voluntary associations, wondered why the country needed organization to impose temperance, guard the Sabbath, and convert sinners to Christianity. Reliance on association suggested that communities, churches, and families had failed to enforce moral standards and promote civic virtue. Antimasons did not repudiate the principle of association; they relied on it to purify the country. But they insisted on judging the legitimacy of any association by the standards of Christian Republicanism, a test so vague yet so all-encompassing as to make its application certain to engender conflict.

The intense resistance to Antimasonry, combined with the power and prestige of its opponents, gave Antimasons a sense of being an embattled minority, courageously brooking bitter controversy to spread the truth. Antimasons formed a subculture of citizens who stuck loyally by the cause, subscribed to Antimasonic newspapers, attended Antimasonic meetings and lectures, took advantage of Antimasonic reading rooms, fraternized especially with those of like mind, and voted the third-party ticket. Like supporters of the temperance and abolitionist movements, Antimasons annually purchased almanacs which mixed practical meteorological, agricultural, and cooking information with propaganda. The possession of an Antimasonic almanac affirmed one's affinity for the "blessed spirit," membership among "the inflexible minority" who battled for Christian Republicanism. Each time one consulted an almanac, it reminded people of the great cause. From these almanacs Antimasons learned, too, the songs of their faith:

Freemen, boldly take your stand;
Spread the truth throughout the land;
Wield the pen with willing hand:
Down with Masonry!

By the blood of Morgan slain,
Victims shall not bleed in vain;
Masonry no more shall reign;
Freemen shall be free![7]

Antimasonry thus gave birth to a political party with roots in a wider social movement—a source of strength but also of weakness. Because many believed one could advance Antimasonic objectives without entering the political arena, the party never attracted a full measure of Antimasonic sentiment. The decline of Masonry, in response to hostile opinion and social pressure, especially women's, rather than political proscription, deprived the single-issue party of a suitable target. Antimasonry was a victim of its own success. By the mid-1830s Antimasonic politics had reached its limits. The decline of Masonry, paralleling the maturation of the Whig and Democratic parties and the crystallization of the economic development issues, also left Antimasonry increasingly isolated and irrelevant. Yet the underlying forces that had brought the movement into being did not disappear; the demise of Masonry revealed that other, more pressing enemies of Christian Republicanism remained on the loose.

In its heyday, a quarter of New England's voters opted for the Antimasonic choice in 1832. The strength of the third party varied among the six New England states. In Vermont it polled a plurality; in Rhode Island it won the balance of power; in Massachusetts William Wirt's vote came close to equaling the difference between the Whigs and the Democrats; while in Connecticut and Maine, Antimasonry was a marginal force, and not even that in New Hampshire.

The demise of the Antimasonic party left some people adrift. In Connecticut an estimated 60 percent gravitated to the Whigs; in Maine half, in Vermont more than 40 percent. Only in Massachusetts did Whigs and Democrats garner an equal share, but in several states many preferred not to vote for either party in 1836: better than two-thirds in Massachusetts, almost half in Vermont and Maine and 20 percent in Connecticut. The high incidence of non-voting suggests that demanding moral standards and persisting antipartisan sentiments repelled many Christian Republicans from the Democratic and Whig ranks. (Table 13.1.[8])

Antimasonic leaders such as Vermont's William Slade, who became a Whig, and Massachusetts's Benjamin Hallett, a Democrat, fought hard to carry Antimasons into their respective parties. Both agreed that Antimasonic principles had largely triumphed, but they could not agree on the proper course for the future. Slade argued that on all issues except Masonry, Antimasons and Whigs shared common ground, and that Whig Masons formed but a small fraction of that party. Hallett insisted that Whig duplicity had forfeited support for that party. Moreover, the most critical issue facing the Republic had shifted from Masonry to slavery, and on that score Massachusetts Whig leaders such as Governor Everett had become allies of the slave power. All Northern voters must rally to Martin Van Buren, he urged, "as the only alternative to saving the country from the dominion of slaveholding nullification." In making an antislavery appeal on behalf of Van Buren, Hallett recognized that many Antimasons agreed that slavery had replaced Masonry as the most pressing national problem.[9]

The links between Antimasonry and abolitionism rested on affinities of ideology, organization, and leadership. "For two evils, great curses are hanging over our country, slavery and murder," Aaron Leland told the Vermont Antimasonic state convention in 1830.[10] As the danger of Freemasonry receded, many transferred their energies to the cause of human freedom. Antimasonry had prepared them for a new, even more demanding crusade.

Abolitionists, like Antimasons, were an identifiable social type. Looking back on the early nineteenth century, the historian of Canaan, New Hampshire, recalled that at the time there was a group of men "whose minds were constantly seizing upon new and unheard of horrors. . . ."[11] Antimasons recognized the affinity too. After noting the achievements of Antimasonry, Samuel D. Greene accounted for Masonry's revival as a result of the antislavery agitation which diverted Antimasons from their original cause.[12]

The two movements overlapped chronologically. Once Antimasonry passed its peak in the early 1830s, abolitionism picked up momentum. Both drew heavily on men and women active in each, such as Myron Holley in Connecticut and western New York, Ray Potter and Henry Tatem in Rhode Island, Edward D. Barber and William Slade in Vermont, Rev. Moses Thacher and William Lloyd Garrison in Massachusetts, David Thurston in Maine, and George Kimball and Nathaniel P. Rogers in New Hampshire. Outside New England, antislavery prominents such as Gerrit Smith and Lewis Tappan also shared Antimasonic sentiments. In Lynn, Massachusetts, a third of the identifiable Antimasonic leaders joined the town's abolitionist society.[13] Similarly, Antimasonic newspapers attacked colonization and displayed sympathy for the abolitionist movement at a time when most papers were hostile.[14]

The nation's foremost abolitionist, William Lloyd Garrison, recognized the Antimasonic affinity for antislavery. Garrison's newspaper, *The Liberator*, defended Antimasons, praised those who petitioned the Massachusetts legislature to investigate the Order, and attacked the *Masonic Mirror* for printing the names of Antimasonic petitioners in order to intimidate them. In 1834 Garrison called on abolitionists to support for Congress Antimasonic candidates such as William Jackson, who was locked in a hard-fought battle against Henry Dearborn, a favorite of Boston aristocracy. At a Jackson meeting, *The Liberator* reported, an orator predicted that once Antimasons such as Heman Lincoln, Nathaniel Borden, and Jackson entered Congress, "We will then see whether the slavery of white people called freemasons, as well as the slavery of colored people, called negroes, cannot both be done away with in the District of Columbia." *The Liberator* also endorsed Amasa Walker, who ran for the Boston congressional seat against the powerful capitalist Abbot Lawrence, whose equivocal views on slavery marked him as unreliable. A vote for Antimasons was a vote against slavery.[15]

Garrison himself had been slow to embrace Antimasonry. In 1829, then editor of a newspaper in Burlington, Vermont, he wondered why people made so much fuss about the murder of William Morgan when two million slaves were subject to murder and kidnapping.[16] By the time Garrison had moved to Boston his views had shifted. In 1832 and 1834 he attended the Massachusetts Antimasonic state conventions as a member of the large Boston delegation. From the Worcester convention in 1832 he sent back enthusiastic reports to *The Liberator*. Hundreds of people descended on the city and "every hotel is literally jammed with strangers," he wrote. Garrison felt at home: "A more substantial, sober, or intelligent body cannot easily be mustered in any Commonwealth," he claimed. Here were men unlike faithless politicians in the major parties who merely mouthed republican pieties and unlike hypocritical Christians shamelessly indifferent to the suffering bondsmen. By contrast, Antimasons were "the last to be suspected of sinister motives, or of seeking popular preferment—the last to abandon the ground of principle and equality." Garrison was "proud in being admitted to a seat" with such citizens.[17]

The links between Antimasonry and antislavery extended into the 1840s when the Liberty and Free Soil parties pushed the slavery question into the electoral arena. The Antimasonic vote of the early 1830s did not correlate strongly with any of the subsequent parties, but there is generally a stronger, positive relationship in the New England states with the antislavery parties than with the Whigs or Democrats. (Table 13.2.[18]) Because of high rates of population mobility and rapid changes in the economic and social structures of New England towns in the 1830s and 1840s, the correlations understate the probable electoral continuities.

Ideology formed another link between Antimasonry and antislavery. Both drew inspiration from uncompromising notions of American republicanism, judged Masonry and slavery, respectively, in conflict with republican norms, and demanded immediate destruction of an institution perceived as immoral. Some Antimasons even charged that Freemasons were behind the Nullification movement in South Carolina in the early 1830s.

Antimasonic pietists shared a strong affinity with the antislavery pietists. Both attacked hypocrisy in churches that refused to purge Masons and slaveowners, and both discovered a similar insincerity. Abolitionists also threatened to split congregations and antagonized powerful community leaders, pillars of the churches. Leading churchmen such as Lyman Beecher and Charles G. Finney were apprehensive of antislavery immediatism, whereas Hopkinsians were among the strongest clerical supporters of the Garrisonian cause. The Mendon Association in southeastern Massachusetts, for example, was a center of abolitionist sentiment. Reverends Moses Thacher, Charles Warren of Attleborough, David Brigham of East Randolph, Thomas Thatcher of Boston, Otis Thompson of Rehoboth, David Sandford of Dorchester, Jacob Ide of Medway, and Thomas Williams of Providence all endorsed immediatism, as did conservative Calvinist Antimasonic stalwarts such as James Milligan of Rye, Chester Wright of Montpelier, Vermont, and Rev. David Thurston of Winthrop, Maine. Moses Thacher's journal the *New England Telegraph,* devoted to upholding Hopkinsian Calvinism, also strongly backed the abolitionist cause. In Cincinnati, Rev. Dyer Burgess, editor of *Infidelity Unmasked* (1831–32), combined Antimasonry with abolitionism.[19] Burgess argued that Antimasonry failed to penetrate the South because those who held men and women in bondage were certain to be hostile to Christian Republicanism. "The mystery of professing religion and holding slaves almost equals the sublime mystery of Freemasonry," asserted a writer in *Infidelity Unmasked*. An "Aged Minister" in the Danville, Vermont, *North Star* defended Antimasonic support for abolitionism because both warred against anti-republican, anti-Christian institutions. The Masons had slain thousands, he argued, but the slaveholders had slain tens of thousands. Masonry and slavery each elevated a few who subverted republican equality, corrupted morals, and betrayed Christianity.[20] Myron Holley spoke for both movements when he argued in the *Free Elector* that "the two greatest evils, which afflict us, are Freemasonry and domestic slavery." And just as moral Antimasonry had failed to uproot Masonry, so, too, vague antislavery sentiments had failed to arrest the peculiar institution. In each case it would take a popular, mass movement to purge the country of sin, for slavery, like Freemasonry, had sunk deep roots, protected by powerful elites and both major political parties. "It has been *the interest* of men, numerous, wealthy, and widely scattered, in the union, to support it," Antimasons explained.[21]

Abolitionists, furthermore, linked the colonization movement, the main alternative to abolitionism, to Masonry. Both attracted businessmen and politicians who sacrificed civic virtue and Christian holiness for worldly interest. The New York *Emancipator* pointed to the *Masonic Mirror and Colonization Advocate* as a sample of "the singular proportion of colonization agents and leading advocates who were members of the Masonic fraternity." There were other links. In 1827 the American Colonization Society praised Freemasons for their support. A Kentucky subscriber to the *Masonic Mirror* insisted that colonization and Masonry should march "hand in hand." Antislavery immediatists claimed that colonizationists were hypocrites who did not favor ending bondage, nor believe in racial brotherhood, but designed a strategy to leave slavery untouched while diverting antislavery sentiment into harmless channels.[22]

The main barrier to immediate abolition was the unbridled self-interest of Americans, sanctified by hypocritical churches which refused to subordinate worldly interest to Christian Republicanism. Yet professed Christians accommodated both institutions because self-interest took precedence over moral and civic duty. The social sources of abolitionism are complex and require fresh empirical study, but historians who locate them in the northern evangelical churches must explain why a majority of evangelicals rejected immediatism.[23]

An uncompromising social perfectionism, moral absolutism, and ambivalence towards modernization united Antimasons and abolitionists and distinguished them from other pietists. "We are thoroughly convinced that the race to which we belong, can never be improved by inequality of conventional privileges, or ranks, by hereditary transmissions of authority, or by a factitious and lasting separation from the common lot," proclaimed Myron Holley in the *Hartford Intelligencer*. In explaining why Lynn, Massachusetts, a hotbed of Antimasonry, became a hotbed of abolitionism, William Lloyd Garrison argued that Lynn's citizens "are not the men to be sneered at by a purse-proud aristocracy," who turned loose a mob in Boston against abolitionists. For such folk, Antimasonry and abolition were equally compelling causes.[24]

The mobs who attacked the abolitionists, Antimasons argued, represented the same forces that had earlier tried to suppress Antimasonry. Once again gentlemen of property and standing employed violence to block freedom of speech and assembly. "Freemasonry has done more than all other causes combined to bring upon the country the state of anarchy which is showing itself in the various quarters of the union," asserted the Danville *North Star,* explaining the wave of anti-abolitionist rioting. These mobs, agreed the *Lynn Record,* were "a masonic concern, composed of freemasons and their humble devotees who would undoubtedly stop free debate . . . here, as well as in New York and elsewhere, had they but the requisite strength."[25]

In all these ways, through continuities in leadership and voting, ideological affinity for Christian Republicanism, and violent resistance from powerful forces, the Antimasonic and abolition movements shared common ground. It was no surprise that the Antimasonic members in the United States Congress, claimed the *Boston Advocate,* were "the only public men who have any true moral courage" whereas others were afraid to "say a word against abolishing slavery." The Antimasons "have made the only appeals . . . against the slave trade. . . ."[26]

No one better typified the linkages than North Wrentham's veteran Antimason, Rev. Moses Thacher, founder and officer of the Massachusetts Antislavery Society. Garrison described his comrade as "a gentleman of great modesty and worth—great moral courage in every good cause—great perseverance, industry, and talent." Thacher's Hopkinsian theology, his penchant for crossing swords with the powerful, and his tribulations as an Antimason, prepared him for leadership in the antislavery movement. His *New England Telegraph* (1835–36) espoused both causes. Racial prejudice was the driving force behind African colonization, Thacher's journal argued. "Unless we are willing to place our colored brethren upon a par with ourselves, admit them into our families, to our tables, into our schools, academies and colleges, and to all the rights and immunities of free citizens, we are but the abettors of slavery and all our professions of philanthropy are vain and hollow-hearted."[27]

Thacher's adoption of abolitionism could only have added to his troubles. His leadership of the Antimasonry movement split his church and later cost him his pulpit. Suffering repeated attacks on his character, Thacher left Wrentham in 1838 after fifteen years. He wandered across New York and Pennsylvania, stopping at nine different churches, averaging three to four years at each. Insecure, short tenures were the common lot of early nineteenth-century clergymen; Thacher's Hopkinsianism, Antimasonry, and abolitionism made the odds even worse. In 1864 he was in Peru, New York, preaching on his favorite theme which had earlier brought him triumph and disaster: "Christianity and Freemasonry Antagonistic." Some "dear brethren and sisters have thought and said, that the subject [of Masonry] ought to be passed over in silence," he told his congregation, because "discussion would stir ill feelings and strife . . . and be injurious, if not disastrous, to our feeble congregation." Thacher refused to keep still even at risk of "violence . . . inflicted upon my own person. . . ." For months, he explained, "I have been assailed in private circles, and in the most public and frequented places of resort in this community." As a citizen and Christian *"imperative duty* impels me to speak. . . ." Thacher marshaled once more the familiar arguments against Masonry: it promoted infidelity, committed blasphemy, practiced indecency, held women in contempt, endangered the morals of youth, and its "barbarous and bloody oaths" placed men under the most "horrible slavery . . ." Turning to the young men in the church, Thacher concluded, "you will remember that an old clergyman gave you the timely admonition." Within two years Thacher left Peru for his last pulpit.[28]

During his active years in the Antimasonic movement Thacher must have encountered Henry Dana Ward. Both attended Antimasonic conventions in Massachusetts and Rhode Island in 1830, and each published important Antimasonic journals. Ward's career differed. Whereas Thacher entered the ministry as a Hopkinsian and remained one, Ward's development was more troubled. The son of Thomas W. Ward, sheriff of Worcester County from 1805–24, he came from a prominent county family. His father's brother was General Artemas Ward, of revolutionary war fame. Henry Dana graduated from Harvard in 1816, received a Master's degree and entered the ministry. His sympathies appear to have been liberal. He settled at an Ohio university as a professor of history and philosophy and joined the Masons, hoping they would provide financial assistance for the school as they had for Allegheny College at Meadville. In 1827, back in Massachusetts, responding to the Morgan case, Ward attacked Masonry in the Boston Unitarian organ, the *Christian Register*. He renounced the Order and moved to New York City, where he edited the *Antimasonic Review and Magazine* which emerged as the most important compendium of Antimasonic propaganda, a clearing-house that diffused material from all over the country. Ward became the movement's most famous "missionary." He traveled extensively and encouraged Antimasons to enter politics, offering personal, informal coordination for a movement that had spread spontaneously. In 1830 he went to Boston to deliver an Antimasonic speech in Faneuil Hall, but the Masons shouted him down. That only made Antimasons more determined. As a member of the third party's national committee in 1836, he hoped to stave off the party's demise by nominating a candidate in the forthcoming presidential election. Thereafter the trail becomes obscure until Ward surfaced as a leader of the Millerites, followers of William Miller, who believed that the millennium was set to unfold in 1843 or 1844. In 1840 Ward chaired the Millerites' General Conference in Boston, which prepared for the great day. After the millennium failed to arrive on time, Ward retained adventist convictions while serving as a minister in the Protestant Episcopal church. Teaching and writing religious books occupied the remainder of his life. Ward's drift from liberal Congregationalism to Antimasonry, from Millerism to Episcopalianism suggest a man cut adrift, deeply troubled by the moral and material directions of his age. His sons adapted to the new order with greater success. One became a federal judge and another an advertising man, publisher of *The Grocer's Encyclopedia* (1911).

Like others during the Great Transition, Thacher and Ward found in Antimasonry a vision for restoring moral discipline and communal harmony that a post-Revolutionary generation was in danger of forsaking. Ward's transition from Antimasonry to Millerism suggests a pessimistic conclusion: there was simply no hope of national salvation short of Judgment Day.[29]

Thacher's relentless Antimasonry and Ward's pessimism had ample grounds. By the 1840s Freemasonry began to revive throughout the northeastern United States where it had only recently suffered its deepest wounds. Despite its short-term success, Antimasonry's long-run failure was unavoidable. The permanent suppression of Masonry seemed impossible, for Freemasonry embodied powerful currents modernizing the United States. For a moment, Masonry succumbed to assault in many parts of the country, but even short-run success gave Christian Republicans no peace. The sin of human slavery reminded them that the underlying spirit of Masonry remained alive even as the institution went underground.

By the eve of the Civil War, Freemasons had regained confidence and experienced renewed growth. In 1857, on the hundredth anniversary of the founding of St. John's Lodge in Providence, Rhode Island, 1500 Masons, including brothers from as far away as Kentucky, marched in colorful attire past buildings draped in bunting and streets decorated with flags. At 1 p.m. the procession entered the Baptist church. From the gallery, packed with women, one could observe an impressive spectacle of Knights Templars, Royal Arch Masons, and members of the Encampment of the Holy Sepulchre filling the seats below. Episcopal Bishop George M. Randall gave a stirring address, which dwelled on the excitement a quarter-century earlier. "Masonry came out of the conflict in triumph," the reporter summarized, "because it is founded in the holiest principles . . . the Golden Rule." After the services, thirteen hundred sat down to dinner at Railroad Hall, where Gov. William Hoppin, not a Mason, praised the Order, followed by Mayor William M. Rodman who gave a toast: "To the Masonic Order. Like the evening dew, secret in its operation, benevolent and beautifying in its revelations of love." In 1859, Providence Masons built a new hall, another sign of renewed prosperity, signaled some years earlier by the formation of What Cheer Lodge. Every June the brothers of What Cheer assembled as though they were part of a large New England family listening to letters from absent members and encouraging brothers to express, through charity and love, devotion to Masonry.[30] A few old enough to remember the Masonic Feast Day more than twenty years earlier when the Antimasons engaged two Afro-Americans to dress up outlandishly as Knights Templars to mock a Masonic procession, could only wonder, as many have since, why so many Americans had once succumbed to paranoid delusions now better forgotten.

Note on Statistical Sources

Election data are town-level and come from the New England state archives supplemented by newspaper returns. Demographic data come from a variety of sources. Population and occupational data are from the United States Census, 1820–40, and for Massachusetts from the manufacturing census of 1837. Town valuation data will be found in state registers and church membership in annual reports published by the major denominations. The church data are problematic because the figures are probably inflated, including persons kept on the rolls after they departed. Since this flaw probably afflicts every denominations' data, and their relative strength is the vital information, the data seemed worth using. Yet there is still a further problem: church members reported in one town may reside and vote in another nearby community. At best the religious data give a rough approximation of denominational impact on voting. Multiple regression statistics were generated by the step-wise procedure in SPSS. Data were put in percentage and per capita forms to standardize for differences in town size. Tests for non-linearity were run selectively. Because the multiple regression statistics were produced from a data set designed to explore the demographic characteristics of voting in the period 1830–60, one could look at long-term patterns. These reveal a good deal of volatility in the relationship between party preference and explanatory variables, such as religion and occupation. This suggests the risks of inferring electoral behavioral patterns from single elections. Data for the collective biographies of Masons and Antimasons came primarily from town and county histories, city directories, biographical compendia, and genealogies.

Notes

Preface

1. Lee Benson, *The Concept of Jacksonian Democracy, New York as a Test Case* (Princeton, 1961), 15.
2. *Ibid.*, 24ff., 193ff.
3. Whitney R. Cross, *The Burned-Over District* (Ithaca, 1950), 117, 121–122.
4. Ronald P. Formisano, *The Birth of Mass Political Parties, Michigan, 1827–1861* (Princeton, 1971), 46, 62.
5. Ronald P. Formisano, *The Transformation of Political Culture, Massachusetts Parties, 1790s–1840s* (New York, 1983), 197, 198, 217, 218ff.
6. Kathleen Smith Kutulowski, "Antimasonry Reexamined: Social Bases of the Grass-Roots Party," *Journal of American History* 71 (Sep. 1984), 289, 290.
7. John L. Brooke, "The Bone and Muscle of the Nation: Society and Antimasonry in Central Massachusetts, 1825–1835," 48–49, paper given at the Organization of American History Meetings, April 1985.

Chapter 1. The Emergence of Antimasonry

1. The best study of the genesis of Antimasonry is a masterful article by Ronald P. Formisano and Kathleen S. Kutolowski, "Antimasonry and Masonry: The Genesis of Protest, 1826–1827," *American Quarterly* 29 (1977), 139–65. See also William Preston Vaughn, *The Antimasonic Party in the United States, 1826–1843* (Lexington, 1983), 1–20; George Blakeslee, "History of the Antimasonic Party" (Ph.D. Diss., Harvard University, 1903), ch. 1.
2. *Legislative Investigation into Masonry . . . before a Committee of the General Assembly of Rhode Island . . .* (Boston, 1832), 6, hereafter *R.I. Legislative Investigation*.
3. J. M. Roberts, *The Mythology of the Secret Societies* (London, 1972), 8.
4. For studies of the Antimasonic party see Charles P. McCarthy, "The Antimasonic Party: A Study of Political Antimasonry in the United States, 1827–1840," *Annual Report of the American Historical Association*, 2 vols. (Washington, D.C., 1902) I: Leland M. Griffin, "The Antimasonic Persuasion: A Study of Public Address in the American Antimasonic Movement, 1826–1838" (Ph.D. Diss., Cornell University, 1950); Michael F. Holt, "The Antimasonic and Know-Nothing Parties," in Arthur M. Schlesinger, Jr., ed., *History of U.S. Political Parties*, 4 Vols. (New York, 1973), I, 585–620.
5. *Masonic Mirror*, 10 April 1833.
6. *Boston Daily Advocate*, extra, *Addresses of the Antimasonic Republican State Convention to the People of Massachusetts . . . Sept. 5, 6, 1832* (n.d., n.p.).
7. *North Star* (Danville, Vt.) 26 May 1829.
8. Griffin, "Antimasonic Persuasion," 620.

9. *Masonic Mirror*, 20 March 1830.

10. *R. I. Legislative Investigation*, 14.

11. *Maine Free Press*, 18 Jan. 1833.

12. John C. Palmer, *The Morgan Affair and Antimasonry* (Washington, 1924), 85.

13. *Masonic Mirror*, 20 March 1830.

14. *Ibid.*, 9 Aug. 1833.

15. Griffin, "Antimasonic Persuasion," 605.

16. *Masonic Mirror*, 2 April, 29 Oct. 1831; Griffin, "Antimasonic Persuasion," 574.

17. *Lynn Record*, 7 Aug. 1830.

18. *Masonic Mirror*, 7 May 1831. See also Blakeslee, "History of the Antimasonic Party," 101–2, 126; *North Star*, 11 March 1833.

19. Samuel D. Greene, *The Broken Seal; or, Personal Reminiscences of the Morgan Abduction and Murder* (Chicago, 1873), 167ff., 225ff.; *Masonic Mirror*, 29 May 1830. See also *Maine Free Press*, 22 March 1833 for another case of alleged Masonic persecution.

20. Greene, *The Broken Seal*, 160ff.

21. Documentation for this and the following paragraphs will be found in more detailed treatments in later chapters.

22. The pioneering modern scholarly work on American Freemasonry is Dorothy A. Lipson, *Freemasonry in Federalist Connecticut, 1789–1835* (Princeton, 1977); for a later period see Lynn Dumenil, "Brotherhood and Respectability, Freemasonry and American Culture, 1880–1930" (Ph.D. Diss., University of California, Berkeley, 1981); and for useful compendia from a Masonic perspective, see Henry L. Stillson, ed., *History of the Ancient and Honorable Fraternity of Free and Accepted Masons* (Boston and New York, 1892), and Robert F. Gould, *The Concise History of Freemasonry*, rev. ed. (New York, 1924).

23. For Masonic statistics see Stillson, *History of Masons*, 877–92.

24. *Masonic Mirror*, 27 Nov. 1824.

25. *Ibid.*

26. Rev. Cheever T. Felch, *An Address Delivered before Mount Carmel Lodge, at Lynn, June, 1821* . . . (Boston, n.d.), 7.

27. Thomas S. Webb, *The Freemason's Monitor: or Illustrations of Masonry* (Salem, 1821), 14. Other useful antebellum guides to Masonry published for the use of Masons are Jeremy L. Cross, *The Masonic Chart* (New York, 1854); Albert G. Mackey, *The Principles of Masonic Law* (New York, 1859); and *The Ahiman Rezon or Book of the Constitution, Rules and Regulations of the Grand Lodge of Pennsylvania* (Philadelphia, 1857).

28. *Masonic Mirror*, 27 Nov. 1824.

29. Webb, *Freemason's Monitor*, 14.

30. Robert Macoy, *General History, Cyclopedia and Dictionary of Freemasonry* (New York, 1869), 468.

31. Webb, *Freemason's Monitor*, 70.

32. *Ibid.*, 31.

33. *Ibid.*, 32.

34. *Ibid.*, 34.

35. *Ibid.*, 58.

36. *Ibid.*, 57.

37. *Ibid.*, 25n.

38. *Masonic Mirror,* 27 Nov. 1824.

39. See Lipson, *Freemasonry in Connecticut, passim,* and Dumenil, "Brotherhood and Respectability," *passim.*

40. For Jews see Jacob Katz, *Jews and Freemasons in Europe* (Cambridge, Mass., 1970), and for Afro-Americans, William A. Muraskin, *Middle Class Blacks in a White Society, Prince Hall Freemasonry in America* (Berkeley, 1975).

41. Webb, *Freemason's Monitor,* 22.

42. Stillson, *History of Masons,* 734; Lipson, *Freemasonry in Connecticut,* 7ff., 240ff., 36ff.

43. Kurt H. Wolff, ed., *The Sociology of Georg Simmel* (Glencoe, 1950), 361.

44. Lipson, *Freemasonry in Connecticut,* 243.

45. Webb, *Freemason's Monitor,* 17, 42.

46. *Ibid.,* 23.

47. *Ibid.,* 24.

48. Lipson, *Freemasonry in Connecticut,* 43–44, 200–201, 216ff.

49. *Ibid.,* 163–76.

50. *The Ahiman Rezon,* 85.

51. Webb, *Freemason's Monitor,* 52.

52. *North Star,* 28 July 1834.

53. See Lipson, *Freemasonry in Connecticut,* 258–60; and for samples of Masonic song, Luke Eastman, *Masonick Melodies* (Boston, 1818).

54. Lipson, *Freemasonry in Connecticut,* 189ff. See Chapter 4.

55. *Ibid.,* 234ff.

56. See *Records of the Grand Lodge of Free and Accepted Masons of the State of Vermont from 1794 to 1846 Inclusive* (Burlington, 1879), especially the biographies of founding Masons, 3–53.

57. *Ibid.,* 72.

58. *Ibid.,* 126ff.

59. *Ibid.,* 290.

60. *Ibid.,* 125.

61. *Ibid.,* 149.

62. *Ibid.,* 221, 314.

63. *Ibid.,* 231.

64. *Ibid.,* 327–28.

65. *Ibid.,* 376.

66. *Ibid.,* 403.

Chapter 2. *Guardians of the Revolution*

1. Amasa Walker, *An Oration Delivered at Stroughton, Mass., July 5, 1830* (Boston, 1830), 24.

2. *An Abstract of the Proceedings of the Anti-Masonic State Convention of Massachusetts, Held in Faneuil Hall, Boston 1829–30* . . . (Boston, 1831), 9ff., hereafter cited as *Massachusetts Antimasonic Convention, 1829–30; An Abstract of the Proceedings of the Antimasonic State Convention of Massachusetts, Held in Faneuil Hall, Boston* . . . (Boston, 1831), 52.

3. William Slade, *An Oration Pronounced at Bridport, July 4, 1829* (Middlebury, 1829), 3–4.

4. *Brief Report of the Debates in the Anti-Masonic State Convention of* . . . *Mas-*

sachusetts, 1829–30 (Boston, 1830), 16, 28; *Proceedings, The Anti-Masonic State Convention, Holden at Montpelier, June 23, 24 & 25, 1830* (Middlebury, 1830), 17; *Proceedings of the Antimasonic State Convention Holden at Montpelier, Vermont, June 26, 27, 1833* . . . (Montpelier, 1833), 32.

5. Vernon Stauffer, *New England and the Bavarian Illuminati* (New York, 1918).

6. For a brilliant exploration of the intellectual history of conspiratorial thinking see Gordon S. Wood, "Conspiracy and the Paranoid Style: Causality and Deceit in the Eighteenth Century," *William and Mary Quarterly* 39, 3rd ser.; (July 1982), 401–41; David B. Davis, "Some Themes of Countersubversion: An Analysis of Anti-Masonic, Anti-Catholic, and Anti-Mormon Literature," *Mississippi Valley Historical Review* xlvii (Sep. 1960), 205–24; Formisano and Kutolowski, "Antimasonry and Masonry," *passim.*

7. Marvin Meyers, *The Jacksonian Persuasion, Politics & Belief* (New York, 1960), and for the workingmen, Edward Pessen, *Most Uncommon Jacksonians* (Albany, 1967).

8. Gordon S. Wood, *The Creation of the American Republic 1776–1789* (Chapel Hill, 1969); Drew R. McCoy, *The Elusive Republic, Political Economy in Jeffersonian America* (New York, 1980); Lance Banning, *The Jeffersonian Persuasion, Evolution of a Party Ideology* (Ithaca, 1978); J. G. A. Pocock, *The Machiavellian Moment, Florentine Political Thought and the Atlantic Republican Tradition* (Princeton, 1975), 506ff.

9. McCoy, *Elusive Republic;* cf., Joyce Appleby, *Capitalism and the New Social Order, the Republican Vision of the 1790s* (New York, 1984).

10. Stillson, *History of Masons,* for statistics, 877ff. See Part II of this book for analysis of the social sources of Freemasonry in the New England states.

11. Walker, *Oration Delivered at Stoughton,* 4, 22, 28.

12. E. D. Barber, *An Address, Delivered before the Rutland County Antimasonic Convention* . . . *June, 1831* (Castleton, 1831), 8, 14.

13. *Proceedings of the Antimasonic Republican Convention of the State of Maine, Held at Hallowell, July 3rd & 4th, 1834* (Hallowell, 1834), 18, 28.

14. Barber, *Address before Rutland County Antimasonic Convention,* 7.

15. *Ibid.,* 14.

16. *Antimasonic Review,* I, No. 9, p. 287.

17. *Proceedings of the Antimasonic State Convention, Holden at Montpelier, June 15 and 16, 1831* (Montpelier, 1831), p. 11.

18. Walker, *Oration Delivered at Stoughton,* 26.

19. Chauncey Whittlesey, *Gen. Chauncey Whittlesey's Renunciation of Freemasonry and Appeal to the Public* (n.p., 1834), 2; Walker, *Oration Delivered at Stoughton,* 26 and note; *Massachusetts Antimasonic Convention, 1830,* p. 17.

20. *Massachusetts Antimasonic Convention, 1830,* p. 17; *Vermont Antimasonic Convention, 1830,* p. 14; *Maine Antimasonic Republican Convention, 1834,* pp. 14, 21; *Antimasonic Review,* No. 3, pp. 72ff.; *Vermont Antimasonic Convention, 1831,* pp. 12, 20.

21. *Vermont Antimasonic Convention, 1832,* p. 20.

22. *Maine Antimasonic Convention, 1834,* p. 11; *Massachusetts Antimasonic Convention, 1831,* pp. 33, 36ff.

23. *Maine Free Press,* 20 July 1832; *Vermont Antimasonic Convention, 1830,* p. 26.

24. Whittlesey, *Renunciation,* 8.

25. *Vermont Antimasonic Convention, 1830*, pp. 27–28. See also Chapter 5.

26. *Ibid.*, 33; *Maine Free Press*, 31 Aug. 1832; *Vermont Antimasonic Convention, 1833*, pp. 28, 31.

27. *Vermont Antimasonic Convention, 1830*, p. 13.

28. *Ibid.*, 5, 6; *Vermont Antimasonic Convention, 1833*, pp. 6, 23.

29. *Brief Report of the Massachusetts Antimasonic Convention, 1829–30*, p. 8.

30. *Vermont Antimasonic Convention, 1830*, p. 6.

31. *Lynn Record*, 16 July 1834.

32. *Rhode Island Legislative Investigation*, 5.

33. *Massachusetts Antimasonic Convention, 1831*, p. 5.

34. *Ibid.*, 14.

35. *Antimasonic Intelligencer* (Pawtucket), 21 April 1829.

36. *Massachusetts Antimasonic Convention, 1832*, p. 8.

37. *Vermont Antimasonic Convention, 1831*, p. 15.

38. Edward D. Barber, *An Address Delivered before the Rutland County Antimasonic Convention . . . June 1831* (Castleton, 1831), 13; *Vermont Antimasonic Convention, 1830*, p. 17; *Vermont Antimasonic Convention, 1831*, p. 22; *Vermont Gazette*, 2 July 1831.

39. *Massachusetts Antimasonic Convention, 1832*, p. 18.

40. *Maine Antimasonic Convention, 1834*, p. 3.

41. *Masonic Mirror*, 29 Jan. 1830.

42. *Lynn Record*, 29 Sep. 1830.

43. *Antimasonic Republican Convention, of Massachusetts Held at Boston, Sept. 11, 12 & 13* (Boston, 1833), 3; *North Star*, 8 July 1833.

44. *New England Telegraph* (1835–36), 362; for other examples of Antimasonic anxiety over the younger generation's attraction to Freemasonry see *Antimasonic Review*, I, No. 7, p. 229; *Lynn Record*, 27 Feb. 1830; *Vermont Antimasonic Convention, 1831*, pp. 16, 18, 22.

45. Timothy Fuller, *An Oration Delivered at Faneuil Hall, Boston, July 11, 1830* (Boston, 1831), 6, 4, 10; Charles Capper, "Margaret Fuller, The New England Years" (Ph.D. Diss., University of California, Berkeley, 1984), 49 and Ch. I *passim*.

46. Samuel F. Bemis, *John Quincy Adams and the Union* (New York, 1956), 273; John Quincy Adams, *Letters on the Entered Apprentice's Oath . . .* (Boston, 1833), 19.

47. Richard Rush, *A Letter on Freemasonry, by the Hon. Richard Rush to the Committee of the Citizens of York County, Pennsylvania* (Boston, 1831).

48. John P. Kennedy, *Memoirs of the Life of William Wirt*, 2 Vols. (Philadelphia, 1854); *Boston Advocate*, 27 Dec. 1831. See also the biography in William Wirt, *The Letters of the British Spy*, 10th edition (New York, 1832), 9–91.

49. Kennedy, *Wirt*, I, 102, II, 314–15, 387–88.

50. William Wirt, *The Old Bachelor* (Richmond, 1814), 32 and see below, Chapter 5.

51. Kennedy, *Wirt*, II, 323–4.

52. Wirt, *Letters of the British Spy*, 101–2.

53. *Ibid.*, 144–45; Kennedy, *Wirt*, I, 251. Wirt explained to Jefferson why he proposed to write a life of Henry in 1811: "Mr. Henry seems to me a good text for a discourse on rhetoric, patriotism, and morals. The work might be made useful to young men who are just coming forward into life."

54. Wirt, *Letters of the British Spy*, 192–94; see Rhys Isaac, *The Transformation*

of Virginia, 1740–1790 (Chapel Hill, 1982), chs. 6–8, 11, 13, for an evangelical critique of gentry leadership.

55. William Wirt, *A Discourse on the Lives and Characters of Thomas Jefferson and John Adams who both died on the Fourth of July 1826 . . .* (Washington, 1826), 6.

56. William Wirt, *An Address Delivered July 20, 1830, before the Peithessophian and Philoclean Societies of Rutgers College,* 5th ed. (New Brunswick, 1852), 25, 46.

57. Kennedy, *Wirt,* II, 240ff., 259–63.

58. *Boston Advocate,* 20 Sep. 1836.

59. *Boston Advocate,* 11 Aug. 1832; *Taunton Gazette,* 10 March 1837; and for other appraisals of Wirt, see *Lynn Record,* 3 Oct. 1832, and *Antimasonic Republican Convention for Massachusetts, Held at Boston, Sept. 10 and 11, 1834* (Boston, 1834), 17–18.

Chapter 3. Antimasonry and the Great Transition

1. Quoted in Randolph A. Roth, "Whence This Strange Fire? Religious and Reform Movements in the Connecticut River Valley of Vermont, 1791–1843" (Ph.D. Diss., Yale University, 1981), 253.

2. *Masonic Mirror,* 12, 19 March 1831.

3. *A Serious Call or Masonry Revealed . . .* (Boston, 1829), 34–35; *Pawtucket Chronicle,* 20 March 1830; *Masonic Mirror,* 3 Aug. 1833.

4. *Report of the President, Vice Presidents, and Several Directors of the Bunker Hill Monument, from June 1831 to June 1832* (Boston, 1832); *Boston Advocate,* 16 June 1832, 27 March 1832.

5. *Boston Advocate,* 11 May 1833, 13 Dec. 1833, 19, 25 Feb. 1834. And see the *Boston Advocate,* 26 Sep. 1834, for another contest in Middlesex County in 1834 between Heman Lincoln, the Antimason, and Samuel Hoar, the National Republican. Lincoln was a prominent Baptist layman who had never held office; Hoar was a Unitarian lawyer from Concord close to the National Republican clique in the metropolis. Contrasting Lincoln with Hoar, Antimasons argued: "No pernicious social influence has drawn him away from the people." See also the *Boston Advocate,* 6 June 1833, for an Antimasonic attack on a National Republican candidate for Congress alleged to be "always . . . repulsive and distant," approachable only "by those who pride themselves by ranking with the better class of society."

6. The *Boston Advocate* gave good coverage to the Workingmen's party. See *Boston Advocate,* 18, 23, 24 Oct. 1833, 25 Jan. 1834. For the *Boston Advocate's* views on unions see 28 April, 23 June 1834.

7. The concept of "industrial society" used throughout this work refers to the increasing importance of production for markets, competition in labor and commodity markets, and the growth of manufacturing and commercial sectors, with concentrations of population not just in large cities but also in small factory villages and market towns. Advances in technology and in the scale of enterprise, notably the large textile factories such as those at Lowell, Massachusetts, were not the essential characteristics of industrial society though were often identified with it. As industrial society matured, they became more important. For an excellent discussion of the concept of industrial society in France, where a majority still lived in rural areas in 1850, see William H. Sewell, Jr., *Work and Revolution in France, The Language of Labor from the Old Regime to 1848* (New York, 1980), ch. 7, pp. 143ff.

8. D. Hamilton Hurd, comp., *History of Norfolk County, Massachusetts* (Philadelphia, 1884), 358.

9. Information comes from the occupational data in United States Census for 1820, 1830, and 1840, and *Statistical Tables of Industry in Massachusetts* (Boston, 1838), 127–28.

10. Hurd, *History of Norfolk County*, 365.

11. Dana M. Winsor, *Three Hundred Years of Quincy* (Boston, 1926), 41.

12. Hurd, *History of Norfolk County*, 359.

13. *Ibid.*, 366, 371ff.

14. For the role of Masonry and similar organizations in British society in the eighteenth century, see John Brewer, "Commercialization and Politics," in Neil McKendrick *et al.*, *The Birth of a Consumer Society, The Commercialization of Eighteenth Century England* (Bloomington, 1982), 218ff., 228ff.

15. The history of class formation in the early nineteenth century is in its infancy. The following works are useful: Stuart Blumin, "The Hypothesis of Middle-Class Formation in Nineteenth-Century America: A Critique and Some Proposals," *American Historical Review* 90 (April 1985), 299–338; Fred C. Jaher, *The Urban Establishment* (Urbana, 1982); Peter Dobkin Hall, *The Organization of American Culture, 1700–1900* (New York, 1982); Robert Doherty, *Society and Power, Five New England Towns, 1800–1860* (Amherst, 1977); Ronald Story, *The Forging of an Aristocracy, Harvard and the Boston Upper Class, 1800–1970* (Middletown, 1980); Gary J. Kornblith, "From Artisans to Businessmen: Master Mechanics in New England, 1789–1850" (Ph.D. Diss., Princeton University, 1983); Jonathan Prude, *The Coming of Industrial Order, Town and Factory Life in Rural Massachusetts, 1810–1860* (Cambridge, England, 1983); Thomas Bender, *Community and Social Change in America* (New Brunswick, 1978); Paul E. Johnson, *A Shopkeeper's Millennium Society and Revivals in Rochester, N.Y., 1815–1837* (New York, 1978); Mary P. Ryan, *Cradle of the Middle Class, The Family in Oneida County, New York, 1790–1850* (Cambridge, England, 1981).

16. On the declining status of the elderly see David H. Fischer, *Growing Old in America* (New York, 1977), chs. 1–3, and a critique of Fischer in W. Andrew Achenbaum, *Old Age in the New Land* (Baltimore, 1978), 25.

17. For a subtle and sensitive contrast between colonial America and the early nineteenth century see Prude, *Coming of Industrial Order,* chs. 1–6 *passim.* For colonial New England see among the large body of literature Michael Zuckerman, *Peaceable Kingdoms, New England Towns in the Eighteenth Century* (New York, 1972); Edward J. Cook, Jr., *The Fathers of the Towns, Leadership and Community Structure in Eighteenth Century New England* (Baltimore, 1976); Robert A. Gross, *The Minutemen and Their World* (Boston, 1976); Robert E. Mutch, "Yeoman and Merchant in Pre-industrial America: Eighteenth Century Massachusetts as a Case Study," *Societas* 7 (Autumn 1977), 279–302.

18. Blumin, "The Hypothesis of Middle-Class Formation," 312.

19. For transformations in agriculture see a seminal article which clarifies the pre-capitalist phase: James A. Henretta, "Families and Farms: *Mentalité* in Pre-Industrial America," *William and Mary Quarterly* XXXV (Jan. 1978), 3–32; and for the development of commercial agriculture see Percy W. Bidwell, *Rural Economy in New England at the Beginning of the 19th Century,* Transactions of the Connecticut Academy of Arts and Sciences XX (April 1916); Clarence H. Danhoff, *Change in Agriculture: The Northern United States, 1820–1870* (Cambridge, Mass.,

1969); Christopher Clark, "The Household Economy, 1800–1860," *Journal of Social History* 13 (Winter 1979); Richard L. Bushman, "Family Security in the Transition from Farm to City, 1750–1850," *Journal of Family History* (Fall, 1981), 238–56; Richard Holmes, *Communities in Transition: Bedford and Lincoln, Massachusetts, 1729–1850* (Ann Arbor, 1980).

20. Jonathan Prude, "Town-Factory Conflicts in Antebellum Rural Massachusetts," in Steven Hahn and Jonathan Prude, eds., *The Countryside in the Ages of Capitalist Transformation* (Chapel Hill, 1985), 71–102, provides an excellent account, esp. 76ff.

21. In Bedford 25% of taxpayers were propertyless in 1810 compared to more than half in the 1830s. See Holmes, *Communities in Transition*, 89ff.; Roth, "Whence This Strange Fire?," ch. 3; Doherty, *Society and Power*, 46ff.; Prude, *The Coming of Industrial Order*, 161ff. *Cf.* Alan Dawley, *Class and Community* (Cambridge, Mass., 1976), 60–62.

22. For hat-making, see Thomas Dublin, "Women and Outwork in a Nineteenth Century Town: Fitzwilliam, New Hampshire, 1830–1850," in Hahn and Prude, *Countryside*, 51–70.

23. Webb, *The Freemason's Monitor*, 14; William F. Brainard, *Masonic Lecture Spoken before the Brethren of Union Lodge, New London* 3rd ed. (Boston, 1830), 7.

24. *North Star*, 24 June 1828. On Masonry's social functions see Roth, "Whence This Strange Fire?," 125ff.; Dorothy A. Lipson, *Freemasonry in Federalist Connecticut*, 65ff.

25. *Infidelity Unmasked*, I, 11 Feb. 1832. See Karen Halttunen, *Confidence Men and Painted Women* (New Haven, 1983), for a brilliant exploration of strategies employed by an emerging bourgeoisie to develop standards of dress, deportment, and manners that identified respectability and differentiated the genuine from the bogus middle class.

26. Gross, *Minutemen*, 177; Holmes, *Communities in Transition*, 105ff.; Prude, *Coming of Industrial Order*, 21ff.; Doherty, *Society and Power*, 33ff.

27. Quoted in Lois K. Mathews, *The Expansion of New England* (New York, 1962, reprint ed.), 146; on outmigration from southern Vermont from 1790 to 1812, see Lewis D. Stilwell, *Migration from Vermont, 1776–1860*, Proceedings of the Vermont Historical Society, V (1937), 123–24.

28. Prude, *The Coming of Industrial Order*, 8.

29. Roth, "Whence This Strange Fire?," 107–8, 123–28, 183ff.; Doherty, *Society and Power*, 36ff. For Masonry's role in Britain in facilitating the business of members, see Brewer, "Commercialization & Politics," 203ff.

30. Cheever T. Felch, *An Address Delivered before Mount Carmel Lodge*, 14.

31. Paul Dean, *An Address Delivered before the Fraternity at Fall River Troy, Mass. . . .* (Boston, 1825), 5–7.

32. Bernard Whitman, *An Address Delivered May 30, A.D. 1832, at the Dedication of the Masonic Temple in Boston* (Cambridge, 1832), 12.

33. Kornblith, "From Artisans to Businessmen," *passim.*

34. *Ibid.*, 508ff.; Roth, "Whence This Strange Fire?," 275ff.; Ronald P. Formisano, *The Transformation of Political Culture, Massachusetts*, 222ff.

35. Gross, *Minutemen*, 174–75.

36. James R. Jackson, *History of Littleton, New Hampshire*, 3 Vols. (Cambridge, Mass., 1905), II, 439ff. Biographical information in this book on the leading members of Littleton's two library societies indicates that 10 of 14 for whom religious data

are available were Congregationalists and three were officers in that church; 18 of 29 for whom occupational information is available held public office, 7 were Freemasons, 2 attended college, 10 were farmers, the rest businessmen (5), professionals (3), artisans who may have been masters (3), and farmers who also engaged in business or a craft (2).

37. Story, *The Forging of an Aristocracy*, 13–19, 160–64, 175.

38. Jaher, *The Urban Establishment*, ch. 2; Story, *The Forging of an Aristocracy, passim;* William H. and James H. Pease, "Paternal Dilemmas: Education, Property, and Patrician Persistence in Jacksonian Boston," *The New England Quarterly* LIII (June 1980), 147–67.

39. Story, *Forging of an Aristocracy, passim.*

40. Samuel E. Morison, *Three Centuries of Harvard* (Cambridge, Mass., 1936), 198.

41. Story, *Forging of an Aristocracy*, 131, 128.

42. Although Story's book is valuable, he exaggerates when he writes about the "monopolization of the Harvard student body by the Boston elite. . . ." His own figures show no monopoly. Cf. Morison, *Three Centuries of Harvard*, 199: "The College in the early nineteenth century was largely composed of boys from New England families of middling fortunes and the swells were outnumbered by horny-handed lads from the country districts," but this appears to be an impression, not the result of quantitative study. Morison later noted the calendar change (201), and justified the high tuition as necessary to train "gentlemen." He also reported George Bancroft's savage attack on Harvard in the 1840s for narrow social and religious exclusivity, 258ff., but prefers President Quincy's unconvincing full-page rebuttal. "Brave 'old Quin'," cheers Morison, 259. For the English traveler, see Ronald Story, "Harvard and the Boston Brahmins: A Study in Institutional and Class Development, 1800–1865," *Journal of Social History* 8 (Spring 1975), 108; for Henry Adams, *The Education of Henry Adams* (New York, 1931), 64ff. For an excellent statistical study of the changing social composition of the Harvard student body, see Stephen Thernstrom, "Poor but Hopefull Scholars," *Harvard Magazine* (Sep.-Oct. 1986), 115ff.

43. Story, *Forging of an Aristocracy*, 30.

44. *Ibid.*, 31, 107.

45. Holmes, *Communities in Transition*, 79; Doherty, *Society and Power*, 82ff.

46. Prude, *The Coming of Industrial Order*, 166, see also 29ff.

47. The most suggestive are the essays in Neil McKendrick, *et al., The Birth of a Consumer Society* 11 and *passim.*

48. Arthur W. Calhoun, *A Social History of the American Family*, 3 Vols. (New York, c. 1945), II, 229 and also 203, 234. In *The Domestic Manners of the Americans* (New York, 1949), Frances Trollope observed the American devotion to French fashions, c. 1830, pp. 350–51, 420ff.

49. Thomas Dublin, *Women at Work, The Transformation of Work and Community in Lowell, Massachusetts, 1826–1860* (New York, 1979).

50. Calhoun, *Social History of the American Family*, II, 236–37.

51. Kornblith, "From Artisans to Businessmen," 355. "Why buy a plated soup tureen for forty dollars?" asked the *National Advocate* in 1819, when one of china for five dollars would do as well. Such "eccentricities of fashion are ruining families by the wholesale." See Calhoun, *Social History of the American Family*, II, 234.

52. David Jaffee, "One of the Primitive Sort: Portrait Maker of the Rural North," in Hahn and Prude, *The Countryside,* 108, 113, 131.

53. Story, *The Forging of an Aristocracy,* 9, 16–17, 19, 166–67; Cleveland Amory, *The Proper Bostonians* (New York, 1957), 257; Halttunen, *Confidence Men and Painted Women,* 124ff.

54. *Antimasonic Intelligencer,* 17 Sep. 1833. The social reformer, Walter Channing, brother of the great Unitarian divine, William Ellery Channing, was critical of consumerism: "By our modes of life—our house—our dress—our purpose; in short by what is strictly external to us, men detach themselves from their neighbors—withdraw themselves from the human family . . . in its every recognized relationship of brotherhood." Quoted in David J. Rothman, *The Discovery of the Asylum* (Boston, 1971), 179.

55. Richard D. Brown "The Emergence of Urban Society in Rural Massachusetts, 1760–1820," *Journal of American History* LXI (March 1974), 29–51.

56. *Ibid.,* 40–41. On the significance of associations see Ryan, *Cradle of the Middle Class,* 53.

57. For the defense of Masonic charity see Joseph Jenkins, *An Address Delivered before the Grand Lodge of Massachusetts at the Installation of Officers, Dec. 28, 1829* (Boston, 1830), 11ff.; Bernard Whitman, *Address . . . at the Dedication of the Masonic Temple,* 11; Brainard, *Masonic Lecture,* 7ff.; David Benedict, *An Address Delivered before the Grand Lodge of Rhode Island at the Anniversary of St. John the Baptist, Thursday, June 23, 1830* (Pawtucket, 1830), 14; for criticism, see *The Antimasonic Review and Magazine,* I, No. 2, p. 17; *An Investigation into Freemasonry by a Joint Committee of the Legislature of Massachusetts, House Report, No. 73,* March 1834 (Boston 1834), 64–65; Pliny Merrick, *A Letter on Speculative Freemasonry* (Worcester, 1829), 12.

58. For how the manual labor movement addressed itself to the declining respectability of manual labor see below, Chapter 10.

59. Sean Wilentz, "Artisan Republican Festivals and the Rise of Class Conflict in New York City, 1788–1837," in Michael H. Frisch and Daniel J. Walkowitz, eds., *Working Class America* (Urbana, 1983), 37–77.

60. Kornblith, "From Artisans to Businessmen," 498ff.

61. *Ibid.,* 472.

62. *Ibid.,* 527ff.; Roth, "Whence This Strange Fire?," 355–56.

63. Donald M. Scott, *From Office to Profession, The New England Ministry, 1750–1850* (Philadelphia, 1978), 79; Donald M. Scott, "The Popular Lecture and the Creation of a Public in Mid-Nineteenth Century America," *Journal of American History* 66 (March 1980), 791–809. For the ambitions of young women see Dublin, *Women at Work,* 33ff.: "I can never be happy there among so many mountains," wrote young Sally Rice in 1838, who migrated from Somerset, Vermont, to Lowell. "You may think me unkind but how can you blame me for wanting to stay here. I have but one life to live and I want to enjoy myself as well as I can while I live," 37.

64. David J. Allmendinger, *Paupers and Scholars, The Transformation of Student Life in Nineteenth Century New England* (New York, 1975), *passim.*

65. *Ibid.,* 2.

66. *Ibid.,* 65.

67. *Ibid.,* 81–82, 84–86.

68. Scott, *From Office to Profession, passim.*

Chapter 4. Purging the Republic's Churches

1. For Warren's testimony see *An Investigation into Freemasonry by a Joint Committee of the Legislature of Massachusetts*, appendix, 11–18; for the Royal Arch oath, see *Rhode Island Legislative Investigation*, 41; for Warren's career, see *Congregational Quarterly*, I (1859), 356.

2. For the Mendon association see Rev. Mortimer Blake, *A Centurial History of the Mendon Association of Congregational Ministers . . .* (Boston, 1853), 7–40, 182, and for a case study of Antimasonry in one town within the association see below, Chapter 9.

3. For renunciations, see, for example: *North Star*, 6 May 1833; *Lynn Record*, 12 Oct. 1831; *Masonic Mirror*, 23, 30 Jan. 1830; *Maine Free Press*, 27 Jan., 24 Feb., 18 May, 2 Nov., 1832; *Antimasonic Review* I, No. 3, p. 100; *Vermont Antimasonic Convention, 1830,* 9.

4. Charles G. Finney, *The Character, Claims, and Practical Workings of Freemasonry* (Cincinnati, 1869), vii; *Boston Advocate*, 22 Mar. 1832.

5. Quoted in Marion L. Bell, *Revivalism in Nineteenth Century Philadelphia* (Lewisburg, 1977), 105.

6. Dorothy A. Lipson, *Freemasonry in Federalist Connecticut*, 293–94, 324–25, 312–16; Whitney R. Cross, *The Burned-Over District*, 117, 121, 124, 125, 136, 137.

7. *Massachusetts Antimasonic Convention, 1829–30*, p. 29; Edward Barber, *An Address Delivered before the Antimasonic Convention of the County of Addison . . . March 12, 1829* (Vergennes, Vt., 1829); Moses Thacher, *An Address, Delivered before the Antimasonic Convention of Delegates for Plymouth County . . . , Dec. 1829* (Boston, 1830), 7–8.

8. *Massachusetts Antimasonic Convention, 1829–1830*, p. 15.

9. *Massachusetts Antimasonic Convention, 1832*, p. 18.

10. *North Star*, 22 Dec. 1834; *Maine Free Press*, 13 July 1833; *Rhode Island Legislative Investigation*, 61; *Maine Antimasonic Convention, 1834*, pp. 7, 19; *Vermont Antimasonic Convention, 1830*, p. 31.

11. *Massachusetts Antimasonic Convention, 1831*, p. 24.

12. *Vermont Antimasonic Convention, 1830*, pp. 26–31.

13. *Massachusetts Antimasonic Convention, 1829–30*, p. 14; *Rhode Island Legislative Investigation*, 12, 143, 28–44; *Maine Antimasonic Convention, 1834*, pp. 9, 22.

14. *Rhode Island Legislative Investigation*, 28–44.

15. *Vermont Antimasonic Convention, 1830*, p. 31.

16. *Ibid.*

17. See *Maine Free Press* and Hartford *Intelligencer*.

18. See Chapter 5.

19. *Rhode Island Legislative Investigation*, 19.

20. *Vermont Antimasonic Convention, 1830*, p. 19.

21. *Massachusetts Antimasonic Convention, 1831*, pp. 24, 27; *Massachusetts Antimasonic Convention, 1832*, p. 25.

22. *Massachusetts Antimasonic Convention, 1831*, pp. 26–27; *Maine Free Press*, 19 Aug. 1831; *Lynn Record*, 22 Sep. 1830, 2 March 1831.

23. James Turner, *Without God, Without Creed, The Origins of Unbelief in America* (Baltimore, 1985), 88 and *passim*.

24. *Ibid.,* 114ff.

25. Paul Kleppner, *The Cross of Culture* (New York, 1970); Richard Jensen, *The Winning of the Middle West* (Chicago, 1971); Sam McSeveney, *The Politics of Depression* (New York, 1972). For the most important early effort to develop an ethno-cultural interpretation of American political history for the Jacksonian period, see Lee Benson, *The Concept of Jacksonian Democracy. Cf.* Paul Goodman, "The Social Basis of New England Politics in Jacksonian America," *Journal of the Early Republic* VI (Spring 1986), 31–41.

26. For a more extended treatment of this problem see Goodman, "The Social Basis of Politics," and the references cited there. Among the best overviews of the history of denominationalism are Sidney Ahlstrom, *A Religious History of the American People* (New Haven, 1972); William G. McGloughlin, *New England Dissent, 1630–1833,* 2 Vols. (Cambridge, 1982); Edwin S. Gaustad, *Historical Atlas of Religion in America* (New York, 1962).

27. Robert W. Doherty, *The Hicksite Separation* (New Brunswick, 1967); George Marsden, *The Evangelical Mind and the New School Presbyterian Experience* (New Haven, 1970); Wade C. Barclay, *History of Methodist Missions,* 3 Vols. (New York, 1949), II; Russell E. Miller, *The Larger Hope: The First Century of the Universalist Church in America, 1770–1870* (Boston, 1979); Byron C. Lambert, *The Rise of the Anti-Mission Baptist* (New York, reprint, 1980).

28. Sidney E. Mead, *Nathaniel W. Taylor* (Hampden, Conn., reprint, 1967); Barbara M. Cross, *Horace Bushnell, Minister to a Changing America* (Chicago, 1958); Joseph S. Clark, *A Historical Sketch of the Congregational Churches in Massachusetts* (Boston, 1858); Ann C. Rose, *Transcendentalism as a Social Movement, 1830–50* (New Haven, 1981); Richard E. Sykes, "Massachusetts Unitarianism and Social Change" (Ph.D. Diss., University of Minnesota, 1966).

29. These are available on microfilm in the American Periodicals on Microfilm Series.

30. *Boston Recorder,* 27 July 1831; *Boston Advocate,* 2 June 1829; *Christian Register,* 8 Oct. 1831. *Maine Free Press,* 3, 10 Feb. 1832. See advertisement for the *Antimasonic Christian Herald* in *Pawtucket Herald,* 10 Dec. 1828.

31. Table 4.1. There were too few cases and too much missing data for inclusion of Rhode Island, and New Hampshire did not develop an Antimasonic party which generated a vote appropriate for analysis. The Massachusetts Congregationalist membership data, derived from the annual reports of the Massachusetts General Association, did not include data for the churches of the Mendon Association which was not a member, yet these churches were strongholds of Antimasonic sentiment. This illustrates the problematic character of church membership data. The data for Maine and Vermont Episcopalians, all Quaker and Unitarian data, and Universalist data for Massachusetts and Maine come from the 1850 United States Census which counted "accommodations" twenty years after the Antimasonic elections studied. For the problems of using denominational data see Formisano, *The Transformation of Political Culture,* 367–69.

32. Clergy were identified in the proceedings of the Grand Lodge of the various New England states, in the Boston *Masonic Mirror,* and in Antimasonic newspapers, and from lists of Masonic clergy prnited in annual state registers.

33. *Masonic Mirror,* 6 May 1826, 25 July 1829, 8 Oct. 1831; *Rhode Island Legislative Investigation,* 22; *Maine Free Press,* 11 May 1832; *Antimasonic Review,* I, No. 8, p. 237.

Table 4.1. Impact of Church Membership on the Antimasonic Vote in New England, 1832–1833: Multiple Regression Betas (b) and Simple Correlations (r)

	Connecticut		Maine		Massachusetts						Vermont	
	1832 Pres.		1833 Gov.		1832 Gov.		1832 Pres.		1833 Gov.		1832 Pres.	
	b	r	b	r	b	r	b	r	b	r	b	r
Congregationalist	−.158	−.09	.108	.01	−.013	.12	.073	.15	−.105	.01	.002	−.03
Baptist	−.022	.04	.139	.05	−.095	−.04	−.072	−.05	−.116	−.08	.069	.06
Methodist	−.008	−.00	.101	.09	−.137	−.16	−.087	−.13	−.173	−.19	−.064	−.02
Episcopal	−.234	−.23	.002	−.05							−.023	−.07
Free Will Baptist			.095	.07	.011	.02	.000	.00	−.039	−.02	−.053	−.03
Unitarian			.049	.04	−.145	−.06	.002	−.10	.071	.15		
Universalist			−.113	−.07	−.072	−.13	.000	.01	−.061	−.09	.159	.15
Quaker			.024	.06	.184	.12	.023	.14	.164	.13		

34. William Henry Brackney, "Religious Antimasonry: The Genesis of a Political Party" (Ph.D. Diss., Temple University, 1976); *Maine Free Press*, 23 Nov. 1832; Henry Crocker, *History of the Baptists in Vermont* (Bellows Falls, Vt., 1913), 75ff., 120ff.

35. Norman A. Baxter, *History of the Freewill Baptists* (Rochester, N.Y., 1957), 137; *Minutes of the General Conference of the Free Will Baptist Connection* (Dover, N.H., 1859), 103, 248.

36. *Seventh Day Baptists in Europe and America,* 2 Vols. (Plainfield, N.J., 1910), I, 176, 177.

37. For an overview of Beecher's career, see Barbara Cross, ed., *The Autobiography of Lyman Beecher* (Cambridge, 1961); Marie Caskey, *Chariot of Fire, Religion and the Beecher Family* (New Haven, 1978), 3–67. See also *North Star,* 2 Aug. 1831; *Maine Free Press,* 12 Aug. 1831; Daniel W. Howe, *The Political Culture of the American Whigs* (Chicago, 1979), 150–67, esp. 161.

38. *Massachusetts Antimasonic Convention, 1831,* pp. 7–8; Woods and Stuart were among the 4,000 who petitioned the Massachusetts legislature for an investigation of Masonry, see *An Investigation into Freemasonry, 1834,* p. 2.

39. *Masonic Mirror,* 20 Feb., 10, 17 April 1830.

40. See, for example, Clark, *An Historical Sketch of the Congregational Churches of Massachusetts,* 251ff.; Moses Stuart, *Miscellanies* (Andover, 1846), *passim; Facts and Documents in Relation to Harvard College by Hollis and Others* (Boston, 1829); J. H. Fairchild, *Objections to the Deity of Christ Considered* (Boston, 1831); Parsons Cooke, *Unitarianism, An Exclusive System, or the Bondage of the Churches That Were Planted by the Puritans, A Sermon at the Annual Fast 3 April 1828* (n.p., n.d.); Parsons Cooke, *A Remonstrance against an Established Religion in Massachusetts* (Boston, 1831); *Spirit of the Pilgrims,* III (1830), 323ff., 641ff. and *passim.*

41. Bernard Whitman, *Address Delivered at the Masonic Temple in Boston,* 30 and *passim.* See also the exchange between Whitman and Eliphalet Pearson, Deacon of the Trinitarian Congregationalist Church in Waltham and delegate to the 1829 Massachusetts Antimasonic Convention: Eliphalet Pearson, *A Letter to the Candid: Occasioned by the Publications of Rev. Bernard Whitman* (Boston, 1831); Bernard Whitman, *An Answer to 'Eliphalet Pearson's Letter to the Candid'* (Boston, 1832). For Whitman's exchange with Moses Stuart, see *Two Letters to the Rev. Moses Stuart on the Subject of Religious Liberty* (Boston, 1830).

42. *Massachusetts Antimasonic Convention, 1831,* pp. 22, 63.

43. See, for example, cases in Rhode Island, Connecticut, and Massachusetts where Universalists' testimony in court came under challenge as unreliable since they did not believe in the doctrine of future punishments: *Atwood v. Welter,* 7 Conn. 66; *Jeremiah Arnold v. Estate of Samuel Arnold,* 13 Vt. 362; *The Right of Universalists to Testify in a Court of Justice Vindicated by a Member of the Bar* (Boston, 1828). For efforts to provide relief for Massachusetts Universalists: *Massachusetts Centinel,* 11 Feb. 1836, 15 Jan. 1839; Robert S. Rantoul, *Personal Recollections* (Boston, 1916), 337ff. For conflicting views in the denominational press see *Universalist Watchman,* 1 Dec. 1832; *Quarterly Christian Spectator* 11 (Sep. 1829), 438ff; *The Anti-Universalist,* 6 Aug. 1828; *Christian Register,* 21 March 1829.

44. Bertram Wyatt-Brown, *Lewis Tappan and the Evangelical War against Slavery* (New York, reprint, 1971), 69; Daniel W. Howe, *The Political Culture of the American Whigs,* 166; *Hopkinsian Magazine* IV (Aug. 1832), 479.

45. William Dunlap, *History of the American Theatre,* 3 Vols. in one (New York,

reprint, 1963) I, 242ff., 271–72, 368, 409–10; Claudia D. Johnson, "That Guilty Third Tier: Prostitution in Nineteenth-Century American Theatres," in Daniel W. Howe, ed., *Victorian America* (Philadelphia, 1976), 111–20.

46. Bertram Wyatt-Brown, *Lewis Tappan,* 68ff. Barbara J. Berg, *The Remembered Gate: Origins of American Feminism* (New York, 1978), 153–84, 166–67, 185–87, 196–97.

47. Neil Harris, *Humbug, The Art of P.T. Barnum* (Chicago, 1973).

48. Bertram Wyatt-Brown "Prelude to Abolitionism; Sabbatarian Politics and the Rise of the Second Party System," *Journal of American History* 61 (Sep. 1971), 316–41; Paul Johnson, *A Shopkeeper's Millennium,* 75; and for interdenominational support for the sabbatarian movement see *Christian Watchman,* 9 Jan. 1829. For divisions among Unitarians see the *Christian Register,* 14, 21, 28 Feb. 1829 which supported the sabbatarian petition and the *Christian Examiner* VI (May 1829), 226–41 which printed an opposing viewpoint.

49. Daniel Calhoun, *Professional Lives* (Cambridge, 1964), ch. 4; Scott, *From Office to Profession.* For a contemporary view see, for example, Rev. Elijah Waterman in John E. Tyler, *Historical Discourse Delivered before the First Church and Society of Windham, Conn.* (Hartford, 1851), 25ff.; *Hopkinsian Magazine* III (Sep. 1829), 495; IV (Jan. 1831), 9.

50. Kornblith, "From Artisans to Businessmen," 317ff.; Roth, "Whence This Strange Fire?," 61ff.; Bernard C. Steiner, *A History of . . . Guilford, Conn.* (Baltimore, 1897); Marshall W. Leach, *Annals of an Old New England Church . . . Plymouth, Conn.* (Brattleboro, Vt., 1939), 37.

51. For the problem of church discipline see Roth, "Whence This Strange Fire?," 45ff., 61ff.; *Hopkinsian Magazine* II (Aug. 1826), 184ff.; Mary P. Ryan, *Cradle of the Middle Class,* compare 41 with 116 on changes in church discipline.

52. Richard D. Shiels, "The Feminization of American Congregationalism, 1730–1835," *American Quarterly* 33 (Spring 1981), 46–62; Ann Douglas, *The Feminization of American Culture* (New York, 1977).

53. See Chapter 5 for treatment of this theme.

54. Robert J. Dinkin, "Seating the Meeting House in Early Massachusetts," *New England Quarterly* 43 (Sep. 1970), 450–64. The subject is treated in many accounts of the established churches in New England town histories. See, for example, Joseph Merrill, *History of Amesbury* (Haverhill, 1880), 89–90, 141–42, 151; Edward Carpenter and Wilton Morehouse, compilers, *The History of the Town of Amherst* (Amherst, 1896), 38ff., 204ff.; Henry A. Hazen, *History of Billerica* (Boston, 1883), 170, 175ff.; Bradford Kingman, *History of North Bridgewater* (Boston, 1866), 84ff.; Mortimer Blake, *A History of the Town of Franklin* (Franklin, Mass., 1879), 29–30; Francis H. Thompson, *History of Greenfield,* 2 Vols. (Greenfield, 1909), I, 233ff., 286–87, 291, 294, 302.

55. Francis Jackson, *A History of the Early Settlement of Newton* (Boston, 1854), 143.

56. Blake, *Franklin,* 29–30.

57. Samuel Sewall, *The History of Woburn* (Boston, 1868), 186; J. E. A. Smith, *The History of Pittsfield, Massachusetts . . . 1800 . . . 1876* (Springfield, 1876), 315. For the Massachusetts law see *Supplement to the Revised Statutes of the Commonwealth of Massachusetts . . . 1836 to 1849* (Boston, 1849), 358, and *The General Statutes of the Commonwealth of Massachusetts . . .* (Boston, 1860), 204, 624, 688.

58. See, for example, Robert H. Abzug, *Passionate Liberator, Theodore Weld and the Dilemma of Reform* (New York, 1980); Ann C. Rose, *Transcendentalism as a Social Movement, 1830–1850, passim*; Arthur M. Schlesinger, Jr., *Orestes A. Brownson; A Pilgrim's Progress* (Boston, 1939); Charles G. Finney, *Memoirs of the Rev. Charles G. Finney* (New York, 1889), especially the early years of Finney's life and conversion. For competition that threatened religious moral leadership see also Karen Halttunen, *Confidence Men and Painted Women*, 22–23.

59. Roth, "Whence This Strange Fire?," 152; *Minutes of the General Association of Massachusetts Congregationalists, 1838* (Boston, 1838), 13; *Minutes . . . , 1839* (Boston, 1839), 22; Mary P. Ryan, *Cradle of the Middle Class*, 13, 82–83. Cf. Paul Johnson, *A Shopkeeper's Millennium*, whose findings that wage earners comprised a small proportion of church members and converts in the Rochester revivals he studied raise difficulties with the "social control" thesis, that evangelical Protestantism disciplined workers to become conservative, passive instruments of industrial capital.

60. Paul S. Boyer, *Urban Reform and Moral Order in America, 1820–1920* (Cambridge, Mass., 1978), 41–42.

61. There are hundreds of manuals, mostly for Congregational churches, in the Congregational Library, Boston, Massachusetts.

62. Greene, *The Broken Seal*, 124; *North Star*, 25 Feb. 1833.

63. *Massachusetts Antimasonic Convention*, 1832, p. 18; Jacob Ide, ed., *The Works of Nathanael Emmons*, 6 Vols. (Boston, 1842), I, li, hereafter Emmons, *Works*.

64. Sidney E. Ahlstrom, *A Religious History of the American People*, 412, and esp. ch. 25 for treatment of the New Divinity. An extended biography appears in Emmons, *Works*, I; Joseph A. Conforti, *Samuel Hopkins and the New Divinity Movement* (Grand Rapids, Mich., 1981).

65. *Statistical Tables . . . of Industry in Massachusetts . . . 1837*, p. 125; John Hayward, *The Massachusetts Directory* (Boston, 1835), 98–99.

66. Emmons, *Works*, II, 331ff., 348, 489.

67. *Ibid.*, 358.

68. *Ibid.*, I, 259ff., 314–16.

69. *Ibid.*, 260, II, 426. See also the *Hopkinsian Magazine* III (June 1831), 121ff.; IV (June 1832), 422ff.; (July 1832), 441ff.

70. Emmons, *Works*, I, 260–64; *Hopkinsian Magazine* II (Aug. 1827), 482.

71. Emmons, *Works*, II, 321, 331, 333, 373–74, 386, 420; *Hopkinsian Magazine* I (Jan. 1824), iii; *Hopkinsian Magazine* IV (Feb. 1832), 316–17, reprinted an article from the *New England Artisan* which argued from anachronistic notions of political economy that "if employers paid workers what they are worth that would prevent much misery."

72. Blake, *History of the Mendon Association*, 53; Emmons, *Works*, I, 1.

73. *Hopkinsian Magazine* III (Sep. 1828), 209ff.; Emmons, *Works*, I, Autobiography, li ff.

74. Emmons, *Works*, I, l, lxvii, lxxv.

75. *Ibid.*, I, clxvi.

76. *Hopkinsian Magazine* IV (Oct. 1832), 519.

77. *Ibid.*, IV (Jan. 1831), 10. See Chapter 10 for the trials of Rev. Moses Thacher, an Hopkinsian who played a prominent role in the Antimasonic movement.

78. *Masonic Mirror*, 28 May 1831.

79. *Massachusetts Antimasonic Convention*, 1833, p. 48.

80. Robert W. Doherty, *The Hicksite Separation;* Rufus M. Jones, *The Later Periods of Quakers,* 2 Vols. (London, 1921), I, 488ff., 437ff.

81. John Gest, *The Cause, Rise and Progress of the Late Unhappy Division of the Society of Friends Explained* . . . (Philadelphia, 1835), 6. See also John Gest, *A Brief Defence of John the Baptist against Foul Slander and Wicked Libel of Freemasons* (Philadelphia, 1834).

82. Bliss Forbush, *Elias Hicks, Quaker Liberal* (New York, 1956), 249.

83. Gest, *Cause, Rise and Progress,* 51–52.

84. On internal improvements see Forbush, *Hicks,* 281; Doherty, *Hicksite Separation,* 82.

85. Frederick B. Tolles, "The New Light Quakers of Lynn and New Bedford," *New England Quarterly* 33 (Sep. 1959), 291–319.

86. *Massachusetts Antimasonic Convention, 1833,* p. 4.

87. *Appleton Cyclopedia of American Biography,* VI, 155; Ann C. Rose, *Transcendentalism as a Social Movement, 1831–1850,* pp. 23–24, 141; *Dictionary of American Biography,* XIV, 586–87; Jill S. Dodd, "The Working Classes and the Temperance Movement in Ante-Bellum Boston," *Labor History* 4 (Fall 1978), 528.

88. Rose, *Transcendentalism,* 109ff. For Pierpont's attack on the militia, see *New Bedford Mercury,* 29 June 1828.

89. From *Boston Telegraph* reprinted in *Maine Free Press,* 12 April 1833; *North Star,* 6 Oct. 1834.

90. *Maine Free Press,* 15 June 1832.

91. *Vermont Antimasonic Convention, 1830,* p. 24.

Chapter 5. *Women and Antimasonry*

1. Luke Eastman, *Masonick Melodies,* 138–39; Daniel P. Thompson, *The Adventures of Timothy Peacock, Esq.* (Middlebury, 1835), 98.

2. Charles P. Sumner, *A Letter on Speculative Free Masonry* (Boston, 1829), 13–14; *Antimasonic Review,* II, No. 8, p. 282; Danville *North Star,* 27 May 1833; *Vermont Antimasonic Convention, 1833,* p. 30; Griffin, "The Antimasonic Persuasion," 728; Thompson, *Timothy Peacock,* is a picaresque novel about Peacock, a devoted Mason, who filches $10 from a sick, old lady, attempts to seduce Katrinka, an innkeeper's daughter, and shields from the law a brother Mason who killed another man in a dispute over a woman in a brothel. "For to enjoy ourselves" with women outside Masonic protection, Peacock explains, is "only one of the privileges that Masonry bestows on her trusty followers," 92.

3. Lipson, *Freemasonry in Federalist Connecticut,* 188ff., 329ff.

4. Nancy F. Cott, *The Bonds of Womanhood, Woman's Sphere in New England, 1780–1835* (New Haven, 1977); Kathryn K. Sklar, *Catharine Beecher, A Study in American Domesticity* (New York, 1973); Barbara Welter, *Dimity Convictions, The American Woman in the Nineteenth Century* (Athens, Ohio, 1975), 21–41; Carroll Smith-Rosenberg, *Disorderly Conduct, Visions of Gender in Victorian America* (New York, 1985), 129–64.

5. Mary B. Norton, *Liberty's Daughters, The Revolutionary Experience of American Women, 1750–1790* (Boston, 1980); Linda K. Kerber, *Women of the Republic, Intellect & Ideology in Revolutionary America* (Chapel Hill, 1980).

6. *Antimasonic Review,* I, No. 12, p. 363, No. 8, p. 10; *Connecticut Antimasonic*

Convention, 1830, pp. 20–21; Barber, *Address before the Anti-Masonic Convention of the County of Addison,* 6–7.

7. Brainard, *Masonic Lecture,* 13–14.

8. *Connecticut Antimasonic Convention, 1830,* p. 21.

9. *Masonic Mirror,* 30 April 1825; Alexis de Tocqueville, *Journey to America* (Garden City, N.Y., 1971), 232; Barbara Berg, *The Remembered Gate: Origins of American Feminism,* chs. 7–9; Carroll Smith-Rosenberg, *Religion and the Rise of the American City, The New York City Mission Movement, 1812–1817* (Ithaca, 1971); Cott, *Bonds of Womanhood,* 152ff.

10. William Morgan, *Morgan's Freemasonry Exposed . . .* (New York, 1882), 57; *Antimasonic Review,* I, No. 8, p. 237; *Connecticut Antimasonic Convention, 1830,* p. 22; *Maine Antimasonic Convention, 1834,* 6.

11. Danville *North Star,* 25 Aug. 1829; *Infidelity Unmasked,* 10 Sep. 1831; John Gest, *A Brief Defence of John the Baptist,* 11.

12. *A Serious Call or Masonry Revealed; Being an Address Prepared by the Order of the Anti-Masonic Convention, Held at Woodstock on the Anniversary of the Death of William Morgan. To the Citizens of Connecticut* (Boston, 1829), 23–24.

13. *Rhode Island Legislative Investigation,* 17; Lionel Tiger, *Men in Groups* (New York, 1969), 146; *North Star,* 14 Feb. 1831; William Bracknett, "Religious Antimasonry: The Genesis of a Political Party," 237; Thomas Gregor, "No Girls Allowed," *Science* 3 (Dec. 1982), 26ff.

14. Ian R. Tyrell, *Sobering Up, from Temperance to Prohibition to Antebellum America, 1800–1860* (Westport, Conn., 1979); Jed Dannenbaum, *Drink and Disorder* (Urbana, 1984); Ruth Bordin, *Women and Temperance: The Quest for Power and Liberty, 1873–1900* (Philadelphia, 1981); Barbara L. Epstein, *The Politics of Domesticity; Women, Evangelism, and Temperance in Nineteenth-Century America* (Middletown, Conn., 1981); Ian R. Tyrrell, "Women and Temperance in Antebellum America," *Civil War History* 28 (1982), 128–52; Ryan, *Cradle of the Middle Class,* 132–36.

15. *Antimasonic Review,* II, No. 8, p. 282; I, No. 4, p. 213; *Maine Free Press,* 16 Sep. 1831; *Lynn Record,* 13 Feb. 1833; *Boston Advocate,* 6 Feb., 25 Dec. 1833.

16. *Maine Free Press,* 9 March 1832; *Antimasonic Intelligencer,* 21 April 1829; *North Star,* 9 Sep. 1829, 25 March 1833; Moses Thacher, *Masonic Oaths Neither Morally nor Legally Binding, an Address Delivered at Weymouth . . . 1830* (Boston, n.d.), 19–20.

17. Stillson, *History of Masons,* 526; *Masonic Mirror,* 10 April 1830.

18. For a synthesis see Carl Degler, *At Odds* (New York, 1980), ch. 13; Smith-Rosenberg, *Disorderly Conduct,* 129–64.

19. Trollope, *Domestic Manners,* 339, 155, 182, 25, 157, 299, 285, 47–48; Alexis de Tocqueville, *Democracy in America,* 2 Vols. (Garden City, N.Y., 1969), II, 592; Suzanne Lebsock, *The Free Women of Petersburg, Status and Culture in a Southern Town, 1784–1860* (New York, 1984), 224. Modern scholars have also speculated on deep strains in the Victorian family based on fear that marriage entrapped men and exposed women to betrayal. Barker-Benfield suggests that "American history is in several ways the interplay between male activity construed as free with heterosexual obligations of settlement." He draws on Leslie Fiedler, who argued, "The typical male protagonist of our fiction has been a man on the run . . . to avoid . . . the confrontation of man and woman which leads to the fall, to sex, marriage and responsibility." Some even opt for bachelorhood. In *Ik Marvel,* one of the best-sellers of the

1850s, a wandering Kentucky hunter loves his freedom too much to submit to a wife. "The gals! . . ." he says. "They're pooty enough to look at, as picters! but to marry one of 'em, an' have her around all the time, huggin' an' sich like, would be too much for human nater— Turn me into a skeleton if it wouldn't." G. J. Barker-Benfield, *The Horrors of the Half Known Life, Male Attitudes Towards Women and Sexuality in Nineteenth Century America* (New York, 1976), 8ff.; Joe L. Dubbert, *A Man's Place* (Englewood Cliffs, N.J., 1979), ch. 2, esp. 21, 25, 26, 30, 32, 34, 49; David G. Pugh, *Sons of Liberty, the Masculine Mind in the Nineteenth Century* (Westport, Conn., 1983), chs. 1–3.

20. Peter N. Stearns, *Be a Man! Males in Modern Society* (New York, 1979), 40.

21. Halttunen, *Confidence Men and Painted Women;* Greene, *The Broken Seal,* 34; *North Star,* 9 Sep. 1829.

22. Stearns, *Be a Man!,* 42ff.

23. Degler, *At Odds,* chs. 7–12; Carroll Smith-Rosenberg, "Beauty, the Beast and the Militant Woman: A Case Study in Sex Roles and Social Stress in Jacksonian America," *American Quarterly* 23 (Oct. 1971), 562–84; Charles E. Rosenberg, "Sexuality, Class and Role in 19th-Century America," *American Quarterly* 25 (May 1973), 131–53; Louis J. Kern, *An Ordered Love* (Chapel Hill, 1981), chs. 1–3; Stephen Nissenbaum, *Sex, Diet, and Debility in Jacksonian America, Sylvester Graham and Health Reform* (Westport, Conn., 1980).

24. Barbara Berg, *The Remembered Gate,* chs. 7–10; Carroll Smith-Rosenberg, *Religion and the Rise of the American City, The New York City Mission Movement, 1812–1837* (Ithaca, 1971), ch. 4; Ryan, *Cradle of the Middle Class,* 116–27.

25. Lipson, *Freemasonry in Connecticut,* 354.

26. *Maine Free Press,* 12 Aug. 1831.

27. Greene, *The Broken Seal,* 29.

28. Joseph Kett, *Rites of Passage, Adolescence in America, 1790 to the Present* (New York, 1977), chs. 1–4; John R. Gillis, *Youth and History* (New York, 1974); Bernard Wishy, *The Child and the Republic* (Philadelphia, 1972); Halttunen, *Confidence Men,* 27ff.

29. Ryan, *Cradle of the Middle Class,* 232, 89ff., 100ff., 176; Kett, *Rites of Passage,* 79.

30. *Maine Free Press,* 7 Sep. 1832; *North Star,* 20 Jan. 1829.

31. Ryan, *Cradle of the Middle Class,* 89ff.

32. Emmons, *Works,* II, 58–60.

33. Edward T. Fairbanks, *The Town of St. Johnsbury, Vermont* (St. Johnsbury, 1914), 133, for Susanna Mansfield who fought her husband to save her children's souls. Mr. Mansfield hid the family Bible to prevent his wife from inculcating "superstition" but she defied him. See the example of Mary Rackliffe, who in 1804 defied her husband, in Unity, Maine, to assist Rev. Jotham Sewall in establishing a Calvinist church. James V. Vickery, *A History of Unity, Maine* (Manchester, Maine, 1954), 59. See also the case of Lewis and Arthur Tappan, nurtured by their mother in Calvinism in Jonathan Edwards's Northampton but who switched to Unitarianism in Boston, where they became successful merchants. Betraying their mother and causing her grief made them feel guilty until they reconverted to evangelical Orthodoxy. Lewis, who had joined the Masons, renounced. See Wyatt-Brown, *Lewis Tappan.* Calvinists accused liberal husbands of prohibiting wives from attending Orthodox services. Caught between the duty to obey a spouse or obey the Lord, defiant women smuggled evangelical tracts into their homes, risking scolding, even beatings. Some

husbands, the Orthodox alleged, imprisoned their wives at home "in a state of bondage of fear," like women in a Turkish harem. See *Boston Recorder*, 10 Oct. 1831; Epstein, *Politics of Domesticity*, 57–61.

34. Philip Greven, *The Protestant Temper, Patterns of Child-rearing, Religious Experience, and the Self in Early America* (New York, 1977). Greven draws on an impressive body of evidence from early American history, but there is hardly any sense of historical development nor coherent connection between child-rearing models and such variables as class or stages of economic development. The issue of child-rearing ideals and practice remains very much in dispute. For guidance into the thicket see Daniel Scott Smith, "Child-naming Practices, Kinship, Ties, and Change in Family Attitudes in Hingham, Massachusetts, 1641 to 1880," *Journal of Social History* 18 (1984–85), 542.

35. Wishy, *The Child and the Republic*, 3–80; Ryan, *Cradle of the Middle Class*, 159–65, 98–102.

36. Douglas, *The Feminization of American Culture*, esp. chs. 1, 3.

37. Richard D. Sheils, "The Femininization of American Congregationalism, 1730–1835," 47; Winthrop S. Hudson, "Early Nineteenth Century Evangelical Religion and Women's Liberation," *Foundations* 23 (1980), 181–85.

38. Trollope, *Domestic Manners*, 344, 75, 275.

39. For a Trinitarian point of view see Joseph S. Clark, *A Historical Sketch of the Congregational Churches in Massachusetts*.

40. Ryan, *Cradle of the Middle Class*, 81, 80, 94; Cott, *Bonds of Womanhood*, 138ff., 192; Epstein, *The Politics of Domesticity*, 47ff., 57; *Universalist Watchman*, 6 Aug. 1831; Smith-Rosenberg, *Disorderly Conduct*, 129ff.

41. This is based on an examination of membership lists for fourteen Unitarian and Universalist churches during the first half of the nineteenth century in the manuscript collections of Andover Harvard Divinity School Library. Men made up 51% of the membership of churches in the following towns: Langdon, N.H.; Dover, N.H.; Quincy, Mass.; Cambridge, Mass.; Plymouth, N.H.; Providence, R.I.; Second Universalist Church, South Adams; New Bedford, Mass.; Marlboro, Mass.; Roxbury, Mass.; Federal St., Boston; Sommerville, Mass.; Second Universalist, New York City; South Boston, Mass.

42. Whitman, *Two Letters to the Rev. Moses Stuart*, 151ff.; William Morse, *On Revivals of Religion, A Sermon Delivered in New Bedford, 17 April 1831* (New Bedford, 1831), *passim; The Christian Magazine* IV, 114ff.

43. See Chapter 9 for an account of the Wrentham church; *Masonic Mirror*, 19 March, 2 April, 22 Oct. 1831; *Maine Free Press*, 10 May 1833; *Lynn Record*, 11 Jan. 1832.

44. For additional discussion of the Quaker split see above, Chapter 4; Gest, *The Progress of the Late Unhappy Division of the Society of Friends*, 20, 51; Gest, *A Brief Defence*, 11.

45. Lipson, *Freemasonry in Connecticut*, 329–38.

46. *Massachusetts Antimasonic Convention, 1832* (Boston, 1832), 5; *Masonic Mirror*, 9 Oct. 1830.

47. For Fuller, see above, Chapter 2; Douglas, *Feminization*, 318–21; Fuller, *An Oration Delivered at Faneuil Hall*, 6.

48. Douglas, *Feminization*, 319–21, 323, 341, 342, and 313ff.

49. *Dictionary of American Biography*, 10 Vols. (New York, 1937), XIX, 338;

Amasa Walker, *An Address Delivered before the Young Men of Boston* (Boston, 1833), 11, 12, 14, 18, 22, 27, 31.

50. See above, Chapter 2; Kennedy, *Life of William Wirt*, I, 102.

51. Wirt, *The Old Bachelor*, 32, 49, 53, 61.

52. *Dictionary of American Biography*, XVI, 204; Lipson, *Freemasonry in Connecticut*, 334–36; Ann Royall, *The Black Book*, 3 vols. (Washington, D.C., 1828–29), II, 76, 110, 111, 157, 217, 348, 376; II, 244; III, 58, 68.

53. *North Star*, 23 June 1829.

54. Ruth E. Finley, *The Lady of Godey's* (Philadelphia, 1931); Isabelle W. Entrikin, *Sarah Josepha Hale and Godey's Lady's Book* (Philadelphia, 1946); for the Antimasonic attack on the Bunker Hill Monument Association see *Report of the Bunker Hill Monument Association*; Griffin, "The Antimasonic Persuasion, 726–27. On Rev. John L. Blake see *Dictionary of American Biography*, II, 343. On the struggle over the Bunker Hill Monument Association see Chapter 8.

55. *Lynn Record*, 6 March 1830.

56. Douglas, *Feminization*, 7, 111ff.; Finley, *The Lady of Godey's*, 139.

57. Sarah J. Hale, *Northwood; or Life North and South: Showing the True Character of Both* (New York, reprint, 1972).

58. Entrikin, *Hale*, 102; Finley, *The Lady of Godey's*, 193.

59. Douglas, *Feminization*, 52–53.

60. Halttunen, *Confidence Men and Painted Women*, 187ff.

61. Hale, *Northwood*, 359.

62. Catharine Beecher occupies an important niche mediating between evangelical and anti-evangelical currents in women's culture. The daughter of a great evangelical who himself mediated among secular and anti-secularist tendencies, strict and liberal Calvinism among Congregationalists and Presbyterians, Beecher never experienced conversion and found herself spiritually adrift. When she sought to establish a female academy in Hartford, she tried to recruit Zilpha Grant, a pietist whose association with the school would stamp it acceptable in the eyes of evangelical parents and attract their patronage. But Grant refused to become Beecher's assistant because she regarded the school as too secular in design; and Beecher herself followed a secular lifestyle. She was a social butterfly who repeatedly attached herself to upwardly mobile prominent families into whose comfortable homes she invited herself for extended periods, making her one of the most formidable spongers of mid-nineteenth-century America. As the loyal "heretic" in the Beecher family, Beecher's uncertain religious identity also created uncertainty about her sexual identity, given the connection that evangelicals made between piety and womanhood. See Kathryn K. Sklar, *Catharine Beecher, passim,* esp. 92–93.

63. For Thacher, see below, Chapter 10; Royall, *Black Book*, II, 244; *Masonic Mirror*, 5 Sep. 1829, 20 March 1830; Roth, "Whence This Strange Fire?," 256. See also *Masonic Mirror*, 5 Sep. 1829.

64. *Maine Free Press*, 9 March 1832; *Boston Advocate*, 4 July 1832, 26 June 1834.

65. Elizur Wright, *Myron Holley; and What He Did for Liberty* (Boston, 1882), 304, 306–8, 312.

Chapter 6. Emergence of Antimasonic Politics

1. There were legislative investigations in Massachusetts, Rhode Island, and Connecticut. See below in the chapters on those states.

2. *Vermont Antimasonic Convention, 1831*, p. 21; *1832*, p. 4; *1834*, pp. 4–5, 29; *Maine Antimasonic Convention, 1834*, pp. 13, 15, 22; *Rhode Island Antimasonic State Convention, Sept. 14, 1831* (Providence, 1831), 5; *Massachusetts Antimasonic Convention, 1831*, pp. 17, 30, 50–51, 58; *Boston Advocate*, 27 Dec. 1831.

3. For the persistence of anti-party sentiment and the slow evolution of the Second Party System, see Ronald P. Formisano, *The Transformation of Political Culture*, 70ff., 91ff., 341–43. See also Michael Wallace, "Changing Concepts of Party in the United States: New York, 1815–1828," *American Historical Review* LXXIV (Dec. 1968), 453–91; on voting, see Richard P. McCormick, "New Perspectives on Jacksonian Politics," *American Historical Review* LXV (Jan. 1960), 288–301; and for party development see Edward Pessen, *Jacksonian America; Society, Personality, and Politics* (Homewood, Ill., 1969), chs. 7–9, and William G. Shade, "Political Pluralism and Party Development," in Paul Kleppner *et al.*, *The Evolution of American Electoral Systems* (Westport, Conn., 1981), 77–120.

4. *Maine Antimasonic Convention, 1834*, pp. 28, 14, 26, 29; *Rhode Island Antimasonic Convention, 1831*, p. 7; *Connecticut Antimasonic Convention, 1830*, p. 15; *Vermont Antimasonic Convention, 1830*, p. 21.

5. *Maine Antimasonic Convention, 1834*, p. 27; *Massachusetts Antimasonic Convention, 1832*, p. 37.

6. *Maine Antimasonic Convention, 1834*, p. 14; *Rhode Island Antimasonic Convention, 1831*, p. 6; *Massachusetts Antimasonic Convention, 1831*, p. 31.

7. *Vermont Antimasonic Convention, 1833*, p. 5; *Maine Antimasonic Convention, 1834*, p. 13.

8. *Massachusetts Antimasonic Convention, 1833*, p. 33.

9. Table 6.1

10. For the Workingmen's party see Sean Wilentz, *Chants Democratic, New York City and the Rise of the American Working Class, 1780–1850* (New York, 1984) and Formisano, *Transformation of Political Culture*, 222ff. For the theme of ambivalence towards modernization, see Marvin Meyers, *The Jacksonian Persuasion, Politics and Belief*, and James R. Sharp, *The Jacksonians versus the Banks* (New York, 1970).

Table 6.1. Antimasonic Vote in New England (% Total Vote)

	1830 Gov.	1831 Gov.	1832 Pres.	1832 Gov.	1833 Gov.	1834 Gov.	1835 Gov.
Connecticut	22[1]	27	10	26	15	7	.1
Maine		1	1		5	1	
Massachusetts		25	24	23	29	14	2
New Hampshire				14			
Rhode Island			15	14[2]			
Vermont	36	44	41	42	53	48	46

[1] Election of Lt. Gov.

[2] The fifth election, Nov. 21, 1832.

11. Table 6.2

12. Table 6.3

13. Table 6.4

14. Table 6.5

15. For scattered Antimasonic county conventions in 1831 and 1832 and a statewide convention in 1833 that nominated Arthur Livermore, see *New Hampshire Patriot,* 11 Jan., 1 Feb. 1830; and also 13 June 1831; *New Hampshire Post,* 13 Feb. 1833.

16. Donald B. Cole, *Jacksonian Democracy in New Hampshire, 1800-1851* (Cambridge, Mass., 1970), chs. 2–4. *New Hampshire Patriot* at least from 1827 reported in detail the organizational activities at the town and the county levels, printing the proceedings of county nominating conventions, including the names of delegates and resolutions.

17. Phineas Henderson to Samuel Bell, 6 Feb. 1830, Bell Papers, New Hampshire Historical Society (NHHS).

18. *New Hampshire Patriot* claimed on 4 Feb. 1833 that the National Republican tactic was not to run a candidate for governor in 1833 but to field an Antimasonic ticket to confuse and detach some Democrats. For the Antimasonic Convention proceedings, see *New Hampshire Post,* 13 Feb. 1833, and for the call to the convention, *Maine Free Press,* 1 Feb. 1833, and a convention report, 15 Feb. 1833; Cole, *Jacksonian Democracy in New Hampshire,* 138.

19. For the prominence of Masons in New Hampshire politics, see Cole, *Jacksonian Democracy in New Hamsphire,* 45 and n. 51. Prominent Whigs and Democrats can be identified in Gerald D. Foss, *Three Centuries of Freemasonry in New Hampshire* (Concord, 1982) which contains an excellent biographical directory. For Antimasonic complaints that the Nationals were hostile, see the *New Hampshire Post* reprinted in the *North Star,* 15 April 1833, and the *Free Elector,* 3 May 1835, reprinting a complaint from the *Boston Daily Advocate* that the Whigs had nominated a Mason for governor.

20. Foss, *Three Centuries of Freemasonry in New Hampshire,* 370–73, and Stillson, *History of Masons,* 891 for New Hampshire Lodge data and 877ff. for the other states. The leadership of New Hampshire Masonry in 1830 is listed in *New Hampshire Annual Register,* 1830 (Concord, 1830), 122–24.

21. Table 6.6

22. Cole, *Jacksonian Democracy in New Hampshire,* on banking, 106–8, and chs. 5, 8; on railroads, 188ff., 199–200, 209–10; on the tariff, 191–96, 206. For an authoritative expression of Jacksonian views of economic questions in the formative period of the Second Party System see the *New Hampshire Patriot,* 25 Jan., 8 Feb. 1830, attacking manufacturing; 15 Feb. 1830, 28 Feb. 1831, attacking the Portsmouth, New Hampshire, branch of the Bank of the United States; 7 Feb., 18 April 1831, 11 Jan. 1833, opposing the tariff.

23. Table 6.7. See also the analysis of the social basis of the vote in Cole, *Jacksonian Democracy in New Hampshire,* 140ff.

24. See, for example, the clergy who participated in the Democratic-sponsored Fourth of July celebrations described in *The Republican Sentiment of New Hampshire, July 4, 1828 Exhibited in Her Anniversary Celebration* (n.p., n.d.), which included Methodists Elder Blodgett and John Broadhead, Christians Joseph Kellum and Webber Rumney, Baptists Rev. Greenwood, Elder Cummings of Hillsboro, Ira Person of Newport, Rev. Chamberlee of Bow, and Rev. Dean of Nottingham.

Table 6.2. Party Competition in New England, 1827–34 (% Democratic)

	1828 Gov.	1828 Pres.	1829	1830	1831	1832 Gov.	1832 Pres.	1833	1834
Connecticut		24		NA	NA	NA	34	42	43
Maine	92[1]	40	49.4	51	57	54	55	52	52
Massachusetts		17		26	21	24	23	25	25
New Hampshire	47	46	53	55	56	62	57	84	85
Rhode Island	ND	23	ND	62	44	38	36	55	51
Vermont		15		20	18	20	25	NA	26

[1] Bipartisan candidate

Table 6.3. The First and Second Party Systems: Continuity or Discontinuity? (Pearson Correlation Coefficients)[1]

CONNECTICUT

	National Republican/Whig			
	1828 P	1832 P	1836 P	1840 P
Federalist, 1816	.14	.11	.35	.25

MAINE
Democrat

	1830	1833	1837	1840 P
Democratic-Republican, 1810	.43	.20	.30	.34

MASSACHUSETTS

		Federalist/National Republican/Whig						
	1823	1824	1828 P	1832 P	1833	1836 P	1839	1840 P
Federalist 1810	.31	.58	.34	.16	.13	.33	.31	.40

NEW HAMPSHIRE

		Democrat		
	1830	1832 P	1838	1840 P
Democratic-Republican, 1810	.62	.49	.58	.59

RHODE ISLAND

	National Republican/Whig				
	1830	1832 P	1836	1838	1840 P
Federalist, 1810	.08	.08	.14	.30	.34

VERMONT

	National Republican/Whig			
	1828 P	1832 P	1836 P	1840 P
Federalist, 1808	.04	.16	.08	.06

[1] Gubernatorial election, except where noted P (Presidential).

Table 6.4. Where the Antimasonic Vote Came from in New England, 1828–33 (Ecological Regression Estimates)

Antimasonic Vote	National Republicans	Democrats	Nonvoters
Connecticut 1832 Pres.	1%	1828 Pres. 0%	5%
Maine 1833 Gov.	2.6	1830 Gov. .2	0
Massachusetts 1831 Gov.	5	1828 Pres. −2	6
1832 Pres.	5	−2	6
Rhode Island 1832 Pres.	1	1830 Gov. .5	3
Vermont 1832 Gov.	11	1828 Pres. −4	13

Table 6.5. Voter Turnout in New England, 1828–33 (% Adult Males Voting)

	1828 Gov.	1828 Pres.	1829	1830	1831	1832 Gov.	1832 Pres.	1833
Connecticut	14	27	15	19	27	24	46	30
Maine	35	43	55	68	57	65	68	52
Massachusetts	24	24	25	32	36	41	39	39
New Hampshire	68	76	71	70	69	63	72	53
Rhode Island	NC	17	NC	21	31	32	22	32
Vermont	28	54	42	49	54	64	50	60

25. See, for example, the conflict over town church property in J. Bailey Moore, *History of the Town of Candia* (Manchester, N.H., 1893), 213; Leonard A. Morrison, *The Supplement to the History of Windham in New Hampshire* (Boston, 1892), 23; Robert F. Lawrence, *The New Hampshire Churches* (n.p., 1856), 146–47.

26. For Democratic complaints of clerical interference in politics, usually aimed at the Congregationalists, see *New Hampshire Patriot,* 2 April 1827, 3, 17 March, 21 April 1828, 1 June, 22 Feb., 1830, 7 Feb., 25 June, 1 Aug., 10 Oct., 7 Nov. 1831, 12 Nov., 3 Dec. 1832. For appeals to Methodists, Baptists, and Universalists see 2 June, 5 Sep., 27 Oct. 1828, 26 Jan. 1829, 9 Nov. 1830, 19 Sep. 1831, 9 Jan., 18 Feb. 1832, 18 Feb., 29 July 1833, 9 Jan. 1834; and for Democratic party opposition to a "Christian Party" in politics, 2 Feb. 1828, 1 Feb., 6 Dec. 1830, 13 June 1831, 4 March 1833, 25 July 1834, 6 July 1835, 25 April 1836. For anti-Dartmouth agitation, see *New Hampshire Patriot,* 30 April, 2 July 1827, 3 March 1828, 12 Jan., 2 Feb. 1829, 6 Sep. 1830, 2 May, 24 Aug. 1831, 12 Nov. 1832, 2 Jan. 1835, 18 April 1836.

27. For Morrill's renunciation see *Maine Free Press,* 7 Sep. 1832; for his participation in the 1833 Antimasonic Convention, see *New Hampshire Post,* 13 Feb. 1833. For biographical information on Morrill see Robert Sobel and John Raimo,

Table 6.6. Demographic Characteristics of Notable
New Hampshire Freemasons Born before 1820

	%	N
Age at Initiation		
21–30	60	117
31–45	31	60
46–60	8	16
61–	1	2
Education		
College		50
Academy		21
Occupation		
High White Collar	51	79
Low White Collar	1	2
Proprietor	38	59
Mariners	5	8
Farmers	5	7
Public Office		
State and Local		112
Federal		56
Military		57
Religion		
Methodist		4
Episcopal		10
Unitarian		1
Universalist		2
Congregationalist		1

Source: Gerald D. Foss, *Three Centuries of Freemasonry in New Hampshire* (Concord, 1972).

Biographical Directory of the Governors of the U.S., 5 Vols. (New York, 1978–83),
III, 947–48; *Appleton's National Cyclopedia*, VII, 125. For his Hopkinsianism see
Conforti, *Samuel Hopkins and the New Divinity*, 185.

28. This is based on tracing convention delegates listed in the *New Hampshire
Post*, 13 Feb. 1833, to town histories. See, for example, these Antimasonic convention
delegates: William Trickey of Rochester, deacon of the Congregationalist church;
Washington's Ebenezer Smith, a deacon, denomination unknown, and Daniel Farnsworth, a founder of the Seventh-Day Adventist church in 1841; Rev. Nathan Bouton,
who offered prayers at the convention, presided over an Orthodox Congregational
church in Concord; Milan Harris, a prominent manufacturer and active Congregationalist in Dublin and Milan; Samuel Roby, a founder of the Baptist church in
Goffstown; Dudley C. Kimball of Haverhill, who became a deacon of the Congregational church at Wells River; Nathan Vilas, deacon of the Baptist church in
Alstead, was son of the first deacon; William Temple, deacon of the Boscawen church,
denomination unknown, and Jeremiah Gerrish, deacon of the Congregationalist
church; National Currier of Canaan was deacon of the Congregational church and
George Kimball an Antimason, though not a delegate, induced him to renounce
Masonry. John A. Chamberlain of Canterbury was deacon of the Congregational

Table 6.7. Impact of Demographic Variables on the Democratic Vote in New Hampshire, 1830–40: Multiple Regression Betas

	1830 Gov.	1832 Pres.		1838 Gov.	1840 Pres.
Sheep	.006	−.071		−.081	−.131
Pop. Change	−.063	−.054		.005	−.030
Mfg. Labor	−.048	−.084	Agricultural	−.025	−.102
Val. Acres/Poll	−.109	−.006	Mfg. Capital	.317	.314
Cows	−.026	−.027	Commerce	.143	.138
Bank Stock	−.064	−.056		−.030	−.017
Real Estate Val.	−.155	−.087		—	—
Money at Loan	−.063	−.016		−.139	−.152
Temperance Soc. Members	.003	.048		—	—
Congregationalists	−.109	−.135		−.187	−.250
Baptists	.022	−.046		−.061	−.079
Free Will Baptists	.181	.243		.071	.070
Methodists	−.042	.050		.053	.055
Universalists	nd	nd		.053	.043
R2	.15	.14		.21	.27

church and Joseph A. Moody was a founder of the Canterbury Society for the Reformation of Morals organized by Rev. William Patrick, the Congregationalist minister; Jeremiah F. Clough was an Elder in the Canterbury Free Will Baptist church. *Infidelity Unmasked*, vol. 1 (April, 1832), reprinted an article by "An Aged Minister" from the *Boston Telegraph*, edited by Moses Thacher, Antimasonic Hopkinsian minister at North Wrentham, Mass., which attacked Unitarian takeovers of Congregational churches and noted that "Masonic Christians" in Somersworth, N.H., had excluded a member who spoke against Freemasonry.

29. *New Hampshire Post*, 13 Feb. 1833; *North Star*, 4 March 1833. For Morrill's Hopkinsianism see Conforti, *Samuel Hopkins and the New Divinity*, 185.

30. In 1830 there were 130 Congregationalist, 69 Baptist and Free Will Baptist, 44 Methodist, and 18 Christian churches listed in the *New Hampshire State Register, 1830*, 99ff.

31. *Ibid.*, 99, 102–3.

32. *North Star*, 15 April 1833.

33. *Maine Free Press*, 12 Aug. 1831, and for the inaugural editorial, 29 July 1831.

34. *Maine Free Press*, 15 June 1832, 31 May 1833. *The Christian Mirror*, a Congregationalist weekly, defended Freemasonry, 26 Feb. 1829.

35. *Maine Free Press*, 3 Feb. 1832, 9 March, 26 Oct. 1832, 18 Jan., 26 April 1833; *Free Elector*, 19 Aug. 1834. *Kennebec Journal*, 6 Oct. 1833, 3 Sep. 1834, 5 Aug. 1831.

36. *Maine Free Press*, 10 May 1833.

37. *Maine Free Press*, 14 Sep. 1832; *Kennebec Journal*, 3 Sep. 1834. The Antimasonic town-level vote in 1833 correlated with the National Republican vote in 1830 at 0.12 and with the Whig vote in 1840 at 0.11.

38. Stillson, *History of Masons*, 879.

39. *Eastern Argus*, 2 June 1829, 3 July 1829, 8, 25 July, 3, 10 Aug., 7 Oct. 1830, 2 Aug. 1831, 12 Aug., 9 Sep., 19 June 1832.

40. [Reuel Washburn], *History of Oriental Star Lodge, No. 21, Livermore, Maine* (Portland, 1862); *One Hundred Years of Masonry, History of Penobscot Lodge, No. 39, Free and Accepted Mason, Dexter, Maine* (n.p., n.d.), 13, 15ff. for William Frost, Universalist minister in Foxcroft, who was Worshipful Master in 1830. The officers of the Grand Lodge are in the *Maine Register and Legislative Calendar, 1829* (Hallowell, 1829), 147–49. For Mesquier see John T. Hull, ed., *Centennial Celebration of Portland* (Portland, Maine), 139–40; for Zina Hyde and Rev. Seneca White see Henry W. Owen, *History of Bath* (Bath, Maine, 1936), 461ff. See Universalists active in Masonry in Belfast in Joseph Williamson, *History of the City of Belfast, Maine,* 2 Vols. (Boston and New York, 1913), I, 308–9, such as Asa Edmunds, a school teacher and merchant. For Rev. William A. Drew, Universalist pastor who performed the first Masonic funeral in Paris, see William B. Lapham and Silas P. Maxim, *History of Paris, Oxford County, Maine* (Paris, Me. 1884), 351ff. For Elder Samuel Rand, a Grand Chaplain of the Grand Lodge, esteemed by men of all denominations, see William Willis, *History of Portland from 1632 to 1864* (Portland, Maine, 1865), 693; for Stephen Lowell, a Portland Methodist known for tolerance, see *ibid.,* 110 and Josiah H. Drummond, *History of Portland Lodge* (Portland, 1881), 243. For Rev. Jonathan Greenleaf, a Grand Chaplain, and Rev. Seneca White, who presided over liberal churches, see E. E. Bourne, *History of Wells and Kennebunk* (Portland, 1875), 620ff. Other Universalists in Livermore Lodge were Wm. H. Brettin, Sr., a prosperous businessman and moderator of the Universalist church; and Cornelius Holland, a physician with a large practice who served in the legislature and Congress. Another Grand Chaplain was Reuben Nason, a Congregationalist minister, who was principal of Gorham Academy and first master of Gorham's Lodge organized in 1822. Sponsored by eminent local men, judges, lawyers, and doctors, Gorham became the pre-eminent academy in Maine. Nason, a Harvard graduate who did not take to the life of a pastor, preferred to prepare the offspring of the leading families in southern Maine to occupy their station in life. See Josiah Pierce, *A History of the Town of Gorham* (Portland, 1862), 149ff.; Nehemiah Cleveland, *History of Bowdoin College* (Boston, 1882), 77–78.

41. This is based on a comparison of the demographic characteristics of banner Antimasonic towns with those with Masonic Lodges, data drawn from the United States Census for 1820, and from the *Maine Register for 1829*, which lists churches, 119ff.

42. Table 6.8

43. Moses Thacher, *An Address Delivered before the Members of the Antimasonic State Convention . . . Augusta, Maine, July 4, 1832* (Hallowell, 1832), 3, 7, 31.

44. Antimasonry was extremely weak in York County, a Free Will Baptist stronghold and home of Parsonsfield Academy, the denominations' leading educational institution in Maine.

45. *Maine Free Press,* 11 May 1832. And see complaint that only two religious newspapers in New England opposed Masonry, *Maine Free Press,* 15 June 1832. For the Baptists see *Maine Free Press,* 18 May 1832. Henry S. Burrage, in *History of the Baptists in Maine* (Portland, 1904), notes that Baptists were active in the Antimasonic movement but though he gives a detailed history of denominational policy, he does not indicate that the Baptist convention took a position on Masonry.

46. *Maine Free Press,* 3, 10 Feb., 7 Sep. 1832; *Christian Mirror,* 26 Feb. 1829.

Table 6.8. Influence of Demographic Variables on the Party Vote in Maine, 1830–33 (Multiple Regression Betas)*

	1830 Gov. Democrats	Democrats	1833 Gov. Nat. Rep.	Antimasons
Agriculture 1840	−.037	−.055	.049	.050
Commerce	.018	−.011	.033	−.028
Manufacturing	−.006	−.137	.120	−.020
Navigation	.009	−.050	.020	−.091
Valuation 1840	−.249	−.262	.218	.048
Population change 1830	.015	−.030	.014	.168
Fishing 1850	−.001	−.002	.008	.005
Lumber labor force 1850	.120	−.082	−.017	−.045
Shipbuilding 1850	−.099	.119	−.076	−.010
Unitarian Accom. 1850	−.110	−.054	.031	.049
Congregationalists	−.089	−.026	.064	.108
Methodists	.045	.030	−.085	.101
Baptists	.067	.019	−.079	.140
Free Will Baptists	−.000	−.055	−.011	.095
Universalists 1840	.035	.005	.063	−.113
Episcopalians 1850	−.095	−.044	.087	.002
Quakers 1850	.015	.038	−.036	.024
R^2	.14	.12	.13	.07

* None of variables significant at .01 level.

At the 1832 Maine Antimasonic Party Convention, Moses Thacher singled out for attack, Rev. Thaddeus Harris, a prominent Unitarian and Mason. See Thacher, *Address, July 4, 1832,* p. 18.

47. See Thomas Adams, *Sermon Delivered in Augusta, Sept. 11, 1828, at the Annual Meeting of the Kennebec Conference of Churches* (Augusta, 1828), 5, 10, 11, 13, 14 for a post-millennialist Jeremiad.

48. *Maine Free Press,* 20 July 1832; for Sewall's role in the Antimasonic party see the *Maine Antimasonic Convention, 1834,* p. 3; other Hallowell Antimasons can also be found there, *passim.* For the history of Hallowell's churches, especially Old South, and for biographical sketches of Antimasons see Emma Huntington Nason, *Old Hallowell on the Kennebec* (Augusta, 1909), especially 207, 175, 330, 328, 194, for the quote, 193, and sectarian divisions in the church between Liberals and Conservatives, 33, 44, 52, 194. For a list of Hallowell Antimasons, five of whom were members of Old South, see *Maine Free Press,* 7 Sep. 1832.

49. David Thurston, *A Brief History of Winthrop* (Portland, 1855), 157ff., and *passim; Congregational Quarterly,* IX (Oct. 1867), 32. Hallowell's Deacons Gow and Sewall both attended Thurston's ordination.

50. Alfred Cole and Charles F. Whitman, *A History of Buckfield* (Buckfield, 1915), 23, 140ff. For battles over closed versus open communion and standards of discipline, worship styles, and abolitionism, see Rev. Joshua Millet, *A History of the Baptists in Maine,* . . . (Portland, 1845), 157; Henry S. Burrage, *History of the Baptists in Maine,* 189.

51. For Methodists see S. Allen, *History of Methodism in Maine,* 1793–1886 (Augusta, 1887), 406–8; for a Methodist Antimasonic preacher, Samuel Hillman,

see *Maine Free Press*, 5 Aug., 11 Sep. 1831; for a Freewill Baptist minister, Elder Joseph Robinson, see Rev. G. A. Burgess and J. T. Ward, eds., *Free Baptist Cyclopaedia* (Chicago, 1889), 576, 528ff., 326.

52. Paul Goodman, *The Democratic-Republicans of Massachusetts, Politics in a Young Republic* (Cambridge, Mass., 1964), 118ff. Under Maine law the first minister in each town, regardless of denomination, could claim ministerial lands, but the town meeting of Atkinson, Piscataquis County, voted in 1831 to use the proceeds from the sale of lands for a school fund rather than for Elder Nathaniel Harvey, a local minister. See Amore Loring, *History of Piscataquis County* (Portland, 1880), 94.

53. Calvin M. Clark, *History of the Maine Missionary Society, 1807–1825* (Portland, 1926), 13, 152, 181–82, 339. See also complaints of weakness in the *Minutes of the General Conference of Maine* (Portland, 1828).

54. Nehemiah Cleveland, *History of Bowdoin College,* 10ff. For Justice Story's opinion see *ibid.,* 103ff.; *Eastern Argus,* 24 Aug. 1830, 15, 22 Feb., 29 May, 3 June, 16, 23, 30 Aug. 1831, 5 March 1834.

55. L. Dana to Samuel Bell, 19 Jan. 1828, Samuel Bell Papers, NHHS; *Eastern Argus,* 18 June 1830. Both the National Republican and Jacksonian press injected religion into political discussion. Thus in 1828 the Nationals' *Kennebec Journal,* 21 Oct. 1828, accused the Jacksonians of palming their man off as a Methodist, Baptist, and Presbyterian among members of these denominations. Furthermore, by widely circulating the Coffin Handbill, reminding voters that Jackson practiced the Code Duello, violating Christian precepts, the Nationals raised questions about his moral fitness. The Jacksonians depicted the Nationals' claim to be the party of piety as the "mere hypocritical display of desperate sectarians. . . ." *Eastern Argus,* 2 Jan. 1829. See also, *ibid.,* 1 May 1829, and the Democratic tactic of alleging that the National candidate for governor, Jonathan G. Huntoon, was a Universalist among the Orthodox and Orthodox among Universalists, *Kennebec Journal,* 16 Oct. 1829.

56. *Eastern Argus,* 9 Aug. 1831, 4 Sep. 1829. *Eastern Argus,* 26 Feb. 1830, reported that the editor of the *Baptist Herald* incurred censure because he wrote a critical account of Hartford Convention Federalism. The *Eastern Argus,* 22 Jan. 1830, also praised John Leland, the iconoclastic Massachusetts Baptist, for opposition to the Sabbatarian movement and on 1 and 3 Aug. 1830 reprinted an address on behalf of religious freedom by Rev. Daniel Sharpe of Boston. See also Leland's defense of Jackson's Bank Policy, *Eastern Argus,* 28 Sep. 1832.

57. *New Hampshire Patriot,* 18 Jan. 1830; *Eastern Argus,* 16 Feb. 1830. The *Argus* also reprinted Methodist allegations that Calvinists plotted to take control of newspapers and public office, *Eastern Argus,* 27 Feb. 1829, 5, 12 March 1834. See also other efforts by Democrats to cultivate Methodists, *Eastern Argus,* 7, 11 Oct. 1831; F. O. J. Smith to Dr. J. Morrill, 8 Feb. 1835, Smith Mss., Maine Historical Society (MeHS); John Fairfield to wife, 5 Dec. 1835, Arthur G. Staples, ed., *The Letters of John Fairfield* (Lewiston, Maine, 1922), 25.

58. For Fairfield's Universalism, see Joseph Granger to John Fairfield, Calais, 13 Nov. 1831, Fairfield Mss., MeHS; and for Smith, M. Raynes to F. O. J. Smith, 2 June 1834, Smith Mss., MeHS, and A. Bailey to Smith, 20 Aug. 1834, who reported that the Whigs accused Smith among the Universalists of being an infidel while claiming among the Universalists that Churchill, the Whig candidate, was a Universalist.

59. Augustus Haines to John Fairfield, 31 Dec. 1832, Fairfield Papers, MeHS;

Charles Monroe to F. O. J. Smith, 13 April 1834, Smith Mss., MeHS, wrote, "The news of R. P. Dunlap's conversion was like an electric shock, it led his friends to staring and inquiring, and the leading religious fanatics of the day to crowing. . . ." See also Joel Chandler to Smith, 9 April 1834, Smith, MeHS.

60. Judah Dana to F. O. J. Smith, 4 April 1833, Smith Mss., MeHS.

61. See the *Christian Mirror,* 5 April 1832, which claimed it did not engage in politics because the Sabbath and Indian questions were moral, not political issues. See also the 27 Sep. 1832 issue, in which the *Mirror* criticized Christians for failing to do their duty in public life. See also *Kennebec Journal,* 19 Aug. 1831, which defended a National Republican editor from Democratic attacks that he was a "Revival editor," arguing that a person's religious opinions should not be an issue in politics.

62. *Kennebec Journal,* 9 Sep. 1834.

63. *One Hundred Years of Masonry, History of Penobscot Lodge No. 39,* pp. 17–18; Albert Moore, *History of North Star Lodge, No. 29, North Anson, Maine* (North Anson, Maine, 1875), 16–17; [Washburne], *History of Oriental Star Lodge,* 7–8. See also Drummond, *History of Portland Lodge,* for the impact of Antimasonry, 133ff.

Chapter 7. Antimasonry in Vermont

1. Henry S. Dana, *History of Woodstock* (Boston, 1889), 522, 532ff; *Journal of the General Assembly of the State of Vermont* (Woodstock, 1830), 22, 31, 55–6, 64–66, 167–68.

2. For an explanation of Vermont's glacial stability after 1850, see Hal S. Barron, *Those Who Stayed Behind, Rural Society in Nineteenth-Century New England* (Cambridge, 1984).

3. Lee S. Tillotson, *Ancient Craft Masonry in Vermont* (Montpelier, 1920), 15, 83ff.; David M. Ludlum, *Social Ferment in Vermont, 1781–1850* (Montpelier, 1948), 89ff.; Walter H. Crockett, *Vermont, The Green Mountain State,* 3 Vols. (New York, 1921), III, 228ff.

4. Tillotson, *Masonry in Vermont,* 123ff.; *Farmers' Herald,* 14 July 1828, 16 June, 28 July, 26 Aug., 2 Sep., 30 Sep., 7 Oct., 9 Dec., 1829. On the removals see the *North Star,* 6 July, 11 Aug. 1829, and Tillotson, *Masonry in Vermont,* 126.

5. Walter H. Crockett, *Vermont, The Green Mountain State,* 3, II, 611ff.; III, 124ff.

6. The town-level Antimasonic presidential vote in 1832 correlated with the Federalist gubernatorial vote in 1808 at −0.07 and with the National Republican vote in 1828 at 0.30. The National Republican presidential vote in 1828 correlated with 1808 at 0.04. Compare John Spargo, *The Rise and Progress of Freemasonry in Vermont,* who connected early Antimasonry with opposition to the Washington Benevolent Societies, grass-roots Federalist town organizations, c. 1812, pp. 52–56.

7. Table 7.1

8. Ludlum, *Social Ferment,* 112.

9. Table 7.2

10. *Vermont Antimasonic Convention, 1831,* p. 9; *Vermont Antimasonic Convention, 1833,* p. 9.

11. *Vermont Antimasonic Convention, 1833,* p. 29; *North Star,* 25 Aug. 1834.

12. Two-thirds of the 88 towns in which the party won a majority in 1832 gave Antimasons over 60% of their votes. So intense was Antimasonic sentiment that in better than 20% of these towns the party garnered three-quarters or more of the vote.

Table 7.1. Turnout in Vermont, 1828–38: Proportion of Adult White Males Voting

Election	% Adult Males Voting
1828 Gov.	28
1828 Pres.	54
1829 Gov.	42
1830 Gov.	49
1831 Gov.	54
1832 Gov.	64
1832 Pres.	50
1833 Gov.	60
1834 Gov.	60
1835 Gov.	53
1836 Gov.	55
1836 Pres.	53
1837 Gov.	60
1838 Gov.	65

Table 7.2. Where the Antimasonic Vote Came from: Vermont, 1828-32 (Ecological Regression Estimates)

1832 Governor	1828 President			
	Nat. Reps.	Dems. Reps.	Non-Voters	% Electorate
Antimasons	11%	− 4%	13%	20%
National Republicans	17%	1%	− 1%	18%
Democrats	2%	8%	1%	12%
Non-voters	9%	7%	34%	50%
% Electorate	39%	13%	48%	
N = 216 Towns				

13. *Antimasonic Convention, 1829,* quoted in *Antimasonic Review* I, No. 9, 283.

14. Ludlum, *Social Ferment,* 97.

15. *Ibid.,* 99; *Masonic Mirror,* 10 July 1830.

16. John Beckley, *History of Vermont* (Brattleboro, 1845), 161. For a modern historical view, see Barron, *Those Who Stayed Behind,* 23–25, 113, 129, 134.

17. *Bennington Gazette,* quoted in *Masonic Mirror,* 3 Aug. 1833.

18. For this study, Masonic leaders come from *An Appeal to the Inhabitants of Montpelier at the Annual Communication of the Grand Lodge, Oct. 1929* (Montpelier, 1829), 9–12. Antimasons are from lists of delegates at the Antimasonic state conventions, 1831–33. Biographical data come from a wide range of sources too numerous to detail, but primarily from town and country histories and Abbe Hemmenway, *The Vermont Historical Gazetteer,* 5 Vols. (1862–82), hereafter Hemmenway, *Gazetteer.* Occupational data were found for 43 Masons and 54 Antimasons.

19. Table 7.3

20. Plotting Antimasonic strength against modern classification of town land

Table 7.3. Demographic Characteristics of the Party Vote in Vermont, 1828–40: Multiple Regression Betas (b) and Pearson Coefficients (r)

Demographic Variables	1828 President National Republican		1832 President National Republican		1832 President Antimason		1832 President Democrat		1836 President Whig		1840 President Whig	
	b	r	b	r	b	r	b	r	b	r	b	r
Sheep	.072*	.17	.057*	.19	-.015*	.06	-.036*	-.11	.034	.10	.103	.17
Population Change	.049	-.10	-.082	-.23	.173	.19	-.141	-.01	-.062	-.15	-.132	-.23
Valuation	.213	.24	.282	.40	-.077	-.19	-.20	-.17	NC		.115	.19
Agriculture	.053	.01	.054	-.17	.037	.16	-.11	-.03	-.036	-.06	-.045	-.12
Commerce	-.118	-.08	.111	.17	-.131	-.17	.06	.05	-.016*	.02	.027*	.09
Oats	NC		NC		NC		NC		.001	-.02	-.092	-.10
Congregational	.094	.18	.172	.27	.002*	.03	-.181	-.24	.270	.28	.167	.22
Baptist	.288	.31	.045	.08	.069	.06	-.136	-.17	.132	.18	.117	.23
Methodist	-.099	-.04	.006*	-.01	-.064	-.02	.077	.04	-.183	-.17	-.136	-.17
Free Will Baptist	-.157	-.25	-.062	-.16	-.053	-.03	.132	.20	-.015*	-.11	-.163	-.26
Episcopal	.050	.07	.023	.09	-.023*	-.07	.007*	.01	NC		NC	
Universalist	.037	.06	-.121	-.11	.159	.15	-.84	-.08	.154	.13	.133	.13
R²	.23		.23		.11		.15		.17		.13	

* Regression coefficients not significant at 1%.

according to suitability for commercial agriculture shows that the two strongest Anti-masonic counties rank sixth and seventh, about in the middle. When comparing the land quality profile of town with their partisan preferences, Nationals ran best in towns with the best land, Democrats in towns with poor land, while Antimasonic towns fell between. Land classification information comes from William J. Wilgus, *The Role of Transportation in the Development of Vermont* (Montpelier, 1945), 38–39. The election data are from the 1832 gubernatorial returns, Vermont State Archives.

21. *Vermont Antimasonic Convention, 1830,* p. 14.

22. "Documents Relative to Manufactures," *The New American State Papers, Manufactures,* 9 Vols. (reprint, Wilmington, Del., 1972), vol. 5, p. 206ff.

23. Lewis D. Stilwell, *Emigration from Vermont 1776–1800,* (Montpelier, 1937), 64ff., 103ff., 124ff.; Harold F. Wilson, *The Hill Country of Northern New England,* 15ff., 17ff.; William S. Rossiter, "Vermont, An Historical and Statistical Study of the Population of the State," *American Statistical Association,* New Series, 93 (March 1911), 338–454; Ludlum, *Social Ferment,* 4ff.; Crockett, *Vermont,* II, 500ff., III, 195ff., 218ff.; Wilgus, *Role of Transportation,* 33–40, 23; Chester W. Wright, *Wool Growing and the Tariff* (Boston, 1910), *passim.*

24. Wilgus, *The Role of Transportation,* 41ff; for the growth of commercial banking, see Zadock Thompson, *History of Vermont . . .* (Burlington, 1853), Part II, 132ff.

25. Samuel Swift, *History of the Town of Middlebury* (Middlebury, 1859), 95.

26. Stillwell, *Migration,* 124ff., 133–34, 137, 142, 151ff., 171; Ludlum, *Social Ferment,* 26; Roth, "Whence This Strange Fire?," ch. 3; 211ff., 275ff.

27. Roth, "Whence This Strange Fire?," 194ff., table at 229; H. J. Conant, "Imprisonment for Debt in Vermont, A History," *Vermont History* 19 (April 1951), 67–80, and for contemporary comment, *Universalist Watchman,* 13 April 1833. See William Monroe Newton, *History of Barnard,* 2 Vols. (Montpelier, 1928), I, 272–73, for a hill town in Windsor County whose population tripled 1790–1830 and then declined. In the 1830s, 200 migrated to thriving Ware, Massachusetts, and only two returned.

28. Rossiter, "Vermont," 139, 420.

29. Roth, "Whence This Strange Fire?," 30.

30. Tillotson, *Masonry in Vermont,* 127; *North Star,* 20 May, 14 July, 7 Oct. 1828, 23 June 1833.

31. *Rutland Herald,* quoted in *North Star,* 4 Oct. 1831.

32. Tillotson, *Masonry in Vermont,* 127.

33. Information on the location of Lodges appears in *Records of the Grand Lodge of Free and Accepted Masons of the State of Vermont from 1794 to 1846 Inclusive* (Burlington, Vt., 1879), 420; Tillotson, *Masonry in Vermont,* 70–77; data for lawyers and doctors appear in *Walton's Vermont Register and Farmers' Almanac for 1830* (Montpelier, 1830).

34. Roth, "Whence This Strange Fire?," 264ff.

35. *An Appeal . . . by . . . the Grand Lodge,* 1829, pp. 9–12. See, for example, Chapin and Rawsell Keith in Hemmenway, *Gazetteer,* IV, 281, 510; William Barron in Silas McKeen, *A History of Bradford* (Montpelier, 1875), 186ff.; Timothy Hubbard in Hemmenway, *Gazetteer,* IV, 441; Hemmenway, *Gazetteer,* I, 545; John Pomeroy in *ibid.,* I, 543; Butler in *ibid.,* I, 576ff.; Joseph Farnsworth in Rev. Henry Crocker, *History of the Baptists in Vermont* (Bellows Falls, Vt., 1913), 599–600,

and Hemmenway, *Gazetteer,* II, 178–79, 196; Job Lyman in *Vermont Register, 1830,* p. 141; Samuel Elliott in Henry Burnham, *Brattleboro* (Brattleboro, 1880), 79–80 and Hemmenway, *Gazetteer,* V, 79; Sam Goss and Oramel Smith in Hemmenway, *Gazetteer,* IV, 469–71.

36. Ludlum, *Social Ferment,* 110–11; *Farmers' Herald,* 30 Sep. 1830, 20 Jan. 1830; *Vermont Journal,* 18 April 1829; Hemmenway, *Gazetteer,* I, 396; Fairbanks, *The Town of St. Johnsbury, Vt.,* 305ff., 496–97.

37. This is based on tallying the clergymen in the Antimasonic Convention proceedings, *The North Star, Vermont Gazette, Farmers' Herald* and other sources listing ministers. For pro-Masonic clergy, see the list of Grand Lodge Chaplains in Tillotson, *Masonry in Vermont,* 67.

38. Ludlum, *Social Ferment,* 25–62; William G. McGloughlin, *New England Dissent* II, 789–813; Thompson, *History of Vermont,* ch. 9. For two fine accounts of the growth of popular religion in New England after the American Revolution see Stephen A. Marini, *Radical Sects of Revolutionary New England* (Cambridge, Mass., 1982), and Nathan O. Hatch, "The Christian Movement and the Demand for a Theology of the People," *Journal of American History* 67 (Dec. 1980), 545–67.

39. Crocker, *Baptists in Vermont,* 14–15.

40. *Ibid.,* 236–37, 394ff., 429; William B. Sprague, *Annals of the American Pulpit,* 9 Vols. (New York, 1859–69), VI, 411ff.; *Proceedings, Vermont Historical Society* (1919–20), 215–44.

41. Mary G. Canfield, *Early Universalism in Vermont and the Connecticut Valley* (Unpublished ms., 1941), Andover-Harvard Library; Edith F. MacDonald, *Rebellion in the Mountains: The Story of Universalism and Unitarianism in Vermont* (Concord, N.H., 1976); Carol Morris, "A Comparison of Ethan Allen's *Reason the Only Oracle of Man* and Hosea Ballou's *A Treatise on Atonement,*" *Annual Journal of Universalist Historical Society* II (1960–61), 234–69; Marini, *Radical Sects of Revolutionary New England, passim;* William S. Gribbin, "Vermont's Universalist Controversy of 1824," *Vermont History* 41 (Spring 1973), 82–94.

42. Thompson, *History of Vermont,* 180ff., for brief accounts of various denominations.

43. See Table 7.4.

44. *Farmers' Herald,* 8 April 1829.

45. Roth, "Whence This Strange Fire?," 125; Tillotson, *Masonry in Vermont,* 130.

46. *North Star,* 20 May, 3 June 1828, 26 May 1829, 29 June 1830, 27 May 1833. Also see note 18. Congregationalist ministers such as Cabot's Henry Jones, Peacham's Leonard Worcester, West Fairlee's Stephen Herick, and Montpelier's Chester Wright joined the Antimasonic cause, while Williston's James Johnson, Springfield's Robinson Smiley, and St. Alban's Jonathan Nye stuck by the Freemasons. Among Antimasonic Baptists were Chester's Aaron Leland, Waterbury's Ezra Butler, Orwell's Nathaniel Colver, Thetford's Thomas Spaulding, Danvillee's Lewis Fisher, and Georgia's Alvah Sabin; not a single Baptist minister was found sticking by the Masons. Methodist Seth Sterling of Woodstock took the Antimasonic side, but Northfield's Joel Winch defended Masonry, as did Joel Clapp, Episcopal minister at Shelburne.

47. John Spargo, *The Rise and Progress of Freemasonry in Vermont* (n.p., 1944), 49ff.; Crocker, *Vermont Baptists,* 45ff.; Wallace S. Boardman, *Historical Sketch of the Baptist Church in Addison, Vermont, 1797–1919* (n.p. 1919), 5–6.

48. *Masonic Mirror,* 15, 22 Aug. 1829, 2 Nov. 1833.

49. John M. Comstock, *The Congregational Churches of Vermont and Their Ministry, 1762–1914, Historical and Statistical* (St. Johnsbury, Vt., 1915); Samuel Swift, *History of the Town of Middlebury* (Middlebury, 1859), 377ff.; Julian I. Lindsay, *Tradition Looks Forward, The University of Vermont: A History, 1791–1904* (Burlington, 1954); McDonald, *Rebellion in the Mountains,* 64; W. S. Rann, *History of Chittenden County* (Syracuse, 1886), 197ff.

50. *Farmers' Herald,* 23 Dec. 1828.

51. *North Star,* 30 Nov. 1830, *Farmers' Herald,* 1 Dec. 1830; Comstock, *Congregational Churches of Vermont,* 49–50, and for biographical details of Danville's ministers, see the alphabetical list following p. 126. Unless otherwise noted Comstock is the source of similar church and ministerial data for other towns discussed below. *Annual Report,* American Education Society (Feb. 1841), 281–82; Hemmenway, *Gazetteer,* I, 315, and 318–19 for Danville's Antimasonic leaders, Gov. William Palmer and editor Ebenezer Eaton.

52. Ernest L. Bogart, *Peacham, The Story of a Vermont Hill Town* (Springfield, 1948), 207, 204–5, 171, 176–88; *Annual Report,* American Education Society (Feb. 1841), 283; Sprague, *Annals,* II, 455–60; Thaddeus Stevens, a leading Antimason in Pennsylvania, grew up in Danville and Peacham where he attended the academy. His mother, Sarah, was a Baptist of "deep piety." Fawn M. Brodie, *Thaddeus Stevens* (New York, 1959), 23–24.

53. For Barnett, see Hemmenway, *Gazetteer,* I, 271ff. The town's Antimasonic delegates appear in the proceedings of the state Antimasonic conventions and the town's representatives to the Vermont legislature in John M. Comstock, ed., *A List of the Principal Civil Officers of Vermont from 1777 to 1918* (St. Albans, Vt., 1918), 70 and the index which identifies others who held county and state offices. For Ryegate, see Thompson, *History of Vermont,* Part III, 154; Hemmenway, *Gazetteer,* I, 377; Comstock, *Civil Offices,* 205.

54. U. C. Burnap, *Priestcraft Exposed, A Lecture, Delivered in Chester, April 9, 1830. Being the Annual Fast; Together with an Essay on the Clergy of the United States* (Windsor, 1830), 4, 16, 25, 35ff., and *passim.*

55. For Smiley see Hubbard, *History of Springfield,* 124; Comstock, *Congregational Churches,* 168–69; for Johnson, Comstock, *Congregational Churches,* 152–53. The following Masons who defended the order after 1829 were on the Board of Trustees in the 1820s: D. Azro Buck, Daniel Kellogg, E. D. Woodbridge, Joseph D. Farnsworth, Rev. Simeon Parmlet (a Congregationalist), Rev. Joel Clapp (an Episcopalian), and Ezra Meech. Other Masons included faculty and officers such as Dr. John Pomeroy, Prof. James Dean; honorary degree recipients included leading Masons Geo. E. Wales, Rev. Silas McKeen (1828), Jonathan P. Miller (1829), and P. C. Tucker (1835). See, for example, the battle against Freemasonry in St. Johnsbury (75% Antimasonic in 1832), where the Fairbanks family, leading businessmen and Masons, were forced to abandon the Order. Members of the First Church, which had begun with Hopkinsian leaders such as the Fairbanks and others, broke away to establish North Church led by Rev. James Johnson, a Mason and a Harvard liberal trained by the Unitarian leader Henry Ware. By contrast liberals controlled the First Congregationalist Church in Montpelier, with its numerous modernizing bourgeoisie who forced out Rev. Chester Wright, a staunch Antimason, who had received his training under Hopkinsian, Asa Burton. For St. Johnsbury see Fairbanks, *St. Johnsbury,* 216–17, 131ff., 306ff., 402; *Dictionary of American Biography,* III, 249;

McDonald, *Rebellion in the Mountains*, 63; Comstock, *Congregational Churches,* 96–97; *Annual Report,* American Education Society (Feb. 1841), 283–84. *Cf.* Roth, "Whence This Strange Fire?," 260ff.; *Farmers' Herald,* 20 Jan. 1830; *North Star,* 28 Oct. 1831; *Records of the Grand Lodge of . . . Vermont,* 360. For Wright, see Sprague, *Annals,* II, 145; *Vermont Antimasonic Convention, 1833,* p. 3; *North Star,* 26 Aug. 1833, 30 June 1834; Thompson, *History of Vermont,* II, 204; Hemmenway, *Gazetteer,* I, 323ff.; Comstock, *Congregational Churches,* 61, 77; Hemmenway, *Gazetteer,* IV, 251ff., 350–51 for an account of Aurora Lodge with a list of its members.

56. *Extracts from the Minutes of the General Convention of the Congregational and Presbyterian Ministers in Vermont . . . 1830* (Windsor, 1830), 12; *Minutes of the General Convention, 1831* (Windsor, 1831), 9.

57. *Minutes of the General Convention, 1829* (Windsor, 1829), 11ff.

58. *Vermont Chronicle,* 23 Oct., 20 Nov. 1829, 3 Oct. 1834.

59. See the *Minutes of the General Convention of the Congregational . . . Ministers in Vermont . . . 1834* (Windsor, 1834), 8; for 1835, 9ff.; 1836, 11.

60. Spargo, *Freemasonry in Vermont,* 50ff.; Crocker, *Vermont Baptists,* 120–23, 144, 147, 153, 288, 354, 364; for Hurlburt, *North Star,* 17 Feb. 1829; *cf.* Baptists who defended Masonry, *Vermont Journal,* 18 April 1829; for expulsions see the *Records of the Grand Lodge of Free and Accepted Masons of . . . Vermont . . . 1794–1846,* pp. 357, 379; for Leland and Butler see *Vermont Antimasonic State Convention, 1830,* p. 1, 18ff.

61. Crocker, *Vermont Baptists,* 119ff.

62. *Vermont Antimasonic Convention, 1830,* pp. 20, 24.

63. Crocker, *Vermont Baptists,* 288, and for the moderators, 639.

64. Hemmenway, *Gazetteer,* III, 865 and 846ff.; *Annual Report,* American Education Society (Aug. 1841), 38; Crocker, *Vermont Baptists,* 166, 237, 264–65; Nathan T. Sprague, Mt. Holly delegate to the Antimasonic Convention in 1831, served as the representative in the legislature, 1816–17, 1822–25, and 1830. The Masons expelled him in 1831. For economic data on Mt. Holly see the summary of the 1840 census in Thompson, *Gazetteer of Vermont,* 123, and the general list for the town's tax assessment in 1827, found at the end of the *Journal of the General Assembly of the State of Vermont . . . 1827* (Woodstock, 1828), pullout.

65. Rev. Edward B. Rollins, *Antimasonic Tract, No. 3, Containing the Renunciations of Free Masonry by the Rev. Edward B. Rollins, of Strafford, Vermont* (Boston, 1829), 3, 6, 11, *passim.* Rollins addressed his circular "To the People Denominated Christian Brethren." For the Christians, see Nathan O. Hatch, "The Christian Movement and the Demand for a Theology of the People," 545–67; Thompson, *History of Vermont,* 190ff. Daniel Cobb of Strafford was the town's foremost Antimasonic politician and later became a Democrat. Strafford Christians dated from 1811, its Free Baptists from 1793, and its Baptists from 1791. The Universalists, organized in the late 1790s, became the largest society and obtained the glebe lands. It later declined but revived in the 1820s. For Cobb see Hemmenway, *Gazetteer,* II, 805–6 and for Strafford's churches, *ibid.,* 1077ff.

66. Rollins, *Antimasonic Tract,* 12; on the Woodstock Christians, see Dana, *History of Woodstock,* 394ff., 527ff., 533.

67. For Free Will Baptists, Nathaniel King of Tunbridge (56% Antimasonic in 1832), see Hemmenway, *Gazetteer,* II, 1124ff.; *Walton's Vermont Register, 1830,*

listed four Free Will Baptist preachers in Tunbridge. Elijah Dickerman and Deacon Peabody were both Antimasonic leaders in this town, *North Star,* 20 May 1828. For King see also Burgess and Ward, *Free Baptist Cyclopaedia,* 322. For a modern account of the origins of the Free Will Baptists see Marini, *Radical Sects, passim.* For Clafflin see Hemmenway, *Gazetteer* II, 860–61. Nathan Wheatley, son of a town prominent, large landowner and noted for his firm principles and religiosity, was an Antimasonic leader. The Wheatleys were also prominent in the town's political life. See Hemmenway, *Gazetteer,* II, 867. For another Christian who renounced Freemasonry, see *North Star,* 2 June 1829. For a pro-Hicksite Quaker, Seth Griffith, Grand Island, see Hemmenway, *Gazetteer,* II, 532ff. See the discussion of the Hicksites in Chapter 4.

68. *Vermont Antimasonic Convention, 1832,* p. 22; McDonald, *Rebellion in the Mountains,* 151–55; Loveland founded the *Universalist Register* (1820) and trained several preachers.

69. *North Star,* 6 July 1930.

70. For Flint, see Hemmenway, *Gazetteer,* II, 1058ff.; for Eggerton see *ibid.,* 996–98, IV, 457; McDonald, *Rebellion in the Mountains,* 194. The third Randolph member of the state committee was Calvin Blodget, Hemmenway, *Gazetteer,* II, 1016. For Jennison, see *ibid.,* I, 119; McDonald, *Rebellion in the Mountains,* 59, 197, 199. For Universalist involvement with Norwich University see McDonald, *Revolt in the Mountains,* 41ff., and William A. Ellis, *Norwich University, 1819–1911,* 3 Vols. (Montpelier, 1911), I, 72ff. Jennison was a trustee of Norwich from 1834–49, and several prominent Antimasons also served on the board of trustees, as did Jedidiah H. Harris of Strafford, another Universalist politician.

71. For the number of Universalist societies in Vermont see *Evangelical Magazine* (Utica), 26 Feb. 1831.

72. For an account of prominent Universalist laymen, see McDonald, *Rebellion in the Mountains,* 190ff. In the 1840s Whigs nominated Universalist Carlos Coolidge for presidential elector and governor (1848–50).

73. For evidence of Antimasonic/Whig dealings in the election of Samuel Swift to the U.S. Senate, *Masonic Mirror,* 9 Nov. 1832. See also Whig refusal to back Gov. Palmer again in 1835, *Rutland Herald,* 3 Nov. 1835; *North Star,* 11 Jan. 1836.

74. At the 1836 Antimasonic State Convention the vote to endorse Whig William Henry Harrison for President was 104 to 40. *North Star,* 7 March 1836.

75. The *North Star* of 22 Sep. 1834 estimated that the Antimasons had 115 in the house and executive council to 113 for the combined opposition.

76. Compare *Journal of the General Assembly for Vermont, 1830* (Woodstock, 1830), 11, 18, 20–21, with *Journal of the General Assembly . . . Vermont, 1831,* pp. 69–70. See also the maneuvering in 1833: *Journal of the General Assembly of . . . Vermont, 1833,* pp. 10, 15, 32, 34, 41, 62; for 1834 see *Journals, 1834,* pp. 11, 16, 36; and for 1835, pp. 10, 32; *North Star,* 5 Nov. 1832.

77. Tables 7.4, 7.5

78. *Assembly Journal, 1830,* p. 53; *Laws of Vermont, 1830,* p. 42; *Vermont Laws, 1833,* p. 20.

79. *Assembly Journal, 1831,* p. 27; 1832, pp. 45, 150, 156, 158; 1833, pp. 22, 36, 161, 192, 193, 189.

80. Table 7.6

81. For the numbers of bank requests see the index in the *Vermont General Assembly,* 1830–35, and for the charters granted see the *Vermont Laws* for those years.

Table 7.4. Legislative Appointments to County Office, Vermont 1821–45 (Numbers of Persons, All Counties)

	Clerk of Court	Sheriff	State's Attorney	Probate Judge	Asst. Judge	Total	% Change From Preceding Five Years
1821–25	1	9	20	24	50	104	—
1826–30	3	12	17	18	34	84	20
1831–35	5	25	21	24	47	122	45
1836–40	12	27	29	26	57	151	25
1841–45	7	27	27	20	57	138	−9

Source: John M. Comstock ed., *A List of the Principal Civil Officers of Vermont from 1777 to 1918* (St. Albans, 1918), 300–351.

Table 7.5. Incidence of Long Tenured Legislators, Vermont, 1820–39 (Four Terms+)

Number of long-tenured Legislators	1820–29 118		1830–39 61			
					All Towns' Party	
Long-Tenured Legislators and Party	1820–29		1830–39		Preferences	
	%	N	%	N	%	N
Antimasonic Towns	55	63	56	30	50	109
National Republican Towns	26	30	31	17	30	66
Democratic Towns	18	21	13	7	19	42

Source: John M. Comstock, *A List of the Principal Civil Officers of Vermont*, 71–263, for the town representatives. Towns were classified according to which party won a plurality in the 1832 presidential election.

For the Safety Fund Measure, see *Vermont Laws, 1831*, p. 20, and *Vermont General Assembly, 1831*, p. 23.

82. *Vermont General Assembly, 1832*, p. 44; *1834*, p. 35; *North Star*, 23 Dec. 1833, 30 June, 27 Oct. 1834, 27 July 1835.

83. For the road measure see *Vermont Laws, 1831*, p. 4, and for the roll calls see Table 7.6, note 80.

84. Peter J. Coleman, *Debtors and Creditors in America* (Madison, 1974), 65–73; H. U. Conant, "Imprisonment for Debt in Vermont," 67–80; for legislative consideration see the index to the Vermont *Assembly Journals*, 1830–35, and for the failure to pass a bill in 1835, see *Vermont General Assembly, 1835*, pp. 56, 78, 223–25, 226–27, 228–29. For Gov. Palmer's views, see *Vermont General Assembly, 1831*, p. 27; Bell's report appears in the *Assembly Journal*, 1834, p. 224.

85. *Masonic Mirror*, 3 Aug. 1833; *North Star*, 7 Sep. 1830, 18 Aug. 1834; The *North Star* printed many attacks on African colonization: 1 April, 8 July, 27 May, 18 March 1833, 31 March, 7 April, 23 June, 18 Aug. 1834.

86. *Rutland Herald*, 17 Nov. 1835.

87. *Journal of the Convention Holden at Montpelier, 1836,* (St. Albans, Vt.,

Table 7.6. Cohesion in the Vermont House of Representatives, 1831–35 (Indices of Cohesion)

	National Antimasons	Republican/Whigs	# Democrats	Roll Calls
1831	16	17	33	6
1832	23	48	55	3
1833	42	NC	NC	8
1834	15	24	22	7
1835	28	42	63	10
1831–35	26	31	42	34
		Banking Roll Calls		
1831–35	17	25	39	12
		Social Issue Roll Calls		
1831–35	37	NC	NC	10
1831–35	24	45	45	5

Note and sources: Perfect cohesion = 100. The party identification of legislators is based on the town's vote in the 1832 presidential election since, except for 1833, there were no organizational roll calls that permitted identification. Comparing this indirect method of identifying a legislator's party affiliation with the 1833 roll call produced little disagreement in identifying Antimasons but since Whigs and Democrats combined in the 1833 roll call, they could not be distinguished, and were not included in the table for that year.

Sources:

Year	Roll Call	Vermont General Assembly, *Journal,* page
1831	To charter Middlebury Bank, second reading	125–26
	To repeal road commissioners law	141–42
	To incorporate Bellows Falls Bank	163–64
	To postpone bill to abolish debt imprisonment	164–65
	To dismiss wild land tax	153–55
	To refer to next session Bellows Falls Canal Bill	158–59
1832	To incorporate Bank of Manchester	97
	To incorporate Essex Bank	126
	To postpone anti-oath bill	156
1833	To instruct United States Senators on Internal Improvements	129–31
	To postpone liquor license bill	143
	To dismiss witness competency bill	163
	To dismiss resolution opposing slave trade	191
	To dismiss bill to ban extra-judicial oaths	189
	To pay Rev. T. Spicer for Election Sermon	25–26
	To abolish Election Sermon	118
	To postpone incorporation of Farmers' Bank	167–68
1834	To dismiss resolution opposing slavery and slave trade	49
	To dismiss resolution requiring bank reporting	135
	To charter Poultney Bank	175–76
	To charter Farmer and Mechanics Bank	146
	To charter Brandon Bank	172–73
	To dismiss bill to ban small bills	189
	To amend repeal of license law	190
1835	Rep. Buck's amendment for speaker to invite Montpelier clergy as chaplains	11–13
	Second reading to create Lamoille County	76
	To dismiss charter for Vermont Life Insurance Co.	106
	To postpone St. Alban's Bank recharter	168

1836), for the proposed amendments, 1off., the roll call on the senate, 41–44; and popular election of probate judges, 76–79. For earlier demands for reform, see the *North Star*, 3 April 1827, *Vermont Journal*, 24 May 1828, 11 July 1829; Pliny White to David Crawford, Montpelier, 7 Jan. 1835, Putney Town Papers, Vermont Historical Society (VtHS). The *North Star* ran a pro-amendment series, 2, 16 Nov. 1835.

88. *Constitutional Convention, 1836*, pp. 22–35 for the Censors' address.

89. Tillotson, *Vermont Masonry*, 97ff., 105, 148ff.; *Record of the Grand Lodge of Free and Accepted Masons*, 373ff., 392, 399.

90. Tillotson, *Vermont Freemasonry*, 139; *North Star*, 29 Nov. 1831, 4 Aug., 14 July 1834. For a thoughtful Whig view see William Henry to Reuben Washburn, Ludlow, 11 Oct. 1833, Washburn Royce Papers, VtHS.

91. *North Star*, 21 July 1831, 8 July 1833.

92. *Masonic Mirror*, 16 Sep. 1833; *Vermont Gazette*, 12, 26 July 1833; *North Star*, 22 July, 27 Aug., 9 Sep. 1833.

93. Julius Y. Dewey to David Crawford, Putney, 7 May 1834, Putney Town Papers, VtHS; *Vermont Gazette*, 23 Nov. 1835; *Rutland Herald*, 14 July 1835, 28 July 1835. H. F. Jarvis to S. S. Crafts, Waterbury, 6 July 1835, appealing for Whig support for Palmer, VtHS. *Letters of Mr. William Slade to Mr. Hallett, Feb. 1836* (Washington, D.C., 1836), was an important pamphlet by an Antimasonic Whig attacking the efforts of Benjamin Hallett, a Massachusetts Antimason, editor of the *Boston Advocate*, to lure Antimasons into the Democratic party.

94. *Rutland Herald*, 28 July, 11 Aug. 1835, 2 Feb., 1 March, 1836; Zimri Howe, to William Slade, Castleton, 21 Jan. 1836, Sheldon Library, Middebury, Vt.; Carlos Coolidge to [?] Williams, Windsor, 25 July 1836, Coolidge Papers, University of Vermont; *North Star*, 8 Feb., 7 March 1836.

95. Table 7.7

96. See Table 7.3. The Free Will Baptist statistic for 1836 is puzzling and deviates from the pattern 1828–40, similar to findings in other New England states showing strong affinity for the Democrats.

97. *North Star*, 22 Feb., 11 April, 23 May, 6 June, 11, 25 July, 15 Aug. 1836, and for an interesting post-mortem after the Democratic defeat, *North Star*, 26 Sep. 1836, and the *Boston Advertiser*, 12, 15 Sep. 1836, which blamed the defeat on the Democrats' failure to nominate Palmer and other Antimasons.

98. Top Masonic Democrats included Nathaniel Haswell, Ebenezer Englesby, John Hollenbeck, and Philip C. Tucker. Haswell and Tucker were Grand Masters. Tucker was an Episcopalian, Englesby a Unitarian, and Haswell is described as sympathizing with both denominations. Tillotson, *Vermont Masonry*, 148ff., 162ff.,

---

Table 7.7. Where the Antimasonic Vote Went: Regression Estimates: Vermont 1832–36

1836 President	1832 Governor				
	Antimasons	Whigs	Demo	% Non-Voters	Electorate
Whigs	9	14	0	9	31
Democrats	2	− 1	11	8	21
Nonvoters	10	4	1	34	48
% Electorate	21	17	12	51	

N = 214 Towns

169, 174ff.; Hemmenway, *Gazetteer,* I, 545, 627. For Haswell's efforts to make the Bank of Burlington a pet bank, see N. P. Haswell's Private Memorandum on his mission to Washington (1833); E. J. English, Pres. of the Bank of Burlington, to Secretary of the Treasury, no date; A. C. Flagg to William T. Barry, Albany, 24 Oct. 1833, VtHS. And for Hollenbeck's involvement in Democratic party strategy see his letter to [?] Whittmore, Burlington, 25 May 1836, VtHS, in which he opposed making a direct appeal to Antimasons, though he was willing to put Antimasons on the ticket. He advised: "Be sure and not nominate any two-sided skunk who after he was elected would refuse to vote for our whole ticket."

99. *History of Rising Sun Lodge No. 7, Royalton Vt.* (n.d., n.p.), 4.

100. Tillotson, *Vermont Masonry,* 131, n. 51.

101. *Ibid.,* 115. The Antimasonic 1832 vote which correlated with the Whig vote in 1836 and 1840 at 0.27 and 0.17 correlated with the Liberty party in 1840 at 0.13 and in 1844 at 0.19. In 1848 the Antimasonic vote correlated with the Free Soil Party at 0.17 and with the Whigs at 0.08. Many leaders of the Vermont abolitionist and later political antislavery movements had earlier supported the Antimasonic movement, such as E. D. Barber, Lawrence Brainerd, Revs. Chester Wright and Alvah Sabin.

102. *Constitution of the Antimasonic Society, of Windham County, Vermont,* Uncatalogued Mss., VtHS.

Chapter 8. Massachusetts Antimasons

1. For "Masonic Murders," see *Eaton's Antimasonic Almanac for 1834* (Danville, Vt., n.d.), not paginated [32–35]; *Masonic Mirror,* 3, 10, 17, 24 April 1830; *Lynn Record,* 1 May 1830; *Massachusetts Antimasonic Convention, 1831* (Boston, 1831), 9–10. A copy of the Anderton Handbill appears with the *Daily Advocate Extra, Addresses of the Antimasonic Republican Convention to the People of Massachusetts,* Sep. 5, 6, 1832 (n.d., n.p.).

2. For valuable narrative histories of the Massachusetts Antimasonic party see Formisano, *Transformation of Political Culture,* 197–221, and Vaughn, *The Antimasonic Party in the United States,* 115–32. *Massachusetts Antimasonic Convention, 1829–1830, passim;* Charles P. Sumner, *A Letter on Speculative Free Masonry . . .* (Boston, 1829); *Pawtucket Herald & Independent Inquirer,* 7, 28 Jan. 1829.

3. *Columbian Centinel,* 16 Oct. 1830.

Table 8.1. The Antimasonic Elections in Massachusetts, 1831–34

		Nat. Rep/Whig	Dem.	Antimason	Workingmen	Turnout
1828	Pres.	83	17			24
1831	Gov.	54	21	25		36
1832	Pres.	53	23	24		39
1832	Gov.	53	24	23		41
1833	Gov.	40	25	29	6	39
1834	Gov.	58	25	13	3	46

4. Formisano is especially valuable on this distinction, *Transformation of Political Culture,* Part Two, "Social Movements and the Formation of Mass Parties," 173ff.

5. On the decision to enter politics, see *Massachusetts Antimasonic Convention, 1831,* Abner Phelps, 17ff., and John Bailey, 29ff.; on the tract society, 61; "Reply to the Declaration of the 1200 Masons," *Boston Daily Advocate,* Extra, 5 Oct. 1832.

6. Table 8.1

7. Samuel F. Bemis, *John Quincy Adams and the Union* (New York, 1956), 291ff.; John Q. Adams, *Letters on the Entered Apprentices Oath.*

8. *Investigation into Freemasonry by a Joint Committee of the Legislature of Massachusetts,* 13, 74–75.

9. Daniel Webster to John Davis, Boston, 14 Aug. 1834, *The Writings and Speeches of Daniel Webster* 18 Vols. (Boston, 1903), vol. 16, pp. 242–43; *Columbia Centinel,* 16, 23 Aug. 1834, 10, 17 Sep. 1834.

10. One of the richest sources of information on Massachusetts politics in the 1830s are the papers of Edward Everett, available on microfilm. See especially Everett to Alexander Everett, Washington, 4 Dec. 1832, 13 Feb. 1833; Everett to the Antimasons of Middlesex County, Philadelphia, 12 March 1833; Everett to Daniel Webster, Washington, 9 Aug. 1833; Webster to Everett, 11 Aug. 1833; Everett to Caleb Cushing, Wash., 8 Dec. 1832, Everett Papers, Reel 5; *Massachusetts Centinel,* 17, 20 July 1833.

11. Edward Everett and Antimasonry, *M.H.S. Prod.,* 2 ser. 18 (1903–1904), 108–109.

12. The best account of Massachusetts politics in this period is Formisano, *Transformation of Political Culture,* chs. 3–8. See also Arthur B. Darling, *Political Changes in Massachusetts 1824–1828* (reprint, Cos Cobb, Conn., 1968), chs. 1, 2. Andrew R. L. Cayton, "The Fragmentation of a Great Family," *Journal of the Early Republic* II (Summer 1982), pp. 146–67.

13. Justin Winsor, *Memorial History of Boston,* 4 Vols. (Boston, 1880–81), III, 236.

14. For the confusion in politics, see Joseph S. Buckingham, *Personal Memoirs and Recollections of Editorial Life,* 2 Vols. (Boston, 1854), II, 13–14; Theodore Lyman, Jr., to Levi Woodbury, 22 Dec. 1828, Woodbury Papers, Library of Congress (LC).

15. Ebenezer Seaver, to Levi Woodbury, Roxbury, 28 March 1830, Woodbury Papers, LC.

16. For evidence of factionalism, see Samuel E. Morison, *The Life and Letters of Harrison G. Otis,* 2 Vols. (Boston, 1917), II, 237, 290; Buckingham, *Personal Memoirs,* II, 12ff.; Robert McCaughey, *Josiah Quincy, 1772–1864* (Cambridge, Mass., 1974), 103ff.; R. Bacon to John Bailey, Boston, 14 Jan. 1828, Washburn

Table 8.2. Continuity or Discontinuity in the Party Vote? Massachusetts 1810–40 (Pearson Correlation Coefficients)

		National Republicans/ Whigs	Antimasons		
		1828P	1831G	1832P	1833G
Fed.	1810G	.34	.10	.06	.08
Fed.	1823G	.22	.23	.21	.09
Fed.	1824G	.36	.24	.17	.30
NR	1828P	—	.32	.27	.34
NR	1831G	.24	—	−.37	−.21
NR	1832P	.31	−.45	—	−.44
NR	1833G	.21	−.39	−.49	—
W	1836G	.41	−.44	−.06	−.09
W	1839G	.35	−.01	−.06	−.15
W	1840P	.46	.09	.04	−.03

Papers, 13, Massachusetts Historical Society (MHS); *New England Galaxy,* 31 Oct., 7 Nov. 1828; J. B. Davis to John Bailey, Boston, 4 April 1828, "Letters to John Brazer Davis, 1819–1831," *Massachusetts Historical Society Proceedings* 49 (1916) 210.

17. For religion see McLoughlin, *New England Dissent,* II, 1065–88; for economic policy, Oscar and Mary F. Handlin, *Commonwealth, A Study of the Role of Government in the American Economy: Massachusetts, 1774–1861* (New York, 1947); for workers, Formisano, *Transformation of Political Culture,* 222ff.; and temperance, Robert L. Hampel, *Temperance and Prohibition in Massachusetts, 1813–1852* (Ann Arbor, 1982).

18. Table 8.2

19. Table 8.3

20. For John Quincy Adams see *Mr. Adams' Address to the People, Assigning His Reasons for Having Accepted Their Nomination for Governor . . . ,* Printed by *Free Press and Boston Weekly Advertiser,* 5 Jan. 1834, Houghton Library, Harvard University; Bemis, *John Quincy Adams,* 291ff.; for Charles F. Adams, see *ibid.,* 302 n.121; Martin Duberman, *Charles F. Adams* (Boston, 1960), 56ff. One can best trace Charles F. Adams's involvement in Antimasonic politics through Marc Friedlander and L. H. Butterfield, eds., *Diary of Charles F. Adams,* 6 Vols. (Cambridge, Mass., 1964–74), especially the index references to Antimasonry in vol. 6; Leonard L. Richards, *The Life and Times of Congressman John Quincy Adams* (New York, 1986), 27ff.

21. John Q. Adams, *Address to the People,* 5 Jan. 1834; Rev. George Allen, *Thoughts on 'The Excitement' in Reply to a Letter to Hon. Edward Everett* (Worcester, 1833), 12, 14, 15, 30, 40, 41, 43, 44 for the theme of selfishness; also Peter Sanborn, *Minutes of an Address Delivered before the Anti-Masonic Convention of Reading, Mass., Jan. 15, 1829* (Boston, 1829), 6, 15; *Pawtucket Herald,* 7, 28 Jan. 1829; *An Investigation into Freemasonry by a Joint Committee of the Legislature of Massachusetts, 1834,* p. 13.

22. *Massachusetts Antimasonic Convention, 1834,* pp. 11, 15.

23. *Proceedings of the Most Worshipful Grand Lodge of Free and Accepted Masons of the Commonwealth of Massachusetts for the Years 1815 to 1825 Inclusive,*

Table 8.3. Where the Antimasonic Vote Came from in Massachusetts: Ecological Regression Estimates, 1828–33

1831 Governor	1828 President			
	Nat. Rep.	Dem.	Nonvoter	% Adult Males
National Republican	10	0	10	19
Antimason	5	—2	6	9
Democrat	1	4	3	8
Nonvoter	5	3	57	65
N = 255 towns				

1833 Governor	1828 President			
	Nat. Rep.	Dem.	Nonvoter	% Adult Males
National Republican	10	—.5	7.5	17
Antimason	7	— 2	7	12
Democrat	1	4	5	10
	.3	0	2	2
Nonvoter	3	3.5	54	60
N = 253 towns				

1832 President	1828 President			
	Nat. Rep.	Dem.	Nonvoter	% Adult Males
National Republican	14	0	7	21
Antimason	5	—2	6	9
Democrat	.8	5	4	9
Nonvoter	1	1	58	60
N = 253 towns				

2 Vols. (Boston, 1826–44), I, 8, 26, 58, 86–87, 104–5, 138, 233, 401–3, 452ff., 485ff., II, 59.

24. See above, Chapter 2.

25. This is based on tracing to demographic sources the list of Boston Freemasons in the *Boston Daily Advocate,* 9 Oct. 1832, and the Boston Antimasons in the *Boston Mirror,* 8 March 1833. Occupational data come from the *Stimpson's Boston City Directory,* 1822, 1837; wealth data come from City of Boston, *List of Persons, Co-Partnerships, and Corporations Who Were Taxed Twenty-Five Dollars and Upwards . . . 1830* (Boston, 1831). Occupations for 347 Masons and 170 Antimasons were found and tax assessment data for 390 Masons (22% of the list) and 338 Antimasons (10% of the list).

26. This is based on tracing to demographic sources the list of Boston Masons in the *Boston Daily Advocate,* 9 Oct. 1832; the Antimasons, excluding Bostonians, come from the delegate lists at the Antimasonic state conventions, 1829–34. Biographical information comes from a wide variety of sources, mostly town and county histories too numerous to cite.

27. *Report of the Bunker Hill Monument Association.* For the cornerstone-laying ceremony of the monument, see the colorful description in the *Masonic Mirror,* 25 June 1825; *Boston Advocate,* 16 June 1832, 11 April 1836.

28. *Pawtucket Herald,* 21 Jan. 1829; *Massachusetts Antimasonic Convention, 1829–30,* p. 5; *Dictionary of American Biography,* X, 529–32; Morison, *Three Centuries of Harvard,* 169–72, 185, 222–23; Paul Goodman, *The Democratic-Republicans of Massachusetts* (Cambridge, Mass., 1964), 168; William C. Lane, "Dr. Benjamin Waterhouse and Harvard University," *Proceedings of the Cambridge Historical Society* (Jan.-Oct. 1909), II, 5–22. Waterhouse was a staunch supporter of John Quincy Adams in the *Boston Patriot* during the 1820s, according to Joseph Buckingham, *Memoirs,* II, 11.

29. Reuben G. Thwaites, *Early Western Travels, 1748–1846* (Cleveland, 1905), xxi, 79, 93, 97, 102–5; Morison, *Three Centuries,* 223.

30. Edward L. Pierce, *Memoir and Letters of Charles Sumner,* 4 Vols. (Boston, 1878–93), I, 76, 109; Sumner, *A Letter on Speculative Free Masonry,* 11–13. David Donald, *Charles Sumner and the Coming of the Civil War* (New York, 1961), 5–6 for Sumner's father, but Donald's interpretation of Sumner's career as a reformer de-emphasizes his early affinity for benevolence and stresses other factors. Like Sumner, two other leading figures in the formation of the Republican party had Antimasonic connections. Thaddeus Stevens was a prominent Antimason in Pennsylvania and Salmon P. Chase was amanuensis and protégé of William Wirt. Stevens grew up in Caledonia County, Vermont, the strongest center of Freemasonry in the strongest Antimasonic state. See note 63, Chapter 7. Wirt attracted Chase as an Old Republican, a living link to the Founding Fathers. Chase attributed Wirt's political downfall to a decline in public virtue. In the late 1820s he wrote: "The day has past, I fear, forever past in this country when a man will be rated according to his intellectual strength, extensive experience [and] moral excellence." Andrew Jackson's success suggested as much. Chase sensed that the 1820s were a watershed, ushering in a new period in which "strangers will succeed" and in which "distrust has come in place of confidence and reserve instead of frankness." When Chase moved to Cincinnati in the 1830s, he attended Lyman Beecher's Presbyterian church, another sign of his affinity for Christian Republicanism, which, Peter F. Walker's interpretation suggests, was a wellspring of his later free-soil and antislavery convictions. Free soilism held forth the possibility for him, as for Charles Sumner, of redeeming the Republic, which had strayed from the virtuous course set by the Founders. See Peter F. Walker, *Moral Choice, Memory, Desire and Imagination in Nineteenth Century American Abolitionism* (Baton Rouge, 1978), 310ff., 323–26.

31. *Diary of Charles Francis Adams,* III, 150–51; Justin Winsor, *Memorial History of Boston,* IV, 132; *Proc. Massachusetts Historical Society* (hereafter *Proc. M.H.S.*), First Series, I, 614n.; Williams's associational activities were traced in the *Massachusetts Register & United States Calender for 1838* (Boston, n.d.) and John Hayward, *The Massachusetts Directory* (Boston, 1835). For Williams's views on the Bank of Ten Million, see *Boston Daily Advocate,* 24, 25, 31 March, 2 April 1836.

32. *Diary of Charles F. Adams,* IV, 120; Justin Winsor, *Memorial History of Boston* IV, 119ff.; *Historical Catalog of Brown University, 1764–1894* (Providence, 1895), 351; *Masonic Mirror,* 18 Sep. 1830. For Phelps's importance, see his role in the proceedings of the Antimasonic conventions cited above; Formisano, *Transformation of Political Culture,* 217–18.

33. *Proc. M.H.S.*, Second Series, XVI (1902), 328 n.5; *Boston Daily Advocate,* 9 Dec. 1833.

34. *Proc. M.H.S.*, Second Series, 49 (1915–16), 246, 248, 250.

Chapter 9. Religious Sources of Massachusetts Antimasonry

1. The best account is in McGloughlin, *New England Dissent,* II, chs. 57–63.

2. For pro-Masonic clergy see the Declaration of 1200, *Columbian Centinel,* 16 Oct. 1830.

3. Edward Everett to Alexander Everett, Washington, 5 Apr. 1830, Edward Everett Papers, Microfilm, Reel 4. For Baptist opposition to Sabbatarianism see the Baptist leader at Newton Theological Seminary, John Kennick, Newton, to John Bailey, 26 Aug. 1830, Washburne Papers, 12, MHS. There is no adequate life of Everett, but see Paul R. Frothingham, *Edward Everett* (Boston, 1825); [Rev. George Allen], *Thought on 'The Excitement' in Reply to a Letter to Hon. Edward Everett* (Worcester, 1833). *Proc. M.H.S.*, Second Series, 18 (1903–4), 108–9.

4. Clark, *A Historical Sketch of the Congregational Churches in Massachusetts,* 244–76.

5. Moses Stuart, "Letters to William E. Channing, D.D., on the Subject of Religious Liberty," in *Miscellanies,* 361 and also 311ff., 327ff., 350ff. Stuart reprinted his 1830 letter to Channing 16 years later, suggesting how deep the divisions went. For other Orthodox attacks on Harvard see *Spirit of the Pilgrims,* III (1830), 323–30 and the *Boston Recorder,* 19 Jan., 2, 9, 23 Feb. 1831; 31 July 1830. Marcus Morton, the perennial Democratic gubernatorial candidate in the 1830s, cultivated Orthodox support. Until he became an Episcopalian, he was a prominent Orthodox layman, serving on the Board of Trustees of Amherst and as an officer of Orthodox benevolent associations. Gov. Lincoln appointed him to the Supreme Judicial Court in part to appease Orthodox grievances against Unitarian domination. Morton cultivated for political purposes Orthodox influentials such as Prof. Moses Stuart at Andover Theological Seminary. He advised presidential hopeful, John C. Calhoun, to seek Orthodox support and claimed he had "a good deal of influence with a powerful religious sect which possibly I might be of some little service in directing into the right channel. . . ." Marcus Morton to John C. Calhoun, Morton Letter Book, MHS. See also Morton to Moses Stuart, Boston, 7 Mar. 1831, *ibid.*

6. Cooke, *Unitarianism, an Exclusive System,* 1–2, and *passim*; Parsons Cooke, *A Reply to a Letter in the* Christian Examiner *Addressed to the Rev. Parsons Cooke* (Boston, 1829), 24 and *passim*; Cooke, *A Remonstrance against an Established Religion in Massachusetts,* 24 and *passim*.

7. Darling, *Political Change,* 92; *Mass. Centinel,* 9, 12 Nov. 1831.

8. Meyer, *Church and State in Massachusetts,* 206–7; George Bliss, Springfield, to J. B. Davis, 12 Oct. 1831, "Letters to John Brazer Davis," *Proc. M.H.S.,* 49 (1916), 240–43; William S. Hastings to Davis, Mendon, 29 Oct. 1831, *ibid.,* 245 see also 244, 247.

9. *Memorial Biographies of the New England Historical and Genealogical Society* (Boston, 1880), I, 323ff.; Buckingham, *Personal Memoirs,* I, 34ff.; Charles F. Adams, *Diary,* III, 45.

10. *Massachusetts Centinel,* 25 Oct. 1831 for a National Republican defense of the party's record on religious freedom, and 11 Feb., 10 March 1832 for the house and senate votes on disestablishment; for Amherst see *ibid.,* 15 Feb. 1832.

11. H. Crosby Englizian, *Brimstone Corner, Park Street Church* (Chicago, 1968), 45; Stuart, *Miscellanies,* 350.

12. Beecher, *Autobiography,* I, 385, II, 55; *Boston Recorder,* 10 Oct. 1831.

13. Beecher, *Autobiography,* II, 107–8.

14. *Spirit of the Pilgrims* (1830), III, 641ff., 645, 651.

15. Stuart, *Miscellanies,* 311ff.; Bernard Whitman, *National Defense, A Discourse Preached before the Ancient and Honorable Artillery Company, 1 June 1829* (Cambridge, Mass., 1828), 15ff., 21, 27; *A Discourse on Christian Union, Delivered at the Installation of Rev. Adin Ballou . . . Mendon, May 3, 1832* (Boston, 1833), 21 and *passim,* 35ff., 66, 67.

16. For Tappan's renunciation, see *Antimasonic Review,* No. 3, p. 100. For the Tappans' career see Bertram Wyatt-Brown, *Lewis Tappan and the Evangelical War against Slavery* (New York, 1971), especially chs. 1–4; Lewis Tappan, *Letter from a Gentleman in Boston to a Unitarian Clergyman of that City* (Boston, 1828), 12 and *passim.* For a Unitarian rebuttal, see *Reply of Unitarian Clergyman to the Letter of a Gentleman in Boston,* 4th edition (Boston, 1828); [J. P. Blanchard], *Review of a Letter from a Gentleman in Boston to a Unitarian Clergyman of That City* (Boston, 1828).

17. *Massachusetts Antimasonic Convention, 1829–30,* pp. 29ff. for Ethan Smith, and *Massachusetts Antimasonic Convention, 1832,* pp. 17–18 for Emmons. For the extent of Hopkinsian influence, especially in southeast Massachusetts, see Blake, *Mendon Association,* which contains biographies of ministers who belonged to the association and lists the churches where they served. Some left the area of the association to take churches elsewhere, extending the influence of Hopkinsianism into other parts of the state. Among towns which employed Hopkinsians in the period 1820–40 and also voted heavily for the Antimasons are Abingdon, Buckland, Canton, Concord, Charlemont, Dighton, Framingham, Freetown, Dartmouth, Hawley, Hanover, Holliston, Medway, Randolph, Weymouth, and Wrentham.

18. Blake, *Mendon Association,* 177–78; *Brown University Historical Catalogue, 1794–1894,* p. 82. Thacher's brother, Tyler, was also an Hopkinsian and served in Hawley 1834–43, where Antimasons polled 96% of the vote in 1832. For Tyler Thacher, see Blake, *Mendon Association,* 198; Otis Thompson, *A Sermon, Preached at the Ordination of the Rev. Moses Thacher as Pastor of the Church in the North Parish of Wrentham, Aug. 20, 1823* (Providence, 1823).

19. *Journal of American Education Society* (Aug. 1835), 46, 57–58; Hayward, *Massachusetts Directory, 1835,* p. 102; *Statistical Tables . . . ,* 131; Enoch Pond, "Wrentham, Massachusetts, Sketches of Its Ecclesiastical History," *Congregational Quarterly* 10 (1870), 323–33.

20. *Rhode Island Legislative Investigation,* 6.

21. John Ferguson, *Letters Addressed to the Rev. Moses Thacher; Together with the Result of an Ecclesiastical Council, Convened at North Wrentham, Dec. 14, 1830* (Boston, 1831), 6; Moses Thacher, *An Address to the Church and Congregation, Under the Care of the Author, on His Seceding from the Masonic Institution, Delivered May 24, 1829, passim.*

22. *Rhode Island Legislative Investigation,* 13.

23. *A Report of the Committee of St. Alban's Lodge, Wrentham, Mass., Appointed to Investigate the Proceedings of Rev. Moses Thacher Relative to the Masonic Institution* (Boston, 1830), 11.

24. Moses Thacher, *An Address Delivered before Montgomery Lodge in Medway,*

Mass. . . . (Boston, 1829), 5; Moses Thacher, *Letters Addressed to a Brother in the Church, on Renouncing the Secret Principles of Freemasonry . . .* (Boston, 1829), 3, 10.

25. Thacher, *Address before Montgomery Lodge,* 3, 7ff., 11, 12, 16–17; *A Report of the Committee of St. Alban's Lodge,* 8ff., 11ff.

26. Thacher, *An Address of the Church and Congregation,* 7ff., 12.

27. *A Report of the Committee of St. Alban's Lodge,* 3ff.; Thacher, *Letters Addressed to a Brother in the Church,* 7, 8, 14ff.

28. Thacher, *Letters Addressed to a Brother in the Church,* 7.

29. See the series by Fenelon in the *Masonic Mirror,* 5, 12 Nov. 1831, and also 8, 15, 22 Oct. 1831; *A Report of the Committee of St. Alban's Lodge,* 23.

30. For the council of 14 Dec. 1830 see Ferguson, *Letters,* 24ff., and for the Thacherite position, see *Reasons Assigned by the Church in North Wrentham for Withdrawing from Their Masonic Brethren and Others . . .* (Boston, 1830), especially 15ff., 49.

31. *Reasons Assigned by the Church in North Wrentham,* 4.

32. Ferguson, *Letters,* 29, 15ff.

33. *Reasons Assigned by the Church in North Wrentham,* 2, 7n; *Masonic Mirror,* 19 March, 22 Oct. 1831; Thacher, *An Address to the Church and Congregation,* 11–12; Moses Thacher, *Masonic Oaths, Neither Morally nor Legally Binding. An Address Delivered at Weymouth, South Parish . . .* (Boston, n.d.), 18ff., 23, 29.

34. *New England Telegraph and Eclectic Review,* Jan. 1835, p. ii; Oct. 1836, p. 477.

35. *Ibid.,* 26 Feb. 1831.

36. *New England Telegraph,* April 1835, p. 112; Feb. 1836, p. 9; May 1836, pp. 202ff.; July 1835, pp. 213–14; *Masonic Mirror,* 22 Oct., 12 Nov. 1831.

37. *Report of the Case of Rev. Moses Thacher vs. Gen. Preston Pond, for Slander, in Charging Him with Committing the Crime of Adultery* (Dedham Patriot and Boston Times, 1838), 3–6, 7.

38. *Ibid.,* 12–19.

39. *Ibid.,* 21–24, 12ff., 19ff., 30.

40. *Massachusetts Antimasonic Convention, 1831,* p. 10.

41. *Lynn Record,* 17 July 1830, 30 April 1832.

Chapter 10. Antimasonry and Industrial Society

1. For Washburn see Rev. Henry T. Cheever, *Autobiography and Memorials of Ichabod Washburn* (Boston, 1878), especially 115–20, 177, and Kornblith, "From Artisans to Businessmen," 384ff. For Thwing see Edward P. Thwing, *A Memorial of Thomas Thwing* (Boston, 1868), 20–25, and for the setting in which Thwing lived, Philip F. Gura, "The Reverend Parsons Cooke and Factory Village: A New Missionary Field," *New England Genealogical Register* (July 1981), 122–212, and for the demographic changes see Doherty, *Society and Power,* 32–35, 82ff., 87.

2. *North Star,* 23 Feb. 1828.

3. Records of the Fall River Antimasonic Reading Room, Jan. 1829, and Minutes of a Meeting of the Citizens of Fall River Village Favourable to the Antimasonic Cause, 13 Dec. 1828, Fall River Historical Society.

4. *The Massachusetts Directory, 1835,* pp. 30–32; Frederick M. Peck and Henry H. Earl, *Fall River and Its Industries* (Fall River, 1877), 1–56; *Our Country and*

Its People, A Descriptive and Biographical Record of Bristol, County, Massachusetts (Boston, 1899), 96–168.

5. *New Bedford Mercury*, 2 Dec. 1831, 23, 30 March 1832; Benjamin Pierce, *Recollections of a Long and Busy Life, 1819–1890*, Clara Boss, ed. (Newport, 1890), 34, 35, 43ff.; Formisano, *Transformation of Political Culture*, 229.

6. *New Bedford Mercury*, 23 March 1832. For earlier labor unrest in the textile region see Chapter 11.

7. Frederick B. Tolles, "The New Light Quakers of Lynn and New Bedford, *New England Quarterly*, 32 (Sep. 1959), 291–319, but esp. 304ff.; *Providence Journal*, 4 June 1831; *Boston Advocate*, 6 Jan. 1835; Forbush, *Elias Hicks*, 209; *Pawtucket Chronicle*, 29 Oct. 1830; *A Descriptive Record of Bristol County*, 469, 491; *Fall River and Its Industries*, 62. The best sources of biographical information for Fall River Antimasons are the two last items. Allied with Ruggles and the New Lights were some leading Fall River businessmen who belonged to the Orthodox Congregational church whose minister, Thomas Smith, renounced Masonry. The most influential was David Anthony, director of Ruggles's bank, president of another, the town's foremost manufacturer, and a church deacon. The Bordens, another important manufacturing family, also embraced Antimasonry. For Anthony see *Descriptive Record of Bristol County*, 451, 561–63 and *passim; Fall River and Its Industries*, 11, 64, 76, 118, 122, 223. Anthony and other Antimasons can be found in the delegate lists of the Antimasonic state conventions, 1829–34, and traced in *Fall River and Its Industries* and *A Descriptive Record of Bristol County, passim.* Anthony and other Antimasonic Congregationalists are in *The Confession of Faith and Covenant of the First Congregational Church, Fall River* (Fall River, 1864), which contains a membership list. Benjamin Pierce recalled Anthony as a blue-law Presbyterian who forced his two sons to spend Sundays all day in church. See Pierce, *Recollections*, 65. For the Bordens see *Dictionary of American Biography*, I, 458–60; *Fall River and Its Industries*, 235, 236. For Borden's congressional campaign see *Boston Advocate*, 20, 21, Oct., 13, 15 Nov. 1834.

8. *New Bedford Mercury*, 13 Jan. 1832, 2 Sep., 28 Oct. 1831, 1 April 1831; for a defense of Ruggles as a supporter of the American System see *Boston Advertiser*, 1 Jan. 1832; *Providence Daily Advertiser*, 18 Aug. 1831.

9. Ruggles's opponent in the heated congressional elections of 1831–32 was James Hodges, a Taunton lawyer and Freemason. Forty-one Taunton men signed the Declaration of 1200 Freemasons in 1831, including Reverend Luther Hamilton, Unitarian pastor at the Congregational church.

10. *Lynn Record*, 17 April 1833. The best account of antebellum Lynn is in Paul G. Faler, *Mechanics and Manufacturers in the Early Industrial Revolution, Lynn, Massachusetts, 1780–1860* (Albany, N.Y., 1981); see also Dawley, *Class and Community*, chs. 1–3. The reminiscences of David N. Johnson, *Sketches of Lynn* (Lynn, 1880) are also valuable.

11. Faler, *Mechanics and Manufacturers*, 109–10, 222–33, and especially ch. 6; *Lynn Record*, 9 Feb. 1831.

12. *Lynn Record*, 20 Feb. 1830.

13. *Ibid.*, 22, 30 May, 19 June, 7 Aug. 1830; for the men's union and for the women, *ibid.*, 1 Jan., 26 Feb., 2 April, 4 June 1834; *Lynn Mirror*, 22 May, 14 Aug. 1830.

14. *Lynn Record*, 9 July 1834; *Lynn Mirror*, 3 Jan., 21 Feb. 1829.

15. On social mobility see Faler, *Mechanics and Manufacturers*, 62–66; Johnson, *Sketches*, 121.

16. *Lynn Record*, 9, 20 Oct. 1833. For the temperance movement see 3 April, 10 July, 1830, 2 Jan., 13 Feb., 11 Sep., 2 Oct. 1833.

17. *Ibid.*, 6 April 1834; Abzug, *Passionate Liberator, Theodore Dwight Weld & The Dilemma of Reform*, 59–62, 66–69, 84–85.

18. Lewis, *Lynn*, 200, 220, 227; *One Hundred Years, Mt. Carmel Lodge, Ancient Free and Accepted Masons of Lynn, Massachusetts* (n.p., 1905); *Lynn Record*, 13 March 1830, 11 Jan., 6 April 1831, 12 March 1835.

19. Faler, *Mechanics and Manufacturers*, 56–57 and ch. 3 *passim.*, for comparatively low rates of geographic mobility, see 139–43; *Lynn Mirror*, 8 Oct. 1831; *Lynn Record*, 26 Feb. 1834.

20. Faler, *Mechanics and Manufacturers*, 36–38, 41, 43–44, 47.

21. *Lynn Record*, 19 Oct. 1831, 1 Oct. 1834.

22. *Ibid.*, 19 June 1830, 18 Dec. 1829.

23. Alan Dawley and Paul Faler, "Working Class Culture and Politics in the Industrial Revolution: Sources of Loyalism and Rebellion," *Journal of Social History* 9 (Summer 1976), 466–80.

24. This is based on occupational data for 48 Antimasons, 49 Masons, and 90 Democrats, and real property for 60, 55, and 77 of the three groups, and personal property for 59, 57, and 77 of the respective groups. For the names of Masons, see *Lynn Record*, 22 Feb. 1832; *Masonic Mirror*, 12 Nov. 1831; Democrats, *Lynn Record*, 22 Feb. 1832; Antimasons come from the *Lynn Record* reports of third-party candidates and activists, 1829–36; the cordwainers' leaders, *Lynn Record*, 27 Oct. 1835. Occupational data are from the *Lynn Directory* (1832); wealth data are from Lynn Tax Assessment Records, 1836, Lynn Historical Society. For church members, names were checked against Faler; *Manual of the First Congregational Church in Lynn* (Lynn, 1874); Newhall, *History of Lynn, passim;* "Names of Preachers and Members That Have Joined the South St. M.E. Church," *The First Universalist Parish of Lynn* (n.p., 1980); "Constitution of the First Baptist Church in Lynn, 1816," Ms., Lynn Historical Society; Charles W. Blackett, "History of the South St. Methodist Church, Lynn, 1906," Ms., Lynn Public Library; Sallie H. Acker, "The Friends, Laws & Social Customs of the Quakers," Ms., Lynn Historical Society.

25. *Lynn Record*, 15 Dec. 1830; and for the connection between Antimasonry and the churches see 20 Feb., 15 Dec. 1830, 3, 10 Sep. 1834, 2 March 1831, 19 Sep. 1832. For the religious affiliations of members of the Mt. Carmel Lodge see *One Hundred Years, Mt. Carmel Lodge, passim.*

26. *Lynn Mirror*, 12 Nov. 1831.

27. *Ibid.*, 12, 26 Nov., 17, 24 Dec. 1831, 4, 25 Feb., 10 March 1832; *Lynn Record*, 10 Nov. 1831. For the New Lights see Frederick B. Tolles, "The New Light Quakers of Lynn and New Bedford"; *Trial of Benjamin Shaw, John Alley Junior, Jonathan Buffum, and Preserved Sprauge for Riots and Disturbance of Public Worship, in the Society of Quakers, at Lynn, Massachusetts . . . March 16, 1822* (Salem, 1822).

28. *Lynn Record*, 2, 16 July 1834.

29. *Ibid.*, 29 Jan. 1834, 3 Sep. 1834.

30. "Minutes of the Lynn Antislavery Society," Ms., Lynn Historical Society; *Lynn Record*, 30 July 1834, and see also 16 April 1834, 23, 30 July 1834, 20 Aug.,

Table 10.1. Where the Massachusetts Antimasonic Vote Went, 1832–36, Ecological Regression Estimates

	1832 President				
1836 President	Nat. Reps.	Anti-masons	Dem.	Nonvoters	% Electorate
Whigs	19	4	3	−1.5	24
Democrats	5	4	12	−1	19
Nonvoter	31	15	8	3	57
N = 288 Towns					

	1833 Governor					
1836 President	Nat. Reps.	Anti-masons	Dem.	Working-men	Non-voters	% Elec-torate
Whigs	14	1	.7	1	7	24
Democrats	.3	2.5	9.5	.3	7	19
Nonvoter	2	8	0	.4	47	57
N = 275 Towns						

22 Oct. 1835. And for a sympathetic treatment of Garrison and the abolitionists see for example *Lynn Record,* 23 Jan., 22 May, 20 Feb. 1830, 11 July 1832, 9 Nov. 1836, 2 Aug. 1837.

31. *Lynn Record,* 13 March 1830.

32. For Antimasons and the Nationals, *Lynn Record,* 24 Nov. 1830, 30 March 1831, 26 Dec. 1832, 2 April, 16 July 1834. For the Democrats and the Young Men's ticket see *Lynn Record,* 30 April, 14 May 1831.

33. For the deadlocked town election see the *Lynn Record,* 2 April, 23 July 1835. And for amalgamation with the Democrats, 29 Oct., 5, 12 Nov. 1835, 7, 21 Sep. 1836, 15 Aug. 1838; *Lynn Freeman,* 17 Nov. 1838.

34. Table 10.1

35. For movement towards Antimasonic coalition with the Democrats see the *Boston Advocate,* 10 Dec. 1833, 24 Nov., 1 Dec. 1835, 7, 15, Jan., 8 March, 5 Sep. 1836; for support of Van Buren, 21 May 1835, 14 Jan., 1, 10 Feb. 1836; for Antimasons who refused to go along, 20 Feb. 1836. See also *Providence Journal,* 20 Feb., 7 Nov. 1834, 14 Jan. 1836.

36. Table 10.2

37. *Boston Advocate,* 21 Nov. 1836; Parsons Cooke, *A Discourse . . . on the Occasion of the Death of William Henry Harrison . . .* (Lynn, 1841). For Jackson, *Boston Advocate,* 11 Oct. 1836.

38. *Boston Advocate,* 7 Jan., 29 April, 26 Sep. 1834.

39. *Ibid.,* 21 June 1834, 23 Feb., 30 Jan., 1, 23 Feb. 1835.

40. *Ibid.,* 6, 16, 25 Feb. 1835.

41. *Ibid.,* 15 Jan. 1836, 24 May, 16, 25 Aug., 5 Sep. 1836; Adams, *Diary,* IV, 79.

42. *Boston Advocate,* 8 June 1835.

43. *Ibid.,* 23, 25 Feb. 1935, 10 Aug. 1835, 10 Feb., 27, 30 April, 14 Nov. 1836,

and for Hallett's speech, Benjamin Hallett, *An Oration . . . July 4th, 1836, At Palmer, in Hampden County . . .* (Boston, 1836), 46.

44. *Boston Advocate,* 1 Feb., 17 Sep. 1836; Hallett, *Oration,* 46.

45. *Proceedings of the Most Worshipful Grand Lodge . . . of Massachusetts . . . 1826–1844,* II, 392–95, 345–47.

Chapter 11. The Antimasons of Rhode Island

1. For an excellent history of Rhode Island Antimasonry, see Susan Porter Benson, "A Union of Men and Not of Principles. The Rhode Island Antimasonic Party, 1829–1838" (M.A. Thesis, Brown University, 1971). Benson did not probe the social sources of Antimasonry, arguing that Rhode Island Antimasonry had no underlying programmatic, ideological, or sociological basis, yet her study is a valuable narrative history. See also Vaughn, *The Anti-Masonic Party,* 133–52.

2. For the growth of Freemasonry in Rhode Island, see Henry W. Rugg, *History of Freemasonry in Rhode Island* (Providence, 1895), *passim,* 86ff.

3. Joshua B. Rathbun, *Address Delivered before the Grand Lodge of Rhode Island at the First Congregational Meeting-House in Providence on the Anniversary Festival, June 24th, 1835* (Providence, 1835), 8, 10–11, 12, 23–24.

4. *Boston Advocate,* 8 June 1835.

5. *Rhode Island Antimasonic Convention, 1831,* p. 6, for endorsement of the American System.

6. *Rhode Island Legislative Investigation.*

7. Patrick T. Conley, *Democracy in Decline, Rhode Island Constitutional Development, 1776–1841* (Providence, 1977) is the best political history for this period; see also Peter J. Coleman, *The Transformation of Rhode Island, 1790–1860* (Providence, 1963); Edwin F. Sweet, "The Origins of the Democratic Party in Rhode Island, 1824–1836" (Ph.D. Diss., Fordham, 1971); Philip A. Grant, Jr., "Party Chaos Embroils Rhode Island," *Rhode Island History* 26 (Oct. 1967), 113–25, vol. 27 (Jan. 1968), 24–33.

8. Christopher Allen to John B. Francis, 19 April 1836, Francis Papers, Rhode Island Historical Society (RIHS); see also 9 Oct. 1835 for an example of election treating; Burrington Anthony to Levi Woodbury, 5 Sep. 1835, Levi Woodbury Papers, LC. For an extraordinary day-by-day picture of Rhode Island politics, see the papers of John Brown Francis and Elisha Potter, Sr., and Jr., in the Rhode Island Historical Society. Because Rhode Island was a small state, the number of voters limited, and personal influence potent, successful politicians such as Francis and the Potters kept close tabs on political conditions and opportunities in every community where they had allies or "connections." For the classic account of aristocratic politics in England, see Sir Lewis B. Namier, *England in the Age of the American Revolution,* 2nd ed. (London, 1961), and *The Structure of Politics at the Accession of George III,* 2nd ed. (London, 1961).

9. Seth Luther, *An Address on the Right of Free Suffrage . . . Delivered at Providence, April 16, 19, 1833* (Providence, 1833); *Providence Journal,* 28 March 1832 for the Providence Association of Workingmen; Joseph Brennan, *Social Conditions in Industrial Rhode Island, 1820–1860* (Washington, D.C.), 53.

10. Conley, *Democracy in Decline,* 197ff., 237ff.; Marvin E. Gettleman, *The Dorr Rebellion* (New York, 1983); George M. Dennison, *The Dorr War* (Lexing-

Table 10.2. Influence of Demographic Variables on Party in Massachusetts, 1823–40: Multiple Regression Betas.

	1823 Gov.	1824 Gov.	1828 Pres.	1832 Gov.		
			Nat.	Nat.		Anti-
	Fed.	Fed.	Rep.	Rep.	Dem.	mason
Pop. change	−.106	−.089	.008*	.159	−.042	−.118
Commerce	.082	.063	−.061	−.058	−.037	.080
Manufacture	.037*	−.083	−.058	−.097	.176	−.034*
Maritime	−.027*	−.102	.016*	.266	.061	−.291
Agriculture	.041	−.064	−.081	−.007*	.155	−.102
Textile	.020*	.019*	−.123	.039	−.072	.014*
Boot and shoe	.189	.133	.035	.022	−.016*	−.009*
Fishery	−.007*	−.024	−.018	−.095	−.002*	.090
Cong. Acc.**	.263	.269	.116	−.028*	−.066	.073
Baptist	−.072	−.117	−.219	−.049	.173	−.072
Methodist	−.081	−.151	−.110	−.003*	.133	−.087
Free Will						
Baptist	.118	−.084	−.108	−.079	.090	.011
Univ. Acc.**	−.113	−.096	.061	−.006*	.064	−.037
Unit. Acc.	−.008*	−.064	.055	.150	−.132	−.048
Quaker Acc.	.018*	.072	.018*	−.176	−.010*	.170
R²	.15	.19	.14	.14	.10	.13

* Regression coefficient not statistically significant at 1%.

** Acc. = Church accommodations (seats)

ton, Ky., 1976), 15ff.; Coleman, *Transformation of Rhode Island,* 258ff.; *Report of the Committee of the Rhode Island General Assembly on the Subject of an Extension of the Suffrage* (n.p., 1829).

11. Coleman, *Transformation of Rhode Island,* 191ff. for banking; for National Republican resistance to the landholders, see *Providence Journal,* 29 March, 4, 12 April, 28 June 1831, and *Address to the Landholders and Farmers of Newport County Delivered by Hon. Tristam Burgess . . . Tiverton, 7 August 1829* (Providence, 1829); for a Democratic appeal to farmers and defense of the bank tax, see [J. E. Waterman], *To the Farmers and Landholders of Rhode Island,* March 1828, Warwick, J. R. Waterman, RIHS.

12. Benson, "A Union of Men and Not of Principles," 13ff., 37ff. For the Antimasonic conventions see the *Providence Journal,* 26, 27 March 1830; *Masonic Mirror,* 8 Jan. 1831; and see the *Free Press and Pawtucket Herald,* 23 Dec. 1830 for announcements of Antimasonic meetings in Foster, Warwick, Gloucester, Scituate, and Coventry to select delegates to the state convention. For the Francis nomination see *Providence Journal,* 17 Jan., 10 Feb. 1831; John B. Francis to James Simmons, 30 Dec. 1830, and Simmons to Francis, 18 Dec. 1830, 9 Feb. 1831, Simmons Papers, LC, give an exceptionally detailed account of Francis's views on Rhode Island and national politics and Simmons's efforts to lure him into the National Republican camp.

13. For the Fenner tickets' election address, see *The Address to the Freemen of Rhode Island by a Landholder* (Providence, 1831); also for an attack on Arnold, see

1832 Gov.			1832 Gov.			
Nat. Rep.	Dem.	Anti-mason	Whig	Dem.	Anti-mason	Working-men
.096	−.035	−.059	.113	−.006*	−.127	.066
−.005*	−.092	.083	−.061	−.128	.035	.264
.101	.119	−.195	−.003*	.075	−.033*	−.061
.254	.171	−.383	.183	.066	−.288	.013*
.032*	.190	−.192	.032*	.083	−.102	.006*
−.109	.097	.019*	.074	.041	.070	−.062
−.004*	.000*	.032*	.003*	−.012*	−.032	.080
.048	−.051	−.000*	−.097	.045	.050	−.006*
.033	−.002*	−.013*	−.006*	−.025*	−.105	.268
−.085	.203	−.095	−.050	.174	−.116	.026*
.067	.096	−.137	.094	.154	−.173	−.071
−.062	.066	.000*	−.091	.113	.039	.045
.042	.039	−.072	−.047	.126	−.061	−.010*
.249	−.098	−.146	.049	−.119	.071	−.027
−.153	−.051	.184	−.120	−.050	.164	−.035
.17	.12	.16	.08	.13	.14	.14

Examination of Certain Charges against Lemuel H. Arnold, Esq. . . . Candidate for Governor (Providence, 1831); for Arnold's campaign see *Providence Journal*, 25 March 1831, for the Antimasonic endorsement, 29 March 1831, for defense of the tariff, 4 April, 28 June 1831; for Democratic leader E. R. Potter's opposition to an investigation of Freemasonry and National Republican Lemuel Arnold's support, see Benson, "A Union of Men and Not of Principles," 48ff.

14. *Rhode Island Legislative Investigation*, 3, 31, and for Antimasonic charges of bias, see 3, 5–6, 23, 32, 39, 69, 73–74.

15. *Providence Journal*, 12 May 1832, 27 March 1833.

16. *Ibid.*, 6 July 1833.

17. *Ibid.*, 24 Feb. 1832; *Boston Advocate*, 13 January 1832.

18. *Providence Journal*, 26 Jan., 4, 8, 26 Feb., 11, 12, 14, 18, 21 March 1833; Benson, "A Union of Men and Not of Principles," 101ff., especially for Masonry in the Democratic party. For a National Republican attack on Francis as a turncoat, see *The Address of a Farmer to the Honest Men of All Parties in the State of Rhode Island and Providence Plantation* (1833); Christopher Allen to Francis, 5 Jan. 1833, Benjamin Covell to Francis, 7 Feb. 1833, T. P. Ives to Francis, 20 March 1833, John Brown Francis Papers; John Waterman to E. R. Potter, 4 March 1833, Elisha Atkins to E. R. Potter, Newport, 8 Feb. 1833, Potter Papers, RIHS.

19. Thomas W. Bicknell, *The History of the State of Rhode Island and Providence Plantations*, 5 Vols. (New York, 1920), III, 1138.

20. For Francis's views on suffrage, see Francis to E. R. Potter, 7 April 1829, 28 Aug. 1829, Francis Papers, RIHS; Francis to James Simmons, 30 Dec. 1830, Simmons Papers, LC; and for Potter, see *Providence Journal*, 1 July 1833.

21. *Providence Journal*, 3, 6, 7, 16 May 1833; *New Bedford Courier*, 23 April 1833; Joseph J. Smith, comp., *Civil and Military List of Rhode Island, 1800–1850*, 2 Vols. (Providence, 1901), permits comparison of removal patterns from year to year.

22. Potter did not win. For the congressional election see *Providence Journal*, 22 July 1, 22 Aug., 11, 18, 21 Nov. 1833; John R. Waterman to E. R. Potter, 24 Dec. 1833; Dutee J. Pearce to Potter, 2 Aug., 7 Sep. 1833; Christopher Allen to Potter, 23 Sep. 1833, Potter Papers; J. B. Francis to C. G. Champlin, 10 Aug. 1833; William Sprague Jr. to Francis, 17 Aug. 1833, Francis Papers, RIHS.

23. *Providence Journal*, 18, 21 Jan., 3 Feb., 11 May, 31 Oct. 1834; Benson, "A Union of Men and Not of Principles," 104ff., 125, 144ff.

24. *Masonic Mirror*, 8 Jan. 1831; for the most complete list of Antimasonic delegates see *Rhode Island Antimasonic Convention, 1831*.

25. Tables 11.1 A and B

26. Table 11.2

27. The Masons are from *Boston Advocate*, 16 Sep. 1832; the Antimasons from the *Memorials to the Honorable General Assembly of the State of Rhode Island . . . January Session, 1833*, in bound volume, *Masonry and Antimasonry, 1833–34*, R.I. Archives. Demographic data from the U.S. Census, 1850. The number of Masons traced to the 1850 census is 127 and Antimasons, 296.

28. "Votes Given in at Election, November 21, 1832," South Kingston, Shepley Papers, 45, RIHS.

29. Kulik, "The Beginnings of the Industrial Revolution in America: Pawtucket, Rhode Island, 1672–1829," 50ff., 154ff. and *passim* for a sensitive account of the impact of manufactures; Rev. Massens Goodrich, *Historical Sketch of the Town of Pawtucket* (Pawtucket, 1876), 133.

30. See note 27 for the sources of Masons and Antimasons. Occupational data from *The Providence City Directory* (Providence, 1830, 1836) and *A List of Persons Assessed in the City of Forty Thousand Dollars* (Providence, 1829, 1835). The 1840 data come from the Providence Poll Book, 1840 Presidential Election, RIHS; occu-

Table 11.1A. Where the Antimasonic Vote Came from and Went, Rhode Island, Pearson Correlations, 1810–40

	Antimasons 1832	
	Governor	President
Federal 1810 Governor	—.11	—.14
Federal 1812 Governor	—.26	—.25
NR 1830	.26	—.05
Whig 1834 Governor	—.08	—.42
Whig 1836 President	.06	.02
Whig 1838 Governor	.11	.16
Whig 1840 Governor	.34	.09
Whig 1840 President	.09	—.11

Table 11.1B. Rhode Island Ecological Regression Estimates, 1830–36

1832 President	1830 Governor			
	Whig	Democrat	Nonvoter	Electorate
Whig	5%	0%	9%	14%
Democrat	0	6.5	2	8
Antimason	1	.5	3	4
Nonvoter	2.5	3	69	74
N = 23 Towns				

1834 Governor	1832 President				
	Whig	Democrat	Antimason	Nonvoter	Electorate
Whig	13%	0%	0%	3%	16%
Democrat	0	10	6	−3	13
Nonvoter	1	−2	−2	74	71
N = 21 Towns					

1836 Governor	1832 President				
	Whig	Democrat	Antimason	Nonvoter	Electorate
Whig	3.5%	0%	−2%	9%	10%
Democrat	−5.5	8	2	8	13.5
Nonvoter	15	1	4	57	76
N = 28 Towns					

Note: Because of the small number of cases—Rhode Island had 31 towns in 1830, diminished further by missing data—these statistics should be read with caution.

Table 11.2. Party Competition and Turnout in Rhode Island, 1829–40[*]

	NR/W%	Turnout
1828 P	77	17%
1830	32	21
1831	56	31
1832	49	32
1832 P	48	22
1833	45	32
1834	49	31
1835	49	33
1836	42	30
1836 P	48	24
1837	25	15
1838	53	31
1839	47	24
1840	58	32
1840 P	61	34

[*] Gubernatorial elections except where P (President) noted.

pational and wealth data from the city directories and tax lists. There were 169 Masons and 96 Antimasons on the Providence lists. Occupational data were found for 139 Masons and 86 Antimasons, real wealth data for 102 Masons and 45 Antimasons, personal wealth for 100 Masons and 44 Antimasons. See Goodman, "Social Basis of New England Politics in Jacksonian America, 1838–1852."

31. Associational affiliations are from *Providence City Directory* (Providence, 1829, 1836); religious affiliations are from town histories and church records.

32. *Providence Journal*, 25 April 1832, 11 March, 12 April 1833.

33. See the list of participating clergy at the Grand Lodge of Rhode Island celebration, *Providence Journal*, 26 June 1830; and for the chaplains of the Grand Lodge, see Rugg, *History of Freemasonry in Rhode Island*, 270ff., and the list in the *Rhode Islander and Antimasonic Republican*, 25 Nov. 1829; *Rhode Island Legislative Investigation*, 60, for testimony by Rev. Lemuel Burgess, a North Kingston Episcopalian. At least 22 of 92 Episcopal laymen who served as delegates to the church's annual statewide meetings in the 1820s and 1830s were Freemasons. See the *Journals of the Convention of the Rhode Island Episcopal Convention* (Providence, 1819–35).

34. *Masonic Mirror*, 21 April 1832; *Providence Journal*, 18, 21 July 1831; David Pickering, *Address Delivered before the Citizens of Providence in the Universalist Chapel on the Fifty-Second Anniversary of American Independence* (Providence, 1828), 13–15. Pickering had earlier engaged in controversy with the great Hopkinsian Antimason, Nathanael Emmons. See David Pickering, *Sermon on the Perdition of Judas, by Nathanial Emmons, D.D. of Franklin, Ms., with a Review of the Same* (Providence, 1827). Hopkinsians in Massachusetts and other orthodox Christians appear as agents for the *Anti-Universalist,* published in Boston in the late 1820s. See, for example, 6 Aug. 1828, which lists such Hopkinsians from southeastern Massachusetts such as Revs. Thomas Williams, John Ferguson, and Otis Thompson, and Rhode Island Antimasons such a Rev. Ray Potter of Pawtucket. For a liberal Baptist defense of Freemasonry, see David Benedict, *An Address Delivered before the Grand Lodge of Rhode Island at the Anniversary of St. John the Baptist, Thursday, June 24, 1830* (Pawtucket, 1830), 20.

35. David Benedict, *Fifty Years among the Baptists* (New York, 1860), 95, 160.

36. The most widely discussed conversion from the First Baptist Church in Providence to Unitarianism was by Samuel Eddy, a Democratic politician. See Samuel Eddy, *Reasons Offered by Samuel Eddy, Esquire, for His Opinions to the First Baptist Church in Providence from Which He Was Compelled to Withdraw, for Heterodoxy,* 1st ed. (n.p., 1818); Eddy's pamphlet went into four editions. Benedict, *Fifty Years among the Baptists,* 139ff., 144ff.

37. Benedict, *Fifty Years among the Baptists,* 172ff., 261; Benedict, *Address Delivered before the Grand Lodge, passim;* 10 April 1830; *Providence Journal,* 6 April 1830. For Deacon Kent, see the account of the Antimasonic meeting in the *Pawtucket Herald and Independent Inquirer,* 31 Dec. 1828.

38. For the origins of the society, see Richard Bayles, *History of Providence, Rhode Island,* 2 Vols. (New York, 1891), II, 74; Benedict, *Fifty Years among the Baptists,* 21, 22, 59, 60, 70, 96, 345ff.; McLoughlin, *New England Dissent,* II, 1136.

39. Benedict, *Fifty Years among the Baptists,* 172ff., 175, 177, 59, 77, 165–6, 261; Bayles, *History of Rhode Island,* II, 91.

40. *Rhode Island Legislative Investigation,* 17ff., 34–35; *Providence Journal,* 5 Aug. 1831.

41. *Free Will Baptist Cyclopedia,* 238, 538; *Lynn Record,* 26 Sep. 1832; *North*

Star, 24 Feb., 13 Oct. 1829; *Boston Daily Advertiser,* 29 July 1831, 13, 15 Aug. 1831; Ray Potter, *Memoirs of the Life and Religious Experience of Ray Potter, Minister of the Gospel, Pawtucket* (Providence, 1829), contains the letter to Rev. Lorenzo Dow, 4 June 1829, appended to the end of the volume.

42. Kulik, "The Beginnings of the Industrial Revolution in America: Pawtucket," 356–57; *Rhode Island Legislative Investigation,* 69; Potter, *Memoirs,* for an advertisement listing his endorsers, vi, 164ff., for the dispute with the Greenes, 193–94.

43. Potter, *Memoirs, passim,* 200ff. for his spiritual odyssey, 267ff. on congregational polity, and 282–83 on his millennialism. For his post-Antimasonic troubles, when his character came under attack and he admitted committing adultery, see Ray Potter, *Admonitions from the Depths of the Earth, of the Fall of Ray Potter, in Twenty Four Letters; Written by Himself to His Brother Nicholas G. Potter* (Pawtucket, 1838).

44. *Rev. H. Tatem's Reply to the Summons of the R.I. Royal Arch Chapter, Warwick, 1832,* 3rd ed. (n.d., n.p.), 5, 6, 8, and *passim.* In eight pages Tatem compressed most of the major themes in the Antimasonic persuasion in compelling language. Oliver P. Fuller, *The History of Warwick* (Providence, 1875), 351. For the Union Conference, see the *Free Will Baptist Cyclopedia,* 112ff.; *Providence Journal,* 5 Aug. 1831; for John Prentice, a Providence merchant tailor and perhaps representative of the "middling interest," see Boston *Daily Advertiser,* 29 July 1831; *Providence Journal,* 28 April 1830; *Rhode Island Legislative Investigation,* 60ff., at which Prentice testified, "I believe the original object of Masons to have been to meet together to have a high frolic, and look after each other's interests, to the exclusion of all others of the community," p. 61. Eleven members of the Maple Root Baptist Church in Coventry, including three deacons, made up a third of the town's Antimasonic petitioners in 1833, whereas only one turned up as a defender of Masonry. For the membership of the Maple Root Baptists, see the list in James N. Arnold, ed., *Vital Records of Rhode Island,* 20 Vols. (Providence, 1891–   ), 10, 245ff.; for the clerks of three Six Principle Baptists who were Antimasons, John Wood of Coventry, Nathan Sweet of Johnston, and Horace Battey of Scituate, see *The United States Baptist Annual Register for 1832,* I. M. Allen, ed. (Philadelphia, 1833), 79.

45. On Moses Brown see *Providence Journal,* 4, 6 April 1831, 6 April 1833; for Potter, see *Rhode Island Legislative Investigation,* 27ff., where he's described as a "Hickory Quaker," a reference to the Hicksites. Isaac Wilbour was the leading Antimasonic Quaker. He presided over the first Antimasonic convention and represented Little Compton, a strong Antimasonic town in Newport County, where Quakers were numerous. Another Quaker, Elisha Matthewson, from Scituate, chaired the 1832 Antimasonic Convention. For Wilbour, see *Biographical Cyclopedia of Representative Men of Rhode Island* (Providence, 1881), 167; Benjamin F. Wilbour, *Little Compton Families* (Little Compton, R.I., 1967), 736. For a South Kingston Quaker who renounced Masonry after joining the Friends, see *Pawtucket Herald,* 4 Feb. 1829.

46. Rev. Henry Edes of the First Congregationalist Church (1805–32), was a Harvard-trained liberal and active Mason. Conservative Calvinism, however, persisted and nourished Antimasonry. In Barrington, for example, Joshua Bicknell was an Antimasonic leader and deacon of the Congregationalist church. The church long enjoyed conservative leadership under Rev. Luther Wright, Jacob Ide's predecessor in Medway, Massachusetts, and then Thomas Williams, a student of Nathanael Emmons and a founder of the Rhode Island Evangelical Consciation. Another Em-

mons student, Emerson Paine, served at Little Compton from 1822–35; Paine's predecessor, Rev. Mase Shepard (1787–1821), was a friend of the great Rev. Samuel Hopkins in nearby Newport. Thomas Burgess, deacon of Paine's church, was one of the town's Antimasonic leaders. For Edes, see Sprague, *Annals of the American Pulpit*, VIII, 95, and for Rev. Fred Farley at Westminster Church see 174ff.; for Bicknell, see Thomas W. Bicknell, *A History of Barrington, R.I.* (Providence, 1898), 580. For Barrington's clergy, see Blake, *History of the Mendon Association*, 170ff. For Little Compton's clergy see Blake, *History of the Mendon Association*, 288, and Sprague, *Annals*, II, 367, and for Deacon Burgess, see *Antimasonic Rhode Islander*, 6 May 1829.

47. Bicknell, *History of Rhode Island*, I, 5. Most information on the Spragues comes from Benjamin Knight, *History of the Sprague Families of Rhode Island, Cotton Manufacturers and Calico Printers, From William I to William IV* (Santa Cruz, Calif., 1881); the quote concerning Amasa is on p. 18; *Dictionary of American Biography*, IX, 474–76; Bicknell, *History of Rhode Island*, III, 1138–39, 1143–44.

48. The best account of Pawtucket is by Kulik, "The Beginnings of the Industrial Revolution in America: Pawtucket, Rhode Island," 255, *passim; Massachusetts Directory*, 1835, 34.

49. *Pawtucket Herald and Independent Inquirer*, 31 Dec. 1828; *Rhode Island Legislative Investigation*, 32, 33, 55, 64, 69, 73.

50. *Ibid.*, 33, 34, 55, 72.

51. Kulik, "The Beginnings of the Industrial Revolution," 50ff., 146ff., 340; *Rhode Island Legislative Investigation*, 34, 65.

52. Kulik, "The Beginnings of the Industrial Revolution," *passim;* Rugg, *History of Freemasonry in Rhode Island*, 798.

53. Kulik, "The Beginnings of the Industrial Revolution," 279–80, 292, 293.

54. *Ibid.*, 255, 275, 278, 300ff.

55. *Ibid.*, 360ff.

56. *Pawtucket Chronicle*, 5 June 1830, 9 March 1832; Kulik, "The Beginnings of the Industrial Revolution," 372. These included William Harris, a manufacturer who married Abraham's daughter, Sarah; Frederick A. Sumner, who married another daughter, Lydia, and was a lawyer; still another daughter, Ann, married Nathan Lazell, a Bridgewater, Massachusetts, Antimasonic businessman and devout Orthodox Congregationalist; Benjamin Fessenden, another Pawtucket Antimason, who married a daughter of Isaac Wilkinson. He abandoned the Unitarian ministry and became a manufacturer and devout Calvinistic Baptist.

57. David Benedict, *Historical and Biographical Sketches of Some of the Early and Succeeding Inhabitants of Pawtucket* (n.d., n.p.), 41; Rev. Israel Wilkinson, *Memoirs of the Wilkinson Family* (Jacksonville, Ill., 1869), 223ff.; Bayles, *History of Providence County*, II, 245, 440; Thomas Steere, *History of Smithfield* (Providence, 1881), 106–11; Edward A. Fessenden, *The Fessenden Family in America* (n.p., 1979), 706ff.; for Lazell, see *Boston Advocate*, 14 May 1835.

58. Bayles, *Providence County*, II, 17ff., 21, 851; Rev. Israel Wilkinson, *Memoirs*, 517. For the names of Pawtucket Freemasons and Episcopalians see notes 27 and 33; Bicknell, *History of Rhode Island*, II, 831; *Appleton Biographical Cyclopedia*, vol. 8, 302.

59. Calvin Philleo, *Light on Masonry and Antimasonry and a Renunciation of Both, with Undissembled Esteem for Masons and Antimasons* (Providence, 1831), 16, also 7, 10, 13–15.

Table 11.3. Where the Antimasonic Vote Went, Rhode Island, 1836–38: Ecological Regression Estimates

1838 Governor	1836 Governor			
	Whig	Antimason/Democrat	Nonvoter	Electorate
Whig	3	2	12	16
Democrat	1	8	5	14
Nonvoter	7	3	60	70
N = 23 Towns				

See also Table 11.1.

60. *Ibid.*, 7.

61. *Ibid.*, 21–23.

62. Christopher Allen to John B. Francis, 7 April 1834, T. P. Ives to Francis, 14 April 1834, Francis to Byron Diman, 4 April 1834; Francis to Dexter Randall, 21 March 1834, Christopher Allen to Francis, 19 Aug. 1834, J. B. Francis Papers, RIHS; E. R. Potter, Jr., to E. R. Potter, Sr., 27 March 1834, Potter Papers, RIHS; *Providence Journal,* 14, 18 April 1834, 12, 15 May 1834.

63. *Boston Advocate,* 7, 18 April 1834, 9, 14 April, 15, 16 May, 4 June 1835; Christopher Allen to Francis, 10 Feb. 1834, Francis Papers; Francis to John Waterman, 1 Jan. 1834, E. R. Potter to John Waterman, 25 Feb. 1834, Warwick-Waterman RIHS; John Waterman to E. R. Potter, 4 March 1834, Potter Papers; *The Address to the People of Rhode Island from the Convention Assembled at Providence on the 22nd Day of February . . . to Promote the Establishment of a State Constitution* (Providence, 1834). To compare appointments in 1833 with 1835, see Smith, comp., *Civil and Military List of Rhode Island, 1800–1850,* II, 482–97, 510–524.

64. William Sprague to John B. Francis, 11, 20 Jan., 8 Feb., 13 June, 12 July 1837; Christopher Allen to Francis, 8, 20, 24 Aug. 1837; Francis to Gov. Marcy, 23 Jan. 1837; E. R. Potter to J. B. Francis, 1 Feb. 1838, 13 June 1837, Francis Papers; Dutee J. Pearce to Silas Weaver, 18 July 1837, Weaver Papers, RIHS; Christopher Allen to Jonas Titus, 25 Oct. 1837, RIHS.

65. Table 11.3

66. Dutee J. Pearce to Levi Woodbury, 14 Aug., 1 Sep. 1837, Woodbury Papers, LC. For factionalism among the National Republicans, see *Political Frauds Exposed or a Narrative of the Proceedings of "The Junto in Providence," Concerning the Senatorial Question from 1833–1838 by Aristides* (n.p., n.d.) and the Knight-Burgess Papers, in the John Hay Library, Brown University.

67. *Chronicle of the Times,* 28 Sep. 1831.

Chapter 12. Antimasonry in Connecticut

1. The best overviews are Lipson, *Freemasonry in Federalist Connecticut,* especially 267ff. and Vaughn, *The Anti-Masonic Party,* 161ff. For the growth of Connecticut Masonry see Stillson, *History of Masons,* 878–92.

2. *Antimasonic Intelligencer,* 14 April 1829, 26 May 1832.

3. *Ibid.*, 3 Jan. 1833.

4. *Free Elector*, 28 Jan. 1834.

5. *Ibid.*, 18 Feb. 1834.

6. *Ibid.*, 18, 25 Feb. 1834.

7. *Ibid.*, 1 April 1834.

8. *Ibid.*, 21 May 1834.

9. *Ibid.*, 25 Nov. 1834.

10. *Ibid.*, 31 March 1835.

11. See for example the *North Star*, 13 Jan., 10 March 1829, *Pawtucket Herald*, 25 Feb. 1829.

12. *Antimasonic Intelligencer*, 9 June 1929.

13. *Connecticut Antimasonic Convention, 1830*, p. 15.

14. Tables 12.1A and 1B

15. Table 12.2

16. Richard J. Purcell, *Connecticut in Transition: 1775–1818* (Middletown, Conn., 1963), remains an extraordinarily useful work, especially 211ff., 236ff.; also useful are Jarvis M. Morse, *A Neglected Period of Connecticut's History, 1818–1850* (New Haven, 1933), and Allen Brownsword, "Connecticut Political Patterns, 1817–

Table 12.1A. How Connecticut Antimasonic Voting Correlated with Other Parties, 1816–48: Pearson Correlations

Other Parties	Antimasonic 1832P
1816G Federalist	.02
1818 For Toleration Constitution	.06
1828P National Republican	.04
1836P Whig	.15
1840P Whig	—.02
1844P Whig	—.06
1844P Democrat	.03
1844P Liberty	.03
1848P Whig	—.18
1848P Democrat	.10
1848P Free Soil	.09

Table 12.1B. Where the Antimasonic Vote Came From, Connecticut, 1828–32 (Ecological Regression Estimates)

1832 Presidential	1828 Presidential			
	Whig %	Democrat %	Nonvoter %	Electorate %
Whig	1	1	24	25*
Democrat	1	1	15	17
Antimason	1	0	5	6
Nonvoters	1	2	50	53
N = 90 Towns				

* Rounding error

Table 12.2. Turnout and Party Competition in Connecticut 1828

Year	% Adult Males Voting	Democrat %	Antimasonic %
1828	14	NA	
1828G	27	24	
1829	15	NA	
1830	19	NA	
1831	27	NA	27
1832	24	NA	26
1832P	46	34	10
1833	30	42	15
1834	51	43	7
1835	59	53	0
1836	52	54	0
1836P	52	51	0
1837	62	53	0

1828" (Ph.D. Diss., University of Wisconsin, 1962). For the emerging Jacksonian party, John Niven, *Gideon Welles, Lincoln's Secretary of Navy* (New York, 1973), gives an exceptionally detailed picture reflecting the extraordinary richness of the Gideon Welles Papers for reconstructing the local political conditions, tangled factionism, and rival party-building strategies.

17. Lipson, *Freemasonry in Federalist Connecticut*, 294ff.; for Antimasonic certification of Tomlinson, see *Antimasonic Intelligencer*, 9 June 1829; for Pitkin's refusal to run as an Antimason see *Masonic Mirror*, 29 Jan. 1830; for his nomination, *Antimasonic Intelligencer*, 18 Dec. 1830; and for a later attack on Pitkin for supporting the National Republicans, see *Antimasonic Intelligencer*, 8 Oct. 1832.

18. For reports of Antimasonic-Whig unity see Andrew Judson to Welles, 21 Jan. 1833, William H. Ellis to Welles, 29 Dec. 1832, Welles Papers LC; for discussion of the proper Antimasonic strategy towards the Whigs and evidence of amalgamation, see *Free Elector*, 4, 11, 18, 25 March, 29 April, 28 Oct., 18 Dec. 1834; for the failure of the anti-oath bill, *Free Elector*, 10, 17 June 1834; on Whig appointments, *Free Elector*, 13, 24 June 1834.

19. Table 12.3

20. Gideon Welles to Samuel Simonds, 18 April 1831, Welles LC.

21. For the history of Congregationalists and other denominations see *Contribu-*

Table 12.3. Where the Antimasonic Vote Went: Connecticut, 1832–36 (Ecological Regression Estimates)

1836 Pres.	1832 Presidential				
	Nat. Rep.	Dem.	Antimason	Nonvoter	% Electorate
Whig	17	0	3	6	26
Dem.	10	7	1	9	27
Nonvoters	−1	10	1	37	47
N = 122 Towns					

Table 12.4. Influence of Demographic Variables on Party Vote in Connecticut, 1828–32: Multiple Regression Betas

	1828 Pres. Nat. Rep.	1832 Pres.		
		Dem.	Whig	Antimason
Money-at-Loan	.015	.162	−.199	.120
Temperance Society	.044	−.175	.079	.052
Population Change	−.048	.018	.019	−.043
Land Val.	−.157	−.061	−.080	−.051
Stores	−.214	−.002	.067	−.085
Distillery	−.160	.086	−.073	.020
MFG Val.	−.019	.037	−.172	.197
Fish Val.	.186	.076	.022	−.096
Cong.	.030	−.124	.201	−.158
Bapt.	−.273	.234	−.144	−.022
Meth.	−.036	−.029	.026	−.008
Episc.	−.102	−.268	.347	−.234
R2	.20	.21	.26	.14

tions to the Ecclesiastical History of Connecticut . . . (New Haven, 1867) 125ff., 151ff., 163ff., 183ff., 191ff., 260ff., and Edward Beardsley, *The History of the Episcopal Church in Connecticut,* 2 Vols. (Boston, 1880), II, *passim;* for the New Light tradition in the eighteenth century, see Richard H. Bushman, *From Puritan to Yankee* (Cambridge, Mass., 1967).

22. Table 12.4

23. Names of Antimasons taken from *Connecticut Antimasonic Convention, 1830,* pp. 28–31, and "Minutes of the Antimasonic State Convention, held at Hartford, Conn., Oct. 15, 1834," Ms., Conn. Historical Society. Demographic information comes from town and county histories. Occupational data were found for 43 people, age data for 22, and religious affiliation for 35.

24. *Connecticut Antimasonic Convention, 1830,* p. 26; *North Star,* 21 Feb. 1832.

25. *Ibid.,* 24.

26. *Antimasonic Intelligencer,* 5, 19 May 1829, 26 April 1831.

27. *Ibid.,* 6 Aug. 1833; *North Star,* 13 Jan., 10 Feb. 1829, *Free Elector,* 28 Jan. 1834.

28. *Antimasonic Intelligencer,* 19 May 1829.

29. *Free Enquirer,* 16 Dec. 1834.

30. *Gen. Chauncey Whittlesey's Renunciation of Free Masonry;* David D. Field, *Centennial Address* (Middleton, 1853), 212.

31. *Antimasonic Intelligencer,* 5 May 1829.

32. D. Cooley to Gideon Welles, 22 March 1832, Welles Papers, LC; Frederick C. Norton, *Governors of Connecticut* (Hartford, 1905), 176ff.; G. Welles to Wm. H. Ellis, April 1830, Welles, Conn. State Archives.

33. Beardsley, *History of the Episcopal Church,* II, 19, 26, 98ff., 119, 123, 139ff., 161ff., 247ff., 280ff.; *Hartford Courant,* 17, 30 May, 28 June 1831.

34. *Contributions to the Ecclesiastical History of Connecticut* (New Haven, [1867]), 269; Morse, *A Neglected Period,* 163; Duane H. Hurd, *History of Fairfield County* (n.p., 1881) 658.

35. Morse, *A Neglected Period*, 101–2, 104–5, 134; P. T. Barnum, *Struggles and Triumphs of Forty Years' Recollections* (Buffalo, 1873); for a Jackson celebration at a Universalist church see *Hartford Courant*, 15 Jan. 1833, and for Democratic support by Universalists, see William S. Holabird to Welles, 8 March 1833: "Our success in this town is truly gratifying. We ran Capt. Thayer against the combined efforts of Calvinism, Methodism, Antiism, federalism and Clayism. They cried out down with the Universalists. . . ." For objections by some Democrats to the party's nomination of a Baptist minister, see Charles Arnold to Welles, 14 March 1834, Welles, LC.

36. *Trumpet of Freedom*, 27 June 1829; Morse, *A Neglected Period*, 105; for Democratic complaints against the political activities of Congregationalists (Presbyterians), see Z. Wildman to G. Welles, 3 Dec. 1832, R. R. Hinman to Welles, 25 Nov. 1832, Welles, LC.

37. *Masonic Mirror*, 5 March 1831.

38. Beardsley, *History of Episcopal Church*, II, 180, 280ff.

39. For location of Masonic Lodges, see *The Connecticut Register*, 1818 (New London, n.d.), 84, and for churches see 86 and *The [Connecticut] State Register . . . 1831* (Hartford, n.d.), 76; Lipson, *Freemasonry in Federalist Conn.*, 130; J. E. Johnson, *Newton's Connecticut History*, 243ff.; *Ecclesiastical History of Conn.*, 446–47; *Antimasonic Intelligencer*, 2 June, 12 July 1833, for two pro-Masonic Episcopal ministers.

40. Beardsley, *History of the Episcopal Church*, II, 130.

41. *Ecclesiastical History of Conn.*, 190ff., 205ff.; *Antimasonic Intelligencer*, 20 April 1830.

42. For Taylor see Mead, *Nathaniel W. Taylor*. For Boardman, see Lipson, *Freemasonry in Federalist Connecticut*, 122, 131–32; Noah Webster was elected an alternate delegate to the 1831 Antimasonic National Convention, see *Connecticut Antimasonic Convention, 1830*, p. 26.

43. For Rev. Nathan D. Strong, see J. Hammond Trumbull, *Memorial History of Hartford County*, 2 Vols. (Boston, 1886), I, 285ff.; *Antimasonic Intelligencer*, 5 May 1829, 26 April 1831.

44. Daniel Dow, *Free Inquiry Recommended on the Subject of Freemasonry: A Sermon, Preached at Woodstock, September 11, 1829 . . .* (Norwich, 1829); Lipson, *Freemasonry in Federalist Connecticut*, 164, 262–63, 287–89, 291, 294; *Appleton's Cyclopedia*, 11, p. 405; Sprague, *Annals*, II, 369ff.; Richard Bayles, *History of Windham County* (New York, 1889), 670; Daniel Dow, *Semi-Centennial Sermon, Preached in Thompson, Conn., April 22, 1846* (New Haven, 1846); Daniel Dow, *The Duty of Praying for All That Are in Authority, Illustrated, A Sermon Preached before His Excellency Oliver Wolcott . . . May 4, 1825* (Hartford, 1825), 17–18; see Dow's ordination sermon, *Ministers of the Gospel Should Take Heed, a Sermon . . . at the Ordination of Rev. Stephen Crosby, . . . Spencer, Mass., June 9, 1819* (Leicester, Mass., 1819), 12, 14, in which he warned the candidate not "to turn one's sails to the wind and float with the tide." The more a minister labored "for the salvation of sinners, the more the opposition of the world is excited against him." For Thompson, see Ellen D. Larned, *History of Windham County*, 2 Vols. (Worcester, Mass., 1874, 1880), II, 351, 441ff., 530ff., 535ff.; John W. Barber, *Connecticut Historical Collections* (New Haven, 1836), 441–43.

45. Daniel Dow, *New Haven Theology, Alias Taylorism, Alias Neology in Its Own Language* (Thompson, 1834); for East Windsor, see *Evangelical Magazine*

(Hartford), II (1833–34), 289ff., 386–87, 568–71. For Hosmer, see Trumbull, *Memorial History of Hartford*, I, 432.

46. *North Star,* 30 June 1829; *Antimasonic Intelligencer,* 5 May 1829. For reluctance by the Stonington Association in 1813 to take a stand, see McGloughlin, *New England Dissent,* II, 1016. For other Baptist Antimasons, see Rev. Joshua Williams of Harwinton, later president of Western Reserve College; *Antimasonic Intelligencer,* 30 June 1829; R. Manning Chipman, *The History of Harwinton* (Hartford, 1860), 73ff., 91, 103. See also Montville's Elder Oliver Wilson and Henry A. Baker, comp., *History of Montville* (Hartford, 1896), 665. Montville was the home of Lorenzo Dow, the eccentric, freelance, anti-sectarian, anti-Calvinist, pro-Masonic preacher. See *ibid.,* 113, 603–4; for Antimasonic Henry Grew, see Trumbull, *Memorial History of Hartford County,* I, 401; *Centennial Memorial History of First Baptist Church* (Hartford, 1890), 192ff.

47. *Minutes of the General Association of Connecticut, 1833* (Hartford, 1833), 15; 1835, p. 14; 1836, pp. 14–15.

48. Professor Olmstead, "Memoir of John Treadwell," *American Quarterly Register* XV (Feb. 1843), 225–53; for Pitkin, see *Dictionary of American Biography,* VII, 639; Purcell, *Connecticut in Transition,* 24, 86, 153, 180, 181, 182, 186, 204, 206, 214, 237ff., 262n. for Treadwell, and 232, 237, 238–39, 240, 245, 254 for Pitkin; Trumbull, *Memorial History of Hartford County,* II, 195ff.; *Ecclesiastical History of Conn.,* 151.

49. J. W. Pardee to James Dodd, 9 May 1833, Welles, LC; Christopher P. Bickford, *Farmington in Connecticut* (Canaan, N.H., 1982), 206.

50. Minutes, Antimasonic State Convention, 1834, p. 8, Conn. HS. Information on Farmington Antimasons comes from Trumbull, *Memorial History of Hartford County,* II, 190ff.; 329; Bickford, *Farmington,* 296, 213, 245. Simsbury's Congregational church also provided Antimasonic leaders such as Federalist Calvin Barber and Deacon Salmon Eno. See Lucius I. Barber, *A Record and Documentary History of Simsbury* (Simsbury, 1931), 362, 364; *Hartford Memorial Biography,* 102, 152ff.; Rev. Allen McLean, *A Discourse on the 50th Anniversary of his Ordination as Pastor* (Hartford, 1859). McLean claimed that Simsbury had "nothing like an overbearing aristocracy; all are on a peaceful, common level. . . . We have no overbearing higher ones, and no crushed and discouraged low ones," p. 25. The members of his church were mostly farmers, less prone to sudden changes of fortune than people in manufacturing villages. "We must be harmonious, we must not divide," was claimed by McLean to be the local motto (p. 28).

51. Trumbull, *Memorial History of Hartford County,* II, 501; for Terry, see Purcell, *Connecticut in Transition,* 73, 187, 188.

52. Irvin W. Sandford, *An Historical Sketch of Salisbury, Conn.* (New York, 1899), 14ff.; Payne K. Kilbourne, *A Biographical History of the County of Litchfield* (New York, 1851); D. Hamilton Hurd, *History of Litchfield County, Conn.* (Philadelphia, 1887), 486ff., 492; Norton, *Governors of Connecticut,* 243; Alexander Holley's Autobiography, 1 Jan. 1862, Holley Papers, Conn. HS.; *Ecclesiastical History of Conn.,* 473; *One Hundred Fiftieth Anniversary of the First Congregational Church;* John M. Holley to Horace Cowles, 9 Aug., 21 Oct. 1833, Holley to Nathaniel Terry, 22 Jan. 1833, Holley Papers, Conn. HS.

53. Elizur Wright, *Myron Holley and What He Did for Liberty* (Boston, 1882), *passim.* And for his social thought, 21, 22, 17, 155, 295–96, 316.

54. *Ibid.,* 157.

55. *Ibid.*, 185, 223, and for his religious views, see also 40, 132, 208, 295–96, 316.

56. *Free Enquirer*, 3, 28 Oct. 1834.

57. Wright, *Holley*, 295–96.

58. *Ibid.*, 306–8, 312, 304.

59. George S. White, *Memorial of Samuel Slater* (Philadelphia, 1836), 126–28.

60. Larned, *History of Windham County*, II, 445; Daniel Hunt, *History of Pomfret* (Hartford, 1841), 16 for Deacon Holbrook.

61. Larned, *Windham*, II, 548.

62. Larned, *Windham County*, II, 514–15; *Ecclesiastical History*, 510. For an interesting picture of Smith Wilkinson, who attended the Rhode Island Antimasonic convention in 1832, see the *Providence Literary Subaltern*, 14 Jan. 1831, which described him as monomaniacal on the subject of Freemasonry, so unbalanced that he walked through Providence distracted, suffering from moody melancholy. Tense and nervous, the sight of an artisan in a leather apron frightened him, for he mistook it for Masonic regalia. The dangers of Freemasonry, he imagined, lurked everywhere.

63. *Free Elector*, 30 Sep. 1834.

64. John Niven, *Gideon Welles, Lincoln's Secretary of the Navy* (New York, 1973); 98ff.; Jarvis M. Morse, *A Neglected Period*, 103; Gideon Welles, Historical Sketch of Leading Newspapers in Connecticut, 1853, Conn. HS.

65. *Free Elector*, 31 March 1835.

66. *Ibid.*, 29 April 1834.

Chapter 13. The Antimasonic Legacy

1. Walter M. Merrill and Louis Richards, eds., *The Letters of William Lloyd Garrison* (Cambridge, Mass., 1971–81), I, 164.

2. William Preston Vaughn, *The Anti-Masonic Party in the United States*, found no evidence of Antimasonry in the South. See, for example, the states cited in the index, 233.

3. Eric Hobsbawm, *Workers, Worlds of Labor* (New York, 1984), 18.

4. Steven Hahn, *The Roots of Southern Populism* (New York, 1983).

5. Rev. Peter Sanborn, *Minutes of an Address Delivered before the Antimasonic Convention of Reading, Mass., Jan. 15, 1829* (Boston, 1829), 19.

6. Leland M. Griffin, "The Antimasonic Persuasion," 411ff.; *Diary of Charles Francis Adams*, IV, 97, 98, 107, 109, 124, 154.

7. *Eaton's Antimasonic Almanac for 1834* (Danville, Vt., n.d.), not paginated [29]. The publishers of an Antimasonic Almanac in Rochester, N.Y., claimed 20,000 copies had been sold, *Hartford Intelligencer*, 17 March 1831.

8. Table 13.1

9. *Letters from Mr. William Slade to Mr. Hallett*, 7 and *passim*. For Hallett's side, see the *Boston Advocate*, 25 May 1835, 16 Sep. 1836. For the demise of Antimasonry nationally, see Vaughn, *The Antimasonic Party*, 173ff.

10. *Vermont Antimasonic Convention, 1830*, p. 19; Ronald P. Formisano, *Transformation of Political Culture*, 327.

11. William A. Wallace, *History of Canaan, New Hampshire* (Concord, 1910), 261.

12. Samuel D. Greene, *The Broken Seal*, 181.

13. See Chapter 10.

Table 13.1. What Happened to the Antimasonic Vote in New England, 1832–36

Ecological Regression Estimates				
Connecticut			**Rhode Island**	
1836 Pres	Antimasons 1832 Pres		1836 Gov	Antimasons 1832 Pres
Whig	3		Whig	−2
Dem	1		Dem	2
Nonvoters	1		Nonvoters	4
Maine			**Vermont**	
1837 Gov	Antimasons 1833 Gov		1837 Gov	Antimasons 1832 Gov
Whig	1		Whig	9
Dem	0		Dem	2
Nonvoters	1		Nonvoters	10

Massachusetts	
1836 Pres	Antimasons 1832 Pres
Whig	4
Dem	4
Nonvoters	15

14. See, for example, *North Star,* 27 April, 11 May 1835. *The Hartford Intelligencer,* 17 Feb., 3 March 1834, reported the formation of the Peacham and Cabot, Vermont, town antislavery societies. The *Boston Advocate,* 24 July 1833, gave publicity to Rev. Amos Phelps of Boston's Pine St. Church, a leading abolitionist Congregationalist, and it reprinted on the front page, 21 Aug. 1834, James G. Birney's letter attacking colonization.

15. *The Liberator,* 19 March, 9 April 1831, 8 Nov. 1834.

16. Griffen, "The Antimasonic Persuasion," 783–84.

17. *The Letters of William Lloyd Garrison,* I, 164–65. Garrison appears in the delegate list in the *Massachusetts Antimasonic Convention, 1832,* p. 43, and 1834, p. 27.

18. Table 13.2

19. Rev. Amos Phelps listed those clergy, mostly New England Congregationalists, who endorsed immediatism in *Lectures on Slavery and Its Remedy* (Boston, 1838), vii–x.

20. *Infidelity Unmasked,* I (June 1831), 10.

21. *North Star,* 11 May 1835.

22. *Free Elector,* 29 April, 1834, 17 Feb. 1835, 31 Dec. 1833.

23. For the most recent study of the churches' response to abolitionism see John R. McKivigan, *The War against Proslavery Religion* (Ithaca, 1984).

24. *Free Elector,* 20 Jan. 1834; *The Liberator,* 2 April 1831.

25. *North Star,* 17 Nov. 1834; *Lynn Record,* 23 July 1834.

Table 13.2. Antimasonic, Whig, and Antislavery Voting in New England: 1828–52 (Pearson Correlations)

Connecticut Antimasons 1832P		Maine Antimasons 1833G		Massachusetts Antimasons		
					1832G	1832P
1828 W	.04	1830 W	.12	1828 NR	.27	.34
1836 W	.15	1837 W	.06	1836 W	—.06	—.09
1840 W	.02	1840 W	.11	1840 W	.04	—.03
1844 W	—.06	1844 W	.12	1844 W	—.03	—.12
L	.03					
1848 W	—.18	1848 W	—.03	L	.21	.13
FS	.09	FS	.33	1848 W	—.12	—.14
1852 W	—.24	1852 W	.05	FS	.29	.24
FS	.27	FS	.26	1852 W	—.04	—.16
				FS	.24	.25

Rhode Island Antimasons			Vermont Antimasons 1832P	
	1832G	1832P		
1830 NR	.26	—.05	1828 NR	.30
1836 W	.06	.02	1836 W	.27
1840 W	.09	—.11	1840 W	.17
			L	.13
1844 W	—.10	—.09	1844 W	.21
			L	.19
1848 W	.17	.13	1848 W	.08
FS	.01	.02	FS	.17
1852 W	.07	.02	1852 W	.13
FS	.12	.08	FS	.14

26. *Boston Advocate,* 10 March 1835.

27. *The Letters of William Lloyd Garrison,* I, 154; *New England Telegraph* (April, 1835), 112.

28. For a fuller account of Thacher's Antimasonic career see Chapter 9; Moses Thacher, *Christianity and Freemasonry Antagonistic, A Discourse Delivered in the Congregational Church, Peru, N.Y.,* 2nd ed. (Cornton, Vt., 1866), 27–29.

29. *Dictionary of American Biography,* X, 422–23; *The Antimasonic Review* (New York, 1828–30). See Brackney, "Religious Antimasonry: The Genesis of a Political Path," 241ff., for an account of Ward that traces his pre-Antimasonic career and suggests he started as a liberal. See an attack on Masonry attributed by Brackney to Ward in the Unitarian *Christian Register,* 3 March 1827.

30. Bicknell, *History of Providence, Rhode Island,* I, 657; *Providence Daily Journal,* 25 June 1857.

Index